HOW RESPONSIVE SHOULD WE BE?

Progress in Self Psychology
Volume 16

Progress in Self Psychology
Editor, Arnold Goldberg, M.D.

Progress in Self Psychology invites articles relevant to psychoanalytic self psychology to be submitted for publication. Send the original manuscript (double-spaced, including references, footnotes, quoted passages, and dialogue) and four copies to:

Arnold Goldberg, M.D.
122 South Michigan Avenue
Chicago, IL 60603-6107

If the article is accepted, a diskette will be required as well. All submissions are refereed. Papers will not be returned if unacceptable.

HOW RESPONSIVE SHOULD WE BE?

Progress in Self Psychology
Volume 16

Arnold Goldberg
editor

THE ANALYTIC PRESS

2000 Hillsdale, NJ London

101 West Street
Hillsdale, NJ 07642

ISBN 0-88163-327-5
ISSN 0893-5483

Printed in the United States of America
10 9 8 7 6 5 4 3 2 1

Acknowledgment

We would like to thank Ms. Christine Susman, who provided secretarial and editorial assistance.

Contents

II CLINICAL

III APPLIED

Contributors

Doris Brothers, Ph.D. is Co-founder and Training and Supervising Analyst, The Training and Research Institute for Self Psychology; Member of Advisory Board, Institute for the Advancement of Self Psychology, Toronto.

Linda A. Chernus, M.S.W is Professor of Clinical Psychiatry, University of Cincinnati, College of Medicine; Adjunct Professor, Smith College School of Social Work.

Mary E. Connors, Ph.D. is Professor, Illinois School of Professional Psychology, Chicago; Private Practice.

James M. Fisch, M.D. is Faculty, Institute for Psychoanalysis, Chicago; Training and Supervising Analyst, Israel Psychoanalytic Institute.

Jill R. Gardner, Ph.D. is Faculty, Postgraduate Education Program, Institute for Psychoanalysis, Chicago; Faculty, Professional Development Program, School of Social Services Administration, University of Chicago.

Mark J. Gehrie, Ph.D. is Faculty, Training and Supervising Analyst, Institute for Psychoanalysis, Chicago; Visiting Professor, University of Chicago, Division of General Studies.

James E. Gorney, Ph.D. is Member, William Alanson White Psychoanalytic Society, New York; Private Practice, Knoxville, Tennessee.

George Hagman, M.S.W. is Faculty, Training and Research Institute for Self Psychology, New York and Member, Connecticut Self Psychology Group.

Hans-Peter Hartmann, M.D. is Member, International Council of Psychoanalytic Self Psychology; Co-founder of European Federation of Self Psychology; Medical Director, Clinic for Psychiatry and

Psychotherapy, Heppenheim; Member, Giessen Psychoanalytic Institute.

Ellen Lewinberg, M.S.W. is Director, Supervisor, and Faculty, Institute for Advancement of Self Psychology, Supervisor and Faculty, Toronto Child Psychoanalytic Program.

Louisa R. Livingston, Ph.D. is Faculty, Training and Research Institute for Self Psychology, New York; Faculty, Training Institute for Mental Health, New York; Private Practice.

Jeffrey J. Mermelstein, Ph.D. is Member, New York University Postdoctoral Society and in private practice, Binghamton, New York.

Wolfgang E. Milch, M.D. is Member, International Council of Psychoanalytic Self Psychology; Head Physician, Clinic for Psychosomatic and Psychotherapy, University of Giessen; Co-founder of European Federation of Self Psychology; Member, Giessen Psychoanalytic Institute.

Joseph Palombo, M.A. is Founding Dean, Institut e for Clinical Social Work, Chicago; Research Coordinator, Department of Pediatrics, Rush-Presbyterian-St. Luke's Medical Center.

Lynn Preston, M.A. is Faculty, Training and Research Institute for Self Psychology, New York and Faculty, Institute for Contemporary Psychotherapy, New York.

Lallene J. Rector, Ph.D. is Associate Professor, Psychology of Religion, Garrett-Evangelical Theological Seminary, Evanston, Illinois; Advanced Candidate, Chicago Institute for Psychoanalysis, .

Ellen Shumsky, M.S.W. is Faculty and Supervisor, Psychoanalytic Psychotherapy Study Center and Faculty, Training and Research Institute for Self Psychology, New York.

Allen M. Siegel, M.D. is Faculty, Institute for Psychoanalysis and Chair, Kohut Memorial Fund, both in Chicago.

Marilyn W. Silin, M.A. is Dean of Students, Institute for Clinical Social Work, Chicago.

Charles B. Strozier, Ph.D. is Professor of History, John Jay College and the Graduate Center, CUNY; Training and Supervising Analyst, TRISP, New York.

Maxwell S. Sucharov, M.D. is Board Member, Western Canada Psychoanalytic Psychotherapy Association and Member, International Council for Psychoanalytic Self Psychology.

Judith Guss Teicholz, Ed. D. is Faculty and Supervising Analyst, Massachusetts Institute for Psychoanalysis.

Eva-Maria Topel, M.A. is Faculty and Supervising Analyst, Süddeutsche Akademie für Tiefenpsychologie and Member, Akademie für Psychoanalyse und Psychotherapie, Munich.

Introduction

Jill R. Gardner

Nearly every introduction to a new volume of *Progress in Self Psychology* makes reference to the increasing range of thought that falls under the umbrella known originally as the psychoanalytic psychology of the self. Numerous metaphors, from wings of a house to streams of a river, have been offered to describe this expanding diversity.

Where Kohut was initially heralded for helping us move away from a positivistic view of the therapist as the possessor of truth, he was later criticized—by some—for still clinging to a one-person psychology that underemphasized relational dynamics. Where two-person psychologies were initially lauded for providing a better reflection of psychological life and the therapeutic process, they were later criticized—again, by some—for still embodying a philosophy of isolated minds. Today those who write from the intersubjective and relational realms of our theory emphasize contextualism rather than a two-person psychology.[1]

Any new idea or paradigm risks an overcorrection in the course of the pendulum swing toward the new idea. Kohut clearly believed that the analysts of his day did not sufficiently emphasize the patient's subjective experience. He sought to correct this. Post-Kohutian intersubjectivists believe that self psychology has not sufficiently emphasized the subjectivity of the therapist. They, too, have sought to correct this. Each point of view has significant implications for clinical practice.

[1] For a fuller description of these ideas, see, for example, Orange, Atwood, and Stolorow (1997).

In her brilliant and extraordinarily clear essay in this volume, Judy Teicholz offers a historical context for and integration of these varying perspectives. Through a discussion of affect as the common denominator in the analyst's empathy, subjectivity, and authenticity, she describes what is gained and what is lost by taking any of these stances too far to the exclusion of the others. She raises the level of dialogue from the question of whether an idea is the same or different from something Kohut said and whether it is or isn't self psychology to the question of what these ideas actually mean in terms of how we understand, react to, and interact with our patients. In addition, Teicholz provides an overview that enables us to orient ourselves to many of the other chapters in this volume.

Sucharov, for example, applies the concept of intersubjective contextualism to all analytic discourse. He believes it is impossible to separate such discourse from the human, subjective contexts in which it takes place. Livingston argues for a flexible, "active responsiveness," not limited to listening, exploring, or interpreting. This responsiveness is based on the patient's need and includes the active and overt use of the therapist's subjectivity. Preston and Shumsky go further, emphasizing the thorough-going bidirectionality of the analytic endeavor. For them, the analytic partnership is at the center of inquiry; a change in either partner can cause changes in the other and in the dyad. Merlmelstein, in contrast, returns to Kohut's concept of prolonged empathic immersion. He offers a fresh view of it as "easy listening" and notes how this process meets the analyst's selfobject needs.

In a chapter rich in complexity and nuance, Gehrie uses a reexamination of one of Kohut's cases to recast the issue of closeness and distance in the analytic relationship. He argues that it is not new dyadic experience but rather a more thorough analysis of "the tie to the negative selfobject" that is required to help patients move beyond schizoid forms of relating.

Gorney, and Hartmann and Milch, respectively, describe how severe bulimia or suicidal rage may be attempts at self-state regulation and the restoration of a sense of efficacy. Each describes how these efforts may be expressed through highly adversarial or negating stances in the treatment relationship. Such stances create particular challenges for the therapist and require interventions solidly grounded in an understanding of the transference meanings of these patient behaviors. Fisch's chapter on the assertive self as manifested in dreams describes the act of dreaming as similarly serving self-reparative functions, in particular the achievement of a sense of mastery.

When Kohut and his collaborators began to formulate the set of ideas that came to be known as self psychology, they were endeavoring to advance the science of psychoanalysis. First and foremost, they were talking about theory; they were also talking about practice, as informed by these new theories. Today, when we say self psychology, we may or may not be talking about psychoanalysis, theory, or even practice.

The appeal of these ideas has resulted in a community of like-minded others which at times resembles more a movement than simply a group of clinicians who adhere to a common psychoanalytic approach. In the introduction to an earlier volume of *Progress in Self Psychology,* Paul Ornstein (1993) described in detail the manifestations of increased interest in self psychology around the globe. Since that time, we have seen the development of a Self Psychology Roster, a European Federation, an annual Newsletter, the first steps toward creating a North American Federation of Free-Standing Institutes, a sharp increase in attendance at our annual conferences, and a web page that gets over 1200 visits a day from all over the world. These are signs of a vigorous self psychology community.

In addition, the ideas embodied in self psychology have been applied to nearly every treatment modality and clinical population, many of which are worlds away from the psychoanalytic practice in which Kohut originally formulated his ideas. Examples in the current volume include Silin's chapter on psychotherapy with placed children, Palombo's on nonverbal learning disabilities, Rector's on twinship and religious experience, and Gardner's and Chernus's on brief treatment. Siegel's creative experiment with supervision via the internet is another example of such expansion. Both Fisch and Palombo also integrate self psychological ideas with concepts from other fields, bringing biology and neuroscience to bear on their topics of dreaming and nonverbal learning disabilities, respectively.

The expansion of self psychology into these varying realms is a reflection of its relevance for our times. For a wide range of clinicians in a wide range of settings, these ideas have proven enormously useful. In short, they work.

They also speak to us. While some people see self psychology primarily as a useful clinical theory, others experience it more as a world view or defining professional identity. In his 1988 Kohut memorial lecture, Ornstein suggested what may lie behind this. He contrasted reactions to Kohut's first book with reactions to other popular, contemporary theories of narcissism and the self. In relation to the latter, people told him, "With this approach I can recognize my patients . . . the descriptions and theories teach me about my patients . . . they speak to my practice." In contrast, he described reactions to Kohut's work as follows: "Kohut speaks to *me* . . . I can see myself in all of this . . . it must be true . . . it is certainly true of me." He added the observation that our prevalent emotional need to make self-reflective contact with our own disturbing subjective experiences drew us strongly and would always draw us strongly to an approach that promised such an understanding. He felt it was for this reason that Kohut's ideas would endure.

I believe it is also for this reason that the ideas embodied in self psychology are so personally compelling to so many people who read them. It is, after all, through our own subjective experience that we find our most cherished beliefs. So it will be with the reader's reactions to the new ideas set forth in this volume.

REFERENCES

Orange, D., Atwood, G. & Stolorow, R. (1997), *Working Intersubjectively: Contextualism in Psychoanalytic Practice*. Hillsdale, NJ: The Analytic Press.

Ornstein, P. (1988), Kohut memorial lecture. Presented October 15th at the 11th Annual International Conference on the Psychology of the Self. Washington, D.C.

——— (1993), Introduction: Is self psychology on a promising trajectory? *The Widening Scope of Self Psychology: Progress in Self Psychology, Volume 9*, ed. A. Goldberg. Hillsdale, NJ: The Analytic Press, pp. 1–11.

Chapter 1

From the Kohut Archives

Charles B. Strozier

This third installment of material from the Kohut Archives at the Chicago Institute for Psychoanalysis includes a range of letters from Kohut's life and work. The selection begins with a 1965 letter to Harry Slochower that indicates the depth of Kohut's appreciation for the subtleties of interpreting literature psychoanalytically. The letter to E. James Anthony is light but shows Kohut's appreciation for eloquence. The 1968 telegram to his friend, Alexander Mitscherlich, is part of Kohut's abiding respect for Mitscherlich's role in the recreation of psychoanalysis in Germany after the war. Kohut had a practice of sending telegrams to his older psychoanalytic friends on their birthdays. The two letters to Lester Schwartz in 1974 are an unusual opportunity to witness Kohut discussing a case, since Thomas A. Kohut (on his father's orders) destroyed all obvious references to case material in the correspondence before a complete set of copies was turned over to the Institute in 1994. The letters to Louis Shapiro, Tilmann Moser, and Bernard Brandchaft are from Kohut's abundant supply of letters to friends and colleagues in the 1970s. He kept up a prodigious correspondence in these years.

I have also included in this selection two letters from Kohut's best friend, Robert Wadsworth. Born on the same day, Kohut and Wadsworth dubbed each other "birthday brothers" when they first met in Chicago through their mutual friend, Siegmund Levarie, on March 5, 1940. There are no extant letters from Kohut to Wadsworth and only a handful from Wadsworth to Kohut (though Levarie has shared with me letters from the 1940s between the two as part of his personal collection). It is not clear why the most important person in Kohut's life outside his family is so absent from his correspondence.

February 3, 1965

Harry Slochower, Ph.D.
Editor in Chief
American Imago
46 East 73rd Street
New York, N.Y. 10021

Dear Dr. Slochower:

Thank you for sending me your manuscript "Symbolism and the Creative Process in Art". I wish that I could have studied it closely and intensively but my time is at the moment so filled with administrative responsibilities that I could only manage to become acquainted with your paper but could not afford the type of concentrated study which it deserves.

I agree with most of your positions and conclusions, and I found the paper easy to read, well written, and enjoyable. As a practicing psychoanalyst (and despite my strong propensity toward the applied field) I find that the greatest weakness of your paper is its generality. This may not be a weakness at all if it is taken as a contribution to esthetics or to the philosophy of science. Most psychoanalysts, however, I venture to guess, will feel that the paper lacks in supplying specific examples—if not from the clinical area, so at least from specific figures some of your views by demonstrating them specifically in vivo, i.e., by quoting from the biographies of creative persons, about supportive details concerning their working methods, or their creative "spells." There are of course others in our field (such as [Heinz] Hartmann) whose writings are devoid of concretely illustrative material. Yet such writers are so much in tune with the known clinical evidence with which the psychoanalytic reader is familiar that they are able to avoid the suspicion of pure speculation.

The second difficulty that I felt when I read your essay concerned the use of the concept symbol, especially your differentiation between the unconscious symbol and the allusions, signs, and signals which are used by the ego. My personal view is that you have approached here a very fruitful focal point for the investigation of creativity, namely how the unconscious symbol is interrelated with, amalgamated with, or transformed into the symbolic processes of the ego (i.e., the symbols consciously used by the ego in the service of communication). To my mind this area needs to be approached theoretically as well as empirically. Theoretically, by differentiating between (1) the gradual transformation of the concrete primary-process symbols into the verbal and other abstractions of the secondary process, and (2) the relationship, within the single mental apparatus of a creative personality, of symbols of widely differing degrees of neutralization (see, for example, Eissler's Appendix U in the second volume of his Goethe[1]). Since I have given a good deal of thought to these questions, permit me to enclose a paper which, I hope, will make the theoretical basis of the preceding considerations a bit clearer. (I am referring to pp. 132–138 of the enclosed chapter, specifically to the diagram on p. 136.[2])

But now I must close. Let me repeat what I said at the beginning: that I enjoyed your fine paper and that I believe your conclusions and views to be sound. Perhaps some of the points which I raise may assist you in integrating some of your thoughts into the framework of certain modern psychoanalytic conceptualizations of mental functioning. With cordial regards,

Sincerely,

Heinz Kohut, M.D.

November 15, 1967

Elwyn James Anthony
8161 Amherst Avenue
St. Louis, Missouri 63130

Dear Jim:

Your address was most enjoyable and kept me pleasurably attentive throughout. I marveled at your ability to hold your significant message so perfectly to the level that the occasion demanded: not trite or superficial, yet never heavy. Congratulations! Am I right in suspecting that you belong to that group of psychoanalysts to whom I referred some years ago in whom "a greater than average need for artistic expression during adolescence and early adulthood is finally channeled into devotion to the science of psychoanalysis"?[3]

With warm regards,

Cordially,

Heinz Kohut, M.D.

---

[1] Eissler (1963).

[2] Kohut probably sent Slochower the paper he wrote with Philip F. D. Seitz, "Concepts and Theories of Psychoanalysis" (1963). The diagram he refers to is probably the one on page 368.

[3] The reference is to Kohut (1960), "Beyond the Bounds of the Basic Rule."

September 20, 1968
Telegram

Professor Alexander Mitscherlich
Mylius Strasse 20
6 Frankfurt/Main
Germany

Dear Alexander: In a world in which foolishness, cowardice, and aloofness seem to ensure victory for ruthless power it is good to know that there are men like you. You are not alone in scholarly [sic] and intelligence and there are others who do not shy away from action. But few indeed will match you in that happy combination of courageous thought and thoughtful courage that has characterized your work and personality. We analysts are proud to reckon you as one of us, and I am proud to count you as a friend. Ad multos annos.[4]

Heinz Kohut

July 31, 1974

Lester Schwartz, M.D.
322 Central Park West
New York, New York 10025

Dear Dr. Schwartz:

Thank you so much for seeing D.R. and for reporting so lucidly about him. I am under pre-vacation pressures and will react only to one point of your letter. You say: "He has spent all of his adult life being controlled by one or another idealized objects–he sees himself now as utterly 'masochistic' in relation to forces outside himself–as if he has no existence of his own. When he focuses on himself he seems to have some frightening disturbances in his sense of continuity. He can't imagine himself changing therefore in any meaningful way, but he thinks it may feel better to have someone to talk to."

If I ponder your initial statement (that you are not at all sure whether D.R. will return to see you after the summer interruption) in the light of your assessment of the severe structural defect in D.R.'s personality, I believe that I can draw this conclusion. He might not come back to see you not because he has not formed a transference, but because he has formed a transference of a particular kind, namely a transfer-

---

[4] Literally: "Toward many years." More colloquially: "May there be many more years."

ence that makes him expect that you will make him come back to see you. Such people rely initially on receiving their motivation from the analyst. To call such a patient by phone, to insist in no uncertain terms that they must come back to see the analyst–that is not undue activity from the side of the analyst-therapist but interpretation through action on the only level of communication that is open and effective. It should be followed, in due course, by verbal interpretations concerning the patient's needs and expectations to be moved by their surroundings the way a puppeteer moves his puppet. (I am sure that it is not an accident that D.R. is now a dancer–and I would use my empathic access to what dancing–a sort of automatic obedience of the body– means to the patient. You might remember, in this context, the initial statement about the puppet theater in my paper on narcissistic rage.[5])

I hope that you will not take it amiss that I have been thinking out loud to you about this fascinating problem. Let me hear from you about him again sometime.

With warm regards and have a nice summer!

Cordially yours,

Heinz Kohut, M.D.

December 3, 1974

Lester Schwartz, M.D.
322 Central Park West
New York, New York 10025

Dear Dr. Schwartz:

Thank you for your very informative letter. I am sorry that the treatment seems to have come to an end. (As you anticipated, I had already learned about this fact from Mr. R.'s mother.) What a fascinating psychological problem! And what specific, peculiar demands which such a patient makes on the therapist! His need to be moved by a power outside himself "like a puppet" is, I would think, the necessary consequence of the fact that he has no self that could function as a reliable center of initiative. His father's abrupt disappearance, and his mother's personality, effectively blocked the development of this central structure of his personality. Insight does not cure this defect. In general, it only helps to start and to maintain the relevant working-

[5] See Kohut (1972).

through processes. Thus, he could not *start* treatment on his own–it had to be on the initiative of someone else and it had to be maintained (e.g., paid for) by someone else. Why the couch hour marked the end of the therapy, I do not know for certain. But I would think of this possibility. The demands that you must for the time being be perceived by him as *his* personality, might have been very taxing, and thus you might have protected yourself from the feeling of being sucked into him (by his *eyes*, for example) by putting him on the couch. He, on the other hand, might have been now deprived of that (at first grossly concrete) possibility to build structure through identification. Visual and oral incorporation wishes of self-building psychological substance might well have become replaced by anal incorporative urges on the couch, as he felt deprived of contact and felt rejected by what he perceived as a break in empathy. (Thus "homosexual" fantasies might have arisen in him as the incorporation needs became intensified and sexualized.) But all this is only speculation.

Thank you so much for tackling this enormously difficult therapeutic problem and for telling me about the events that led to the end of therapy.

Cordially yours,

Heinz Kohut, M.D.

Blind copy to Dr. Paul Ornstein

August 28, 1975

Louis B. Shapiro, M.D.
180 North Michigan Avenue
Chicago, Illinois 60601

Dear Lou:

Your letter which arrived yesterday gave me the greatest satisfaction. It was the response of your total person to my total effort–no piddling nit-picking, which is the last thing that I can use at the present stage of my work. You were the first person to read the first version of the "Rehabilitation" in its entirety.[6] And I take it as a good sign that your feelings about it are so positive.

---

[6] The working title of the book Kohut was then writing was *The Rehabilitation of the Self: Thoughts About the Termination of Analyses and the Concept of Cure*. The final title was *The Restoration of the Self* (1977).

Yes, I know, of course, about the attacks on my work. And I have no doubt that the Rehabilitation, too, will be greeted with anger and derision by many. But if there are some of your caliber who can find in it what, as you have expressed so movingly, you found in it–and you found it even in this first unpublished version–then I can remain hopeful for the worthwhileness of the many hours that I have spent on it (and sometimes the sleepless nights with which I reacted to the problems raised in me as I was writing it).

Many thanks for being so generous in your reactions.

Warmly yours,

Heinz Kohut, M.D.

September 16, 1975

Dr. Tilmann Moser
6 Frankfurt/Main
Humboltstrasse 5
Germany (B.R.D.)

Dear Tilmann:

Your letter gives me food for a good deal of thought, both in the scientific and in the personal sphere. With regard to the scientific problem about group analysis, I have little to offer. I am impressed by your arguments and have no doubt from what you say that there is here a rich field for serious investigative effort which requires the devotion of researchers with specific motivations–whatever their genetic roots!–as you are. I cannot fully follow you with regard to the wholesome effect of a protracted hate-transference. This concept seems to me to rest on some concretistic quantitative theory–as if a certain definite amount of hate had to be discharged so that one can be rid of it. I would, of course, be in agreement if the assertion were made that the affect of hate had to be fully and repeatedly experienced in the transference. But I do not believe that we have reached psychological bedrock at that point. Behind the rage is still the disappointment about the lack of perfect empathic response from the side of the omnipotent, omniscient, and all-good parent who is totally devoted to the child, and to the child alone. Brothers and sisters play important roles because they interfere with the total devotion of the parent, or because they can become parent substitutes, or because the child can see the parental lack of empathy vis-a-vis the brothers and sisters, etc. etc. Yet the bedrock behind the narcissistic rage is still the disappointment in the parental self-object. I also did not understand why other patients or the imagined children of the analyst in the regular analytic situation cannot serve the process of working through. Why does it have to be the excitement of a real group situation? If the analyst is sensitive to the violent hatreds stirred up in the analysand, then the intense endopsychically determined rage can be worked through in the usual analytic situation.

Whatever the merits of my argument might be, however–and I don't see why I should not openly tell you what I think from the point of view of *my* knowledge and *my* experience–, you have no need to assume that I would reject *your* interest in this field. If you think over your experiences with groups carefully, if you go beyond acting and reacting, if you are led to new insights–you have my full blessing, whether you need it or not. But I will not go further into speculations about your wish that I repeat to you that you can be different from me, that you can go your own way, that you can be yourself, without losing my affection for you and for your struggles in life. I am sure that you and your analyst must have asked this question and must be working toward an answer.

And now I will close and go back to my own work which will perhaps, via a different approach, give you some answers to the problems that you raise

I am, as always, your

Heinz Kohut, M.D.

[from Robert Woodman Wadsworth]

Sunday, September 4 [1977[7]]

Dear Heinz,

The Labor Day weekend is passing quietly: yesterday perfect weather and a dinner party with my new Italian-American dancer colleague from the Library[8]; today church as usual[9] (no air-conditioning because the furnace was under repair!) and then some last-minute marketing at the Co-op. Tomorrow I may get to the cemetery in N.P.,[10] which I had

---

[7] At the top of the letter is a handwritten note by Kohut: "Replied 9/13/77." No copy of Kohut's letter is available (in fact, there is no copy of *any* letter from Kohut to Wadsworth extant in the Kohut Archives of the Chicago Institute for Psychoanalysis).

[8] Wadsworth worked for the University of Chicago Library in the Acquisitions Department.

[9] Wadsworth, who was very musical, played the organ at a Lutheran church every Sunday.

[10] Norwood Park, a suburb of Chicago, where Wadsworth grew up. He is probably referring to visiting his mother's grave.

to neglect when I went to New Haven for Memorial Day. My neighbors across the wall are spending the holiday in Washington Island, and I'm standing in as cat-sitter.

As usual in September, the Library is being ripped apart in anticipation of the Autumn Quarter and the new crop of paying guests. Mrs. Regenstein's riches[11] are going for a new "grid" flooring near the doors, to catch what comes in on wet boots, and for a new revolving door. Some of it should go–but will probably not–for an emergency system of electric lights for times of blackout. A week ago everything went off at 4:40 p.m., fortunately in bright daylight; still more fortunate, no one happened to be in an elevator, although I was on my way to one. We shuffled our way out through dark stair wells and dusky passages, and no one suffered; but so large a building needs something better than matches and personal flashlights.

On Tuesday the staff threw a party for a departing member of the Acquisitions staff–going to a new job at Emory, in Atlanta–and the ladies laid themselves out with cookies, cakes, punch, and other delicacies. The high point came when, after having received the gift of a large atlas, the young man found his voice and paid his grateful tributes to (1) his bridge partners at lunch, (2) his "Jewish mammas" (needless to say, the speaker was a Jew), *and* (3), by a surprise turn, no other than "RWW," whom he referred to with respect as a model of "intellectual integrity"!!! I was too much overcome by surprise to do the right thing and rise to my feet, wave my arms, and *bawl* "Hear! Hear!"; but it was nice to hear, particularly (as I wrote to Miss Kangro,[12] who had been here the day before and had talked with the youth) as I noticed with Schadenfreude my Number One Enemy slouching in the door, drinking in these words from one of His Own![13]

Miss Kangro's visit touched off another triumph, for a number of us had dinner at the Quadrangle Club,[14] and the hostess for the occasion (the only club member in the group) was a woman who had given us all concern by two recent suicide attempts. Billings[15] seems to have done well for her. I will admit I felt rather dubious as I watched her disappear into her own apartment that evening (she had been living at Billings and was out on an overnight pass), but she turned up on time on Tuesday and seems to have pulled herself together remarkably well.

---

[11] The University of Chicago Library is named after Mrs. Regenstein.

[12] Amy Kangro, a librarian in the map department.

[13] This is possibly Walter Necker.

[14] The faculty club of the University of Chicago, located across the street from the Library.

[15] The University of Chicago Hospital was named "Billings."

My Last Year[16] is going to be one blaze of entertainment–if such a thing is possible. I have the opera (two tickets still; I'm living it up), the orchestra, the chamber-music series of the Fine Arts Foundation, the Goodman Theatre series, and whatever else I feel like taking on. My teaching will come in the Winter, and if I know D. [Don] Swanson[17] it will continue indefinitely after retirement because no one will wish to upset anything.[18] The outlook in the Library is not good but will probably brighten rather than get worse; there is a story that a one-million-dollar endowment for books is to be expected from Mrs. R.

Paqui was to complete the first course of radiotherapy treatment when I talked to him a week ago. The baby in Seattle is expected any minute, and Jo's mother is ready to fly to the scene. Frank was to go to Albuquerque in this autumn and then later to Brazil.[19] No predictions offered about Paqui's "expectations," and I suppose no one knows what to expect. Bill Earle tells me the two cases in his experience "lasted" for just about a year after surgery.

Tell Tom[20] that Alan Krieger is now editorial assistant on the *Journal of Church History*. We're sorry he can't take over the work of the young hero that delivered the valedictory mentioned earlier, but the editorial experience for a young historian is important, and he can manage this time.

By now Carmel must feel like a second home.[21] I'm sure you must be panting for that First Bath in a month, but make the most of the compensatory features on hand! We've just been drowned with rain.

Best wishes!

Yours,

Robert

[from Robert Woodman Wadsworth]

---

[16] Wadsworth retired from the library in 1978 at 65 years of age.

[17] Don Swanson was the Dean of the Graduate School of Library Science at the University of Chicago.

[18] Wadsworth taught occasional courses in the department of library science but did not have a professorial appointment.

[19] Pacqui is a friend, and Jo and Frank are members of Wadsworth's family.

[20] Thomas A. Kohut, Heinz Kohut's son.

[21] Kohut spent August and much of September in Carmel, California, each year.

Sunday, September 11 [1977?[22]]

Dear Heinz,

Your good letter came yesterday, in the midst of a perfect weekend of bright sun and bracing air. I spent much of the day on the usual neighborhood errands, which were a pleasure under these conditions, and then joined my new dancer friend for an evening program on the North Side, arranged by an earnest group of dedicated young dancers, some of them from Hyde Park. As we rode downtown in the I.C.,[23] I had Berghoff[24] at the back of my head as a suggestion for dinner; but before I could say a thing, he came out with the same suggestion on his own. We feasted on brook trout and sat in a small back room I've never entered before, lined with photographs of what must be all the Berghoff family.

Today, after church, I blew myself to a Super Transfer[25] and went to the Art Institute, returning south by Culture Bus to the Museum of Science and Industry and then continuing by the normal CTA bus for Fifty-Fifth.[26] In the afternoon I used the transfer for a round trip to the lake and walked–and sat–on the Point,[27] basking in the afternoon sun. My nose tells me that hay fever is still with us, but of course the Library is air-conditioned.

There is now a proposal to install a computer-assisted bibliographic search service (similar to MEDLINE) in Regenstein. I'm afraid it's one more case of window dressing, but I've not yet seen the list of "bases" involved. The humanities don't lend themselves to all kinds of "searches."

My dear Lutherans are cooking up another choir, and I'm likely to have rehearsals on Thursdays come October. They're not a total waste, since I get in some practice, and I ordinarily have a ride. I'm still in love with the church.

---

[22] Internal evidence suggests Wadsworth wrote this letter the week after the previous one, but he begins by thanking Kohut for his letter "yesterday." That would seem to contradict Kohut's handwritten note on the letter of September 11 that he replied September 13. This letter therefore may be from 1978.

[23] The Illinois Central Railroad runs between Hyde Park and downtown Chicago.

[24] A popular Chicago restaurant a few blocks from the Art Institute and the symphony.

[25] Wadsworth was fascinated with various forms of travel and loved all trains and buses. When there were still trolley cars in Chicago, he memorized the serial numbers of every car in the system. On trips to New York, he would figure out the most complicated route to take and report on his travels in letters in great detail.

[26] Chicago Transit Authority bus for 55th Street.

[27] The rocky shoreline of Lake Michigan near Hyde Park.

The opera tickets and the orchestra tickets have come: time to think of fall! Make the most of California!

Best wishes!

Yours,

Robert

P.S. On one hurried day this last week I heard bloodcurdling low feline moans of threatening hostility from upstairs. Rebecca[28] proved to be on the porch railing on the third floor, giving the works to the resident cat. She has terrorized the two cats across the hall and has no hesitation about entering their apartment through their cat door. What have I done to deserve all this?

March 25, 1980

Bernard Brandchaft, M.D.
9777 Wilshire Boulevard
Beverley Hills, California 90212

Dear Bernie:

Died the wool analyst that I am, I tried at first to comprehend the impact your letter had on me. But I could make no headway: to grasp the method by which this wonderful communication achieved its effect on me is beyond me. And that is clearly as it should be–just as the analyst sometimes must not interpret mechanisms but only express his understanding for the broad need that the analysand had expressed, so must one sometimes simply accept gratefully a wholesome, joyful experience and not interfere with it by cutting a living whole into lifeless slices. It simply was good to have another mind resonate with mine, thinking and feeling as I do, and courageously facing the disappointments and obstacles of the moment–facing them with the confidence that is nourished by the conviction that we have indeed gotten hold of a valuable set of insights. These insights, we trust, will continue to bear fruit, directly or indirectly, long after we have ceased to support and defend them by our individual efforts. Thank you for your deep convictions, thank you for your courage and your persuasive

[28] One of Wadsworth's cats, stories of whom were a frequent theme in his letters.

example. I'm lucky to have found a colleague and collaborator like you.

Warmest regards from house to house.

Cordially,

Heinz Kohut, M.D.

REFERENCES

Eissler, K. (1963), *Goethe: A Psychoanalytic Study: 1775–1786*. Detroit: Wayne State University Press.

Kohut, Heinz (1960), Beyond the bounds of the basic rule. In: *The Search for the Self: Selected Writings* of Heinz Kohut: *1950–1994, Vol. 1,* ed. Paul Ornstein. New York: International Universities Press.

——— (1972), Thoughts on narcissism and narcissistic rage. *The Psychoanalytic Study of the Child*, 27:360–400. New Haven, CT: Yale University Press. Also in *Search for the Self: Selected Writings of Heinz Kohut: 1950–1994, Vol. 2,* ed. P. Ornstein. New York: International Universities Press, 1978, pp. 615–658.

——— (1977), *The Restoration of the Self*. New York: International Universities Press.

——— & Seitz, P. F. D. (1963), Concepts and theories of psychoanalysis. In: *The Search for the Self: Selected Writings* of Heinz Kohut: *1950–1994, Vol. 1,* ed. Paul Ornstein. New York: International Universities Press, 1978, pp. 337–374.

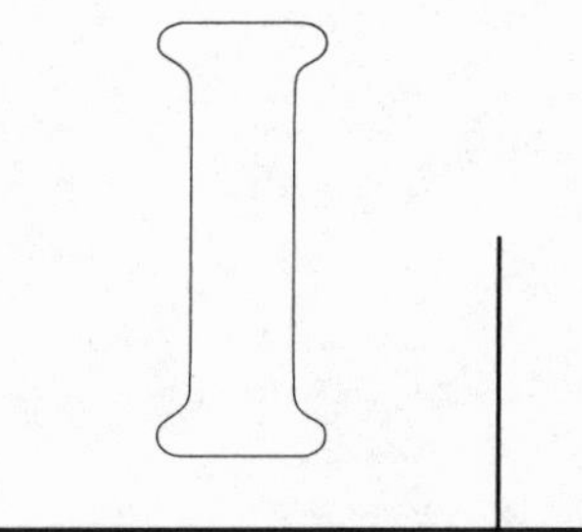

Theoretical

Chapter 2

Forms of Relatedness: Self-Preservation and the Schizoid Continuum

Mark J. Gehrie

This chapter seeks to expand upon and elaborate an aspect of theory that bridges object relations and self psychology and that relates to a domain of experience that has been at the heart of a paradigm shift in psychoanalysis. This "domain" cuts across the range of psychological functioning and is relevant to internal structural as well as relational considerations. It is reflected interpersonally in forms of relatedness that are founded on certain fundamental internal conditions (i.e., on the structural qualities of the self) and that vary with these structural qualities. There are three interrelated levels to consider in the context of this domain of experience: (1) forms of interpersonal relatedness and conscious subjectivity, (2) preconscious and unconscious self-experience pertaining to this relatedness, and (3) self-structure (which is a more abstract level of conceptualization, not part of conscious experience per se, but which is inferred from 1 and 2 above). This domain of experience (which I shall shortly describe) is also relevant to developmental "derailments," to the evolution of character, and to many other conditions that are not most meaningfully viewed as psychopathological. For the purposes of this chapter, I will focus on the dynamics of self-preservation in the context of the analytic process as they pertain to this domain of experience and to a related technical strategy.

The domain to which I refer has been most explicitly described and elaborated in the works of W. R. D. Fairbairn (1940, 1941), Melanie Klein (1946, 1952), Harry Guntrip (1952, 1961, 1962), to some extent by D. W. Winnicott (1951, 1958, 1965), and of course addressed by many others, especially the group known as "Independents" in the British Psychoanalytical Society. While there are clear distinctions in the thinking among these authors, at base there is agreement that "schizoid factors in the personality," to use Fairbairn's (1940) title, or the basic anxiety of the annihilation of the self are core experiences for every human being. In contemporary usage the term *schizoid* has been largely reserved for a particular class of patients who suffer from an overt form of schizoid anxiety and whose lives are dominated by the attempt to defend themselves from this intolerable experience of loss of self through the establishment of emotional distance. I propose to broaden the usage of this term to include a wide range of experience that I believe underlies often familiar symptomatology more commonly conceptualized in altogether different terms. This constitutes a *shift in focus* toward the identification of the role of this core anxiety in both the development of the self and its characterological expressions, subjective self-experience, and the (interpersonal) forms of relatedness that are the inevitable consequences of that development. If, as many authors (including Ferenczi and Rank, 1924; Gedo and Goldberg, 1973; Gedo, 1988; and others) over the years since Freud (1917, 1920, 1921, 1923) have noted, self-preservation is indeed the primary consideration, then this view is not without significant precedent in the work of others except insofar as I wish to extend and generalize its nosological relevance. I am proposing that this domain of experience relates most intimately to the basic integrity of the system that we have come to refer to as "self." It constitutes, I propose, at least a portion of the foundation upon which much subsequent meaning is built (see Goldberg, 1995). Moreover, the contributions of Fairbairn and Guntrip in particular provide a foundation for the exploration of certain central conceptualizations in the psychology of the self, which have remained relatively implicit in the work of Heinz Kohut (1971, 1972, 1977, 1984; see also Bacal and Newman, 1990) and which have to do with the implications of the priority of self-preservation. These assessments will also directly affect our decisions about how and how far to pursue an analytic effort in instances where self-preservation becomes a central concern in the analysis.

The general framework for exploring these isses will be based on the idea of *a schizoid continuum*: whether we are speaking of inferred self-structure, conscious or unconscious self-experience, or forms of interpersonal relatedness, there exists a broad range or spectrum upon which each individual's conscious and unconscious experience of closeness-versus-distance may be located and its implications (for the structure of the self) assessed. Both Fairbairn and Guntrip have noted that, from a certain angle, "everybody without exception must be regarded as schizoid" (Fairbairn, 1940, p. 7). This implies that everyone, to one extent or another, uses defenses that may be characterized as fundamentally schizoid in nature; that is, they operate to establish a form of emotional distance for the purpose of protecting and preserving a conscious or unconscious experience of the self as a vulnerable entity.[1] For Fairbairn, the essential "qualification" is "the mental level which is being considered," that is, at what point in any given personality structure the "splits" become evident. From this perspective, *schizoid* may be thought of as a *kind of mental process,* implying a certain class of adaptive/defensive activities, as well as alluding to a particular domain within the structure of the self, rather than simply as a diagnostic term. It is the *schizoid dimension of experience*, rather than a particular symptomatic expression or character type, that is most central to the idea of a schizoid continuum, and this dimension will inevitably be found in the psychological armamentarium of every individual.

By paying closer attention to the dynamics of closeness-versus-distance (in the broadest sense, and by this I mean not simply closeness or distance from or with other people, but also within and between various facets of a more or less integrated self system), opportunities for effective clinical interventions may be greatly expanded. Consideration of this dynamic as characteristic of the schizoid is derived from Fairbairn's (1940) theory of endopsychic structure, in which regression is understood as "withdrawal from a bad external world, in search of security in an inner world" (p. 55). As is well known (see especially Guntrip, 1952), such withdrawal may take a great variety of forms and may constitute more or less of an interference with other aspects of functioning, but *withdrawal*, nevertheless, remains the key dynamic: a turning away from noxious experience, exemplified by its opposite in the phototropism of plants in which light is turned toward. "Noxious," in the sense that it is used here, is not a moral or societal judgment, but specifically a (subjectively experienced,

---

[1] Among the features most commonly associated with such defenses, as listed by Fairbairn, (1940) are: "1. an attitude of omnipotence, 2. an attitude of isolation and detachment, and 3. a preoccupation with inner reality" (p. 6). These are not necessarily manifest features and may be covered over and concealed in many ways, but they all imply a "splitting of the ego" to one extent or another, the implications of which lie at the heart of the idea that "the basic position in the psyche is invariably a schizoid position" (p. 8).

but often unconscious) stimulus for anxiety that is warded off via withdrawal.

In terms of the three levels on which I have conceptualized this basic turning away, it is apparent that, when such action must be initiated during the earliest periods of the formation of the self, the consequences will be vastly different than when such action is taken after the core structure of the self has been firmly established. If, in other words, the earliest strivings of the infantile self toward essential objects (the first "selfobjects") are fundamentally painful or frustrating and remain so for enough time, then there will develop the *psychological equivalent of an avoidance tropism,* an (unconscious) experiential expectation that relatedness is a source of pain. This (unconscious) expectation will become built into the core organization of self-experience, and it is this phenomenon that may also be described in Fairbairn's terms as "ego-splitting" and in Klein's terms as the schizoid "position." In both characterizations fundamental and irremediable alterations of the basic fabric of the self have occurred and will not only not be outgrown, but will exert a telling and limiting influence on subsequent self-development and relations with objects.[2] This basic "turning away" may also be conceptualized in terms of a continuum of conscious and unconscious self-experience.

Since the same words often do not mean the same things and since we are speaking of the relativity of subjective states (which will also be experienced differently by each *listener*), the descriptive examples that follow must be understood as being representative of a larger context that can only be meaningfully filled out in more extensive case examples. Most typically, self-experience in this domain is expressed in terms of relatedness to others; those who are most reflective and suffer from splits in the self of the least depth will be more likely to recognize the shadow of their self-experience as it falls onto the relational world. At the other extreme, there are those who will insist that their conscious self-experience is solely a function of the relational dynamic. For example, if we collect reports of the first moments of a new analysand's experience of lying on the couch, we are usually, sooner or later, able to understand that report of conscious experience as an expression of his or her character structure or psychopathology. In a similar way, it will also reveal a basic turning away from (or turning toward) the analytic relation, which, if looked into,

---

[2] As Fairbairn has explicated, it is the vulnerability associated with infantile dependence on the early objects which is at the core of the formation of the self (and of psychopathology) and not the vicissitudes of the Oedipus complex which, despite Klein's differences on this point, are a much later phenomenon.

may further reveal a piece of underlying (i.e., not conscious) self-experience. For some, lying down is experienced in terms of fundamental safety and freedom ("Now I can pay more attention to my own feelings without being so distracted by looking at you . . .") as opposed to loss ("I feel all alone here. . .") or danger ("I don't like this . . . it feels scary") and futility ("Nothing is happening . . . I don't know what to do.")

Clearly each of these examples may mean many other things, but for the sake of discussion it is possible to suggest a dynamic that differentiates a range of basic responses to a given situation—responses that reveal an experience, along a continuum, of (relative) safety-versus-danger, closeness-versus-distance, hope-versus-futility, and so on. Such responses, at one level or another, may indicate a basic orientation regarding the experience of the self in relation to another (or in relation to another aspect of the self that may not be accessible to consciousness). These examples of conscious self-experience may (or may not) be supported and verified by subsequent experience in the analytic situation. However, interventions organized around informed ideas about the patient's conscious or unconscious sense of emotional safety in the analytic relationship will have a much greater chance of advancing the analytic process than if this domain is not included as a significant source of meaning, especially since these meanings are often concealed within other kinds of contexts. The concept of "empathy," for example, may be informed by this dynamic insofar as what is considered "empathic" may often be in large part a function of the correct assessment of a patient's need for distance in the interaction and the formulations of interventions based on this judgment.

THE CASE OF MR. M RECONSIDERED

To return to the proposal for a shift of focus: Fairbairn's recasting of psychoanalytic theory (1940, 1941, 1944, 1958) to rest on developmentally earlier (and object-related) emotional experience than that upon which Freud based his models of internalization, ego, and structuralization has great relevance for self psychology. The emphasis in self psychology on the development of the self and the functional tie of such development to critical early object experiences is basically in keeping with Fairbairn's emphasis on what he considered to be crucial formative experience, although the role of the "good" object (the "selfobject" in its more limited definition) in self psychology is more specified in terms of particular developmental needs of the child. Kohut's (1977) description, for example, of the dynamics of the development of early "defects in the self" and the evolution of "compensatory structures" illustrates this point. Kohut (1971, 1977) describes "Mr. M" (Goldberg, 1978), a patient in analysis with a female analyst under supervision by Kohut. Mr. M was 30 years old when he sought analysis, precipitated by his wife leaving him after six years of marriage. He wanted to understand what had happened in his marriage as well as his lack of fulfillment in his professional life as a writer for a TV station. He felt he had a "block" in his ability to be a creative writer and suffered from a sense of inner emptiness. Mr. M was adopted at the age of 3 months, along with his older brother and younger sister, by an immigrant couple who could not have children of their own. He remembers his adoptive mother as chronically ill and his tool-maker father as "passive." According to Kohut (1977),

> Certain transference phenomena . . . as well as childhood memories, indicated that he had experienced his mother's responsiveness to him as insufficient and faulty. He recalled how, on many occasions during his childhood, he tried to look at her suddenly so that she could not have time to cover over by a falsely friendly and interested facial expression the fact that she really felt indifferent about him [p. 8].

He was 11 (Goldberg, 1978, p. 125) when his adoptive mother died, and his father remarried 2 years later to a woman with her own children. The patient felt that he lost his father as well, since he (the father) now became "totally devoted to his new wife and to her family" (p. 125). The patient was not able to think of his father's new wife as his mother.

According to Kohut (1977), the failure of early maternal mirroring left Mr. M with a "defect in the self," which resulted in structuralized incapacities—most notably in the realm of the management of states of overstimulation. A writer, Mr. M's work suffered from his inability to regulate "the grandiosity and exhibitionism that became activated when his imagination was mobilized" (1977, p. 10). (See also Goldberg [1978] for a fuller report on the analysis of Mr. M.) However, the "abilities he employed" (i.e., what he *was* able to accomplish) were present in large part because of compensatory structure: "talents acquired or at least decisively reinforced later in his childhood in the matrix of the relation to the idealized selfobject, the father" (Kohut, 1977, p. 10). In other words, the structure of the self was formed around the relations with the early objects and around both positive and negative valences: the absence of the mother's mirroring responsiveness did not simply yield nothing—it yielded a specific defect, or *structure*, which was as much a part of Mr. M as the more positive idealizing tie to his father. Kohut remarks that a major piece of the working through phase of the analysis had to do with Mr. M accepting that it was "hopeless" to expect the mother's mirroring response (p. 14)—implying that the fact that Mr. M, up until that time in the analysis, "had not given up all hope of the mother's intuneness with him" (p. 9) and this *was at least as significant a factor for him as was the fact of the mother's failure to provide certain selfobject functions.* While Kohut focuses on the "specific maldevelopment" that followed upon the mother's specific failures of empathy, he does not emphasize the impact of the patient's continued hope for the mother's empathic response, a factor that was likely to be as structuralizing in its effects as were the mother's more observable failures. Fairbairn (1943) focuses precisely on this point: that the desperate attempt to engage the unengageable object may become a central and organizing aspect of the self, that the child's "need for relatedness" is a primary motivation (even though exactly what this is is not specified), and that this accounts for attachments to "bad" objects as well as for the fundamental "splits" that develop in the child's ego.

The "selfobject needs" specified by Kohut constitute some of the specific aspects and facets of the child's "need for relatedness" emphasized by Fairbairn. The structuralized, affective consequences noted by both Kohut and Fairbairn form the framework for a view of development, structuralization of the mind, and pathology from the point of view of both the consequences of the attempt by the child to obtain crucial responses, as well as the nature of those specific responses themselves. In other words, the effects of Mr. M's mother's "faulty empathy" (p. 9) created a specific type of emotional environment for Mr. M in which his relationship to his mother—and inevitably to later objects—was dominated by this attempt to evoke the responses that he craved. Kohut concludes that Mr. M remained, as a result of all this, with "a specific maldevelopment in the exhibitionistic sector of his personality" (p. 9) and developed "brittle defensive structures of the all or nothing type" (p. 9). That is, Mr. M either suppressed his exhibitionism at the cost of nearly all pleasure, or there were breakthroughs of "frantic activity and mild sexualized fantasies . . . [in] which the mirroring self-object (always a woman) was under his absolute, sadistically forced control" (p. 10). Such fantasy may be regarded as reparative or restitutive but also as a form of coercion that must be repeatedly invoked because the basic arrangement never shifts. As Fairbairn (1944) noted, "In his [the child's] attempts to control the unsatisfying object, he has introduced into the inner economy of his mind an object which not only continues to frustrate his need, but also continues to whet it" (p. 111). In Kohut's (1977) terms, these strivings remain "archaic" or "unmodified" because of the failure of the development of "modulating, substitution-offering psychic structures" (p. 11). Kohut goes on to discuss the formation of "compensatory structures" in such an instance (in the context of the relative availability of alternate sources—in this case, the father—of important selfobject functions) but notes specifically that the success of the working-through process in the analysis of Mr. M depended upon Mr. M's arriving at "the conclusion that it was hopeless to expect the mother's mirroring responses" (p. 14). However, it seems clear in this case that this "conclusion" was not, in fact, arrived at with certainty or completeness: "Certain layers" of the experience relevant to these early failures of the mother's mirroring responses were not reached, because to reach them "might bring about a perhaps irremediable disintegration of the self" (p. 19).

> I believe he dimly recognized that the activation of certain aspects of the mirror transference would expose him to the danger of permanent psychological disruption through the re-experience of primodial rage and greed, and that he indirectly expressed his awareness of these potential dangers in two ways: by developing a psychosomatic symptom, a rash on his elbow . . . and by saying that remaining in analysis much longer could become "addictive" [pp. 24–25].

This apparent refusal by Mr. M (a conclusion supported by Kohut) to go beyond a certain point in the analysis of the "primary defect" in Mr. M's personality because of the fear of "irreversible regression" (loss of self) is understood by Kohut (1977) as relative to the very early and extensive traumas suffered by Mr. M at the hands of this adoptive mother.

> Not only must he have been traumatized by the repeated failure of his adoptive mother to respond appropriately to his needs during the preverbal period, but behind these layers of frustration there hovered always a nameless preverbal depression, apathy, sense of deadness, and diffuse rage that related to the primordial trauma of his life. Such primal states, however, can neither be recalled through verbalized memories, as can traumata occurring after speech has developed, nor expressed through psychosomatic symptoms, as can the more organized rages of later preverbal experience . . . The effect of the primordial trauma on the patient's psychological organization (the existence of a weakness of the basic layers in his personality) is attested to only by his fear that further analysis would become "addictive"—by the vague dread, in other words, of a regressive voyage from which there is no return [p. 25].

It is in this context that Kohut (1977) remarks on the likelihood of the consequences of the interplay between mother and infant: after describing what the (adoptive) mother's difficulties in establishing a basic connection to Mr. M in the earliest months might have been, he notes:

> In consequence of . . . these restrictions of the mother's capacity to respond to the child, it might have brought about the development of a vicious cycle in the relation between mother and child because the mother's limited ability for phase-appropriate mirroring responses would, in turn, call forth an emotional withdrawal from the side of the baby [p. 27].

This "emotional withdrawal from the side of the baby" is tantamount to what Fairbairn has described as the inevitable consequences of the "basic endopsychic situation:" that the ego of the child becomes "split" in the effort both to maintain the essential tie to the object, which is fundamentally frustrating, and to survive otherwise intolerable emotional states that are a consequence of the nature of the "bad" object tie. This "splitting" occurs in the context of the infant's experience of ambivalence in the relationship to the mother, in which frustration is inevitable, but which must somehow be tolerated in order to preserve the "good" aspects of this essential tie. This leads to the circumstance of the "bad" frustrating object also remaining a "desired" object, and for the child, the consequences of the continuing attempts to generate (evoke) the desired response:

> The unsatisfying object has, so to speak, two facets. On the one hand, it frustrates; and, on the other hand, it tempts and allures. Indeed its essential "badness" consists precisely in the fact that it combines allurement with frustration [p. 111].

Although Fairbairn relies on the theory of internalized objects to elaborate and explain the dynamics of the consequences of this early ambivalent object tie, in my view much of his description of the child's (presumed) subjective experience is of great value even without a reliance on that theory. For Fairbairn, the "only solution" open to the child in the attempt to maintain the "good" aspects of the essential relationship is "to transfer the traumatic factor in the situation to the field of inner reality. . . . This means that he internalizes his mother as a bad object" (p. 110). In the case of Mr. M, for example, the danger that Kohut cites as the fundamental reason that further regression was not encouraged is aptly described by Fairbairn (1944) in terms of the affective state of the child who continuously attempts to regain the "rejecting" mother:

> It . . . becomes a dangerous procedure for the child to express his libidinal need, i.e., his nascent love, of his mother in face of rejection at

> her hands; for it is equivalent to discharging his libido into an emotional vacuum. Such a discharge is accompanied by an affective experience which is singularly devastating . . . The experience is one of shame over the display of needs which are disregarded or belittled. In virtue of these experiences of humiliation and shame he feels reduced to a state of worthlessness, destitution or beggardom. His sense of his own value is threatened. . . . At a still deeper level (or at a still earlier stage) the child's experience is one of, so to speak, exploding ineffectively and being completely emptied of libido. It is thus an experience of disintegration and of imminent psychical death [p. 113].

The child's management of this dilemma will, obviously, reflect not only constitutional factors, but the particular balance and intensity of the circumstance, that is, the extent of the child's frustration in the attempt to gain the response of the object. It is precisely in the evolution of the child's solution to this dilemma that becomes the basis for the characterological template for the structure of future relatedness. Fairbairn (1944) defines the spectrum by elaborating the extremes (in the context of object relations theory):

> Reduced to its simplest terms, the position in which he finds himself placed would appear to be one which, if, on the one hand, he expresses aggression, he is threatened with loss of his good object, and, if, on the other hand, he expresses libidinal need, he is threatened with loss of his libido (which for him constitutes his own goodness) and ultimately with loss of the ego structure which constitutes himself. Of these two threats by which the child feels menaced, the former (i.e. loss of the good object) would appear to be that which gives rise to the affect of depression, and which provides a basis for the subsequent development of a melancholic state in individuals for whom the disposal of aggression presents greater difficulties than the disposal of libido. On the other hand, the latter threat (i.e. loss of libido and ego structure) would appear to be that which gives rise to the affect of futility, and which provides a basis for the subsequent development of a schizoid state in individuals for whom the disposal of libido presents greater difficulties than the disposal of aggression [pp. 113–114].

For Fairbairn, it is the child's internalization of the "bad object" that consitutes the essential outcome of this dilemma, while for Kohut the situation results in a developmental arrest or fixation at the level of the selfobject need. For Kohut (1977), then, the unrequited need remains, in situ as it were, as *a self state that is evidenced by the existence of archaic selfobject transferences.* The "irreversible regression" (p. 26) that he describes as the fear behind Mr. M's reluctance to deepen the analysis may also be seen as Mr. M's fear of reengaging the overwhelming sense of futility that interfered with "the consolidation of the baby's basic self" (p. 27) and the "addiction" to the analyst as the regressive reenactment or reliving of the "bondage" (Fairbairn's term: p. 115) to the mother. Restated, the deepening of the analysis might recreate the pathogenic situation in which the analyst, "as temptress . . . [incites] the very need which she fails to satisfy" (Fairbairn, 1944, p. 115). *This intolerable state is embodied in the sense of futility that lies at the core of the schizoid withdrawal.* It is this essentially schizoid dynamic—the splitting of the self (ego) as a primary protection against very early states of helpless frustration and overwhelming futility—that Kohut postulated at the core of Mr. M's personality and that he characterized in the form of untransformed "archaic strivings," that is, in the form of its *expression*, rather than in its structuralized version as a "state" of the self.

In my view, it is particularly this underlying self state that is at issue and the correct assessment of which is necessary for a meaningful understanding of process as well as for the proper formulation of technical interventions. In particular, technique must take into account the implications of the underlying state of the self, and most specifically the condition of the self being split or of the existence of split-off sectors before meaningful approaches may be formulated.

In Kohut's (1977) theory of cure, "Old experience [must be] repeatedly relived by the more mature psyche" (p. 30), and this is elaborated as follows:

> Under the repeated impact of the archaic strivings, new structures are formed in the ego which are able to modulate and transform the archaic strivings. . . . The analysand, in order to keep open the access of the archaic strivings to his ego . . . uses the analyst as a self-object. . . . Little by little, as a result of innumerable processes of microinternalization, the anxiety-assuaging, delay-tolerating, and other realistic aspects of the anayst's image become part of the analysand's psychological equipment, *pari passu* with the "micro"-frustration of the analysand's need for the analyst's permanent presence and perfect functioning in this respect. In brief: through the process of transmuting internalization, new psychological structure is built [p. 32].

Kohut (1977) stresses that "the optimal result of an analysis not only rests on the aquisition of new structures . . . but that, secondarily, the heretofore isolated pathological sector of the personality establishes broad contact with the surrounding mature sectors" (p. 33). In other words, the split in the self must be able to be healed. But what about Mr. M? Kohut did not recommend continuing the analytic effort with Mr. M, precisely because he suspected that the regressive experience (noted above) might lead beyond a state in which the relived pathogenic situation was containable within the relatedness of the analytic situation because it must not have been clear to Kohut whether Mr. M did in fact possess a rudimentarily organized archaic self which was capable of sustaining the pressures of the analytic "cure" just described. In other words, Kohut's theory of cure rests on a particular set of preexisting psychological conditions, which Mr. M might not have been able to meet; Kohut felt that Mr. M could not tolerate the affects involved if the split were bridged, and this suggests a weakness in the theory: that the optimal frustration of selfobject needs does not address the tie to the *negative selfobject* (Gehrie, 1996). Rather, it may have been that Mr. M *specifically required an analysis of the tie to the negative selfobject that would inform the investigation of self-structure and its consequences for relatedness*; in such an undertaking, the analyst's "empathy" would likely take a different form, for example, a form that would establish a bridge to the experience with the negative selfobject (Gehrie, 1996). In other words, Kohut's concerns about the patient becoming "addicted" to the analyst might more reflect his view of the role of the mirroring selfobject (and its potential to be needed forever to maintain Mr. M's integratedness) than of the possibility presented by the analysis of Mr. M's terrors in the attachment to his analyst: *that the attachment would cost him his self and that any connection to the analyst would be experienced as intolerable and would eventuate in his psychological disintegration.* The analysis of this negative selfobject tie would require the establishment of a connection in which these dangers were not addressed by the attempt to "close the gap" in the emotional distance between patient and analyst, but precisely to permit it and bring it into the interpretive focus. (This might be accomplished by addressing the patient's experience of his *insignificance* in the negative mother transference, his experience of safety in the distance, and the acknowledgement that by permitting the attachment to the analyst Mr. M reopens the possibility of his love feeling meaningless.) This might have been experienced as "empathic" precisely because the anxiety evoked by the analyst's mirroring might not have become so stimulated; he might have felt that, since she understood this dynamic and was not insisting on changing it, it was safer to exist in relation to her.

In other terms, this issue might be seen as reflective of the degree to which early trauma had forced deep and/or unbridgeable splits in the self, which now had to be maintained in order for subjective existence to be tolerable: that crucial objects could be held onto only in accordance with these existing splits, that is, in a state of relatedness in which these splits would *not* be "endangered" or, more precisely, in which intolerable feelings would remain safely away from consciousness. Relatedness thus becomes the dependent variable: dependent upon the conditions obtaining in the underlying self-state and with particular reference to experiences that must remain split off in order for homeostasis to be maintained. In the case of Mr. M, for example, Kohut (1977) extrapolated that "the primordial experience in the orphanage had left him with an increased rage-potential and with a readiness toward quick emotional retreat in response to maternal frustrations. . . . In Mr. M's case, the essential psychological fact . . . was that he experienced his mother, and in the transference the analyst, as traumatically unempathic vis-à-vis his emotional demands and as unresponsive to them" (p. 30).

> Mr. M was afraid that worrying about the analyst's reaction to him indicated that he might become enslaved to her in a similar way (as he had felt with his mother); that he could not express himself freely without being concerned whether or not he had pleased her. . . . [Separations left him with] the feeling that he was on a conveyor belt. They . . . exposed a specific form of narcissistic vulnerability, namely, that the analyst will disregard his feelings, whatever they might be, that what he thought and felt would not matter to her . . . he felt himself becoming passive as his needs for the analyst and the analytic experience increased. This made him vulnerable. He was afraid that the more dependent he became on the analysis, the more vulnerable he would become in relation to the analyst. . . . He feared control and emotional exploitation in all his intimate relationships. . . . He was constantly anticipating the repetition of the feeling that what was important to him could simply be ignored or forgotten by others [Goldberg, 1978, pp. 130, 133–134, 138].

The extent of Mr. M's fear of and vulnerability to intrusion is illustrated by a feeling in one of his dreams that "When I knew you [the analyst] were looking, I fell apart—I woke up, and I literally started losing parts of me, they were falling off, like my arms" (p. 154). In subsequent hours, the analyst remarked to Mr. M how important it was for her to remain at a "comfortable distance"; she should "be there, available, but not intrude with her presence so that he would feel obliged to consider her and to please her" (pp. 154–156).

These early experiences and subsequent transference constellations made it impossible for Mr. M to feel close to the analyst in the negative maternal transference. His experience of mirroring failures was too intense to be accessed and worked through in the ordinary way (without endangering the underlying fragile self-structure by exposing the "primordial trauma of his life" and "risking permanent harm to his psychological equilibrium.") He was caught between the experience of feeling traumatically unresponded to, on one hand, and traumatically overstimulated, on the other. The early traumas (especially his 3-month stay in the orphanage after his birth and the associated feelings of depression, deadness, and lethargy) and associated negative attachments to both adoptive parents (founded primarily on their essentially "faulty" availability in terms of both his mirroring and idealizing needs), combined with (perhaps) "the analyst's feeling temporarily emotionally distant from the patient" (Kohut, 1977, p. 29) left the present too powerfully overlaid with the "template" (Gehrie, 1993, 1996) from the past: that is, the tie to the negative selfobject preserved his balance in a crucial way and forced Mr. M into extra-analytic contexts (which he could manage or control) for the creation of opportunities for relatedness. For example, Kohut (1977) reports that Mr. M took up playing the violin: "In the fantasies that accompanied his playing he offered his grandiose self to the admiring view of multitudes which he experienced as maternal, without being inhibited by the fear that he would suffer the crushing frustration of maternal disinterest, and without the even greater fear that he would become hypomanically overstimulated and thus experience the dissolution of his exhibiting self" (p. 39). It was in this form of "preverbal emotionality" (p. 38) that Mr. M worked through the maternal mirror transference.

These considerations suggest that Mr. M succeeded in structuring a context for relatedness in his analysis that he could tolerate; he clearly wanted more gratifying involvements in his life as well as some understanding of the nature of the failures that he had suffered, and the analysis provided "lived evidence" of the nature of his relational difficulties. The analyst did not push him beyond his capacities to tolerate closeness (and risk a regressive disintegration), and she also permitted extra-analytic solutions to issues, which no doubt she hoped might have been managed in the context of the transference. (Perhaps the analyst's countertransference distance might also be seen as her intuitive response to Mr. M's need for greater distance from her, that he needed a way to avoid his experience of her pursuit in order to preserve his balance.) Hence, what Kohut describes as "a defect in his personality that had in essence remained unanalyzed" (Kohut, 1977, p. 24) and as the patient's "sense" about the nature of the risks involved may also be conceptualized as this patient's intuitive awareness of the relatively fragile nature of his self-structure and the requisite forms of distancing (schizoid) defenses that had to be maintained. This self-structure was the legacy of and contained within in it the tie to the earliest frustrating object, as well as the tie to the the later ones; Mr. M could permit the analysis to loosen the ties to these early objects only insofar as the anxiety that was released in these efforts at integration did not threaten the integrity of his fragile self. Further analysis of these ties would have required permitting the splits to be maintained while the negative selfobject tie was addressed very gradually. This approach would not attempt to decrease or remove the distance that Mr. M required to maintain the integrity of his self, but to elucidate it in an emotional context and expand his repertoire for self-management. This type of condition, in which attempts at analytic integration release unmanageable (as opposed to simply painful or uncomfortable) feelings, represents one point on the schizoid continuum, bringing together the self-state, subjective experience and capacity for relatedness, as well as suggesting implications for technique: the gradual integration of heretofore split apart aspects of the self (Goldberg, 1999) in the context of the understanding and interpretation of the dynamics of closeness and distance in the transference represents a concrete clinical strategy.

REFERENCES

Bacal, H. & Newman, K. (1990), *Theories of Object Relations: Bridges to Self Psychology*. New York: Columbia University Press.

Fairbairn, W. R. D. (1940), Schizoid factors in the personality. In: *Psychoanalytic Studies of the Personality*. London: Routledge & Kegan Paul, 1952, pp. 3–27.

——— (1941), A revised psychopathology of the psychoses and psychoneuroses. In: *Psychoanalytic Studies of the Personality*. London: Routledge & Kegan Paul, 1952, pp. 28–58.

——— (1943), The repression and the return of bad objects (with special reference to the "war neuroses"). In: *Psychoanalytic Studies of the Personality*. London: Routledge & Kegan Paul, 1952, pp. 59–81.

——— (1944), Endopsychic structure considered in terms of object-relationships. In: *Psychoanalytic Studies of the Personality*. London: Routledge & Kegan Paul, 1952, pp. 82–136.

——— (1958), On the nature and aims of psycho-analytical treatment. *Internat. J. Psycho-Anal.*, 34:374–385.

Ferenczi, S. & Rank, O. (1924), *The Development of Psychoanalysis*. New York: Dover Publications.

Freud, S. (1917), A difficulty in the path of psychoanalysis. *Standard Edition*, 17:135–144. London: Hogarth Press, 1955.

——— (1920), Beyond the pleasure principle. *Standard Edition*, 18:7–64. London: Hogarth Press, 1961.

——— (1921), Group psychology and the analysis of the ego. *Standard Edition*, 18:69–143. London: Hogarth Press, 1955.

——— (1923), The ego and the id. *Standard Edition*, 19:12–66. London: Hogarth Press, 1961.

Gedo, J. (1988), The Mind in Disorder. Hillsdale, NJ: The Analytic Press.

——— & Goldberg, A. (1973), Models of the Mind. Chicago, IL: The University of Chicago Press.

Gehrie, M. (1993), Psychoanalytic technique and the development of the capacity to reflect. *J. Amer. Psychoanal. Assn.*,41:1083–1111.

——— (1996), Empathy in broader perspective: A technical approach to the consequences of the negative selfobject in early character formation. In: Progress in Self Psychology, Vol. 12, ed. A. Goldberg. Hillsdale, NJ: The Analytic Press, pp. 159–179.

Goldberg, A., ed. (1978), *The Psychology of the Self: A Casebook.* New York: International Universities Press.

——— (1995), The Problem of Perversion. New Haven, CT: Yale University Press.

——— (1999), *Being of Two Minds.* Hillsdale, NJ: The Analytic Press.

Guntrip, H. (1952), The schizoid personality and the external world. In: *Schizoid Phenomena, Object Relations, and the Self.* New York: International Universities Press, 1969. pp. 17–48.

——— (1961), The schizoid problem, regression and the struggle to preserve an ego. In: *Schizoid Phenomena, Object Relations, and the Self.* New York: International Universities Press, 1969, pp. 49–86.

——— (1962), The schizoid compromise and psychotherapeutic stalemate. In: *Schizoid Phenomena, Object Relations, and the Self.* New York: International Universities Press, 1969, pp. 288–309.

Klein, M. (1946), Notes on some schizoid mechanisms. In: *Envy and Gratitude and Other Works 1946–1963.* New York: The Free Press, 1975, pp. 1–24.

——— (1952), Some theoretical concepts regarding the emotional life of the infant. In: *Envy and Gratitude and Other Works 1946–1963.* New York: The Free Press, 1975, pp. 61–93.

Kohut, H. (1971), *The Analysis of the Self.* New York: International Universities Press.

——— (1972), Thoughts on narcissism and narcissistic rage. *The Psychoanalytic Study of the Child,* 27:360–400. New Haven, CT: Yale University Press.

——— (1977), *The Restoration of the Self.* New York: International Universities Press.

——— (1984), *How Does Analysis Cure?* ed. A. Goldberg & P. Stepansky. Chicago: University of Chicago Press.

Winnicott, D. W. (1951), Transitional objects and transitional phenomena. In: *Collected Papers: Through Pediatrics to Psychoanalysis.* New York: Basic Books, 1958. pp. 229–242.

——— (1958), *Collected Papers: Through Pediatrics to Psychoanalysis.* New York: Basic Books.

——— (1965), *The Maturational Processes and the Facilitating Environment.* New York: International Universities Press.

Chapter 3

The Analyst's Empathy, Subjectivity, and Authenticity: Affect as the Common Denominator

Judith Guss Teicholz

The purpose of this chapter is to respond to a troubling critique of empathy that seems to pervade contemporary psychoanalytic literature. While the various authors of this critique generally *problematize* the analyst's empathy, they consider the authentic expression of the analyst's subjectivity to be essential both to the treatment process and to cure. The analyst's empathy seems almost to be *replaced* by her subjectivity, and therefore any attempt to address the current critique of empathy must also raise questions about the nature of the presumed, mutually exclusive relationship between the analyst's empathy and her subjectivity. For this reason, in what follows I respond to the critique of empathy in the context of examining the relationship between the analyst's empathy, subjectivity, and authenticity in the clinical situation.

EMPATHY, SUBJECTIVITY, AND THE SELF

While empathy remains at the heart of self psychology, its clinical importance is often dismissed and devalued by analysts writing from outside a Kohutian perspective. Coming from a broad spectrum of theoretical paradigms, contemporary analytic authors tend to give a privileged position to the overt expression of the analyst's subjectivity, while pointing out innumerable problems with analytic empathy. Writing from classical/interactional (Renik, 1993), relational/conflict (Slavin and Kriegman, 1992; Mitchell, 1993, 1996; Slavin, 1997), and critical constructivist (Hoffman, 1983, 1998) viewpoints, these authors hold diverse opinions on many analytic issues but speak almost in one voice to recommend that the analyst articulate her differentiated feelings and viewpoint to the patient as part of an authentic engagement in the analytic encounter. This clinical emphasis on the analyst's self-expression would seem to be diametrically opposed to self psychology, in which the analyst uses her empathy to draw out the patient's unique experience, while as much as possible keeping her own subjectivity in the background.

Relational authors argue for the analyst's distinctive self-expression because they believe that interpersonal conflict is universal and will therefore inevitably emerge in the analytic dyad (Mitchell, 1992; Slavin and Kriegman, 1992). They place a high value on openness and authenticity, and they think that the analyst must either confront divisive issues or risk colluding with the patient to avoid them. Building on Sullivan's (1953) concept of *participant-observation,* they believe that the best way to help patients change their painful patterns of relating is through authentic engagement with a distinctive other who participates interpersonally but who also steps back to observe and make comment upon the patient's maladaptive attitudes and modes of behavior (Mitchell, 1992, 1996, 1997). In these exchanges, the analyst's countertransfence is an important aspect of what may be communicated to the patient (Aron, 1990, 1996; Mitchell, 1997). All of these modes of interaction take precedence over the clinical use of empathy.

In other critiques of self psychology, concern has been expressed that empathy too easily becomes ritualized (Hoffman, 1983) or automatized (Slavin and Kriegman, 1992), thereby arousing mistrust in the patient. A further concern has been expressed that the analyst's empathy will undermine the patient's autonomy, while the analyst's openness and self-disclosure are more likely to provide positive models of independent thinking and self-exploration (Renik, 1993, 1995, 1998).

Empathy has also been questioned on the basis of its placement in a broader class of analytic attitudes and activities, which include neutrality, holding, and interpretation. All of these are noted for their failure to take into account such ultimate realities as the irreversibility of time and human mortality (Hoffman, 1998). In the view of Hoffman, for instance, exposure to the analyst's unique thoughts and feelings might nudge an ambivalent patient toward a job opportunity that would otherwise be lost and never present itself again or might push a reluctant patient toward making emotional contact with an elderly or ill parent before it is too late. With concerns such as these in mind, the relational or constructivist analyst does not usually immerse herself in the patient's experience and try to see things from the patient's viewpoint. Rather, she is likely to spell out the extent to which her own feelings and viewpoints *differ* from the patient's. In all of these recommendations, a fuller expression of the analyst's subjectivity seems to have *replaced* her empathy.

This is in marked contrast to Kohut's (1971, 1977) theory of treatment in which the analyst's empathy, and not her subjectivity, facilitates the patient's self-exploration. By virtue of the analyst's efforts to *contain,* rather than to express, her distinctive subjectivity, the patient is allowed the experience of feeling mirrored or "twinned" by one who unconsciously represents an idealized parent figure. The analyst uses her subjectivity primarily in the process of vicarious introspection, toward the goal of achieving an in-depth understanding of the patient's experience. In this process, the analyst may *silently* explore her own feelings but usually refrains from articulating them to the patient, especially in their divergent aspects.

In Kohut's (1984) view, the analyst's empathy or vicarious introspection has a direct impact on the patient's self. It facilitates processes in the patient that lead to both self-exploration and restoration (Kohut, 1977). Although Kohut (1977, 1984) deliberately avoided being pinned down to a singular definition of self, he suggested that the self was at the center of experience, that it had its origins in the earliest interactions between the individual and his caretakers, and that it coincided with but was not identical to "the set of introspectively or empathically perceived inner experiences to which we later refer as 'I'" (1977, p. 311). The more thoroughly and profoundly the analyst empathically perceives and repsonds to the patient's inner experiences, the greater will be the range of inner experiences to which the patient will be able to refer as "I." Another way of saying the same thing is that the analyst's empathy serves to open the patient's mind to a greater breadth and depth of his own thought and feeling, leading in time to an integration of previously disavowed experience and to an increased robustness of self. The analyst's empathy can often obviate the need for interpersonal feedback and confrontation because a strengthened self is both less defensive and more capable of active and accurate self-reflection.

Because Kohut addressed the treatment situation at both phenomenological and metapsychological levels of abstraction, he described curative processes both as they are experienced directly by the patient and as they gradually lead to changes in the patient's psychic functioning and structuralization from the viewpoint of an outside observer. But Kohut did not make a radical distinction between structural concepts such as "self-representation" and experiential concepts such as "sense of self." Rather, he suggested that the term *self* was really nothing more than "a generalization derived from empirical data" (1977, p. 311). His term *structure* referred to stable patterns of intrapsychic experience and functioning. Thus the self was for him both experience and structure, and the two aspects were ineluctably intertwined.

In self psychology, healthy self-structure gives those who possess it a sense of cohesion and continuity and confers on them capacities for self-soothing and affirmation which contribute to a sense of serenity and worth. Individuals possessed of healthy self-structure also feel a forward movement in their lives as they strive to achieve their ambitions and goals and to live up to an internalized set of ideals. This forward movement (or tension arc) gives meaning to life that transcends daily activities and opens doors to creativity (Kohut, 1977, 1978, 1984).

But all of these experiential benefits of self-structure, as well as the structure itself, come about only as a consequence of optimal self–selfobject *experiences* in childhood (Kohut, 1984, p. 53). Thus, Kohut both identified qualities of experience that were associated with healthy self-structure and believed that such structure came into existence only following upon specific kinds of developmental experiences between the child and his primary caretakers. Structure and experience are thus so closely intertwined in his theory that neither can be considered without the other.

Atwood and Stolorow (1984) set out to clarify and expand upon Kohut's self psychology, but, in so doing, they shifted the terminology from *self* to *subjectivity*. Atwood and Stolorow define subjectivity as "organizations of experience," and like Kohut's self, these organizations encompass both structure and experience. In fact, Stolorow, Brandchaft, and Atwood (1987) include in their concept of subjectivity all that Kohut meant by *self* except for "self-as-agent," which they reject because they see it as an experience-distant concept. But Kohut wrote not of self-as-agent so much as of the *experience of self as the center of initiative*. Therefore, it is not at all clear that self-as-agent remains a point of difference between Stolorow et al.'s *subjectivity* and Kohut's *self*.

Like Stolorow et al., Daniel Stern (1985) uses the term *subjectivity* in ways that both overlap with and differ from Kohut's concept of self. Where the two authors converge, Stern's *stages of self* lend support for Kohut's (1984) distinction between *archaic* and *mature* selfobject experiences. Kohut's *archaic* selfobject experience, for instance, has much in common with Stern's *core* or physical self, in which the individual does not yet recognize the separate subjectivity of the other. At this earliest stage of development, the child may indeed recognize the *physical* distinctiveness of the caretaker but does not yet recognize either himself or the other as a separate center of experience. He does not yet understand that both he and his mother are private repositories of unique but sharable thoughts and feelings. In this "pre-self" (Kohut, 1977, 1984) or "presubjectivity" (Stern, 1985) stage of development, a need for omnipotent merger prevails, in which the caretaker's idealized qualities (Kohut, 1971, 1977, 1984) and her emotional availability and responsiveness remain central to the child's psychological well-being (Emde, 1990).

In Stern's developmental schema, subjectivity and intersubjectivity emerge simultaneously with the recognition of separate mind in both self and other. This double achievement leads to the infant's awareness of a previously unrecognized distance between himself and his caretaker. In an effort to cross this gulf, the child newly possessed of subjectivity and intersubjectivity seeks external reassurance that his own thoughts and feelings and those of the caretaker can be shared. It is only through the establishment of *bridges of empathy* between caretaker and child that such reassurance can be secured (Stern, 1985, p. 126). Thus, in Stern's view, the caretaker's empathy continues to be of pivotal importance to the young child, even after intersubjective relatedness has been achieved.

But as the child's subjectivity becomes more consolidated, the caretaker's empathy becomes less of a life-and-death matter. At some later developmental point, the healthy child becomes interested in knowing the details and nuances of the caretaker's distinctive subjectivity. When things go well, Stern argues, an active and robust curiosity about others eventually comes into being.

Although Stern (1985) placed the initial establishment of subjectivity/intersubjectivity at around nine months of age, he saw it as an achievement of considerable psychic complexity, which requires specific, prior kinds of interactions with the human environment in order to unfold. Clearly, in both Kohut's and Stern's theory, then, the young child can be derailed on the path to selfhood or intersubjective relatedness, both of which depend on the adequacy of environmental provision and responsiveness for their initial establishment and continued maintenance.

Because of this vulnerability to developmental derailment, subjectivity and intersubjectivity cannot at all be taken for granted in our patients in a firmly established form. Indeed, Kohut (1984) saw many or most patients as beginning treatment with a fragile self and with archaic, rather than mature or mutual, modes of self–selfobject relating. But when relational and constructivist authors make the general recommendation that analysts express their subjectivity in the clinical situation, they do seem to be taking for granted the establishment of a robust subjectivity and intersubjective relatedness in their patients: they seem, in fact, to conduct their treatments as if each and every patient possessed a subjectivity consolidated enough not only to withstand, but even to benefit therapeutically from, exposure to the articulated experience of a differentiated other. In their enthusiasm for the analyst's distinctive self-expression, they have failed to consider the possibility, pointed out by both Stern (1985) and Kohut (1984), that patients in *archaic and presubjective*—as *opposed to mature, mutual, or intersubjective—states of relatedness* may be unable to make therapeutic use of overt expressions of the analyst's differentiated subjectivity, and might even be harmed by them.

Thus far we have seen that Kohut's term *self* has much in common with Stern's and Stolorow et al.'s subjectivity and that these commonalities, not surprisingly, lead to compatible views of the treatment situation among these various authors. And in spite of previously noted differences between Kohutian and *relational* views of treatment, Kohut's *self* also has conceptual complexities, multiple meanings, and ambiguities that give it much in common with the *relational* view of subjectivity as well. Nevertheless, relational theories do not share with self psychology its phenomenological/metapsychological duality, because in most relational theories subjectivity is an experiential but not a structural or metapsychological concept. And while many relational theorists join Kohut in viewing the expansion of self as a central goal of treatment (Mitchell, 1997), they tend to view the "normal" self as multiple and fragmented rather than as continuous and cohesive. It seems to be little recognized by relational theorists that, although Kohut (1984) did see cohesion and continuity as qualities of experience essential to psychic health and well-being, he did so exactly *because* he recognized "the psyche of modern man [as] . . . multifragmented" (p. 60).

Not realizing that Kohut's theory accounted for both a multiplicity and cohesion of self, relational and constructivist theorists have moved away from Kohut's language of *self* toward a language of the *subject*. This terminological shift represents an effort on their part to emphasize the more open-ended aspects of self (Ogden, 1992a, b) and to avoid conceptual reification, which Kohut (1984) himself wished to avoid. Their term *subjectivity* is particularly intended to connote the unboundedness, multiplicity, fluidity, ambiguity, ineffability, and ever-changing qualities of the self, as opposed to its cohesion and continuity.

In addition to these differences in emphasis between Kohut's *self* and the *relational subject,* there is also a difference in the relative importance placed on the subjective experience of patient and analyst in the analytic situation. Relational theorists explicitly explore the analyst's subjectivity alongside the patient's because they see it as unwittingly contributing not only to the analyst's perceptions of the patient's intrapsychic life, but also to the actual cocreation of unique versions of the patient's psychopathology. They see the analyst's subjectivity, along with the patient's, as codetermining both process and outcome in treatment. They also believe that the patient will not only perceive the analyst's subjectivity, but will have feelings and make interpretations about what he perceives (Hoffman, 1983; Aron, 1996). They think that the analyst should as much as possible bring under analytic scrutiny the patient's inevitable perceptions, feelings, and interpretations concerning the analyst's experience because the only alternative to such scrutiny is to leave their impact on the patient and the treatment isolated from analytic exploration (Hoffman, 1983; Aron, 1996).

But the self psychologist, as well, remains alert to shifts in the patient's affect and thought processes, which she recognizes may have been triggered by spoken or unspoken thoughts and feelings in the analyst. And the self psychologist also encourages the patient to bring these perceptions and reactions to the surface and to put them into words. In fact Kohut (1971, 1977, 1982, 1984) long predated relational and constructivist theorists in recognizing the analyst's subjectivity, but he did so primarily in the context of exploring *the limits of scientific objectivity.* He did not take the further step of placing the analyst's subjectivity on a par with the patient's in the analytic situation. And unlike relational analysts also, his recognition of the contribution of the analyst's subjectivity to the patient's experience in treatment did not lead him generally to recommend the analyst's self-disclosure. The one exception to this was that he did advise analysts to acknowledge their failures of empathy when the affective bond between patient and analyst has already shown signs of having been disrupted by these failures. Whereas the relational analyst might then go on to explore the interpersonal context in which the analyst's "failure of empathy" occurred, however, Kohut seemed to prefer a simple acknowledgement on the part of the analyst with an immediate return to a focus on the depth-psychological experience of the patient.

Similarly, although all intersubjectivity theorists join relational theorists in viewing the analytic situation as a two-person endeavor, intersubjectivists writing from a *self psychological* perspective do not give a generally privileged position to the analyst's self-expression (Stolorow, 1995; Lachmann and Beebe, 1996; Stolorow and Atwood, 1997; Orange and Stolorow, 1998). To do so would be to dispense with empathy as the analyst's primary approach to the patient, which no self psychologist is ready to do. Nevertheless, since intersubjectivity theory does place the analyst's subjectivity on a par with the patient's in the cocreation of the analytic process, a self psychology that includes notions of intersubjectivity must find a way to counter the view that the analyst's empathy and subjectivity, of necessity, oppose one another.

Indeed, a major purpose of this chapter is to propose a conceptualization of the analyst's empathy and subjectivity in which they are not mutually exclusive phenomena but are instead closely related aspects of the analyst's psychic functioning, both of which make important contributions to the analytic situation. This proposal is based on the fact that Kohut himself acknowledged the analyst's subjectivity (1977, pp. 63–69; 1982, p. 400; 1984, pp. 34–46) as well as a two-way influence in the analytic situation (1984, p. 40). But in marked contrast to relational and constructivist theorists, he did not see these phenomena in any way as diminishing the role of empathy in cure.

Relational authors seem to present us with a forced choice: they see either an empathic analyst who is inauthentic and out-of-touch with her subjectivity or an authentic analyst in touch with her subjectivity, but who has put her empathy aside. Rather than accepting these mistaken alternatives, I suggest that the analyst's empathy, subjectivity, and authenticity share common ground in affective experience and stand in complex relationship to one another. The affective experience of both patient and analyst are critically important to the analytic process because the affect of every individual is at the core of both self and subjectivity (Lachmann and Stolorow, 1980; Stechler and Kaplan, 1980; Tolpin, 1983; Socarides and Stolorow, 1985; Stern, 1985; Demos and Kaplan, 1986; Stolorow et al., 1987; Demos, 1988). But even if we agree that affect is an essential component of both empathy and subjectivity, the way we perceive the relationship between empathy and subjectivity is still tied to whether we view psychoanalysis as a one- or a two-person theory. Prior, therefore, to the further elaboration of my central thesis, I shall explore one- and two-person facets of self psychology—admittedly, a controversial issue.

ONE- AND TWO-PERSON ASPECTS OF SELF PSYCHOLOGY

In Kohut's (1971, 1977, 1984) theory of treatment, the *selfobject* concept is central: it refers to the patient's experience of the analyst's psychic functioning as *an extension of the patient's self*. This understanding of selfobject experience, combined with Kohut's depth-psychological focus on the patient's viewpoint, renders inessential the analyst's status as an "outside other" (see Benjamin [1988, 1990] for a critique of this aspect of Kohut's theory). Because in selfobject experience the patient recognizes the psychic functioning of just one person, Ornstein (1991) and Goldberg (1998) argue that self psychology should be seen exclusively as a one-person theory. But among self psychology "revisionists," Lachmann and Beebe (1996) strive to integrate one- and two-person aspects of treatment in a dynamic systems theory derived from infant research. And Stolorow and Atwood (1992) believe that longstanding tensions between the interpersonal and the intrapsychic are resolved by their theory of intersubjectivity, in which the individual is constituted through the dyadic context.

In general, those who emphasize a two-person view of the analytic situation advocate that the analyst articulate unique aspects of her subjectivity in her work and that she engage authentically with the patient; those who see psychoanalysis as a one-person endeavor suggest that the analyst might better contain the more distinctive aspects of her subjectivity, keeping the focus on the patient's experience and striving toward empathic resonance. But those attempting to integrate one- and two-person aspects of psychoanalytic theory must question any such clinical dichotomy, seeking new ways to conceptualize the relationships among the analyst's empathy, subjectivity, and authenticity and their expression in treatment.

Although it may seem to depart from traditional self psychology to suggest that the analyst's empathy, subjectivity, and authenticity have a common denominator in affect, several passages in Kohut's writings suggest that he may have been moving toward a more explicitly intersubjective view of treatment, especially toward the end of his life. Although he never broadly discussed the implications for treatment of the analyst's subjectivity, he did suggest that the analyst's subjectivity, including deeply ingrained "prejudicial tendencies" (Kohut, 1984, p. 38), plays a central role in determining the analyst's choice of theory, his mode of listening, and his selective focus on certain aspects of the patient's communications. He also wrote that "the subjective element . . . is as immanent in the clinical situation as it is in small-particle physics" (p. 39), and he called for "the courage to acknowledge [both] . . . the influence of the observed on the observer and . . . the influence of the observer on the field that he observes" (p. 40). He argued that in clinical psychoanalysis, the depth-psychological observer "by his very presence . . . is a . . . constituent in the field" (p. 39). He also wondered whether the analyst's presence and participation might actually "contribute to the shaping of social reality," even when the analyst is trying only "to describe [the patient's] motivations and reactions with scientific objectivity" (p. 39).

Kohut supplemented his original view of empathy as a mode of observation (1959), with a later focus on empathy's potential for creating a bond between two individuals (1982). And from the start, he defined empathy as *vicarious introspection*. Although Kohut himself did not spell out certain implications of this terminology, I would argue that to the extent the analyst's psychic functioning is *introspective,* it must include her subjectivity, and to the extent it is *vicarious,* it must involve the subjective experience of both patient and analyst.

In his later years, Kohut (1984) felt that self psychology had finally succeeded in shifting the psychoanalytic view away from the Freudian *object* as target of the individual's instinctual impulses to a focus on the *selfobject* as constitutive of the individual's self. He suggested that he had perhaps overemphasized the selfobject dimensions of relationship to correct an imbalance in earlier psychoanalytic theorizing and he thought that the time had come to explore broader relational configurations, beyond either sexual discharge or selfobject need (Kohut, 1984). These shifts in emphasis may indeed have signaled a move in the direction of a two-person theory. But self psychology had always balanced the tensions between "autonomous" *self*-strivings and "embedded" *selfobject* need, and this balancing may have rendered it *both* a one- and a two-person theory from the start (Teicholz, 1999).

For Kohut (1984), a one-person view prevails in *archaic* stages of development and in early phases of treatment. Until the patient is helped to make therapeutic gains toward a more consolidated self-structure, empathy and selfobject function in treatment are not mutual but move rather from analyst to patient. In these earlier phases of treatment also, the subjectivity of the analyst is seen as relevant mainly to the extent that the patient can make silent and unrecognized use of it. While the analyst's therapeutic functioning is certainly understood to emanate from a distinctive subjectivity, what the patient needs from the analyst is itself more *im*personal: the analyst's psychic functioning is "broken down" and metabolized through internalization processes to become uniquely the patient's own (Kohut, 1971, 1977). Self psychology's historical emphasis on these less personal aspects of the analyst's functioning, combined with its primary focus on the patient's experience, has tended to deemphasize the freer and more open-ended expression of the analyst's unique subjectivity.

In Kohut's developmental theory, a failure to integrate normal childhood grandiosity toward establishment of adequate ambitions, goals, and ideals leads to defective self-structure. This rendering of development, if it could stand alone, would contribute to a one-person view of self psychology. But Kohut's view is also a theory of how structures of subjectivity optimally develop in a self–selfobject milieu, how they may be compromised through environmental failures, and how these failures may later be redressed through understanding and explanation in the context of an empathic bond between two persons. In these aspects of his theory, as well as in his descriptions of mature and healthy selfobject relationships, Kohut (1984) leaned more toward a two-person theory.

For instance, in his view of healthy adult relationships, self and other remain open to one another for *mutual* enhancement throughout the lifecycle. The essence of cure is to open "a path of empathy between self and selfobject . . . on mature adult levels" (Kohut, 1984, p. 66) where empathy is bidirectional (p. 52). Kohut also argues that *autonomy* is neither desirable nor possible (i.e., 1984, pp. 47, 52, 61, 63) because the viable self is never without its self–selfobject milieu. Thus, although his theory can be construed as a one-person psychology in the sense that he sees the thrust of development as moving toward individual selfhood, it is also a two-person theory because individual selfhood can only be achieved or sustained through the emotional presence and availability of a significant other, even when that other is not perceived as such. Taken together, the multiple strands of self psychology form a theory in which one- and two-person facets would seem to coexist and interpenetrate.

Since Kohut (1984) himself argued that the analyst's subjectivity and personhood contribute to the affective atmosphere of the treatment and to the specifics of how it is conducted, I shall explore the analyst's empathy, subjectivity, and authenticity in an attempt to become more aware of how these facets of the analyst's "human presence" (p. 36) may relate to one another and how they may even at times be used in concert to facilitate particular treatments.

MUTUAL INFLUENCE AND THE ANALYST'S SELF

Recently, infant researchers such as Stern et al. (1998) have joined relational analysts in exploring the analyst's spontaneous self-expression and authentic relating, introducing such concepts as the "shared implicit relationship" (p. 910) and "now moments" (p. 911) and seeing these aspects of experience as potentially curative. Although initially a source of support for the tenets of traditional self psychology, infant research has increasingly been taking a turn toward the intersubjective and relational. Indeed, some of the new psychoanalytic emphasis on intersubjectivity has its origins in mounting evidence from infant researchers of *mutual influence* between parent and child. In relational theories of treatment, this mutual influence is understood to create multiplicities, fragmentation, and lack of stability in even the healthiest of selves, whether patient's or analyst's.

In contrast to this view, Kohut's theory of treatment sees the patient gaining cohesion and continuity through internalization of selfobject function in the analytic encounter. In the self psychological view of more mature relationships, a mutual exchange of selfobject function yields self-consolidation and enhancement for both partners. Thus, Kohut sees a self *strengthened* through its relationships, while relational theories see the self as repeatedly decentered and destabilized through its intrapsychic multiplicities and through its relationships of mutual influence with others.

Although the empirical findings of infant researchers do seem to lend credence to the primacy of a destabilizing mutual influence in relationships (Beebe and Lachmann, 1988b), the same researchers also point to *continuities* in the infant–mother relationship: continuities that contribute importantly to the development of representational mentation and psychic structure in the child (Stern, 1985; Beebe and Lachmann, 1988b, 1994; Beebe, Lachmann, and Jaffe, 1997).

Infant research, then, would seem to support Kohut's own emphasis on *continuity in the context of flexibility and change*. It is for this reason that recognition of mutual influence in self psychology neither detracts from the analyst's basic stance of empathy and responsiveness nor leads to a general privileging of the analyst's self-expression. Self psychology has *always* recognized the analyst's contribution both to the patient's experience and to what transpires between patient and analyst. It was with this influence in mind that Kohut advised the analyst to help the patient to articulate his own feeling states *and* to communicate how they may have been triggered by the *analyst's* words or behavior.

But while Kohut never lost sight of the patient as the focus of analytic attention, contemporary analysts have begun to explore the effect of mutual influence on the *analyst*. Slavin and Kriegman (1998) even argue that in order to help the patient, the analyst must change. It does of course require flexibility in the analyst to depart from her usual modes of seeing and doing, and such changes in the analyst may indeed help to move an analysis forward. But since lasting psychic change is a hard-won achievement, most changes in the analyst, in the course of her work, are probably *transient* rather than permanent. In fact, Fosshage (1995) has suggested that, while it is essential that we immerse ourselves in our patients' experience, it may be equally important that we are able to move back to our own perspectives. Empathy as vicarious introspection would seem to *exemplify* such back-and-forth movement in the analyst's mind, between her own and the patient's subjectivity. This psychic agility in the analyst might call to mind the movements of a dancer:

> It's the establishment of a clear center that enables the great dancer to move. Freely and fully, she explores the range outside of her metaphoric centerline. Reaching in multiple directions, she leaps and lifts with an absolute commitment to that center. It is being grounded in her own center that allows the dancer to take flight.
> [Jacob's Pillow program notes, 1997].

I would suggest that, as analysts, the more we operate from our own centers, the more gracefully will we be able transiently to accept our patients' unfamiliar attributions (Lichtenberg, Lachmann, and Fosshage, 1996) and the greater will be our ease in making leaps toward the patient's different and difficult experience. But even if we agree that the analyst moves *internally* between her own and the patient's subjectivity, we are still left with questions concerning whether, or to what degree, the analyst should openly articulate her personal feelings and viewpoint to her patients.

THE ANALYST'S SELF-EXPRESSION AND SELF-CONTAINMENT

In the analyst's back and forth movements between her own and the patient's subjectivity (Fosshage, 1995), she transiently keeps selective aspects of her own subjectivity in the background or puts them aside. But many relational theorists argue that the analyst neither can nor should "set aside" her subjectivity in the interests of the patient, seeing such efforts as both inauthentic and antitherapeutic (i.e., Renik, 1993, 1995, 1996, 1998; Bass, 1996). They believe, rather, that the patient's exposure to overt expression of the analyst's distinct subjectivity is inherently facilitative of psychic growth (Benjamin, 1988, 1990; Bollas, 1989; Slavin and Kriegman, 1992; Renik, 1993, 1996, 1998; Mitchell, 1993, and 1996; Hoffman, 1994; Aron, 1996).

In contrast to such self-expression on the part of the analyst, the self psychologist usually foregoes the overt and differentiating expression of her unique subjectivity, in recognition of the patient's archaic selfobject need. Such self-containment on the analyst's part is deliberately intended to protect the patient from premature awareness of his need for psychic provision from a separate other. Since the analyst's differentiated self-articulation or his interpersonal observations and feedback tend to highlight the analyst's separateness from the patient, Kohut suggests that the analyst must often refrain from these kinds of communications. Instead, the analyst's self-containment or silent affective resonance may allow the patient to feel implicitly held and accepted and may lead to a gradual strengthening in the patient's sense of self.

Because relational theorists do not recognize archaic selfobject need, they see in the self psychologist's deliberate curtailment of her self-expression the *sacrifice, rather than the containment, of her distinctive subjectivity* (Teicholz, 1999). They fail to see that the analyst can *silently* recognize, use, grapple with, and enjoy her subjective experience while not overtly articulating or expressing it to the patient. They also make no distinction between the patient's *unconscious* use of *unexpressed* aspects of the analyst's subjective experience, on the one hand, and his more *overt* use of the analyst's revealed subjectivity, on the other. Although they tend to cite Stern's (1985) research, they ignore his arguments for a stage of *non*recognition before the initial establishment of subjectivity and intersubjectivity in childhoood. They therefore mistake the *patient's* failure to recognize the analyst's separate subjectivity as a failure on the analyst's part to recognize her own. They confuse the self psychologist's *deliberate discretion* concerning the overt expression of certain aspects of her subjectivity, with an *absence* of subjectivity or authenticity on her part and confuse the analyst's chosen self-containment with an unawareness or inability to allow her subjectivity to be used on the patient's behalf.

If, however, we understand the analyst's subjectivity to include her conscious and unconscious patterns of organizing experience (Atwood and Stolorow, 1984) as well as her various modes of processing affect (Emde, 1990), then we recognize that the analyst's subjectivity is *inherent* to whatever other kinds of interactions take place between patient and analyst. The analyst's subjectivity is part of the *atmosphere* of a treatment, part of what she is as opposed to what she does (Kohut, 1984, p. 15), and Kohut argued that these aspects of the caretaker's subjectivity do make a significant contribution, either in original development or in cure.

As an important aspect of the analyst's subjectivity, her *processing of affect* includes soothing, mirroring, or acceptance of idealizations (Kohut, 1971, 1977, 1984). These processes may at times be even more important than what the analyst either interprets or discloses. In Kohut's theory, it is the patient's unconscious use of these processes toward development, maintenance, or enhancement of self that constitutes a selfobject experience. In omnipotent merger, for instance, a patient suffering the terror and chaos of defective self-structure may be soothed if he can have the experience of feeling included in the analyst's affective calmness and serenity (Kohut, 1984, pp. 8–9).

The analyst's job, of course, is not all silent processes and affective resonance. Even going beyond her spoken understanding and explanation, an analyst may sometimes give overt expression to selective aspects of her unique subjective experience and thereby facilitate or enhance a needed mirroring, twinship, or idealizing experience for a particular patient. Following a long-enough period of the analyst's empathic immersion and responsiveness, certain patients may also be helped by the analyst's differentiated self-expression to begin a process of self-definition or delineation (Trop and Stolorow, 1992) in contra-distinction to the analyst as a separately perceived other (Teicholz, 1995, 1996). In Lichtenberg's (1989) view of multiple motivational systems, every patient will at some point even have need of *aversive* selfobject experiences. In general, though, there will always be countless details and aspects of any analyst's subjectivity that would, if revealed, traumatically interfere with a given patient's needed selfobject experience and sense of well-being.

The analyst's explicit self-expression is thus a powerful mode of participation that can be used either for ill or good and should be thoughtfully considered for both its therapeutic and destructive potential. It should neither be placed off-limits nor recommended as a general principle of analytic practice. Rather, selective aspects of it may be articulated (or not) only on the basis of a profound, detailed, and nuanced appreciation of the individual patient and the unique analytic dyad (Stolorow, 1995; Stolorow and Atwood, 1997; Orange and Stolorow, 1998).

THE ANALYST'S EMPATHY, SUBJECTIVITY, AND AUTHENTICITY

The widening scope of psychoanalysis has, in some circles, led to a demand for a parallel expansion of analyst participation. But even if we agree to such expansion, on what basis can analysts of any theoretical orientation sort through the multitude of possible responses to their patients? I would suggest that only an empathic stance can provide the starting point and therapeutic platform from which the analyst makes further clinical judgments concerning whether or to what degree she will deliberately articulate aspects of her distinctive subjectivity.

Especially in response to patients in archaic states of relatedness, empathy leads the analyst to articulate mainly those aspects of her subjectivity that are congruent with the patient's viewpoint or to show aspects of her subjectivity that are resonant with the patient's affect and meet the patient's need. Empathy can guide the analyst toward silence and stillness in the interpersonal arena or toward expression of understanding and explanation. But empathy might also on occasion guide the analyst toward giving the patient interpersonal feedback or toward articulating some idiosyncratic detail of her personal experience as it relates to the patient's most salient concerns. Although when the analyst is functioning optimally, her self-expression is never random and is always fine-tuned to the patient's current needs and feelings, it does not routinely lead her to say what the patient on the most superficial level wants to hear. An example of interpersonal feedback is Kohut's (1984), own "You are an idiot!"—exclaimed to a patient who was speaking of the breakneck speed at which he had driven to his session. This comment was spoken in the context of a longstanding empathic immersion; indeed it derived from that very empathy itself.

Although Kohut (1984) insisted on the importance of emotional atmosphere, human presence, and the analyst's *being,* as opposed to doing, he also saw the analyst's empathy as a guide to *action.* He stated, for instance, that it is "the mother's *action, guided by empathy*" (1982, p. 397), that fosters the child's self-development. He thereby claimed an analytic place for both being and doing, for both presence and action, at least in the symbolic realm (see also Teicholz, 1989, 1999; Gehrie, 1996). Holding in mind this analytic potential for either being or doing, we may think of the analyst's empathy as allowing maximal contact with both her own and her patient's subjectivity, as allowing immediate *intrapsychic* use of the analyst's subjectivity on the patient's behalf, and as leaving room for the explicit *interpersonal* use of the analyst's subjective experience when an ongoing immersion in the patient's experience seems to lead her in that direction.

Many relational and constructivist analysts, however, do not acknowledge empathy as an essential guide to interacting with their patients (Hoffman, 1983; Slavin and Kriegman, 1992; Renik, 1993; Mitchell, 1996). In their view, the analyst's empathy stands in the way of the analyst's freer self-expression and may even prevent her from having inner access to her own subjectivity. They see empathy as inauthentic and as inessential to interpersonal engagement.

To counter this broad critique of empathy, let us follow Kohut in viewing *vicarious introspection* as the first step toward understanding another: the analyst looks inside herself, searching for what she might feel had she shared the patient's history and were she in the patient's current situation. The analyst may say nothing overtly to the patient about her personal experience, but by suggesting an understandable link between the patient's current and early experiences or by connecting the patient's current feelings to something the analyst may have done to elicit them, she is in some way saying, "No wonder you feel that way" (Teicholz, 1995): the analyst conveys that she might feel something similar, were she in the patient's shoes.

To name the patient's likely feelings with acceptance and understanding is thus to make a simultaneous revelation about the analyst's own affective experience. The analyst's empathic resonance is always grounded in her affective experience, and affective experience is necessarily subjective. The processes involved in feeling or expressing empathy are therefore subjective phenomena, and any expression of empathy is to some degree an expression of the analyst's subjectivity as well. As with the analyst's subjectivity, so with her authenticity: the bearer of an authentic self is someone in touch with her feelings, someone whose behavior is synchronous with her affect. Thus, between empathy and authenticity, as between empathy and subjectivity, the common denominator is affect.

But along with these commonalities between empathy, subjectivity, and authenticity, there are also differences. Although the analyst's empathy necessarily includes aspects of her subjectivity and authenticity, the expression of subjectivity or authenticity does not inherently involve empathy. We noted earlier, for instance, that it may be grossly unempathic to reveal certain aspects of a particular analyst's subjective experience to a given patient. There are further asymmetries as well: empathy is by definition an act of attention to the feelings of another, while either authentic behavior or the expression of subjectivity may be enacted with no attention whatsoever to the feelings of anyone else. Authenticity refers to the affective genuineness of a single subjectivity, whereas empathy refers to an affective connection between two subjectivities. Authenticity devolves from the feelings of just one subject, while empathy devolves from the point at which the feelings of two subjects converge.

Because of these differences in their points of origin and in what they reflect, the analyst's authenticity and her empathy often do diverge in treatment. When this happens, empathy should be of *therapeutic* concern, *especially* for analysts whose theories highlight two subjectivities. In fact, it remains a mystery why relational theorists, who above all emphasize psychoanalysis as a two-person endeavor, should critique the clinical use of empathy, which necessarily involves two persons, and instead favor the more individualistic expression of the analyst's unique subjectivity and authenticity. But one might also wonder why a self psychology whose primary therapeutic goal is the achievement of *mutual* empathy (Kohut, 1984) insists on retaining its status exclusively as a one-person theory.

SOME CONCLUDING THOUGHTS

We have seen that, in the writings of many relational theorists, the analyst's empathy is set up in opposition to her differentiated self-expression and authentic engagement. Following upon this dichotomy, however false, self psychologists and relational analysts tend to line up either on the side of the analyst's empathy or on the side of her more open self-expression. But I propose that admirable ideals may be reflected in both these stances. Those who argue for greater empathy and self-containment on the part of the analyst have in mind such ideals as nonimpingement, nonintrusion, the avoidance of overstimulation, and the creation of ample safety, time, and space for the blossoming of (selfobject) transferences and the unfolding of multifaceted aspects of the patient's self. Those arguing for the analyst's fuller self-expression and relational engagement hold forth such ideals as the therapist's authenticity, spontaneity, and playfulness as factors in the patient's enhanced capacity for self-expression and establishing new patterns of relating.

Kohut wrote of the analyst's natural warmth and responsiveness (1971, 1977, 1984) as important aspects of the therapeutic atmosphere, and he expected the patient's capacity for humor (1971) and playfulness (1978) to be enhanced by successful treatment: I think he might easily have argued that parents or analysts could be authentic, spontaneous, playful, and engaged while acting in concert with a child's or a patient's developmental or therapeutic goals. It may therefore be in keeping with self psychology to argue that there are many ways to be either a good parent or a good analyst, provided they are built on a foundation of empathic immersion and resonance.

REFERENCES

Aron, L. (1990), One-person and two-person psychologies and the method of psychoanalyis. *Psychoanal. Psychol.*, 7:475–486.

——— (1996), *A Meeting of Minds*. Hillsdale, NJ: The Analytic Press.

Atwood, G. & Stolorow, R. (1984), *Structures of Subjectivity: Explorations in Psychoanalytic Phenomenology*. Hillsdale, NJ: The Analytic Press.

Bass, A. (1996), Holding, holding back, and holding on. *Psychoanal. Dial.*, 6:361–378.

Beebe, B. & Lachmann, F. (1988a), The contribution of mother–infant mutual influence to the origins of self and object representations. Psychoanal. Psychol., 5:305–337.

——— &——— (1988b), Mother–infant mutual influence and precursors of psychic structure. In: *Frontiers in Self Psychology: Progress in Self Psychology, Vol. 3,* ed. A. Goldberg. Hillsdale, NJ: The Analytic Press, pp. 3–26.

——— &——— (1994), Representation and internalization in infancy: Three principles of salience. *Psychoanal. Psychol.,* 11:127–165.

——— ——— & Jaffe, J. (1997), Mother–infant interaction structures and presymbolic self and object representations. *Psychoanal. Dial.,* 7:133–182.

Benjamin, J. (1988), *Bonds of Love: Psychoanalysis, Feminism, and the Problem of Domination*. New York: Pantheon.

——— (1990), An outline of intersubjectivity: The development of recognition. *Psychoanal. Psychol.,* 7:33–46.

Bollas, C. (1989), *Forces of Destiny*. London: Free Association Books.

Demos, E. V. (1988), Affect and the development of the self: A new frontier. In: *Frontiers in Self Psychology: Progress in Self Psychology, Vol. 3*. ed. A. Goldberg. Hillsdale, NJ: The Analytic Press, pp. 27–54.

——— & Kaplan, S. (1986), Motivation and affect reconsidered: Affect biographies of two infants. *Psychoanal. Contemp. Thought,* 10:147–221.

Emde, R. (1990), Mobilizing fundamental modes of development: Empathic availability and therapeutic action. *J. Amer. Psychoanal. Assn.,* 38:881–914.

Fosshage, J. (1995), Countertransference as the analyst's experience of the analysand: Influence of listening perspectives. *Psychoanal. Psychol.,* 12:375–391.

Gehrie, M. (1996), Empathy in broader perspective: A technical approach to the consequences of the negative selfobject in early character formation. In: *Basic Ideas Reconsidered: Progress in Self Psychology, Vol. 12,* ed. A. Goldberg. Hillsdale, NJ: The Analytic Press, pp. 159–179.

Goldberg, A. (1998), Self psychology since Kohut. *Psychoanal. Quart.,* 67:240–255.

Hoffman, I. Z. (1983), The patient as the interpreter of the analyst's experience. *Contemp. Psychoanal.,* 19:389–422.

——— (1994), Dialectical thinking and therapeutic action in the psychoanalytic process. *Psychoanal. Quart.,* 63:187–218.

——— (1998), *Ritual and Spontaneity in the Psychoanalytic Process: A Dialectical-Constructivist View*. Hillsdale, NJ: The Analytic Press.

Jacob's Pillow Program Notes (Summer 1997).

Kohut, H. (1959), Introspection, empathy, and psychoanalysis. *J. Amer. Psychoanal. Assn.,* 7:459–483.

——— (1971), *The Analysis of the Self*. New York: International Universities Press.

——— (1977), *The Restoration of the Self*. New York: International Universities Press.

——— (1978), Psychoanalysis in a troubled world. In *The Search for the Self, Vol. 2,* ed., P. Ornstein. New York: International Universities Press.

——— (1982), Introspection, empathy, and the semi-circle of mental health. *Internat. J. Psycho-Anal.*, 63:395–407.

——— (1984), *How Does Analysis Cure*? ed. A. Goldberg & P. Stepansky. Chicago: University of Chicago Press.

Lachmann, F. & Stolorow, R. (1980), The developmental significance of affective states: Implications for psychoanalytic treatment. *Annual of Psychoanal.*, 8:215-230.

——— & Beebe, B. (1996), Three principles of salience in the organization of the patient–analyst interaction. *Psychoanal. Psychol.*, 13:1–22.

Lichtenberg, J. (1989), *Psychoanalysis and Motivation.* Hillsdale, NJ: The Analytic Press.

——— Lachmann, F. & Fosshage, J. (1996), *The Clinical Exchange: Techniques Derived From Self and Motivational Systems.* Hillsdale, NJ: The Analytic Press.

Mitchell, S. (1992), Commentary on Trop and Stolorow's "Defense analysis in self psychology." *Psychoanal. Dial.*, 3:441-453.

——— (1993), *Hope and Dread in Psychoanalysis.* New York: Basic Books.

——— (1996), When interpretations fail: A new look at the therapeutic action of psychoanalysis. In: *Understanding Therapeutic Action: Psycho-dynamic Concepts of Cure,* ed. L. Lifson. Hillsdale, NJ:The Analytic Press, pp. 165–186.

——— (1997). *Influence and Autonomy in Psychoanalysis.* Hillsdale, NJ:The Analytic Press.

Ogden, T. (1992a), The dialectically constituted/decentered subject ofpsychoanalysis. I: The Freudian subject. *Internat. J. Psycho-Anal.,* 73:517–526.

——— (1992b), The dialectically constituted/decentered subject ofpsychoanalysis. II: The contributions of Klein and Winnicott. *Internat. J. Psycho-Anal.*, 73:613–626.

Orange, D. & Stolorow, R. (1998), Self-disclosure from the perspective of intersubjectivity theory. *Psychoanal. Inq.,* 18:530–537.

Ornstein, P. (1991), Why self psychology is not an object relations theory. Clinical and theoretical considerations. In: *The Evolution of Self Psychology: Progress in Self Psychology, Vol. 7,* ed. A. Goldberg. Hillsdale, NJ: The Analytic Press, pp. 17–30.

Renik, O. (1993), Analytic interaction: Conceptualizing technique in the light of the analyst's irreducible subjectivity. *Psychoanal. Quart.,* 62:553–571.

——— (1995), The ideal of the anonymous analyst and the problem of self-disclosure. *Psychoanal. Quart.,* 64:466–495.

——— (1996), The perils of neutrality. *Psychoanal. Quart.,* 65:495–517.

——— (1998), Getting real in analysis. *Psychoanal. Quart.,* 67:566–593.

Slavin, M. (1997), Discussion of case presentation by Carolyn Stack, Ph.D. Boston Institute for Psychotherapy, Nov. 8.

——— & Kriegman, D. (1992), *The Adaptive Design of the Human Psyche: Psychoanalysis, Evolutionary Biology, and the Therapeutic Process.* New York: Guilford.

——— & ——— (1998), Why the analyst needs to change: Toward a theory of conflict, negotiation, and mutual influence in the therapeutic process. *Psychoanal. Dial.,* 8:247–284.

Socarides, D. & Stolorow, R. (1985), Affects and selfobjects. *Annual of Psychoanal.*,12/13:105–120.

Stechler, G. & Kaplan, S. (1980), The development of the self: A psychoanalytic perspective. *The Psychoanalytic Study of the Child*, 35:85–106. New Haven, CT: Yale University Press.

Stern, D. N. (1985), *The Interpersonal World of the Infant.* New York: Basic Books.

——— Sander, L., Nahum, J., Harrison, A., Lyons-Ruth, K., Morgan, A., Bruschweiler-Stern, N. & Tronick, E. (1998), Noninterpretive mechanisms in psychoanalytic therapy: The "something more" than interpretation. *Internat. J. Psycho-Anal.*, 79:903–922.

Stolorow, R. (1995), An intersubjective view of self psychology. *Psychoanal. Dial.*, 5:393–400.

——— & Atwood, G. (1992), *Contexts of Being.* Hillsdale, NJ: The Analytic Press.

——— & ——— (1997), Deconstructing the myth of the neutral analyst: An alternative from intersubjective systems theory. *Psychoanal. Quart.*, 66:431–449.

——— Brandchaft, B. & Atwood, G. (1987), *Psychoanalytic Treatment: An Intersubjective Approach.* Hillsdale, NJ: The Analytic Press.

Sullivan, H. S. (1953), *The Interpersonal Theory of Psychiatry.* New York: Norton.

Teicholz, J. G. (1989), Broadening the meaning of empathy for work withprimitive disorders. Presented at Spring Meeting of Div. 39, American Psychological Association, Boston, April 9.

——— (1995), Loewald's "positive neutrality" and the affirmative potential of psychoanalytic interventions. *The Psychoanalytic Study of the Child*, 50:48–75. New Haven, CT: Yale University Press.

——— (1996), Optimal responsiveness: Its role in psychic growth and change. In: *Understanding Therapeutic Action: Psychodynamic Aspects of Cure*, ed. L. Lifson. Hillsdale, NJ: The Analytic Press, pp. 139–161.

——— (1999), *Kohut, Loewald, and the Postmoderns: A Comparative Study of Self and Relationship.* Hillsdale, NJ: The Analytic Press.

Tolpin, M. (1983), Corrective emotional experience: A self psychological reevaluation. In: *The Future of Psychoanalysis*, ed. A. Goldberg. New York: International Universities Press, pp. 363–380.

Trop, J. & Stolorow, R. (1992), Defense analysis in self psychology: A developmental view. *Psychoanal. Dial.*, 2:427–441.

Chapter 4

The Active Exploratory and Assertive Self as Manifested in Dreams

James M. Fisch

In this chapter I will look at the use of dreams in psychoanalysis from the perspective of the psychology of the self, and I will suggest that one of the central functions in both dream formation and dream interpretation is the restoration of a sense of active mastery to the dreamer. Support for this hypothesis comes from an extension of Kohut's concept of self-state dreams, from child observation studies that posit a motivational system organized around exploration and assertiveness and the search activity concept of Rotenberg, which is derived from experimental/empirical studies in man and animals.

Kohut's (1971) concept of a vigorous, firm, and cohesive self as the center of initiative and experience represents the most systematic and consistent study of the self in normal and pathological development. In Kohut's metapsychology, the healthy assertiveness of the self is presented as an alternative to Freud's pseudobiological concept of an aggressive/destructive drive. Although the self is an experience-near concept derived from empathic immersion in the patient's subjective experience, it is also used in the more abstract sense, referring to an intrapsychic structure. Clinically, the condition of loss of vitality (empty depression) is the antithesis of vigor and assertiveness, which is experienced as joy. Kohut describes the pathological defenses and

An earlier version of this chapter was published in German in Psychoanalytische Blätter, 9:123–139, 1998.

environmental failures that prevent the self from fulfilling its inherent plan and developing healthy ambitions. The effect of selfobject failures during development is a self that is threatened by fragmentation; defends itself against further traumatic selfobject experiences; and, deprived of essential narcissistic supplies, remains devitalized.

Kohut (1977) also made a specific contribution to dream studies with his concept of the "self-state dream":

> Basically there exist two types of dreams: those expressing verbalizable latent contents (drive wishes, conflicts, and attempted conflict solutions), and those attempting, with the aid of verbalizable dream-imagery, to bind the nonverbal tensions of traumatic states (the dread of overstimulation, or of the disintegration of the self [psychosis]) [pp. 108–109].

Kohut further elaborated that, in the case of the second type of dream, the self-state dream, additional free association does not lead to unconscious, hidden layers of the mind: "At best they provide us with further imagery which remains on the same level as the manifest content of the dream" (p.109). He went on to discuss the mechanism of the dream formation, where "the healthy sectors of the patient's psyche are reacting to a disturbing change in the condition of the self—manic overstimulation or a serious depressive drop in self-esteem—or to the threat of the dissolution of the self" (p. 109). Kohut also referred to transitional and mixed forms of self-state dreams, for example, dreams in which certain elements (often the total setting of the dream, its atmosphere) portray aspects of the archaic self that have emerged.

Although Kohut discusses two distinct categories of dreams, one related to structural conflict, the other to self-dissolution, his emphasis in both categories is on the disturbing theme that leads to the formation of the dream. By emphasizing the disturbing theme, even in the self-state dream, Kohut is focusing on the traditional self-experience of anxiety and threat. However, if the self-state dream demonstrates the psychic capacity to visually represent the state of the self with the means of verbalizable dream imagery, might not this same capacity also be available when the self has emerged from a recent threat with a sense of capacity and vitality? In other words, when there is no immediate disturbing theme, but rather a motivation to portray the self-state with the self-feeling of pride and competence. Fosshage (1983), in a similar vein, has presented a revised psychoanalytic model of dreams, which states, "The supraordinate function of dreams is the development, maintenance, (regulation), and when necessary, *restoration* of psychic processes, structure, and organization" (p. 657; italics mine). In particular, it is the restoration function of dreams that is being explored here. At this point a brief review of the exploratory–assertive motivational system is in order.

Lichtenberg (1989) has presented a theoretical model of the self as organized around basic needs, with five distinct motivational systems: (1) the motivational system organized around the need for physiological regulation, (2) the motivational system organized around the need for attachment, (3) the motivational system organized around the need for exploration and assertiveness, (4) the motivational system organized around the need to respond aversively (withdrawal and antagonism), and (5) the motivational system organized around the need for sensual and sexual pleasure. Each system of motives interacts and overlaps with others. Lichtenberg's concept of "systems" is derived from his integration of a vast number of contemporary infant observation studies with psychoanalytic developmental and clinical theories of the self. He presents a systematic and highly cogent argument for the usefulness of viewing the clustering of needs into these five major categories which can be observed throughout the life cycle.

Lichtenberg begins his discussion of the exploratory–assertive system by citing Broucek's (1979) study that found infants actively respond to a problem-solving experimental situation and were able to quickly recognize potentials in the situation for their assertive response and that "acting on this recognition, they explored the possibilities for establishing an efficient contingent relationship between their activity and an occurrence in the environment" (p. 125). Infants were observed to sustain an activity that seemed to amplify their pleasure, which derived from the experience of efficacy or competence. He also cites Papousek and Papousek's (1975) classic experiment with 4-month-old infants who, after being oriented to bursts of interesting multicolored light and discovering that they were able to activate the light by a particular sequence of head motions, continued the activating response even when they were no longer interested in the light itself. These experiments with infants suggest that the experience of active assertiveness is in itself pleasurable, to the extent that it is central to one of the systems of motivation. Lichtenberg (1989) states:

> By virtue of the self-organization of what I call the exploratory–assertive motivational system, the infants are able to initiate new behavioral organizations that have the qualities of "real" and of "own". The affective marker for this experience lies in competence and efficacy pleasure. Expressed in the language of later life, this might be: I can recognize it, I can match it, I make it go on or off, or I have discovered it and I have altered it, and so on, exploration being closer to the "ha!" of insight, and assertion being closer to power and mastery [p. 129].

Lichtenberg's exploratory–assertive system draws on the earlier psychoanalytic concept of Hendrick (1942), who proposed an instinct for mastery, and White's (1959) concept of "competence," the capacity to interact effectively with the environmnent, which White suggested could not be motivated wholly "from sources of energy currently conceptualized as drives or instincts" (p. 297). In accordance with his relational and self psychological orientation, Lichtenberg sees the exploratory–assertive system emerging out of the normal infant–caregiver regulatory patterns based on affect signals. Infants are motivated, at a very early presymbolic age, to experience themselves with a sense of agency as the activators of their environment, and the caregivers, by their empathic reinforcement and affect regulation function, allow this system to develop as a firm component of the healthy self. Competence is associated with the pleasure of efficacy in problem solving (p. 144). Observing infants at play, novelty and variety are one source of prolonging a play episode. Another source is an infant's awareness of being the cause of a desired alteration in the environment.

All of these aspects of exploration and assertion are in the service of learning to interact competently with the environment. Play, as Lichtenberg (1989) suggests, is serious business, but the affect triggered by it is a positively toned feeling of efficacy. He distinguishes between play and work, by defining play as when there is the pleasure of a feeling of efficacy along with the pleasure of a feeling of intimacy. Work is an exploratory–assertive activity in which the dominant affect is restricted to efficacy and competence (p. 145).

In summary, infant research studies lead to the conclusion that there is in-born capacity in all humans for problem solving, exploring, and asserting active control over the environment, which is associated with the affective experience of pleasure. The pleasurable affect of exploration–assertiveness becomes organized into a central motivational system and forms a core component of the sense of competence, which is central to sense of self.

The above conclusion leads to a number of interesting questions: If exploration–assertion is a central motivational system, shouldn't we observe its operation in all forms of both conscious and unconscious human behavior? How can we conceptualize the mechanism by which exploration–assertiveness expresses itself in the healthy self? Can it be demonstrated that exploration–assertion, associated as it is with the sense of competence and self–esteem, facilitates adaptation and resistance to illness? How is exploration–assertion related to dream content and dream function?

DREAM STUDIES

One body of work that appears to be addressing these questions from the perspective of dream research and behavioral studies is the work of Vadim Rotenberg and his associates. In a series of papers (Rotenberg and Arshavsky, 1979b; Rotenberg, 1984, 1992, 1993; Rotenberg and Boucsein, 1993) Rotenberg has presented a central explanatory theory of brain function as it relates to health and disease, which he calls the Search Activity Concept. Search activity is a healthy capacity found in both man and animals for dealing with situations of uncertain outcome. The healthy individual will be oriented toward actively changing this situation or his attitude, while simultaneously and continuously monitoring the effects of his actions. This combination of activity in the absence of the capacity to predict outcome, plus monitoring (a form of feedback cycle), is called search activity. Search activity is a concept that bridges neurophysiological, behavioral and psychological phenomena and can be studied in animal models, in sleep and dream studies, and in the clinical situation. Based on such studies, search activity can be seen as a component of many different forms of behavior: self-stimulation in animals and creative behavior in humans, as well as exploratory and active defense (fight/flight) behavior in all species (Rotenberg, 1984, 1993, 1996).[1]

Rotenberg (1996) describes four possible behavioral responses to the situation of indefinite outcome: (1) search (as described), (2) stereotyped response (a rigid application of logical or previously applied actions, without monitoring of the outcome), (3) disorganized response (panic behavior), and (4) renunciation of search (freezing, withdrawal, emotional collapse). One of the best indications of search activity in animals such as rats or cats is a high-amplitude and well-organized hippocampal theta rhythm. All forms of behavior that are accompanied by hippocampal theta rhythm (orienting, learning, searching for food, searching for a sexual partner or for security, alarm) include search activity, whereas stereotyped behavior, panic, and freezing are accompanied by the desynchronization of hippocampal electrical activity (p. 191). Rotenberg concluded that all forms of behavior that include search activity, but differ in other respects, increase body resistance to disease or breakdown, while all forms of behavior that

---

[1] Fred M. Levin (1991, 1995) has proposed a model of learning that integrates psychoanalysis with neuroscience, which correlates very well with Rotenberg's Search Activity Concept. A detailed comparison of these two models is beyond the scope of this chapter.

include renunciation of search as a common feature decrease body resistance, especially in stressful situations, and predispose the subject to psychosomatic disorders (Rotenberg, 1984; Rotenberg and Korosteleva, 1990; Rotenberg and Boucsein, 1993). In this model, renunciation of search is seen as a form of clinically or subclinically manifested depression, or giving-up complex (Engel and Schmale, 1967) correlated with decreased body resistance to psychosomatic illness, whether accompanied by either positive or negative affect. In his comprehensive review of sleep and brain studies, Rotenberg (1996) reasons that

> Since search activity is so important for survival, and renunciation of search so destructive, it would be reasonable to assume a natural brain mechanism that can restore search activity after temporary renunciation of search. I suggest that REM sleep and dreams fulfill this function. A covert search activity in dreams compensates for the renunciation of search and ensures the resumption of search activity in subsequent wakefulness [p. 192].

Rotenberg then lists the findings from many sleep studies that support the above hypothesis (Rotenberg and Arshavsky, 1979b; Rotenberg, 1993) and concludes that there is an inverse relationship between search activity during wakefulness and the need for REM sleep. He states: "Both in man and in animals renunciation of search increases REM sleep requirement" (1996, p. 192) and to support the connection between REM sleep and search, he cites the work of Morrison (1982), who demonstrated that, when the *nucleus coeruleus* in the brain stem is artificially destroyed so that muscle tone does not drop during REM sleep, animals demonstrate complicated behavior (they appear to be participating in their own dreams), which can generally be described as search behavior (p. 193). Another finding was that healthy human subjects with normal search activity during wakefulness participate actively in their own dreams (there is a high correlation of increased heart rate and eye movement density) (Rotenberg, 1988), whereas depressive subjects tend toward a passive stance in their own dreams. The dreams of healthy subjects represent a very specific kind of search activity: *the subject is active in his dream. . . . He is struggling, discussing, running, manipulating, and so on.* (Rotenberg, 1993). The contribution of dreams to creativity is not seen in terms of task solution, but rather in the restoration of search activity, which is a crucial component of creativity: "What is important for the subject is to perceive himself as a problem solver, a conqueror" (p. 194). The ability to continue search with a negative outcome is more important than a positive outcome without search. Thus, according to the search concept, the essential value of search is in the activity itself, not the outcome, which differentiates search from adaptation, where success of outcome is essential.

CLINICAL STUDIES

In clinical studies, absence of search has been highly correlated with states of depression and the level of catecholamines in the brain. A minimum starter level of brain catecholamine is necessary to initiate search activity, which in turn stimulates further production of catecholamines (Rotenberg and Arshavsky, 1994b). The state of clinical depression is associated with an increased need for REM sleep (which in animal studies is also associated with the hippocampal evidence of search activity), suggesting that search activity in dreams is an unconscious, physiologically based, self-reparative function that opposes depression (or the tendency toward renunciation of search). Additional highly correlative data from split brain studies suggests that search may be related to the right-brain function, which is responsible for polysemantic and complex thinking (Rotenberg and Arshavsky, 1991,1994a). Clinical studies of adjustment problems in new immigrants demonstrated a positive correlation between search and successful adjustment, and interventions which strengthened search were therapeutic (Rotenberg et al., 1996; Venger, Rotenberg, and Desiathikov, 1997). In a study of top-class athletes, REM sleep was longer following profound athletic failures that might have caused a reaction of surrender (Rotenberg and Arshavsky, 1979a). And another behavioral study showed that, on the postexamination night, REM sleep lasts longer only in students who show signs of unproductive emotional tension, and after a sleep with an extensive REM phase, the signs of such tension disappear (Rotenberg and Arshavsky, 1979a). The cumulative weight of this data suggests that search is a definite, neurophysiologically structured internal system that is intimately related to complex, creative problem solving and positive self-esteem.

The above summary from a wide range of brain and behavioral studies of search activity leads to the following hypothesis: that a stable, reliable system of search activity is the neurophysiological basis for the exploratory–assertive motivational system, and together they work to restore the sense of self-cohesion and competence to the self threatened by enfeeblement or fragmentation. One way that search activity and assertiveness can be activated is through the dream state, and the capacity for symbolic representation enables the active self of the dreamer to be pictorially represented in dream images, in the form of the self-state dream described by Kohut. A reasonable corollary to the above hypothesis is that one of the goals of any depth psychological treatment should be the restoration and stabilization (structural change) of both the search and exploratory–assertive systems. The above hypothesis may have important implications for clinical technique.

Kohut described the self-state dream as one that used dream imagery to represent the state of the self. He emphasized the self struggling with enfeeblement or fragmentation (the disturbing theme), whereas I am looking at the self portraying its sense of vitality (the exploratory–assertive theme) and being actively engaged in search activity by producing the dream. The self-state dream cannot be analyzed by the process of free association to a deeper level of symbolic meaning. The dream symbols already convey the deepest meaning regarding the state of the self. If the waking self has recently been confronted with problems of indefinite outcome (the usual problems of life that require understanding and some form of decision making) and has not been able to elaborate a creative, active response because of conflict, fatigue, depression, or the unavailability of a needed selfobject, then according to the search concept, REM sleep would be stimulated. The dream itself would be the active response, at a physiological level, to the problem, and the dream content may or may not also portray the self in a state of search activity. I would further suggest that in the situation I am describing, the dream would most likely be long, rambling, somewhat incoherent, with many changes of location and portray the dreamer in a state of movement. Often, clinicians experience this type of dream as unanalyzable and motivated primarily by resistance to the analytic process, an example of a "special purpose dream" (Conigliaro, 1997, p. 330). An understanding of the reparative, vitalizing function of such a self-state dream would enable the analyst to remain in empathic attunement with the patient's need for a sense of competence. The following clinical vignette is offered to illustrate both the occurrence of the active self-state dream and its meaning within the clinical interaction.

CLINICAL ILLUSTRATION

The patient is a 25-year-old professional woman in exploratory psychotherapy treatment with a female therapist because of panic attacks and difficulties with relationships. Recently, reacting to a deepening sense of attachment to the therapist and to a current boyfriend, the patient impulsively decided to reduce the frequency of her sessions. After doing so, she experienced an attack of acute anxiety and called to restore her original schedule. She reacted with indignation and remorse when she imagined the therapist to be saying that she was running away from therapy and associated to her mother's depression, which frightened her with images of deadness and helplessness. In the same hour, she also talked about the deep feelings of longing aroused by her attachment to her boyfriend's loving and supportive family. In the next session, she reported the following dream:

> She's on vacation at a seaside resort and is in the water with a group of people. . . . the water is a beautiful blue color. . . . She wasn't far from the city where she lives [actually a far distance away]. . . . She sees a snorkeler with sophisticated new equipment. . . . A beautiful turtle swims by. There are children there. She fears they might be afraid of the turtle. They don't see it or react. . . . She decides to go to her room to get her equipment. . . . Her mask comes apart. She fixes it . . . sees her aunt, who gives her a lift back to her own home . . . tells a friend she wants to go back to the beach. . . . Her boyfriend comes and with sign language he communicates that he wants her to give him the camera. . . . She goes inside and realizes the door has been unlocked all along; maybe her house has been broken into. . . . She checks; everything is OK.

The patient does not refer to the dream content, not in the session it is reported, nor does she associate to any of the dream elements in subsequent sessions. However, and this is the main point, *the themes that stimulated the patient's panicky behavior prior to the dream, such as the intensity of her need for the therapist, her anxiety about the deepening relationship with her boyfriend, her identification with the depressed mother, and so on, remained in focus in the therapeutic dialogue and the treatment moved forward.* To repeat, even though the patient did not offer associations to the dream content, the act of dreaming, and perhaps the specific active dream content, were coincident with the patient's recovery from a threatened state of disequilibrium and lowered self-esteem. The disorganized, panic reaction to the threat of depression (renunciation, devitalization, fragmentation) appears to have stimulated a search response in the form of REM sleep active content, which facilitated the restoration of self-cohesion.

DISCUSSION

The dream is produced at a point where the patient is confronted with the revival of anxiety about her depressed, devitalized mother and her need for a stable attachment, which seems to be possible with the current boyfriend. She anticipates a decision regarding whether to marry, a decision fraught with danger, where the outcome is unpredictable. She begins to experience disorganizing panic and reacts with a stereotypical behavior pattern of avoidance and emotional distancing. This unsatisfactory solution leads to further anxiety; she returns to the therapist; who calmly helps her to process the inner and outer meanings of her current situation (search), and in this state of near-panic and threat of renunciation of search, associated with feelings of loss of competence (depression), she has the beach dream. The image of the self in the dream is active. She and those around her are in motion (swimming, driving, walking, checking). Children are oblivious and unafraid of a large turtle. She is able to actively repair a broken mask. She reports the dream in therapy; there is no interest in exploring the content, and the whole process signals recovery from the recent panic and forward thrust in treatment. There may be deeper themes of a longing for a nonverbal, empathic communication with the boyfriend, suggested by the signalling via sign language, but since there is no interest in this level of dream exploration, there is no way of knowing whether this may be an example of a mixed dream that is both self-state and symbolic of underlying conflict. What is significant in terms of the point being illustrated is that the theme of helplessness and enfeeblement of the self is not depicted in this dream, although it was clearly evident in the waking concerns of the patient prior to the occurrence of the dream. The dream appears to be reparative, both in the function it serves at a psychophysiological level as it is formed and in the image of activity and repair that is portrayed in the dream content.

SUMMARY

Psychoanalysts have a language and orientation of their own derived from the unique setting in which they work, where depth psychological meanings are possible, which allows for the prolonged empathic immersion in the deeper levels of experience with their analysands. Kohut was strict in his insistence that psychological theory had to be confined to what was learned by empathic observation, essentially within the analytic situation, and he therefore did not utilize data from other sources, such as direct infant observation. Although I fully agree with Kohut's defining position that "we designate phenomena as mental, psychic, or psychological if our mode or observation includes introspection and empathy *as an essential constituent*" (Kohut, 1959, p. 461), in this chapter I have tried to bring together several theories of human motivation derived from distinctly different observational methods: psychoanalysis, infant observation, sleep and behavior studies. I believe the three theories (self psychology and the self-state dream, the exploratory–assertive motivational system, and the search activity concept), although derived from vastly different methodologies, share a similarity in terms of their cohesiveness and explanatory power. Each of these theories has the potential to be a conceptual bridge that may facilitate interdisciplinary communication between psychology, infant research, and biology, and together they may provide additional leverage in the clinical understanding of certain moments of dream interpretation. A clinical vignette was presented to illustrate the integrated use of the three concepts.

REFERENCES

Broucek, F. (1979), Efficacy in infancy: A review of some experimental studies and their possible implications for clinical theory. *Internat. J Psycho-Anal.*, 60:311–316.

Conigliaro, V. (1997), *Dreams as a Tool in Psychodynamic Psychotherapy: Traveling the Royal Road to the Unconscious.* Madison, CT: International Universities Press.

Engel, G. & Schmale, A. (1967), Pschychoanalytic theory of somatic disorders. *J. Amer. Psychoanal. Assn.*, 15:344–365.

Fosshage, J. (1983), The psychological function of dreams: A revised psychoanalytic perspective. *Psychoanal. & Contemp. Thought,* 6:641–669.

Hendrick, I. (1942), Instinct and the ego during infancy. *Psychoanal. Quart.*, 11:33–58

Kohut, H. (1959) Introspection, empathy, and psychoanalysis. *J. Amer. Psychoanal. Assn.*, 7:459–483.

——— (1971*), The Analysis of the Self.* New York: International Universities Press.

——— (1977), *The Restoration of the Self.* New York: International Universities Press.

Levin, F. M. (1991), *Mapping the Mind: The Intersection of Psychoanalysis and Neuroscience.* Hillsdale, NJ: The Analytic Press.

——— (1995), Psychoanalysis and knowledge: Part I. The problem of representation and alternative approaches to learning. In: *The Annual of Psychoanalysis, ed. J. A. Winer.* Hillsdale, NJ: The Analytic Press.

Lichtenberg, J. (1989), *Psychoanalysis and Motivation.* Hillsdale, NJ: The Analytic Press.

Morrison, A. (1982), Central activity states: Overview. In: *The Neural Basis of Behavior,* ed. A. F. Beckniin. New York: Spectrum, pp. 3–17.

Papousek, H. & Papousek, M. (1975), Cognitive aspects of preverbal social interaction between human infant and adults. In: *Parent–Infant Interaction* (Ciba Foundation Symposium), ed. New York: Associated Scientific Publishers.

Rotenberg, V. S. (1984), Search activity in the context of psychosomatic disturbances of brain monoamine and RFM sleep function. *Pavlov J. Biologi. Sci.*, 19:1–15.

——— (1988), Functional deficiency of REM sleep and its role in the pathogenesis of neurotic and psychosomatic disturbances. *Pavlov J. Biolog. Sci.*, 23:1–3.

——— (1992), Sleep and memory 1: The influence of different sleep stages on memory. *Neurosci. & Biobehav. Rev.*, 16:497–502.

——— (1993), REM Sleep and dreams as mechanisms of the recovery of search activity. In: *The Functions of Dreaming,* ed. A. Moffat, M. Kramer, & R. Hoffman. Albany: State University of New York Press, pp. 261–292.

——— (1996), The psychobiological dream functions: A new solution for old contradictions. In: *Sense and Nonsense, Philosophical, Clinical and Ethical Perspectives,* ed. J. J. Rozenberg, Jerusalem: Magnes Press, Hebrew University, pp. 187–197.

——— & Arshavsky, V. V. (1979a), REM sleep, stress and search activity. *Waking & Sleeping,* 3:235–244.

——— & ——— (1979b), Search activity and its impact on experimental and clinical pathology. *Activitas Nervosa Superior* (Prague), 21:105–115.

——— & ——— (1991), Psychophysiology of hemisphere asymmetry: The "entropy of right-hemisphere activity. *Integrat. Physiolog. & Behav. Sci.*, 26:183–188.

——— & ——— (1994a), An integrativc psychophysiological approach to brain hemisphere functions in schizophrenia. *Neurosci. & Behav. Rev.*, 18:487–495.

——— & ——— (1994b),The revised monoamine hypothhesis: mechanism of antidepressant treatment in the context of behavior. *Integrat. Physiolog. & Behav. Sci.*, 29:182–188.

——— & Boucsein, W. (1993), Adaptive vs. maladaptive emotional tension. *Genet., Soc. & Gen. Psychol. Monog.,* 119:207–232.

——— & Korosteleva, I. S. (1990), Psychological aspects of the search activity and learned helplessness in psychosomatic patients and healthy testees. *Dynamische Psychiatrics/Dynamic Psychiatry,* 120:1–13.

——— Tobin, M., Krause, D. & Lubovkov, I. (1996), Psychosocial problems faced during absorption of Russian-speaking new immigrants into Israel: A systematic approach. *Isr. J. Psychiatry Relat. Sci.*, 33:40–49.

Venger, A., Rotenberg, V. S. & Desiathikov, Y. (1997), Evaluation of search activity and other behavioral attitudes in indefinite situations. *Dynamische Psychiatrics/ Dynamic Psychiatry,* 160/161:368–377.

White, R. (1959), Motivation Reconsidered: The Concept of Competence. *Psychoanal. Rev.,* 66:297–333.

Chapter 5

The Development of the Dyad: A Bidirectional Revisioning of Some Self Psychological Concepts

Lynn Preston
Ellen Shumsky

Development has traditionally been equated with linear, sequential, universal movements through life stages. As psychoanalysis relinquishes its claims on the universal and the safe rationality of predictable sequences (see Mitchell, 1997), new metaphors of therapeutic development—connoting a process of healing, growth, and change—are needed. Moving from an exploration of the individual self to an emphasis on a more relational self requires a new look at how relatedness unfolds. We are proposing the idea of a developing dyad—the evolution of the analytic partnership—as one lens through which the analyst can envision the movement of therapy. We focus this lens on specific self psychological theoretical constructs: selfobject experience, rupture and repair, therapeutic impasse, and optimal responsiveness. Our purpose is to add our voice to those who posit an interactional dimension to self psychological psychoanalytic theory. We want both to preserve and expand the above-mentioned constructs, which we have found to have profound clinical efficacy.

The working assumptions that underlie our use of the lens of the developing dyad as a metaphor have been drawn from an amalgam of psychoanalytic relational theories—based on an understanding of the human experience as inherently interactive and intersubjective. Three basic presuppositions are as follows: (1) The growth of a relationship promotes the growth of the individuals within it, and the growth of individuals within a relationship promotes the growth of the relationship. (2) Each dyad is unique and develops uniquely. There are no universal developmental steps or stages. (3) The growth of a relationship is measured by increasing intimacy, aliveness, vitality, resiliency, flexibility, depth, the capacity to negotiate conflict and difference, the building of trust and openness, the capacity to include a wider spectrum of feelings, and the expansion of each individual's relational repertoire.

Self Psychology/Intersubjectivity Theory is emerging from a positivist, unidirectional concept of psychoanalytic process. The patient has been seen as the one who needs healing and, with proper application of analytic theory and technique, as the one who changes. The contribution of intersubjectivity theory has facilitated a growing understanding of the fuller implications of a process of psychological growth as a relational experience. The analyst—no longer neutral, objective, abstinent—has increasingly become a coparticipant in a system of mutual influence that organizes and creates a dyadic relational field. In the process both partners are changed.

Kohut (1977) took a first step into developing this paradigm by recognizing that the analyst's response, far from neutral, was influencing the patient's self-experience. Stolorow and Atwood (1992) leapt into the domain of interactive field theory by viewing psychoanalysis as a process emerging from the interplay of two differently organized subjectivities—an intersubjective phenomenon—which further highlighted the analyst's participation in psychoanalytic process and invited renewed attention to the issue of countertransference, which is increasingly understood, not as an impediment to healing, but as inevitable and co-determining of the transactional field. Bacal and Thomson (1996) explicitly address and include the selfobject needs of the analyst as a dimension of the analytic field, further crediting the participation of both patient and analyst in cocreating the psychoanalytic matrix. The work of Beebe and Lachmann (1994, 1996) on early mother–infant interactions clarifies the interlocking and reciprocally delimiting contributions of self- and mutual regulation in a dyadic system. Natterson's (1991) analytic writings fully embrace an intersubjective schema as he states that the "subjective life of the therapist is co-equal to that of the patient in creating the therapeutic transaction" (p. vii). Orange (1995) proposes the term cotransference, rather than countertransference, to convey her understanding that the organizing activity of patient and analyst are "two faces of the same dynamic" (p. 67). Lessem and Orange (1993) stress the importance of the particularity of the analyst who cogenerates the selfobject bond with the particular patient. Sucharov (1996) further extends the idea of mutuality in the psychoanalytic endeavor by proposing that "empathic undertanding is bilateral. Understanding and being understood by the other is an indivisible process that is mutually regulated on a moment to moment basis" (p. 1). Fosshage (1995) proposes replacing the narrow and confusing term *countertransference* with a more totalist expression, "the analyst's experience of the patient . . . [which] more fully captures the complexity of the analyst's involvement" (p. 375). Preston (1996) explicitly states that the emotional and intellectual investments of the analyst are a determining factor in the cocreation of selfobject experience. Orange, Atwood, and Stolorow (1997) most recently propose that "the intersubjective field of the analysis made possible by the emotional availability of *both* patient and analyst, becomes a developmental second chance for the patient" (p. 8; emphasis added). Clearly, the thrust of intersubjectivity theory is in the direction of refining and expanding understandings of the psychoanalytic engagement as a thoroughly bilateral system of mutual influence.

Positing the psychoanalytic endeavor as a fully intersubjective phenomenon introduces new challanges for conceptualizing psychoanalytic change. The analytic process has become a two-way, instead of a one-way, engagement—a process of mutual influence, of cotransference. A new unit, the dyad, has become a focus of exploration. Concepts of growth/healing/transformation/development need to be thought about in dyadic terms that include the analyst as well as the patient. Relational psychoanalysts are in the process of articulating a language that captures a dyadic vision of development, which in turn creates a bidirectional lens through which we see our work anew.

Stolorow, Brandchaft, and Atwood (1987) located analytic process as occurring at the intersection of the subjectivities of patient and analyst (p. 1). This was offered as a value-neutral inevitability. With this as a starting point, we are exploring the idea that the expansion of the patient–analyst relational matrix is one way of envisioning therapeutic change. Sucharov (1996) spoke of bringing "forth the intersubjective field as a conceptual lens that facilitates the rediscovery of the therapist's subjectivity in the psychoanalytic process." (p. 18). We are trying to bring forth the evolution of a dyadic interchange as a conceptual lens to delineate, detail, and elaborate the clinical workings of therapeutic process.

In this chapter we shall examine some fundamental self psychological constructs through a bidirectional lens, demonstrating ways in which both patient and analyst cocreate the interactional field. It is another way of viewing psychoanalytic process that includes the analyst's as well as the patient's contributions and the ways in which they influence each other.

Beebe and Lachmann (1994, 1996) have drawn on the findings of empirical infant research to produce a powerful model that helps in understanding the processes of psychotherapeutic action in an interactive system. They address the developmental necessity for integrating self- and mutual regulation and propose their inseparability. They include in their definition of self-regulation a capacity for self-soothing and predictable organization of behavior. Mutual regulation refers to "a model in which both partners actively contribute to the regulation of the exchange, although not necessarily in equal measure or like manner" (1996, p. 124). "Each partner influences the process through his or her own self regulatory range and style and through specific contributions to the pattern of interaction" (1996, p. 124). We understand this to mean that the relational universe that the analytic dyad inhabits is cocreated and delimited by the intersecting subjectivities of both participants. An expansion of one partner's self-regulatory range broadens that person's relational capabilities. For example, an increased ability to self-soothe can lead to a greater capacity to tolerate the empathic failures of the other. Either partner's expanding relational capabilities alters the shape of the dyadic universe, which then allows for the possibility of new self-experience for the other partner. In an alive interactive system, there will be pushes and pulls from *both* directions as each participant tries to expand or modify the self-regulatory system of the other and therefore the dyadic universe, to make possible the inclusion and reception of more self-experience. From this perspective, therapeutic development can be seen as the experience of the cogeneration of evolving mutual regulations, which then broaden the self-regulatory ranges of the participants or vice versa. As the partnership evolves in complexity, depth, and flexibility, each participant also evolves. Dyadic development results in individual development, and individual development expands dyadic development.

We are suggesting that the self psychological metaphor for growth as the accretion of internal structure through selfobject experience facilitated by optimal responsiveness can also be conceptualized in a way that reflects the bidirectional nature of the analytic endeavor. We can think of growth as the patient's accretion of relational flexibility, which results in a more resilient, alive partnership and a more cohesive delineated self.

In the language of intersubjectivity theory (which has replaced notions of intrapsychic structure with the concept of invariant organizing principles that are socially formed and socially maintained, we can say that in the psychoanalytic process the patient's organization of experience changes as the patient's sense of herself in relation to the analyst is altered in the dyadic process. In an effective analysis, there is a transformation of relational expectations resulting from participation in a new selfobject relationship (Bacal, 1990). In other words, the analytic relational experience offers the patient, and often the analyst, new possibilities in the human world.

SELFOBJECT EXPERIENCE

A most striking example of the evolution of a self psychological intersubjective perspective can be seen in changing understandings of the pivotal construct of selfobject experience. Kohut's (1977) definition, emerging from a classical frame was clearly a unidirectional vision. "The analysand, in order to keep open the access of the archaic strivings to his ego . . . uses the analyst as a self-object . . . ie., as a precursory substitute for the not-yet-existing psychological structures (p. 32). Eighteen years later, Bacal (1995b) describes the therapeutic process in self psycholgy as "centrally entailing a continuous dynamic experience of complex selfobject interaction between analyst and analysand" (p. 361). Kohut, operating from a unidirectional assumption, refers to the patient's use of the analyst as a selfobject. Bacal's emphasis is on mutual selfobject interaction—the activity of a partnership. The image of the analyst as provider is changed to the experience of a particular kind of patient–analyst interaction (see Fosshage, 1995).

A premise of this chapter is that selfobject experience is not a unidirectional process in which the therapist gives and the patient receives empathic understanding (see Sucharov [1995] for a fuller discussion of the bidirectional nature of empathy). We view selfobject experience as the intrapsychic dimension of an interactional giving/receiving process—the experience of successful mutual regulation.[1] Bacal (1995a), drawing upon the work of Suttie (1988) refers to the selfobject need for vitalizing self-experience through giving, sharing, and entering into "reciprocal relatedness" (p. 403). In our view of selfobject experience, the mutual regulatory activity of the partnership—the participation in the give and take of relationship building—

[1] This is in contrast to Shane and Shane (1996) who view the selfobject dimension of relatedness in the clinical situation to be "distinctly onesided" (p. 13).

constitutes a growth experience for both partners (see Preston, 1996). Both partners struggle to provide what the other needs for partnership, and both struggle to accept what the other has to offer. When selfobject experience has been achieved, both may experience their contribution as valuable to themselves, to the other, and to the relationship. This participation in a creative, intimate, deeply honest endeavor is the developmental second chance or, as Spezzano (1997) puts it, "the first chance to address the dialectic between affect and relationship that is the foundation of human psychology" (p. 611).

Case Example: Sandra/Ruth

To illustrate the application of the idea of an interactive giving–receiving matrix as the carrier of selfobject experience, we will consider the following brief piece of clinical process. (The patient's self-expression is often vague, elusive, tangential, and difficult to follow. The analyst, whose self-organization is threatened by states of confusion, has trouble understanding the patient and wishes she would get to the point. She believes that the patient's scattered productions are an expression of anxiety about her relationship with the analyst.)

Sandra: Things are messy with all the women in my life.
Ruth: I wonder if that includes me.
Sandra: I sometimes think perhaps I should find a guru and study Buddhism or yoga.
Ruth: Tell me about the mess between us.
Sandra: I know what will happen. I'll tell you everything that is troubling me and you'll dispassionately nod or ask a series of questions.
Ruth: I invite the feelings and don't engage with them.
Sandra: You seduce and disappoint. I tell you about a movie that was meaningful to me. You seem interested in it but never refer to it again.
Ruth: What you are saying is very important.
Sandra: Yes and you will never come back to it. You are so laid back. It's like nothing matters.
Ruth: I can see why you feel that way. I'd like to talk more about it, but it's time to stop.
Sandra: (As she is paying the analyst) Where are you going on vacation?
Ruth: Spain.
Sandra: Make sure you see the Andalusian horses.
Ruth: You know, in Ireland last year I looked for and found the wild ponies you told me about. But I never shared that with you. I can see why you feel that you don't matter. You have no idea how much you are with me. I never see a horse without thinking of you.
Sandra: Now I feel like hugging you.

Let's look at what is happening here from the point of view of mutual giving/receiving. The therapist is asking for what she needs in the partnership, which is for the patient to get to the point, that is, to talk about their relationship. The patient first responds indirectly to the analyst's need and then gives the analyst a pointed personal expression of criticism and disappointment about the analyst's distance. The analyst receives this contribution and responds empathically, giving the patient needed validating responsiveness. The patient continues with an indirect request for something she has been sorely needing—for the therapist to pursue her more consistently. This request again satisfies the analyst's need for the patient to get to the point, and she again offers the patient legitimizing affirmations. The patient then spontaneously takes the risk of inviting personal contact. The analyst responds with heartfelt self-expression that is a powerful corrective of the patient's complaint. The patient receives the analyst's gift and responds with a gift of affection. The session ends on a note of warm connection. This partnership has been struggling with the challenge of expanding possibilities for personal expressivity through pulls and pushes from both sides. The relationship has taken a small step toward greater openness.

The give and take of relatedness that constitutes the intersubjective field of the analysis can also be viewed as an incrementally evolving spiral of increased bidirectional risk taking, understanding and trust. Brothers (1995) refers to a dyadic vision of selfobject experience in the development of her ideas about trust. She includes not only the patient's need to trust the analyst, but the patient's need to feel trusted by the analyst. She defines trust as "the hope or wishful expectation of obtaining and providing the selfobject experience necessary for the development, maintainence, and restoration of cohesive selfhood" (p. 33). She sees trust as the "glue" of self-experience and views psychotherapy as a bidirectional trust-building voyage. The clinical vignette above can also be seen as a sequence of mutual risk taking, acceptance, and trust building.

The patient risks making a generalization in which she indirectly refers to difficulties in the analytic relationship. The analyst personalizes it. The patient further indirectly risks, indicating that she is not getting what she needs from the analysis. The analyst wants to know more. The patient finally risks a direct personal expression of her disappointing experience of the analyst's inconsistency and unreliability. The analyst is interested but ends the session. The patient then moves forward into a personal engagement with the therapist. The therapist, inspired by the patient's courage, risks an emotional expression of her connectedness to the patient. (Perhaps, having stepped outside the analytic frame, the analyst is also freed from expressive constraints imposed by her adherence to theory that discourages self-disclosure). The patient has gotten needed responsiveness from the analyst and wants more closeness. The dyad has taken a step of trust.

RUPTURE AND REPAIR

The traditional self psychological view of therapeutic process is that the self develops through the accretion of structure as a result of rupture, repair, and transmuting internalizations. Seen through a dyadic lens, one could say that growth occurs through a process of the mutual regulation of rupture and repair—both people make the mess and both people clean it up—which leads to a stronger, more flexible, self-righting dyad.

In the traditional self psychological model, the focus of the analytic work is on the emotional life of the patient. None the less the emotional life of the analyst is always implicitly cocreating the interactional field. Because we focus on the patient, we tend to notice disturbances in the field through our experience of the patient. Often, the rupture or disturbance is unconscious for the patient. We notice that the patient comes late, forgets to pay, seems flattened, feels more hopeless. The analyst may take this as a signal that there has been an empathic failure and investigate what might have happened. The conclusion of the investigation is some interpretation by the therapist about what she did or didn't do that was experienced by the patient as an empathic failure. How were the selfobject needs of the patient not adequately met? The patient feels recognized and understood by the interpretation and is perhaps flooded with memories of other such failures. The treatment is back on track. The therapist takes responsibility for the rupture. She identifies the empathic failure, and she repairs it through an interpretation that acknowledges her participation in its creation.

How might a treatment disturbance be seen through a dyadic lens in which both the rupture and repair are cocreated? The disturbance, an empathic failure, has begun before the analyst starts noticing it in the patient's behavior. The process of mutual regulation is endlessly ongoing. The analyst may have unconsciously become misattuned, may experience tension, or may become aware of feelings of discomfort, restlessness, sleepiness, annoyance or boredom (see Bacal and Thomson [1996] on signal disruption). In some way, the patient's participation has been frustrating the selfobject needs of the analyst and the analyst may be trying to self-right. The ongoing dyadic experience consists of disruptions, misunderstandings, and misattunements that are negotiated by both people. Problematic patterns of interaction can often be understood as either participant's habitual archaic attempt to restore a disrupted bond.

Case Example: Susan/Janet

Susan wants to focus her session on a recognition she has just had, that she never goes after what she wants. She has a flood of associations, and as the session ends, she indicates that the session was disappointing because she didn't get clarity about the nature of her wanting disorder. Janet says, "I felt you sitting on something throughout the session." The next week Susan comes late to session and says she had a strong urge not to come at all. In fact, she is not in touch with wanting anything. Janet recalls the way the last session ended. In the ensuing discussion she comments, "When I said you were sitting on something throughout the last session, perhaps you felt I was saying it was your own fault that you hadn't gotten what you wanted." Susan is engaged by this and comes alive.

Let's look at what happened here from a dyadic perspective. This therapist has been unconsciously working from an early organizing belief that she is an inadequate responder. She was disturbed by the patient's dissatisfaction with the session. She felt blamed. She defensively handed the blame back to the patient, "I felt you sitting on something." (The subtext is, "It's not my fault, it's yours.You stopped yourself from getting what you wanted.") The therapist's selfobject need to be mirrored for her efficacy wasn't met by the patient. Because the analyst is focusing on the patient, the point at which she becomes aware of the disturbance is when the patient is trying, in her way, to repair it. The patient stops wanting. She stops making demands on the relationship. She accepts the blame and disengages. That's her major symptom—the self-limiting way she has learned to restore a selfobject tie by accepting full responsibility for the relational difficulty and withdrawing her needs. The analyst notices something is wrong when she notices this typical way the patient has of repairing ruptures. Then she coparticipates in repair by taking responsibility for her defensiveness. Embedded in her review of the session is an implied interpretation: the patient lost her wanting because she accepted the blame for the last session not going well.

The analyst's noticing, taking responsibility, and interpreting are her ways of participating in repairing the rupture. The acceptance of responsibility for the analyst's discomfort and emotional disengagement are some ways the patient tries to repair the rupture. Additionally, when the analyst refers back to the previous session, the patient has to empathically grasp the reaching out of the therapist, make a place for the therapist's way of seeing things, and take the risk of trusting that the therapist is not invested in remaining rigidly in a defended position.

Aron (1996) has pointed out that the "analysis is asymmetrical in terms of differences in power and responsibility between patient and analyst" (p. 99). However, mutuality resides in the reality that both participants make their contributions to the creation of the rupture. And both participants offer characteristic, as well as tentative, new contributions to its repair. This partnership has been struggling with issues of blame and responsibility. A step has been taken toward a new experience of responsibility as "the ability to repond," not as the assignment of blame.

OPTIMAL RESPONSIVENSSS

Howard Bacal's (1990) concept of optimal responsiveness has largely replaced Kohut's original idea of optimal frustration as a fundamental therapeutic structure-building activity of self psychology. In Bacal's model, optimal responses are therapeutic contributions of the analyst that facilitate curative selfobject experience for the patient (p. 364). Interpretive activity is but one way of being optimally responsive.

A dyadic approach to optimal responsiveness entails the analyst thinking not only about responses to the patient, but also about responses to the dyad. By this we mean that, in addition to attending to the patient, the analyst is also attending to the struggle of the partnership to form a healing connectedness. As Sucharov (1995) says, "We must listen to the dance while dancing" (p. 11). The analyst reflects on the process—patterns and sequences produced by the intersecting subjectivities of patient and analyst. It is in this responsibility of the analyst that relational asymmetry is most apparent. These reflections, an expression of the analyst's subjectivity, are, however, incomplete without the additional inclusion of the patient's experience.

Optimal responsiveness has primarily been associated with analytic empathic interpretations, which are "you" statements. A broadened lens would also include "we" statements and "I" statements. Spezzano (1997) advocates the use of the word *we* as a way of locating "aspects of unconscious activity where they first appear: not interiorly, but in the intersubjective field" (p. 616). He goes on to say that the use of "we" statements as therapeutic interventions is what distinguishes relational from nonrelational practice. We view "we" statements as not only an attempt to discover the patient's unconscious, but also as a way to locate the "us"—to identify the immediate challenge of the partnership in its striving for connection, safety, and freedom. The response that is optimal for the dyad takes into account the needs and requirements of both partners, as well as the relational developmental struggle of the dyad. The developmental tasks of the dyad are determined moment-by-moment by the intersection of the needs and constraints of both people. The hurdles and challenges at each step are unique for each partnership. "Yours and mine assume their particular shape in our relatedness" (Orange, 1995, p. 24). Optimal responsiveness to the dyad appreciates the validity of both partners' ways of organizing their own experience.

The partnership negotiates these uniquely constructed developmental tasks through the ongoing discovery and cocreation of maps and tools. It is the coauthoring of vital, deeply personal metaphors through collaborative meaning-making that is a primary tool for this journey. Spezzano (1997) remarks that metaphor is the link between affect and words (p. 607).

Case Example: Karen/Jake

The patient, Karen, has been in treatment for six months. She often falls into long silences. The analyst, Jake, grew up as a lonely child and is uncomfortable with silences. Karen has just asked Jake a question, which Jake answered. Karen is silent. Jake becomes increasingly uncomfortable, not knowing whether Karen is thinking about what he said or has drifted off in isolation. He finally asks Karen what she is thinking.

Karen: Nothing. I went blank.
Jake: Did you have any thoughts about what I said?
Karen: I liked what you said.
Jake: What happened after that?
Karen: I thought about it and then I went blank.
Jake: It seemed like an uneasy silence between us. Did it seem like that to you?
Karen: Yes. I get anxious when I have nothing to say.
Jake: Did you think of looking to me for input?
Karen: Do you want me to do that?
Jake: Well, I don't know. I would like to understand what is happening between us when you go blank.
Karen: I think it is very bad of me to have silent expectations of you.

Jake: What are the silent expectations?

Karen: It's bad of me to want you to help me. I should do it myself.

Jake: What is so bad about wishing for help?

Karen: My foster mother who I lived with as a teenager told me how hurtful and mean it was for me to have silent expectations of her. It made her feel bad.

Jake: I guess you are concerned that your silent expectations of me are making me feel bad.

Karen: All my life I've been told to speak up. But I can't.

Jake: You seem to get lost and wait there quietly, hoping I'll come and find you.

Karen: I'm afraid to look at you and ask for help.

Jake: You seem to get frozen in your tracks. I feel fine about helping you, but I get uncomfortable when I think I may be intruding upon your silence.

Karen: I'm hoping that you'll ask me a question.

Jake: We seem to get stuck when you are afraid to ask for help, and I am afraid that offering it will feel like an intrusion.

A challenge of this dyad is to negotiate the silences. Embedded in these silences are the patient's conflict between a wish for help and an emotional conviction that this unspoken wish is unacceptable and the analyst's discomfort with silence and her fear that she will intrude her need for connection into the patient's need for silence. The patient's introduction of the evocative term *silent expectation* allows the couple to identify a conflict. The analyst's use of the metaphor of the "lost patient waiting to be found," seems to allow the patient to articulate her fear of asking for help. The interpretation of the dyadic struggle brings into focus the treatment as a partnership.

Optimal responsiveness to the dyad can also be facilitated through the analyst's use of personal "I" statements previously referred to as "expressive relating" (Preston, 1996). The personal expression of the analyst, arising out of her moment-to-moment experience of the interaction, can be a powerful conveyor of the relatedness and intimacy that fosters selfobject experience. Aron (1997) describes the task of the relational psychoanalyst as holding the tension between understanding the patient (empathic interpretations) and being a new object for the patient (personal interactive participation). These processes are, of course, inextricably connected. Along with empathic understanding, the analyst's personal expressivity can be a potent carrier of a new relational experience. In the above-mentioned case example, Jake's inclusion of his own subjectivity disconfirmed Karen's relational expectation and expanded the interactive possibilities of the dyadic universe.

IMPASSES

One of the clearest explications of the clinical workings of an intersubjective approach is found in the paper "Impasses in Psychoanalytic Therapy: A Royal Road" (Atwood, Stolorow, and Trop, 1989). The authors describe a therapeutic impasse as a situation in which the absence of "reflective self awareness" on the part of the therapist contributes to the establishment of rigid interaction patterns. When the emotional convictions organizing the experience of both partners can be investigated and illuminated, the impasse provides a "unique pathway—a royal road—to analytic understanding" (p. 54). The authors are suggesting that the analyst's ability to reflect on his own contribution to the impasse begins the process of dyadic righting. The case examples cited indicate that this self-reflection enables the analyst to reposition himself—to change the way in which he participates in the relationship. The way that we understand this is that the analyst's new self-awareness enables him to provide a new experience that alters the dyadic universe so that a change in the patient's self-experience becomes possible. In other words, the therapist takes a step out of rigidified interactional patterns and broadens his own self-regulatory range, simultaneously impacting on the patient.

Mitchell (1997), addressing the issue of analytic impasses, also speaks about the need for the analyst to go first "to break out into a different emotional state, to want more" (p. 61). He speaks of an "outburst . . . from the confines of options that all seem unacceptable" (p. 57). For Mitchell it is often the analyst's emotional response to the constraints of the impasse that ushers in a new lived experience characterized by analyst and patient working together to broaden the options available to them. From our perspective, Mitchell's "outburst"—an emotional expression of the analyst's response to the impasse and his commitment to the dyad—contributes a new element that alters the dyadic universe, thus offering new possibilities for the patient. It serves the same analytic function as Atwood et al.'s application of reflective self-awareness.

Both Atwood et al. and Mitchell speak of the necessity for meta-understanding of the impasse. Both indicate that the therapist is usually the one who has to make the first change. The intersubjectivists emphasize the importance of the analyst's exploration of his own contribution as coconstructor of the impasse. Mitchell highlights the patient's investment in maintaining the imprisoning constraint but views the shared experience of imprisonment as a necessary dimension of the analytic journey.

A synthesis of the intersubjectivist and Mitchell's interpersonal contributions to the understanding of therapeutic impasses gives a clinically helpful schema of dyadic movement. Elements of this schema are (1) a need for the analyst's introspection to see his own contribution, (2) an exploration of how the analyst's contribution fits with the patient's understanding of the impasse, and (3) the need for the therapist to "go first" in taking some new action, which may be an interpretation or an emotional expression of the analyst's subjectivity.

Another evocative lens through which to view impasses is Searles's (1975) idea, expanded by Sucharov (1995), that the patient unconsciously strives "to cure the analyst of those problematic aspects that would interfere with the analyst's therapeutic function for the patient" (p. 3). This speaks to the dimension of impasse in which the *patient* is trying to break out of the dyadic constraints imposed by the limitations of the self-regulatory range of the analyst. This is not the equality of a Ferenczi co-analysis, but the mutuality of a coconstructed partnership in which the roles and responsibilities of each participant are different. As Orange et al. (1997) say, "One is primarily guide and the other seeks to organize and reorganize experience in less painful and more creative ways. Nevertheless, each is a full participant and contributor to the process that emerges" (p. 9).

Case Example: Mary/John

Mary is a bright, attractive young therapist. Her early meaningful selfobject tie was with her father who was alternately warm or withdrawn and absent. Mary experiences her analyst, John, alternately as caring and deeply in tune with her, and detached and withdrawn. In the latter state he resorts to a much more classical stance of abstinence or authoritarian technical interpretations. As a child, Mary tried to get her parents to see beneath the surface of what was going on. In her analysis she works very hard to get her analyst to recognize his own moodiness and inconsistent way of being with her. She wants him to understand how restimulating and retraumatizing it is for her when he withdraws. Mary alternates between acting like the clingy hysterical young child, pulling John in to care for her, and being the insightful therapist who points out his deficiencies. John had, as a child, struggled to maintain a sense of his own autonomy in the face of a needy, demanding, and highly seductive mother. He alternated between falling under her spell and resisting her pull on him.

In a moment of emotional vulnerability in Mary's analysis, John acknowledged the validity of her perceptions of him. He acknowledged that he does go through periods of withdrawal and that he feels very anguished at the pain he has caused her. She then, feeling justified at being angry at him and perhaps testing the sincerity of his change of heart, suggested that he give her extra sessions free of charge to process this cyclical interaction. She felt that she had invested so much time and energy through the years getting him to take responsibility for his problematic participation in their relationship that reparations were due her. He became stiff and silent at her suggestion. She pointed out that he was withdrawing in the same old way again. He did not respond, and she became angrier and angrier. Finally, he told her that she wasn't taking responsibility for her anger. He said that he would not allow her to criticize and yell at him and that she was out of control. This left her feeling frantic, crazy, and fragmented. She sought help from another therapist.

John had offered Mary an emotional self-disclosure. Perhaps he wanted to be rewarded by her acceptance as an antidote to the experience of his mother's demanding neediness. One interpretation of Mary's angry reaction is that she is railing against the limitations of John's self-regulatory range, battering at the walls of his self-protection that prevent her from having the selfobject experience she needs. His inability to empathically explore the meanings of her desperation results in her spiraling anger, which can be seen as a disintegration byproduct. Mary took John's expression of responsibility and vulnerabilty as a signal that he was a grownup and she could now be a raging child. One line of speculation is that she was testing to see if he could be the strong father who could tolerate her criticism and anger and stay connected to her. This partnership was strained to the breaking point in its inability to negotiate hurt and anger.

There are several advantages to the inclusion of a perspective that views the patient as trying to broaden the analyst's self-regulatory range: (1) It adds another dimension to the understanding of the complex workings of the indissoluble unity of patient and analyst. (2) It encourages the analyst to look for the patient's developmental strivings in what can seem like purely self-defeating behavior. (3) It invites the analyst to use painful, frustrating stalemates as vehicles for personal growth. As Mitchell (1997) puts it, "One of the best kept secrets of the psychoanalytic profession is the extent to which analysts often grow (in corrective emotional experiences) through a surrender to the influence of patients" (p. 26). (4) It can act as a scaffold, preventing the treatment from falling into cycles of withdrawal, retaliation, or collapse. The legitimization of the therapist's use of the analytic platform to gain access to aspects of himself that have been out of awareness supports the analyst's efforts for continued engagement. It has the potential to energize an embattled or frozen treatment.

CONCLUSION

In radically rejecting "the notion that psychoanalysis is something that one isolated mind does to another, or that development is something that one person does or does not do" (Orange et al., 1997, p. 18), we come face to face with the challenge of reconsidering and reconceptualizing time-honored, profoundly useful, but unidirectional clinical concepts such as selfobject experience, rupture and repair, and optimal responsiveness. We view these constructs through a bidirectional lens because we believe these "old bottles" are excellent containers for relational theory. A full consideration of the implications of psychoanalytic bidirectionality is unfamiliar and complex. It can be as exciting and disorienting as stepping from a three-dimensional world into the fourth dimension.

We use the idea of self- and mutual regulation introduced by infant research to elaborate the dimension of mutual influence in these basic self psychological concepts. We view selfobject experience as interactive (the experience of a successful mutually regulated giving and receiving matrix); rupture and repair as a complex interweaving of mutual empathic striving toward dyadic self-righting; and optimal responsiveness as, at times including the expressive use of the analyst's subjectivity ("I" statements) and the entity of the analytic couple ("we" statements).

Self psychologists are certainly not alone in grappling with the new relational paradigm in psychoanalysis. As Aron (1996) points out, there is a great deal of cross-fertilization in the rich dialogue between theoretical perspectives resulting from this paradigm shift. We believe that self psychology and intersubjectivity theory continue to have unique and invaluable contributions to make to this new relational integration.

REFERENCES

Aron, L. (1996), *A Meeting of Minds: Mutuality in Psychoanalysis*. Hillsdale, NJ: The Analytic Press.

——— (1997), Intersubjectivity: Clinical implications. Presentation, New York City, December 12th.

Atwood, G. E., Stolorow, R. D. & Trop, J. L. (1989), Impasses in psychoanalytic therapy: A royal road. *Contemp. Psychoanal.*, 25:554–574.

Bacal, H. (1990), The elements of a corrective selfobject experience. *Psychoanal. Inq.*, 3:347–372.

——— (1995a), The centrality of selfobject experience in psychological relatedness. *Psychoanal. Dial.*, 5:403–410.

——— (1995b), The essence of Kohut's work and the progress of self psychology. *Psychoanal. Dial.*, 5:353–366.

——— & Thomson, P. (1996), The psychoanalyst's selfobject needs and the effect of their frustration on the treatment: A new view of countertransference. In: *Basic Ideas Reconsidered: Progress in Self Psychology, Vol. 12,* ed. A. Goldberg. Hillsdale, NJ: The Analytic Press, pp. 17—35.

Beebe, B. & Lachmann, F. M. (1994), Representation and internalization in infancy: Three principles of salience. *Psychoanal. Psychol.,* 11:127—165.

——— & Lachmann, F. M. (1996), The contribution of self- and mutual regulation to therapeutic action: A case illustration. In: *Basic Ideas Reconsidered: Progress in Self Psychology, Vol. 12,* ed. A. Goldberg. Hillsdale: NJ: The Analytic Press, pp.123—140.

Brothers, D. (1995), *Falling Backwards: An Exploration of Trust and Self Experience.* New York: Norton.

Fosshage, J. L (1995), Interaction in psychoanalysis: A broadening horizon. *Psychoanal. Dial.,* 5:459—478.

Kohut, H. (1977), *The Restoration of the Self.* New York: International Universities Press.

Lessem, P. & Orange, D. (1993), Self psychology and attachment: The importance of the particular other. Presented at the 16th Annual Conference on the *Psychology of the Self,* October 28–31, Toronto.

Mitchell, S. A. (1997), *Influence and Autonomy in Psychoanalysis.* Hillsdale, NJ: The Analytic Press.

Natterson, J. (1991), *Beyond Countertransference: The Therapist's Subjectivity in the Therapeutic Process.* Northvale, NJ: Aronson.

Orange, D. (1995), *Emotional Understanding: Studies in Psychoanalytic Epistomology.* New York: Guilford.

——— Atwood, G. E. & Stolorow, R. D. (1997), *Working Intersubjectively: Contextualism in Psychoanalytic Practice.* Hillsdale, NJ: The Analytic Press.

Preston, L. (1996), Expressive relating: The intentional use of the analyst's subjectivity. In: *Progress in Self Psychology,* ed. A. Goldberg. Hillsdale, NJ: The Analytic Press, pp. 203–218.

Searles, H. (1975), The patient as therapist to his analyst. In: *Tactics and Techniques in Psychoanalytic Therapy,* Vol. 2, ed. P. Giovacchini. New York: Aronson, pp. 95–151.

Shane, M. & Shane E. (1996), Self psychology in search of the optimal: A consideration of optimal responsivemess; optimal provision; optimal gratification; and optimal restraint in the clinical situation. In: *Basic Ideas Reconsidered: Progress in Self Psychology, Vol. 12,* ed. A. Goldberg. Hillsdale, NJ: The Analytic Press, pp. 37–54.

Spezzano, C. (1997), The emergence of an American middle school of psychoanalysis: Commentary on Karen Rosica's paper. *Psychoanal. Dial.,* 7:603–618.

Stolorow, R. D. & Atwood, G. E. (1992), *Contexts of Being: The Intersubjective Foundations of Psychological Life.* Hillsdale, NJ: The Analytic Press.

———, Brandchaft, B. & Atwood, G. E. (1987), *Psychoanalytic Treatment: An Intersubjective Approach,* Hillsdale, NJ: The Analytic Press.

Sucharov, M. S. (1995), The patient's empathic understanding of the therapist: A bilateral systems view of empathic process. Presented at the 18th Annual Conference on the *Psychology of the Self,* October 19–22.

——— (1996), Listening to the empathic dance: A rediscovery of the therapist's subjectivity. Presented at the 19th Annual Conference on the *Psychology of the Self*, October 19th.

Suttie, I. D. (1988), *The Origins of Love and Hate*. London: Free Association Press.

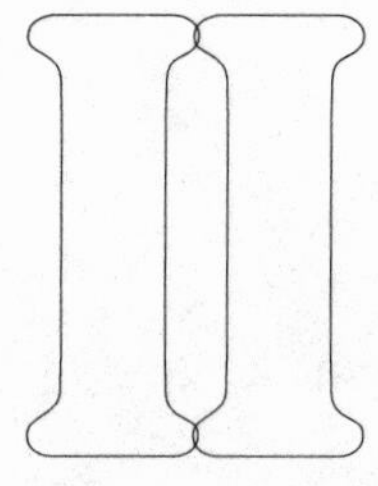

Clinical

Chapter 6

The Need for Efficacy in the Treatment of Suicidal Patients: Transference and Countertransference Issues

Hans-Peter Hartmann
Wolfgang E. Milch

This chapter will focus on the role of efficacy and agency selfobject experiences in the prevention of suicide. Selfobject experiences mostly have in common that they refer to the self as recipient of some action of the selfobject. Wolf (1988) described another kind of phenomena that proceed in the opposite direction, that is, phenomena characterized by the self as actor and the selfobject as acted upon. The essence of these phenomena is the self's experience of being an effective agent in influencing the object that Wolf defined as efficacy experiences. Exploring the self-state of suicidal patients, the therapist is confronted with their loss of agency in a state of despair and deep feelings of helplessness. When suicidal patients experience being an effective agent in influencing the object, their selves become more cohesive and the

---

This paper is dedicated to Dr. Christel Schöttler, Giessen.

The authors wish to thank Drs. Lotte Köhler, Anna and Paul Ornstein, Harvey Freed and Ernest S. Wolf for their thoughtful assistance.

suicidal ideation is less imminent. Some borderline patients try to manipulate their surroundings. Other suicidal patients are found to act on the therapist by attacking him (Milch, 1990b). These attacks are not meant to destroy the therapist but, rather, aim at making contact with him and, by doing so, experiencing personal agency. When these attacks are unconscious, the neediness of the patient is split off (vertical split). In the countertransference, the manipulating behavior and the attacks of the patients provoke defensiveness in the therapist, who might feel insulted and acted upon. The patient's wish to make contact and to sense his own agency via hidden or open attacks is often experienced as so hurtful by the therapist that he himself might wish to get rid of the patient or even that the patient might die. On the other hand, the patient often expects to be rejected (see case vignettes later) as a protection against disappointment and therefore loses his last hope. This whole course of events is, in our view, a kind of pathological accommodation (Brandchaft, 1998).

In 1910, shortly after Freud developed the concept of transference, a member of his circle, Wilhelm Stekel, emphasized that one of the best preventions of suicide of students was by establishing a transference. Today, we would conceptualize this prophylactic curative transference as a selfobject transference that helps to establish a therapeutic bond with suicide-prone patients, thereby providing a steadying factor (Reiser, 1986). An impaired core self is prone to rapid fragmentation in the face of disrupted narcissistic homeostasis, and suicide may occur as a consequence of disintegration in several different types of core selves (Maltsberger, 1986; Reiser, 1986). Suicidal behavior may be an expression of despair caused by the loss of a sustaining selfobject experience (Kohut, 1984). Narcissistic injuries with severe states of envy or shame (Kohut, 1971, 1972), loss of attachment (Ornstein, 1994), or inhibition of self-assertion (Wolf, 1988) are frequently observed as precipitants of suicidal ideation. Patients whose self reached only a fragile state of cohesion are much more vulnerable to selfobject losses or narcissistic mortification than solidly cohesive selves. Fragile selves react with narcissistic rage for the sake of their assertiveness because they don't have self-righting mechanisms at their disposal.

The lack of selfobject experiences, then, can lead to a state of extreme helplessness, fragmentation, and narcissistic rage. Suicidal behavior is the result of a final attempt to evoke a reaction of the selfobject, to experience one's own efficacy, and to regulate the self-state. In a fantasy of archaic grandiosity, the body and the personal world may be destroyed, and in this act the sense of one's own agency is rescued.

COUNTERTRANSFERENCE CLUES TO SUICIDE RISK

Suicidal patients have a higher than usual need to maintain a consistent responsive selfobject experience for the maintenance and protection of their fragile selves. The suicidal patients' highly ambivalent attempts at establishing a relationship with the therapist create significant transference and countertransference problems. Some suicidal patients mobilize a selfobject transference by means of attacks on the therapist. These attacks upon the setting or the therapist seem innocent or they are uttered in a friendly tone because the aversive content underlies a vertical split. The patients are not aware of the aggressive connotation and often react with astonishment when the therapist interprets the attacks in a later phase of therapy. But these subtle attacks may give rise to a countertransference in the therapist. The therapist may experience a change in his self-state or an altered sense of self as a result of the patient's challenges (perhaps the patient's first hint of a threatening suicide). The self psychologically informed therapist, of course, goes beyond his own experience in trying to understand his patient's perspective.

But in many cases an important sign for the danger of suicide lies in the therapist's personal embarrassment, which is already there before the process of further understanding of the patient's perspective is fully developed. The hidden attacks are very troublesome to the therapist's own feeling of self-worth, and his state of self may express its vulnerability (Wolf, 1979; Köhler, 1984). In a psychiatric clinic, the detection of these countertransference reactions of the therapist are systematically used for the prevention of suicide in patients who are not aware of their suicidal ideation because this is split off. We also think that these countertransference problems are part of the reason why suicidal patients rarely find a psychotherapist who is willing to take them into therapy. The nature of these attacks are difficult to recognize because the contact seems to be friendly in the foreground, while the background is dominated by hatred and rage. Mostly, therapists are unable to escape from these affects. In many cases therapists talk with suicidal patients for the first or second time without knowing the background. It is, therefore, a danger to perceive those feelings of hatred and rage in isolation because of the lack of understanding in the course of a long therapeutical relationship.

Clinical Vignette

A clinical example serves to demonstrate this point. A female borderline patient told the analyst in an inoffensive tone: "Doctor, help me, give me an injection that will cause my death!" At first, the analyst tried empathically to understand the need of the patient, but his efforts were offended by the patient remarking: "If this cannot take place (i.e., the injection), send me to the gas chamber." The analyst experienced himself helpless, numb, and inhibited, as if he had inwardly turned to stone or was powerless. He felt rejected in his attempts to cure and was mortified that his intention was not recognized by the patient. He heard very upsetting remarks from her; for example, she asked him to transfer her to a forensic ward, where she could stay with murderers and criminals. She also mentioned that this would be a chance for her to be killed. This was extremely disturbing because it, too, affected the therapist's own feeling of self-worth and was experienced by him as insulting. The therapist experienced feelings of guilt, shame, restlessness, and an inability to concentrate—in short, a self that was no longer functioning well. It seemed that the patient had stopped providing a confirming selfobject experience for the therapist, and the latter's self began to fragment with the above-mentioned symptoms. Apparently, the therapist's relative helplessness led to some rage and he confronted the patient with her deprecating behavior. This acting out of the therapist was a countertransference reaction that was, however, mild enough for the therapist to recognize and control. He told the patient in controlled, but no uncertain, terms that he felt insulted by her. The patient was quite surprised by this reaction, and she realized that this expression of his feelings, which were obviously a result of his own sense of injury, was completely sincere. It turned out that the patient was longing for such a reaction just as she had unsuccessfully tried to move the stone-like face of her depressed mother. His response to her attacks was in tune with her need to be able to provoke a reaction.[1] Later on, she told the analyst that she had hoped for empathic responses from her parents when she first attempted suicide. Both therapist and patient learned more about the patient's need to be an agent and her reasons for trying to provoke an emotional exchange, which, in her case, took the form of attacking and inciting the analyst, an example of a need for an efficacy selfobject experience, maybe as a consequence of an until then not fully func-

---

[1] This could correspond to findings of baby watchers in the "still-face" experiment (Tronick and Adamson, 1980), which illustrates how crucial it is for the infant to be an agent, able to influence the mother and restore contact with her. In this experiment mothers of 3- to 6 month-old babies are asked to show no facial reaction to their babies. The babies try to evoke a reaction, get upset and enraged, and finally resigned (efficacy selfobject experience).

tioning mirroring selfobject experience. This vignette is also an example of the interactive mode that characterizes much good clinical therapeutic work.

COUNTERTRANSFERENCE PRECIPITATED BY MOBILIZATION OF THERAPIST'S NEEDS

As this example shows, an attack can be understood as an effort on the patient's part to make contact with the therapist. The aggressive form of the patient's need explains why such an effort is so readily misunderstood. When these needs of the patient are not met and the therapeutic efforts fail, as a reaction to the attacks, the therapist's countertransference sometimes puts him in danger of insulting the patient. Often, patients are very sensitive to the therapist's weak spots. The therapist may feel rejected because his endeavor is not validated by the patient. His needs to be mirrored or idealized by the patient are frustrated, and his feelings of self-worth and professional competence can be badly affected. Consequently, the therapist may experience the patient as so intolerable that he sends him away to a colleague. One of our studies showed that suicidal patients were transferred from one ward to the other far more than nonsuicidal patients (Milch, 1990a).

TESTING THE THERAPEUTIC AMBIENCE FOR SAFETY VERSUS PROVOKING THE THERAPIST

In this context, we make a distinction between the provocative behavior of a suicidal patient and a "testing" in the sense that Weiss and Sampson (1986) use this concept. Testing behavior is easily confused with psychological attacks of suicidal patients, but in detail they differ in their etiology, pathology, transference, countertransference, and the appropriate therapeutic response. Patients test the therapist in the initial stages of the therapy to assess the quality of what the relationship will be. The "testing" behavior is based upon the wish for reliability and security. This wish is close to consciousness and might be understood and interpreted. The aversive behavior, however, is a recapitulation of an attempt to elicit a response from the childhood selfobject. The testing can also lead to countertransference reactions: the therapist may become angry and consider the patient to be incurable, but unlike a selfobject countertransference (Wolf, 1979; Köhler, 1984) this does not alter his sense of self.

GENETIC CONSIDERATIONS: DEVELOPMENTAL ORIGIN OF AGGRESSIVE BEHAVIOR AND RAGE AS A MEANS OF OBTAINING THE DESIRED RESPONSE

In family therapy with 30 patients who had attempted suicide during hospitalization, we could observe that the quality of the attachment behavior of the parents to the patients was unstable, ambivalent, or disorganized. Even for the therapists, the parent's behavior was very difficult to validate or predict (Milch, 1990b). We had assumed that in their childhood most of these patients had experienced severe disruptions in the relationship with their parents. For instance, the parental responsiveness was faulty because of a depression or a psychosis of the mother. To establish contact and to obtain a responsive reaction from the mothers, the children often threw tantrums.[2] The provocative behavior, later seen in therapy, may therefore represent a model scene of infancy or childhood (Lichtenberg, 1989).

In some cases we heard from our patients that their expressions of rage received no response from the parents. One woman, whose analysis will be described later, tried as a child to elicit an emotional response from her mutistic mother. Even when she used her small fists to beat on her mother, she could not provoke a reaction. In other cases we heard from patients about how their early efforts to contact their parents by crying was traumatically disrupted by extreme over- or understimulation. In the above-mentioned example, when the baby cried, the father yelled into the baby buggy until she was quiet.

Apparently, parents must not only be able to respond to the need, but also to the attack that results when the need is not met. If the attack is not responded to either, the child will first respond with narcissistic rage, and the next phase (for the adult) might be despair and/or suicide.

It is possible, then, to understand how narcissistic rage, in an attempt to establish contact with a selfobject, can turn into self-destructive behavior in later life. In committing suicide, it is the narcissistic rage that threatens to destroy the self. The tendency for murderous rage turns into the drive to commit suicide (Freud, 1917). In self psychology terms: the patient needs to end the state of unbearable helplessness by an assertion that destroys.

---

[2] This is in keeping with infant observations: when babies are left alone, their crying may serve to call for attention. If they are not heard, the crying is intensified. It seems to become a protest. Eventually, the babies become resigned to the fact.

CURATIVE FANTASIES IN SUICIDAL BEHAVIOR

In this context suicidal behavior may be seen to have two curative aspects: The first would be mobilizing aggression to win back a selfobject. When working with suicidal patients, a curative fantasy often can be elaborated when the patient speaks about possible reactions of important selfobjects after their own imagined death. The fantasy is that their longing for selfobjects is understood. The selfobject is, of course, needed for their narcissistic equilibrium. The second curative aspect of suicidal behavior might be the attempt to regulate the state of self by efficacy.

When there is no hope that the situation will change or that a psychic development will occur and there is no prospect of finding new selfobjects, then the experience of being one's own agent through suicidal behavior is vitalizing and strengthens the fragmentation-prone structure of the self. But before it gets this far, the patient may try both to restore a sense of agency and to recreate the lifesaving selfobject bond, though by inappropriate means. As we described, the patient attacks the therapist in order to provoke a reaction and thus prove that he or she can achieve a selfobject experience.

If the analyst can understand the true meaning of the countertransference, thus provoked, he will not dismiss the patient, as others did in the past who were the target of the patient's attacks. Now under different circumstances in the therapy, the patient may stabilize selfobject maintenance and self-regulation and thereby enhance the cohesion of his or her self. Though the patient dreads to repeat the old trauma (Ornstein, 1974, 1991), the therapeutic situation provides a chance to mutually experience the inner state of the patient, that of an "incompetent" and rejected child who is feeling unbearably helpless. By experiencing the archaic needs and states in the transference, a new quality of hope for sustaining stable selfobjects becomes established in the patient. The experience of being empathically understood strengthens the self so that seemingly unbearable affects become tolerable. Being the source of his own competence and initiative gives the patient a sense of coherence and vitalization.

CASE REPORT

A 27-year-old married woman had specifically asked for psychoanalysis after having been referred by a female behavior therapist, who thought psychoanalysis would be a better form of treatment for her.

The patient was a slim, good looking young woman, with long brown hair down to her waist, who wore white clothing. She appeared to be highly intelligent and clear, but the analyst felt at a distance, as if a wall of glass stood between them. She said, in a condescending tone, that she preferred psychoanalysis with a woman, but she would see whether she could work with a man. Behind her overt kindness, the analyst sensed veiled hostility. Her presenting symptom was an anxiety of losing her father after he had a few heart attacks. Her mother was schizophrenic and she (the patient) had attempted to commit suicide three times during her adolescence. Previous to her first suicide attempt was an incident in which her father had considered her contact with several young men as sexual and had accused her of being a whore. Her attempts to create an independent life were greatly hindered by his need to control her. The patient had initially reacted to this by developing anorectic symptoms. Then, she attempted suicide at the age of 16, after her father failed to react to her loud screaming during a quarrel. It became clear at this initial interview that the disturbed nature of the father–daughter relationship played an important part in the patient's suicidal behavior.

The second suicide attempt occurred after she had been studying hard for a chemistry test with her father and he failed to appreciate her insecurity about the test. Her father's reaction to her abdominal pains several years previously had been similar. He had not taken her to the hospital, and she had subsequently suffered from a perforated appendix. At that time, wrapped in a blanket, she had thrown herself off a balcony and sustained several fractures.

The third suicide attempt, which nearly ended in death, occurred when her father would not give in to her wish to finish high school. She swallowed about 200 pills and had to be treated in intensive care.

Every suicide attempt occurred in a situation where Mrs. A was unable to get through to her father; in all three attempts she experienced a profound sense of helpless rage. Since the father had had heart attacks following her first two suicide attempts, the patient feared that her rage could kill him.

After her last attempt the patient appeared to give up hope to have her father near her, and she could no longer distinguish between her own and her father's wishes. Despite good grades, she was convinced that all she had achieved at school was due to her father. By acting "crazy" she maintained her self-cohesion. Acting the role of her crazy mother made it possible for her to experience the difference between her mother and herself: she only acted mad, whereas her mother was mad, in reality.

Important Factors in the Development of the Patient's Psychopathology

As a small child, Mrs. A was unsuccessful in her attempts to reach her withdrawn and mute mother; she would often strike at her with her fists. On the basis of the patient's narrative, we assume that the patient suffered from a deficiency in self-regulation. On the other hand, she greatly admired her father, who was a headmaster and was considered to be very knowledgeable. He was a decisive factor in the family, and she would often argue with him regarding political matters. He had functioned as her idealized selfobject (concerning more rational than emotional matters), thus partially compensating for the difficulties in her relationship with her schizophrenic mother. This made her fear of losing him understandable: the disruption of this selfobject bond during her adolescence left her desperate and suicidal. Her attempted suicides were efforts to provoke a reaction and to make contact with him. But even by attempting suicide, she was unable to reach her father. He had not reacted with concern when she was admitted to the hospital, but only commented cold-hearted "noblesse oblige," meaning that her suicide attempt was not in accordance with his own moral standards.

The patient felt that the awakening sexuality of her adolescence was not greeted joyfully by her father. Instead, he was threatened by his own sexual insecurity, which intensified his fear of showing his feelings. The strong, archaic wish of the patient to be recognized and accepted contrasted with her father's need to be supported in his view of the world. Consequently, the adolescent arguments between the patient and her father resulted in her weakened cohesive self fragmenting, and she experienced severe narcissistic rage.

The Analysis

Given this information, the analyst felt insecure about the degree of Mrs. A's psychopathology and wondered whether she was treatable by psychoanalysis. He knew that, during the psychiatric hospitalization 10 years ago, a borderline condition had been diagnosed, and the patient was described as negativistic, with flat affects and rigid defenses. But the analyst had another impression during the initial interviews: he had a very positive assessment of her potential. This positive attitude was related to good patient and analyst match; that is, a patient who needed mirroring met an analyst who idealized her.

In keeping with the "good" patient–analyst match, during the first months of treatment, the analyst developed a fear of having a heart attack. He understood this as his countertransference with which he reacted to the patient's fear that her relationship to the analyst could be broken off in the same way as it was to her father.

The provocative behavior so often found in suicidal patients became evident during the first 6 months of the treatment. Mrs. A would often appear 5 or 10 minutes before her appointment and expect the analyst to begin the session earlier. During the sessions she seemed to totally ignore his comments, seemed arrogant, and tried to instruct him how to interpret. She would also irritate him by frequently trying to change the time of her sessions. At times, she wanted to start 15 minutes later. Very often, she would not keep her appointment because of ill health. She would always present her suggestions in a friendly manner and also had very good explanations for missed appointments and lateness. For this reason it took the analyst a long time to recognize his own anger. For a few months he accepted her conditions but felt increasingly dominated by her and began to feel both helpless and very angry.[3] The analyst's tolerance did not get them any further, however, and was, from his point of view, a repetition of the patient's relationship with her unresponsive mother. Eventually, all of this began to irritate and annoy the analyst, and he was able to recognize the countertransference nature of his reactions.

In the 82nd hour, after a longer period of reflection, the analyst expressed his anger (a disciplined spontaneous engagement; Lichtenberg, Lachmann, and Fosshage, 1992) at the many missed and changed appointments. Mrs. A seemed very astonished and assured him that she had not intended to annoy him. Now she had experienced the analyst's authentic emotional reaction in an atmosphere of goodwill. After that her provocative behavior disappeared.

This was only the beginning. Gradually, the patient was able to understand her need to decide things for herself and to act as an agent. Efficacy was very important for her. It was further worked through, by interpretations of the transference, how afraid she was that she would not be able to effect a change in her environment.

From the point of view of the patient, the analyst belonged to her extended self, which was understood by the analyst as a merger transference. She needed to control him to prove her efficacy. Her need for

[3] This example of the analyst's selfobject countertransference is the result of the transference attack of the patient and is not understood in the sense of "testing."

control was also an expression of her great uncertainty about whether she would be unconditionally accepted and mirrored.

When she experienced herself as effective, she was enabled to accept strong feelings of "oneness" with another. On the other hand, she also experienced herself as a center of initiative and for the first time felt fear for herself and not for others (Lachmann and Beebe, 1989) as a sign for the growing intimacy with the self (Lichtenberg, 1999). A process of a therapeutic dialogue developed between patient and analyst because of the analyst's ability to recognize and accept the patient's needs for mirroring in the transference. He and the patient seemed to be pretty much on the same wavelength; for example, when he thought about something, the patient would begin to talk about the same subject. The analyst's empathic listening was supported by strong "vitality affects" (Stern, 1985) on both parts, and now it appeared that there was a good match between analyst and patient. The analyst noted his strong attachment to her, yet at the same time he recognized the absolute necessity to respect her essence and in no way to disturb it.

At this point in the treatment, the patient experienced more interest in sexual interaction with her husband. However, the rediscovery of her sexuality led to a revival of the patient's adolescent problems, with the result that the patient found it difficult to tell the difference between sexuality and affection. In the course of working these problems through, there was a similar situation with the analyst, during which it became clear that the patient's adolescent sexual feelings had been mixed up with her archaic mirror needs. She wanted to be accompanied by the analyst in her sexual development and felt herself misunderstood when he interpreted that she would have sexual feelings toward him (like her father misunderstood her contact with young men during adolescence as sexual and called her a whore). It was clear that this "speech confusion" (Ferenczi, 1933), namely to confuse the need for affection and a close relationship as sexual wishes, was caused by the fact that her archaic needs for mirroring had not been met by her schizophrenic mother. Therefore, they were directed toward her father and confused with sexual wishes. The mother's earlier lack of reaction had left feelings of emptiness and worthlessness in the patient.

Later, the therapist worked on her sense of guilt and responsibility for her mother's illness. Mrs. A was also able at long last to express her feelings to her father without fear that she would be in a suicidal state: "I won't let my life be taken from me anymore."

Mrs. A had started to develop hope that it might be possible for her to live independently. At the same time her subtle anger disappeared in and outside the treatment situation.

In a climate of mutual responsiveness, in which it was always possible to detect and to restore disruptions in the relationship, she really celebrated her birthday, something she had only endured previously. She began painting and started to go out dancing, something that had always frightened her before.

She also began to have regular bodily rhythms and cycles for the first time. She started to menstruate regularly, had a more physiological response to illness (e.g., increased temperature in response to infections), and started to eat and drink normally and with enjoyment. Her marital relationship gradually improved. She shifted slowly from sexualization to sexuality and developed a real interest in sexual intercourse with her partner. She became calmer and less agitated and was able to regulate states of disorganization and fragmentation more effectively on her own, that is, by her own capacity to soothe herself.

After 2½ years of analysis, the sudden death of her father awoke archaic fears of selfobject loss. She called the analyst as soon as she heard of her father's death, and he told her to come by immediately. She was in despair, feeling abandoned and totally unprotected. Her husband had to drive her to the session because she was so disorganized that she was incapable of driving. She was shivering from head to toe so the analyst offered her a cup of hot tea, which she gratefully accepted. He just listened and acted as a sounding-board for her despair and sadness. The day afterward she had a dream: "My father came down the stairs, and I said, Why didn't you fight this time, why not this time? He answered that he couldn't but that she was probably right that he should have fought." The patient, therefore, no longer had the feeling that she was responsible for her father's death.

Mrs. A was able to calm her fears about not being able to live without her father with the idea that he had died as he had lived and that he had wanted to die. She found it difficult to sleep for days and needed the analyst to support and stabilize her. He decided that tranquilizers (for two or three weeks) were necessary. The death of the father was the acid test of the therapy.

There were problems and quarrels over her father's will, but Mrs. A was able to overcome this. The experience of being able to cope with the death of her father without feeling suicidal or without other serious decompensation was growth promoting. Likewise, her ability to argue and to set limits with her mother had strengthened her self and enabled her to go her own way. She went back to high school, passed her exams, studied for two semesters at a college, and then progressed to the university.

CONCLUDING REMARKS

During analysis, Mrs. A tried by means of her aggressive and insulting behavior to experience her agency in the therapeutic relationship and to establish affective contact with and to get closer to the analyst. By such means she attempted to satisfy her archaic selfobject needs, as suggested by Wolf (1988): "From the awareness of having an initiating and causal role in bringing about states of attachment and intimacy, the infant acquires an *experience of efficacy* that in addition to the responsive selfobject experiences—becomes an essential aspect of the cohesive self-experience. It is as if the infant were able to say to himself . . .: I can elicit a response, therefore I am somebody" (p. 62). We understand Mrs. A's intense needs to experience a sense of efficacy as a pathological outcome of her disturbed childhood; we don't see them as normal healthy strivings. We believe that at times the experience of efficacy is at least as important as the experience of being understood, both developmentally and therapeutically. The patient was pleased with the analyst's reaction to her attacks on his self-worth, demonstrating his availability and responsiveness as well as his understanding of the purpose of her attacks. We believe that the disciplined spontaneous reaction (Lichtenberg et al., 1992) of the analyst in the 82nd session on a template of an empathic background signalled to the patient his affective investment in her. This intensified the patient's sense of hope and facilitated the establishment of an archaic merger transference.

The suicidal behavior, while certainly to be understood as an effort to be rescued, also expressed the patient's need to experience herself as competent and effective. This was the prelude to the sense of security required for the establishment of a selfobject relationship without the threat of suicide. Her sense of self as an agent was solidified by her impact on the selfobject analyst. She no longer required the fantasies of self-injury for such strengthening and said, in essence, "If I can no longer have an impact on others, at least I can have an impact on my own body." She developed better capacities for self-righting. Gradually, her preoccupation with death and suicide disappeared. Body rhythms also attained regularity. The analyst's empathic responsiveness facilitated the remobilization of the grandiose–exhibitionistic infantile self. This means she was able to develop stable selfobject transferences, especially in the form of twinship and mirroring transference, which supported Kohut's own view (a personal communication, 1981, cited in Stolorow, Brandchaft, and Atwood, 1987): "Insofar as the therapist is able to build an empathic bridge to the patient, the patient has in a way ceased to be a borderline case . . . and has become a case of (severe) narcissistic personality disorder" (p. 118).

REFERENCES

Brandchaft, B. (1998), The self in developmental trauma. Paper presented at the 21th Annual Conference on the Psychology of the Self, San Diego, CA, October 22–25.

Ferenczi, S. (1933), Sprachverwirrung zwischen den Erwachensenen und dem Kind [Confusion of tongues between adults and the child]. In: *Schriften zur Psychoanalyse,* Vol. II [Final *Contributions to the Problems and Methods of Psycho-Analysis*], ed. M. Balint (trans. E. Mosbacher). London: Karnac Books, 1980, pp. 156–167.

Freud, S. (1917), Mourning and melancholia. *Standard Edition,* 14:243–258.

Köhler, L. (1984), On selfobject countertransference. *The Annual of Psychoanalysis,* 12:39–56. New York: International Universities Press.

Kohut, H. (1971), *The Analysis of the Self.* New York: International Universities Press.

——— (1972), Thoughts on narcissism and narcissistic rage. In: *The Search for the Self, Vol. 2,* ed. P. H. Ornstein. New York: International Universities Press, 1978, pp. 615–658.

——— (1984), *How Does Analysis Cure?* ed. A. Goldberg & P. Stepansky. Chicago: University of Chigaco Press.

Lachmann, F. M. & Beebe, B. (1989), Oneness fantasies revisited. *Psychanal. Psychol.* 6:137–149.

Lichtenberg, J. D. (1989), *Psychoanalysis and Motivation.* Hillsdale, NJ: The Analytic Press.

——— (1999), Intimität mit dem Selbst [Intimacy with the self]. In: *Die Deutung im Therapeutischen Prozess* [*Interpretation and the Therapeutic Process*], ed. W. E. Milch & H.-P. Hartmann. Giessen: Psychosozial, pp. 107–125.

——— Lachmann, F. M. & Fosshage, J. L. (1992), *Self and Motivational Systems: Toward a Theory of Psychoanalytic Technique.* Hillsdale, NJ: The Analytic Press.

Maltsberger, J. T. (1986), *Suicide Risk: The Formulation of Clinical Judgment.* New York: University Press.

Milch, W. E. (1990a), The change of symptomatology in hospitalized suicidal patients. *Crisis,* 11:44–51.

——— (1990b), Suicidal patient's psychological attacks on the therapist. *Bull. Menn. Clin.,* 54:384–390.

Ornstein, A. (1974), The dread to repeat and the new beginning: A contribution to the psychoanalytic treatment of narcissistic personality disorders. *The Annual of Psychoanalysis,* 2:231–248. New York: International Universities Press.

——— (1991), The dread to repeat: Comments on the working-through process in psychoanalysis. *J. Amer. Psychoanal. Assn.* 39:377–398.

——— (1994), Trauma, memory and psychic continuity. In: *A Decade of Progress: Progress in Self Psychology, Vol. 10,* ed. A. Goldberg. Hillsdale, NJ: The Analytic Press, pp. 131–146.

Reiser, D. E. (1986), Self psychology and the problem of suicide. In: *Progress in Self Psychology, Vol. 2,* ed. A. Goldberg. New York: Guilford, pp. 227–241.

Stekel, W. (1910), Contribution about suicide. In: *Minutes of the Vienna Psychoanalytic Society, Vol. 2 1908–1910,* ed. H. Nunberg & E. Federn. New York: International Universities Press, 1974, pp. 500–507.

Stern, D. N. (1985), *The Interpersonal World of the Infant.* New York: Basic Books.

Stolorow, R. D., Brandchaft, B. & Atwood, G. E. (1987), *Psychoanalytic Treatment: An Intersubjective Approach.* Hillsdale, NJ: The Analytic Press.

Tronick, E. & Adamson, L. (1980), *Babies as People: New Findings on Our Social Beginnings.* New York: Collier.

Weiss, J. & Sampson, H. (1986), *The Psychoanalytic Process.* New York: Guilford.

Wolf, E. S. (1979), Transference and countertransference in the analysis of the disorders of the self. *Contemp. Psychoanal.,* 15:577–594.

——— (1988), *Treating the Self.* New York: Guilford.

Chapter 7

eSupervision: Something New Under the Sun

Allen M. Siegel
Eva-Maria Topel

The thing that has been,
it is that which shall be;
And that which is done
is that which shall be done:
And there is nothing new under the sun.
Is there any thing whereof it may be said,
"See, this is new?"

Kohelet (Eccleseastes) 1:9–10

Long valued for their ironic truth, Kohelet's words have lost their hold on the 21st century. eBay, email, eToys, eEveryThing—the sun no longer sets without a cyberspace headline. We learn of cyber-viruses that threaten our world, of cyber-entrepreneurs who morph into millionaires, and of mega-mergers between cyber-companies. Virtual University, Drugstore.com, surely something new is upon the land, only now the land is the entire planet. Expanded by cyberspace, borders have been swapped for Borders.com. Whether in a jungle or atop an ocean, we are no longer removed from office, school, or home.

In his recent book, Thomas Friedman (1999), *New York Times* foreign correspondent, describes what he calls the "democratization of finance, technology and information" and details how these developments have combined to create the world-changing revolution called globalization. Revolutions do not occur without tension, and the intriguing title of Friedman's new book, *The Lexus and the Olive Tree*, conveys the tension that exists between old identities and new technologies. For his title Friedman chooses two of the many stories he tells about people who either participate in or sit out the global revolution. The Lexus refers to a new robotic Japanese automobile factory that produces cars of absolute perfection. The olive tree, on the other hand, an ancient specimen that has carried a Palestinian family's identity for generations, was threatened with extinction by a new technological facility. Friedman describes the dilemma both people and countries experience when they are forced to choose between prosperity associated with new technology and the anchor to one's sacred roots that comes with adherence to old ways.

We in the mental health field do not escape this evolutionary tension as we are confronted with the dilemma of whether to cling to tool and method pride or embrace the new in creative ways that enhance our growth yet retain our identity. We are confronted with the dilemma of whether to explore the use of electronic communication in what we do or insist on the face-to-face, or at least voice-to-voice, encounter as the only possible way to do our work.

The purpose in writing this chapter is to offer our electronically conducted supervisory experience as an example of one possible use of the new technology. We refer to our experience as eSupervision despite the fact that we began our work using a fax and completed it using email. We found the supervisory experience essentially identical using both technologies, although we did notice that the Internet created a sense of immediacy and connectedness that was not as present when we used the fax.

Before moving to our clinical material, however, we will first discuss some of the current literature in an effort to highlight recent discussions concerning supervision and demonstrate that the elements of supervision described in those discussions were present in our work as well. Because there is no currently existing literature about eSupervision, we hope to initiate and stimulate a conversation concerning the special issues involved in an electronic "non-face-to-face" supervisory experience.

We emphasize the non-face-to-face aspect of our work to call attention to the absence, for both supervisee and supervisor, of direct facial, nonverbal, and preverbal communications. Missing in overt expression from our work, for example, were the facial mirroring experiences, as well as the experiences of voice and gesture correspondence that are embedded in a visually related discourse. These informative reassuring and regulating nonverbal communications are the "basic interaction patterns" that usually operate outside the realm of awareness (Beebe and Lachmann, 1994; Lachmann, personal communication, 1999). These nonverbal communications underlie the face-to-face encounter and provide the participants with continuing regulatory information about the ongoing process in the cocreated field. Deprived initially of these early interactive communicative elements in our work, we each coincidentally developed a deeper appreciation of the subtle existence and power, both disruptive and soothing, of the nonverbal exchange. These issues of communication were especially poignant since we worked together on the treatment of a 13-year-old girl who preferred not to speak.

CONCEPTUALIZATION OF THE SUPERVISORY PROCESS

Defined in its most basic form, supervision is the consultative–tutorial process that involves the teaching and learning of psychotherapeutic work. It is a complex endeavor that requires the ability of the supervisor to teach a particular psychology and, in similar fashion, requires an ability on the part of the supervisee to grasp the theory's affective components, as well as its cognitive elements. In addition, supervision is a multitiered process that considers the interactive fields created by the patient–therapist couple, the therapist–supervisor couple, and the impact of each couple set upon the other.

Joshua Levy and Alan Kindler, editors of a recent volume of *Psychoanalytic Inquiry* dedicated to psychoanalytic supervision, note that ideas about psychoanalytic supervision have lagged behind developments in theory and technique (Levy and Kindler, 1995). They suggest that current ideas about supervision must consider recent paradigm shifts, including the interactive nature of the experience, as well as the older and much discussed ideas, such as the learning alliance, that has been described by earlier contributors (Ekstein and Wallerstein, 1959; Dewald, 1987).

The recent paradigm shift Levy and Kindler refer to is one that has been informed by principles embedded in the psychology of the self. It is a paradigm in which the therapeutic ambiance is shaped out of the therapist's attempts to listen for and validate the subjective reality of his or her patient. In addition, it is a paradigm in which continuous attention is paid to the state of the patient's self and to the coconstructed reality that is created out of the interaction between patient and therapist. Supervisors whose therapeutic work is informed by this paradigm approach their supervisory work with attitudes and concerns similar to those they carry into the treatment setting. They are attentive to and affirmative of their supervisee's experiences and to the coconstructed reality that exists among all three participants in the supervisory experience. The stance toward both patient and supervisee suggested by this paradigm differs from the older omniscient psychoanalytic stance that adopts a "view from above" attitude.

The supervisory enterprise is a unique educational experience that involves affective, as well as cognitive, learning. Supervisory education usually includes an intense affective experience that is provoked when psychological issues within the patient resonate with similar issues within the therapist. Often, the awakened psychological issues within the therapist are expressed in a transferential form with the supervisor. This occurs as the therapist traverses a process in the supervision that parallels some aspects of the patient's experiences in the therapy. Another situation that stirs intense affects within the supervisee occurs when the supervisee wishes to learn a new theory because he or she can no longer contain the long experienced disquiet over his or her previously valued theory's limited explanatory power.

Jonathan Schindelheim describes the anxiety he experienced when he sought supervision to help him move beyond the authoritarian, "view from above" listening position he had been taught during his training (Schindelheim, 1995). He courageously describes his painful transition as he left the certainty and comfort afforded by his authoritarian theory to move to the uncertainty engendered by the new and unfamiliar listening stance he sought to learn. His anxiety began as he abandoned the formulaic understandings informed by listening from a position grounded in the analyst's frame of reference and moved to listening from his patient's perspective instead. Schindelheim found that developmental learning occurred within him when he participated in a supervisory experience that was informed by and conducted in accord with the new listening stance he hoped to learn. Comparing the supervisory experience informed by the theory he hoped to learn with the previous supervisory experiences informed by the authoritarian theory he hoped to leave, Schindelheim (1995) describes how it seemed that his new supervisor was, "searching to discover the supervisee in his or her experience rather than insisting that the supervisee find the supervisor in the assumed greater objectivity of a 'higher theoretical reality'" (p. 162).

While Schindelheim (1995) writes of the supervisee's experience, Ernest Wolf, on the other hand, discusses the affective component of supervision from the self psychologically informed supervisor's perspective:

> I do not think that to direct and oversee the performance of another analyst, even one who is still a candidate, is an appropriate aspect of psychoanalytic education. The purpose of so-called supervision in psy-

> choanalytic education should be to facilitate the emergence of those psychological skills and talents as well as to strengthen those personality traits that will enable the analyst to perform and to improve his psychoanalytic work. In essence that describes a process of change via learning . . . .
>
> What do we as psychoanalysts know about the facilitation of learning? We know that anxiety . . . interferes with learning . . . because pain has a tendency to disorganize the structure of the self, that is, to fragment it. . . . Thus, one of the most basic aspects of supervision or consultation should be the reduction of the student-analyst's anxiety and the first aim is the strengthening of the student's self. Teaching has to merge into healing before it will result in learning [pp. 260–261].

Wolf (1995) sensitively discusses supervisees' unexpected disequilibria in the supervisory situation where they

> suddenly find themselves in a totally unexpected ambiance of being closely scrutinized as they expose the very core of their being. They suffer a painful loss of self-esteem. Often they question their value and that of their aims, indeed, that of their self. They may complain of feeling empty, unloved, uncared for, and unable to get close to others. Some become depressed with nightmares, others become paralyzed into fragmented aimlessness against which they may defend by a restless frenetic activity. . . . It is hardly a condition conducive to learning [p. 262].

Since psychoanalysis has not yet developed a theory about learning, Wolf suggests that we pay attention to the processes involved in structural change during treatment, as a step toward the development of such a theory. He asserts that learning involves a structural change and suggests that the process of structural change in supervision is similar to that of structural change in the treatment setting. Wolf conceives of structural change in both settings as the result of a "disruption/restoration" sequence (Wolf, 1983, 1988, 1993). He further suggests that the supervisor who is aware of the disruption/restoration sequence is sensitive to the student's vulnerable self-esteem and supports that self-esteem when appropriate. Wolf adds that this support need not be entirely verbal. He observes that, when the supervisor is sufficiently attuned to the supervisee's vulnerability, the student-analyst senses the emotional safety that has been created and eventually relaxes within the supervisory setting. Wolf calls attention to the inevitable disruptions that will occur in supervision based upon the unavoidable expectations and disappointments experienced by both participants. He assigns the supervisor the responsibility of monitoring the experience and, equipped with sensitivity to these issues, the responsibility of shepherding the supervisory endeavor to a successful conclusion.

Paula Fuqua (1994), in her thoughtful contribution to the supervisory literature, approaches the same subject as Wolf, only she does so at a level of greater abstraction. In her conceptualization, Fuqua articulates several tenets of a supervisory learning model. Her first tenet is that "learning proceeds from a biological baseline and is an inner-generated activity in which the innate need for a tolerable amount of novelty is the motivator" (p. 82). Her second tenet asserts that "learning involves a necessary dismantling of psychological structure," which she believes "is just as much a definitive part of learning as are the adding and restructuring that follows" (p. 82). Fuqua's third tenet addresses the role and function of the teacher. She writes, "The function of the teacher is to serve as a manager of the states of disruption which involves the teacher's various selfobject functions for the learner as well as the presenter of the material that is to be learned" (p. 83). Fuqua asserts that learning is (a) defined by a change in structure, (b) facilitated by some structural disruption, (c) interfered with by too much disruption, and (d) facilitated by the presence of a knowledgeable selfobject who helps manage the level of the structural change.

James Fosshage (1997) considers some specific issues of which the supervisor must be cognizant in his or her function as manager of the supervisee's experiences. Fosshage speaks of the intersubjective system that exists between "analysand, analyst and supervisor which is exceedingly complex and is probably rarely captured through addressing a single linear process" (p. 192). He writes, "The analysand's transferences and, similarly, the analyst's counter-transferences are not distortions but constructions. The analyst selects particular cues, ascribes meaning, and interactively constructs" (p. 200). The awakened multiple transferences in both patient and therapist might, at times, prove overwhelming for the supervisee. In this event Fosshage suggests that "when the analyst's self needs come to the foreground, the supervisor must find a way, directly or indirectly, to attend to the analyst's momentary disequilibrium in order to facilitate the supervisory process" (p. 202). Additionally, Fosshage notes that "mismatches occur that make it difficult for the supervisor to understand the analyst's approach, creating mutually frustrating and undermining scenarios" (p. 197).

The supervisory approach of tending to and helping regulate the supervisee's self-state suggested by Wolf, Fuqua, and Fosshage touches on the issue of what has been called the "teach–treat dilemma," a seeming dichotomy between the student's need to be taught versus the student's need for treatment. Wolf and Fuqua have suggested that the learning experienced in a psychoanalytic supervision involves structural change and that the well-functioning supervisor is attuned to anxieties that attend such a change. They further suggest that affective learning requires the creation of an atmosphere in which the student feels safe and has the experience that his or her narcissistic vulnerabilities are understood and respected.

Sensitivity to a student's vulnerability does not necessarily express a dichotomy between teaching and treating. In psychoanalytic supervision the supervisor's teaching and the supervisor's attunement to the student's narcissistic equilibrium are two threads in the same cloth. They each lead to ongoing self- and mutual regulation at differing levels. Thomas Rosbrow (1997) addresses this seeming dilemma when he writes, "The teach–treat dilemma is a false dichotomy. . . . In a developmental approach, the process of learning in supervision is itself mutative and, in a broader sense therapeutic" (p. 218).

THE eSUPERVISION

This chapter presents the early opening phase of a correspondence we conducted that spanned a period of a year and a half and contained a total of 140 letters. Through the presentation of our early letters, we will demonstrate the way we communicated with each other, the ambiance we created, the regulatory attitude that guided the affective component of the supervision, and the nature of the teaching that informed the cognitive component. We underscore our attempt, in the opening phase, to establish a way to communicate in writing with an unseen, unknown other about very sensitive issues.

Letter 1, Eva

Dear Dr. Siegel,

Dr. Ernest Wolf wrote to let me know that you would be kind enough to do supervision with me through the mail. You will notice that my English is a little bit rusty but I hope that with practice and writing it will soon become better. I am sorry for my mistakes and maybe for inevitable misunderstandings at the beginning.

I have many questions to discuss so I would like to start soon. I, too, have a fax so we could use this quick way to communicate if you agree to do that. Then I have questions about the payment and the setting possibilities, like when will you have time to work with me?

I never did supervision by mail and I felt quite enthusiastic about the idea when Dr. Wolf suggested it to me. Living in the countryside and a farming area, there is no one near me with whom I could talk about self psychological ideas on a regular basis so I am looking forward to doing this by mail.

In order to introduce myself I will tell you of my educational background and clinical experiences. After what you might call high school, I studied at the Freie Universität von Berlin and eventually earned my MA degree in 1971 in psychology, sociology, and educational science. I worked in different educational institutions and psychosomatic clinics and I finished my analytic training at the Munich Akademie für Psychoanalysis und Psychotherapie, e.V.

I first learned about Self Psychology at a congress organized by Dr. Lotte Koehler with Beatrice Beebe and Michael Basch in the summer of 1994. Listening to Beebe and Basch, I realized that there were possibilities for expanding my theoretical frame. I decided to join the International Self Psychology Symposium at Dreieich in 1995 organized by Hans-Peter Hartmann and Wolfgang Milch, where I met Ernest Wolf, Anna and Paul Ornstein, Joe Lichtenberg and Lotte Kohler all for the first time. This January, Frank Lachmann came to Konstanz for a workshop. Now my head is full of the information I obtained by reading and listening—but I feel that this is only one way of learning and not sufficient for understanding the full extent of what self psychology means, especially since my training and my analysis were based on drive psychology.

I am looking forward with excitement to your answer.

With best wishes,

Eva-Maria Topel

Letter 1, Allen

Dear Ms. Topel,

I was delighted to learn from Dr. Wolf that you are interested in self psychology and wish to become involved in supervision through the mail. You needn't worry about your English. Your ability to express yourself in your letter to me was excellent and I don't anticipate that communication will be a serious problem for us. I hear your enthusiasm and am most happy to work with you. I hope that in time your self-consciousness about your English will diminish. There will be two of us involved in this experience and perhaps I should apologize for my lack of fluency in German, which I did study in college. Since America is essentially an island nation, I have not made use of my German since then and I'm afraid my German is way too rusty for us to make use of it in our work now.

To let you know something about me, I had my psychiatric training at Michael Reese Hospital in Chicago between 1966 and 1969. That was a time when Kohut was making his early transition from drive and ego psychology to his psychology of the self. A close relationship existed then between Michael Reese Hospital and the Chicago Institute for Psychoanalysis where Kohut taught; consequently many of my teachers were influenced by Kohut from the very beginning of his work. In 1976 I began my training at the Chicago Institute for Psychoanalysis and I completed it in 1985. Kohut became ill in 1971 and withdrew from his teaching responsibilities in order to spend his time writing, but his influence continued to be strongly felt at the Institute and elsewhere in Chicago. While the formal theory in my psychiatric training was drive and ego psychology, as was your experience, the leit motif that became an ever-growing theme for me was self psychology.

I have just completed a book entitled *Heinz Kohut and the Psychology of the Self* [Siegel, 1996]. It describes the development and evolution of Kohut's ideas from his first paper, written in 1948, to his last publicly spoken words three days before his death. It will be published in October of this year, as part of a series of works about various theoreticians. While self psychology has continued to develop since Kohut, I believe his ideas are seminal and worthy of direct study.

In terms of my own work, I do both psychotherapy and psychoanalysis with adolescents, college students and adults. I also have experience working with couples. I have formally taught psychodynamic psychotherapy and have supervised for many years, but I have never supervised by mail. This will be a new experience for us both. As in any relationship, the first issue will be one of getting to know each other. That will take a little time, as will our becoming accustomed to this form of supervision. I have a great curiosity about it, as do you, so we will see how it evolves. I will leave things open as to how you should begin. Begin any way that you wish and we will work from there. If you require more structure at this point, please let me know and I can provide some direction. For now I think it best for you to start your own way, with whatever you feel is important. In time the blank spaces will fill in.

It just occurred to me that I might use idioms that are unclear. If that happens, please ask me to explain myself. I will be happy to do so. In our work I will consider it my responsibility to be clear and to discuss the ideas and issues we will talk about in a way that is understandable to you. Please do not worry about the language. As I said earlier, your English will not be a problem.

In regard to my fee I do not know how much time will be involved as we work through the mail. I assume I will need more than 45 minutes to read your work and then respond. If you are comfortable with this suggestion, let's keep the issue open for the moment and we will see how much time is involved. I can promise you that it will not be unreasonable in terms of US dollars. Please let me know if that is acceptable to you. Regarding the setting, I assume you are referring to the frequency. Let's keep that open for now so that we can see what you need. I am interested in pursuing this new form of work and am willing to provide the time it requires.

I do have a fax and we certainly can communicate that way. I look forward to our work together. It is an exciting new venture for us both. I hope I can make it a rewarding experience for you.

Sincerely,

Allen M. Siegel, M.D.

P.S. Please let me know how you would like me to address you.

Letter 2, Eva

Dear Dr. Siegel,

My excitement continued as I read your so very friendly response to my letter. It's hard to express my feelings: joy, happiness, hope and curiosity to see what will happen in this process that is so new and strange. As I read I found myself smiling with the thought, "Perhaps this is what I have always been looking for." Then, in the next moment a fear comes up in me that I could be wrong. It was with the help of your words and sincere ideas, which I could read and re-read that I got the courage to collect my thoughts and begin to write.

Now I am in the middle of theoretical confusion. I have drive theory training in my mind yet I feel that empathic responsiveness is the key. My inner world feels like it is wanting change and I am having ideas I never thought of during my training analysis.

I chose the case of a young girl to present to you. She has come to see me once a week for 11 sessions because of selective mutism, accompanied by enuresis nocturna. Her mother told me that she has never been able to stop wetting her bed. Medical investigations have been made and they are without any physical result. Her last doctor worked with something we call "Klingelhose" which the girl wears at night. If it becomes wet it rings a bell. Now, at night, the whole family (she has a brother four years younger and a sister three years older) hears the bell ringing while the patient is firmly sleeping.

When I first saw the girl, I could not believe that she was 13 years old. She looked more like 9, at the most. She walks with her head between her shoulders so that she seems to be smaller than she actually is. The only thing she really likes to do is swimming with some girlfriends, until she is exhausted. She can speak fluently but she doesn't respond to her teachers and adults outside her home. To her mother, she talks only in one word sentences, if at all. The girl is intelligent, as I learned by playing with her, but she withdraws at the very moment negative affect might come up, for instance while losing a game. I have learned to know her very quick disappointments and her retreats by reacting to her inexpressive face and by listening to her nearly inaudible sighs. I react to this way of being in her by feeling stiff, even motionless at times, and I feel restricted in my comments.

At this moment we are able to talk to each other in short sentences and she allows me to talk to her about momentary feelings. For example, if we are playing a game I might tell her I think she feels without hope to win. She might nod her head, smiling in response, and then she continues to play her chosen game, quietly as usual.

Sometimes I feel she wants me to win. Sometimes she seems to like the way I lose or the way I let chances open up for her. Once, when I let her win, she took a deep breath and smiled but she hid her affect as soon as, I think, she felt I saw her smile. Because of this situation I'm no longer sure of what to do or say. At that moment I thought I should give her a response and that she really needs one, but a new one, different from the way it had always been before for her. I feel, if I can't find a new way to connect, she will lose hope. This is the point where I am looking for help. Since I attended the congress in Cologne, I thought self psychology might be able to provide such help. I have the feeling that she is waiting for me and that this interaction will be decisive for the therapy, so I feel pressure and hope and fear arising in the same moment for both of us.

About one hour after our last session I reflected on our meeting and even felt afraid that she could be suicidal because she played as if she wanted to destroy everything she had constructed before. That was the last meeting before her Easter vacation. I will see her again next week, and I have no doubt that she will come! It seems to me though that she is struggling for her self-state and that it can go either in a good direction or in an even worse direction.

When I met with the parents, the girl's mother spoke with very low vitality and, reacting to her sadness over this child, she talked with a sudden, depressed sigh and a kind of smile, "With this girl there will always be sorrow." Even if so, she told me that her daughter gets on her nerves. The mother feels she will always have to look after her daughter! During our meeting, the girl's father sat quite still in his chair and spoke only if I spoke to him. He was friendly but rigid in his words and movements.

It seems that one result of this sad situation of constant mutual displeasure is that the girl withdraws. She is behaving as if not listening to anyone, as if expecting only useless advice. It seems that she no longer wants to be confronted by people who are unable to understand her. When I reflected on one of our sessions I thought that she quietly, but endlessly, demands that if anyone ever wants to be heard by her and get a real reply in response, what they say must be exclusively for the girl and not for anyone else! I am troubled because I feel quite helpless when I sense this special need which now seems to be coming as if it were an angry demand.

I think I will stop here for now because I want to hear what you have to say.

It's OK with me to leave the question about your fee open and to wait for your impression. Since you asked, I would like you to address me by my first name, Eva, if you would like to do that.

Now I anxiously await your reflections. Thanks for listening.

Sincerely,

Eva

Letter 2, Allen

Dear Eva,

I was happy to receive your letter. Your enthusiasm for your work, your concern for the girl and your uncertainty about how to approach her all come through clearly. All of these will be helpful in our work, even your confusion. They all speak about your wish to learn and to understand this child so that you can be of help to her.

As I understand her at this very early point, the girl presents a very troublesome problem. She seems to be a very sad and depressed girl, living in an emotionally deadened home. She seems to be barely verbal but her silence is, nevertheless, a statement of something about her and we need to understand her silence that way. Her silence is a potential problem for the therapy but it does not have to be insurmountable if we understand the silence as a communication. For example, is the girl saying, "Why speak? No one will listen anyhow? Why should I assume this experience with you will be different from anything else I have experienced?"

I am impressed with the authoritarian and somewhat tyrannical way her enuresis has been approached. For me the central question in this problem is, "What does the enuresis mean?" I believe that understanding the meaning of the enuresis is more important than simply training her not to wet her bed. The girl has repeatedly been humiliated by her doctors and by her family for a problem that she is ashamed of herself. If she could control it, she would. She certainly doesn't need a cheering section that tells her how bad she is for something she cannot control. Her problems, of course, are much deeper than simply wetting her bed.

The first task in treating her is to come to some understanding of who she is as a person and what is the nature of the emotional environment in which she lives. To contrast drive theory and psychology of the self for you, drive theory would conceptualize this girl's problems as emanating from a conflict between her forbidden unconscious wishes, contained in unconscious fantasy, and the defensive forces of the ego that oppose them. Drive psychology would view this child primarily as though she were a closed system with an assortment of sexual and aggressive wishes, present from birth. According to drive theory, these basic wishes or instincts must be tamed by the ego so that the child will eventually live in a civilized fashion. In this regard, drive theory mixes the values found in Western religions and principles borrowed from Darwin's biology into its ideas about human mental states. Because of these intrusions into its theory, drive psychology is not a pure psychology. Instead, it is an amalgam of ideas from several different fields.

Kohut, on the other hand, defined psychology as the science that studies the internal life of humankind through the use of empathy, the only instrument we have available to gather data about human emotional experience. Empathy, as Kohut originally defined it, is the way one person can know something about the internal experience of another. Empathy, according to this definition, is a tool that allows us to gather data about other people's emotional experiences. Empathy provides us with information. Once we have the information we need we can then decide what to do or what not do with or for another person. To respond appropriately to any person, we must first be informed about them and empathy is the tool that provides that information.

At this moment, the central issue for us in relation to this child is what is going on with her? Why is she so depressed? Why is she nonverbal? What information do you get when you sit with her, even when she is silent? What is the silence like? Is it calm? Is it angry? Does it make you anxious? What are its qualities?

The sense I get from your material is that this is a girl who has not been understood as a person. It seems that she has given up the hope that she will ever be understood and she has withdrawn. In response to this hopeless withdrawal, I would attempt to establish a kind, gentle and realistically friendly atmosphere with her. In an effort to help her talk about herself, an experience I assume she has not really known, I would comment on her sadness. I would say to her that she seems to be so very sad. Does she know why she is so unhappy? I would ask if she were able to put that into words. I would ask what makes her sad.

What makes her mad? What sorts of things hurt her feelings? What things does she find herself thinking about when she is alone? What troubles her? What makes her happy? What is it like to live in her home? She might respond with one-word answers. If so, I would encourage her to elaborate and I would help her do so, building upon anything she might offer in the way of revealing herself. I would not hesitate to ask her how she feels about her bed-wetting. What is that like for her? I would become her ally in the attempt to help her master it. I would stop the torture devices like the Klingelhose. She does not need to be further humiliated. I would treat the enuresis as the girl's issue alone and, in an effort to get the parents "off her back," I would try to educate them, as well as the girl, that the problem will go away in time. I would tell them, "There are worse things one can do than wet one's bed, so let her be," and I say to you that the girl suffers her own humiliation every time she wets her bed, so let it become her problem with you to help her. Remove the rest of them from the situation, if that is possible.

I would add here that, of course, in working with children, one must have a good working relationship with the parents. The child does not exist alone. This is another point where self psychology differs from drive psychology. The child is not simply a bundle of instincts that must be tamed through an increase of ego capacity. The child lives in a milieu of responsive or non-responsive people. These people perform various psychological functions for the child that the child cannot provide for himself or herself. These psychological functions are essential for the healthy development of the self. The "objects" that provide these essential psychological functions are called selfobjects because they are experienced, by the child, as part of the self in terms of the psychological functions they perform. We will have opportunities to discuss questions concerning selfobjects over time. For now it will help me to know what literature you have read within the field of self psychology. I do not want to be condescending or redundant in what I write to you so I need to know what you know and what you wish to learn.

Returning to the girl, particularly in relation to the games she plays with you and the winning or losing issue, it is important for the game to be real. If she cannot win, that is OK. If she is sad over losing, then that experience will give you the opportunity to talk with her about how she feels when she loses. It will help us learn how she feels about herself. If you let her win, she will probably know what you are doing and that will diminish her trust in you. You must be real with her. If she loses, it's OK. Losing has a meaning and that is what you are after. What is her experience when she loses? Don't worry about protecting her feelings by helping her win. It will backfire. It does not protect her. What will protect her is the experience of being with someone who is truly interested in her and who wants to know what it is like to be her. This experience will provide her with hope over time and that is where the protection lies.

This is all I have to say for now. This is an interesting case with many problems. I am sure we will both learn over time as we attempt to understand her. I look forward to your response to what I have said.

Sincerely,
Allen Siegel

Letter 3, Eva

Dear Dr. Siegel,

Thanks a lot for your clarifying response. It gave me an opportunity to prepare for the next session with L and I am happy to tell you that this time we both spoke even more together. What happened is that I simply did not stop when L stopped speaking! For example, this is how it went.

Me: You look away, maybe you don't like to speak with me today?
L: No, . . . it is just unusual for me.
Me: Unusual? . . . Nobody talking to you like this?
L: (She nods her head affirmatively.)
Me: . . . Reminds me of the time we talked about how speaking has not been a good experience for you.
L: (Again she nods her head, but this time, since her eyes are more in contact with me and she seems a little curious, I took a chance and said:)
Me: Could you tell me about your experiences talking and the reasons you do not speak?
L: Never thought about it.
Me: How could that be?
L: Nobody ever asked me.
Me: Oh . . . why speak if nobody asks as if nobody is interested?
L: (She nods her head affirmatively again and sadly looks away. This time I am different and I continue despite her withdrawal.)
Me: . . . Makes you sad . . . maybe more?
L: Never thought about it.
Me: (I had a hard time knowing how to go on but I noticed that I no longer was thinking about resistance but in terms of how she used her withdrawal. After some time waiting:)
L: I will go swimming.
Me: Oh, you are going to meet your friends there?
L: (More vitally engaged now, and I am too.)
Yes, I joined a swimming group and we train for rescue!

Me: (Responding to the proud tone in her voice, I said:) Oh, good! So you can save a life?
L: Not now. I am not strong enough yet, but I will!
Me: I see. So you are training very hard.
L: (Proudly she nods her head.)
Me: That's fine. You will become strong. Your parents must like it too.
L: I don't know.
Me: Why not?
L: They don't talk about it.
Me: What do they talk about?
L: My taking good notes.
Me: (Again I had a hard time knowing how to go on. Then I tried:) Good notes . . . hmm. . . another area to feel good about?
L: (Nods her head.)
Me: (I reflect for a moment and L takes out a game from the shelf. We play and she seems to be excited. I said:) Exciting, isn't it?
L: (She seems astonished.) Nooo.
Me: No?
L: I don't talk about such things.
Me: How do you feel then?
L: Never thought about it.
Me: Would you like to find out?
L: (She nods her head vitally and after a while said:) Yeah, there is something that I feel. I don't know how to describe it.
Me: Well, here we are now, in a situation where you could be winning the game. Could that be important to you?
L: (She looks ambivalently at me, takes in a deep breath and answers:) Maybe. I don't know. I feel nothing. Hmm . . . but yes, it is exciting. (And then, with more and more joy in her voice she talks about her experience as we play with comments about whether it is exciting for her or not. At the end she summarizes:) For me it is most exciting if both players are at the same point and either of them could win! (This time, at the end of our session, L says good-bye, looks directly at me and shouts in a friendly voice:) Until next week, I guess?
Me: Yes, until next week!

I was very impressed by your formulation: a deadened home! It's a touching symbol. I will write down the literature I have read, but as I am quite aware now, cognitive study does not imply emotional understanding. I really enjoyed your comments and the way you give them. They are a very clear integration of theory and its place in practice. Please go on this way. It is not condescending to me! Once again your letter made me smile. I like to listen to you very much. Furthermore, to have your answer written down is helpful for me, because I can study it as often as I want and need to and, if I need to after some time, I can check it again to see what you said or whether I missed something or mixed something up.

I noticed that my theoretical approach to the girl's problem was not empathic according to your explanation of empathy. What I mean is that the "information" I obtained did not come from L but from the theory I have in my mind. Even though I know about mirroring and the need for acceptance, as you can see I still reverted to the old way of thinking. That's where your theoretical comments were so valuable for me.

At the beginning of L's treatment I already got her mother to agree to stop the "Klingelhose." She understood her humiliation when we talked about it but it was difficult for her to oppose doctors. In our area bed-wetting, even if still a quite usual symptom with children, is seen as a shameful disease and it is also still uncommon and equally shameful for people to apply for psychotherapy for it.

Until now I did not have a comfortable way to ask the girl about herself. As far as I understand you, however, it is possible to ask directly, especially when she does not speak and especially because nobody in her life has asked her about her own affairs. I tried to wait silently and not to interfere with the patient as I had learned to do. Guess we will talk about this issue too. I remember Paul Ornstein saying in a workshop, "Wonderful theory, but what did the patient say?"

It seems so easy to understand that empathy is not possible if you don't know about the patient, but how does one get the data? The two approaches seem to differ so much. No explanation is possible if the therapist only tells about his own insides. I am left with confusion.

It was clarifying for me to think about what a "selfobject" is and what function it serves. I agree with you about what you said concerning being real with her and about what gives hope and what protects, especially after our last session. She lost one game after she was very close to winning. She became very excited and when I asked her about what she felt she said, "All over," and ran to the shelf to fetch another game that she thought she could win. I was glad that she tried again.

I'm sorry that I didn't ask you how you would like me to address you. And as I like having your letter very much, would you too want me to send you my original letter in addition to the fax?

Sincerely,
Eva

Letter 3, Allen

Dear Eva,

Congratulations!

It seems that you and L are beginning to find a way to talk with each other. By the way, it would help me if you gave L a name. If you wish, it need not be her true name but I do need a name to help make the treatment and the girl more real. I find that relating to an initial is disruptive for me.

From what you have written it seems that you will need to overcome parts of your training. Since what we "know" is guided by our theories we tend to tell our favorite theory to the patient who learns our language and then spits our ideas back to us. In this way we get "proof" of the "correctness" of our theory and this gives us confidence that our theory is correct. With this confidence we march on creating a story for the patient who, because she probably has done so all her life, complies with what we say. Our treatment proves our theory but our patient does not benefit. The treatment becomes a repetition of the misunderstanding and compliance our patient has experienced early in life and continues to experience with us today. We need to help L tell us about herself so that we do not create her in our own image.

Your thought that the information you have about L has been coming from your brain and not from L is correct. From what you've written I see that this problem comes from what you have been taught. How can one learn about another person without asking questions? The critical technical issue is when and how to ask the question. The idea that one must wait silently, without interfering, until one can give an interpretation lies in at least two sources. One is the "scientific" medical model that approaches the clinical situation as though it were an experiment conducted in the totally "clean" environment of a vacuum. This view sees the patient as a pure specimen, not to be disturbed by the activities of the analyst. It assumes that the environment does not affect the subject. This is incorrect. In Chapter 2 of Kohut's *Restoration of the Self* (1977), Kohut nicely discusses "scientific objectivity" and how the observer influences the observed. I recommend it to you.

It is a fantasy that we do not influence our patient. The mere fact of our presence as a listening, understanding and appropriately responding person has an effect upon the patient. There is no such thing as a "clean environment." You and the patient exist in a dynamic system. There is a back and forth movement. You affect her, she affects you. We study what goes on in her, in you and between the two of you. There is an active, fluid dynamic in constant motion; even when there is silence. Sometimes the dynamic is present especially when there is silence and that seems to be the case right now with you and L.

Before I expand upon that point though, I said there were at least two sources for the practice of waiting silently one is until ready to make an interpretation. I want to comment on the second source, which I believe has its origin in one of the analyst's own unconscious narcissistic issues. The issue I am referring to is the analyst's unmodified unconscious demands for omniscience. It is a demand that requires one to know things with *a priori* knowledge. The truth is, however, that for example, one cannot know the full blooming of a rose when it is still an unfolded bud. Aside from their variations in color it seems that, at first glance, rose buds have much in common one with another. At that stage they all seem to look alike, but if you've ever grown roses you know that's not the case. Rosebuds open into 5-petal roses and 40-petal roses, fragrant roses and non-fragrant roses, strong roses and fragile roses. One can never know the rose's bloom by its bud. One can never know the unexposed world of the rose before it reveals its unique insides. That surprise is part of the joy of raising roses. The same is true with our patients. To believe we know the patient, without the patient revealing his or her insides to us, is a belief based upon fantasy. An analyst's fantasized omniscience protects the analyst against the terrible anxiety that comes from not knowing, an anxiety that stems from an assault on one's unconscious grandiosity. As an analyst develops and gradually becomes comfortable with not knowing, the acceptance of and comfort with one's ignorance can become a valued part of our analytic selves. Rather than experienced as an assault on our expansiveness, the acceptance of our ignorance makes it possible for us to be an open receiver to what goes on in our patient, in ourselves and between our patient and ourselves.

Now let's look at your material. You began on a good path with L when you said, "Maybe you don't like to speak" and L replied, "No . . . it is just unusual for me." That was an excellent start. Unfortunately, however, you jumped in as you have been trained to do and told L what she was thinking. You did this when you said, "You mean nobody talks to you like this?" That certainly is a true statement and maybe something you might say later on but L had just said something amazing. She told you something about herself when she volunteered that talking about herself was "unusual." I would have tried to help her expand that thought. Rather than give her an answer as you did, I might have responded with, "Tell me about that" or "What do you mean?" Or as you correctly said a little later, "Could you tell me about your experiences talking and the reasons you do not speak?" You were correct in what you said but I believe your impulse, which has been highly developed through your training, was to give her an answer immediately. Unless your patient is overwhelmed with anxiety, it is best to give her a little time and space to see what she does on her own. L seems to want to talk. She needs to learn how to talk about herself and to do this she needs the space to express herself. Her response, "Nobody asks me" is both startling and expectable, given what we know about her. It also is profound in its simplicity. I would pursue that line. To do this I might say, "What do you mean?" "How is that possible?" "Do you have thoughts and ideas that you keep to yourself?" "Would you like to talk about things inside of you?" Once you get the idea you will see that there are many ways to coax a bud into bloom.

I think you had a hard time continuing from this point forward because you had cut L off when you gave her an answer as you've been taught to do. Your observation that she looked sad is important but, again, you told her about it without encouraging her to talk about it herself and this left you with nowhere to go. Instead of closing a door by giving an answer, one might say instead, "You look sad as we talk about this. Is that how you feel?" She might respond with, "I don't know." I would not be put off by that kind of remark. I would expect it since L does not know how to talk about feelings since no one ever helped her with that. I would encourage L to elaborate on her experience. I might help her with, "I know it's hard to talk of feelings since you never have done so, but try, if you can, to put into words what your sadness is like for you." You might be surprised at what L will come up with. Again, once you get the idea it will flow for you.

The next material is very interesting and suggests that we are on the right track. Since L fell silent I might have asked her about her silence by saying something like, "What made you suddenly become quiet?" I believe she told you that she has joined a group that trains for rescue. That was not a chance association. She is talking about you and her. She *has* joined a group that is attempting to save her from drowning within a deadened existence. It is the group she is forming with you. L further said that she is not yet strong enough to save a life but, in a full and strong way that was brimming with hope and confidence, she said that she would become strong. I think she is talking of her hope that you will be able to help her. She senses your interest and your wish to reach her with the lifeline that your understanding provides.

In the next material you introduce the topic of her parents. What made you move in that direction? Why did you introduce the idea that her parents would like her rescue training too? L responded to that by saying that her parents don't speak with her. She has no idea what they think about her interest. She added, in a concise way, that they are mostly concerned that she behave herself, work hard in school and take good notes. She infers here that they do not respond to her internal life, only her behavior. She must perform well. She became quiet and you felt stuck. I believe you were stuck because you touched on something that is difficult for L. Your statement about the notes, "another area to feel good about," seems to be an attempt to enliven L and make her feel better. I don't believe the good notes make her feel better. I think they make her feel worse because they remind her that her parents are not interested in who she is, what she is like, and in what her interests are. They are interested in how she performs. Her role is to be a "good girl" and that burden makes her sad. This is an interesting issue that will come up over and over. Watch for it and be prepared to gently explore it. Your task is to explore rather than to provide answers. I predict that the effect of such an exploration will be to give her hope, rather than to frighten her. It frightens her more if she thinks you have all the answers. She has lived with people who have all the answers about her. They "know" what is best for her and they tell her so "for her own good."

L wants to play the game with you, but the game is the game of communication and relatedness. I believe she conveys this sense when she talks about the games. She said, "For me it is exciting if both players are at the point where either of them could win." She hungers for the exchange and the liveliness of the encounter. This exchange is like oxygen. Further, it is the light and warmth that will allow the bud to slowly come into bloom.

I believe I have given you much to think about so I will stop for now. It sounds as though your previous experience with analytic literature and training is not too different from L's experience at home. The deadened literature you have read in the past strangled your lively interest. That is not an uncommon experience. I was impressed with what you have read so far and what you are reading in self psychology. Some of the material in the field is difficult to understand upon first or even second reading. If you have any questions I will try to answer them.

I am happy to send you the originals of my letters and yes, I would like to have yours, in addition to the fax. I am just thinking about how wonderful it is to have the fax technology that allows us to communicate this way. I believe it enhances our experience. I find that I look forward to your letters, curious about your response to what I have said. In regard to how to address me, please address me in the way that makes you most comfortable.

Sincerely,
Allen Siegel

Letter 4, Eva

Dear Mr. Siegel,

Thank you very much for the fax I received yesterday afternoon. I am glad; you gave me back my curiosity and my joy in my profession. I really would like to call you Allen, if you allow me. In doing so I do not want to be disrespectful, but I want to show my thankfulness for your caring in our working relationship.

When I saw Lisa this time I noticed that something had changed with her. After an initial silent period I realized that she seemed to have grown up. Her movements were more purposeful.

She looked at me somewhat shyly when she first came in. We shook hands as usual and she went to the shelf to find a game to play. As we started to play quietly I noticed that two things were in my mind. One was your touching question, "Why should Lisa assume that this experience with me will be different from that with others in her life?" The other thought was your comment, "Let's have some time to breathe." Then Lisa's stomach made a soft noise, she smiled gently and I began, smiling back at her.

Eva: You're smiling? (Her nodding head and quick glimpse at me through nearly closed eyes encourages me to go on.)
Eva: What makes you smile?
Lisa: My stomach.
Eva: Hmm . . . Is anything going on?
Lisa: (Nodding her head affirmatively again.) Hungry. (For me this was a highly symbolic answer and it made me think too much. Old answers came up, but this time I refused to listen. Without the old answers, however, I did not know how to respond. After a little while I was able to continue.)
Eva: Hungry?
Lisa: Doesn't matter!
Eva: (As you can imagine, I again needed time to know how to respond. I thought, "What doesn't matter?" Is it my speechlessness that doesn't matter? Or is it being hungry that doesn't matter—and hungry for what? Finally I said:) Hmm . . . does not matter?
Lisa: I am not ill. (I don't remember exactly what Lisa said next. She played a little while, wrinkled her brow and I with a low voice asked:)
Eva: What's going on?
Lisa: Not so good!
Eva: Can you explain to me what you mean by "not so good?"
Lisa: (Smiling a little.) Not fine.
Eva: What's not fine now?
Lisa: (Looking at the game we are playing.) I have to go back.
Eva: Oh yes, I see . . . feel something right now?
Lisa: (Looking at me somewhat carefully.) Angry!
Eva: (You can imagine that I was [I can't find the right word] content at this moment.) Oh yes, of course . . . (Lisa continued smiling for a long time. Her smile gave me the impression of her being a "good girl" so I asked:) You're still angry, aren't you?
Lisa: (Nods her head affirmatively.)
Eva: And as I see you, I see that you are smiling.

Lisa: (Nods her head "yes" with her eyes nearly closed but looking in my direction.)
Eva: It seems to me that you think it's better not to show that you are angry.
Lisa: (Smiling gently, she nods her head.)
Eva: Usually there are good reasons if one does not want others to know about one's feelings.
Lisa: (Shakes her head "No.")
Eva: Do you think it could be possible there are good reasons that one would not want people to know?
Lisa: Yeah. (Lisa continues playing)
Eva: Stuff you do not want to talk about?
Lisa: (Nods her head and goes on playing.)
Eva: (A little later the play has a possibility for me to win. Lisa moans a little and I ask:) . . . Something is going on . . .
Lisa: Not so good.
Eva: What could that mean now?
Lisa: Unfair!
Eva: (As you can imagine again, I had a hard moment before I could go on. Then I asked:) What is unfair?
Lisa: Two against one.
Eva: Yes, two against one. (Teasingly I added:) Such unfairness, you know?
Lisa: Lisa then told me about a film she recently saw where three white boys beat up one black boy and hurt him badly. Lisa said she had much sympathy for the black boy. I did not know where she would want to move on to, so I waited and then tried:
Eva: I wonder what you are feeling now?
Lisa: Remains quiet, shaking her shoulders a little bit.
Eva: Not easy to find the words?
Lisa: Turns away from me.
Eva: I should not ask you?
Lisa: Nods her head and smiles.
Eva: Hmm, I see. Maybe there will be another time to talk about it?
Lisa: Nods her head affirmatively and with this we went on playing.

I want to stop the verbatim report here because I do not remember the following very well. But I do remember Lisa's serious mood which was more calm than quiet as we ended the session. When she left, Lisa turned toward me for a friendly goodbye. The next session will be on Monday.

I am impressed about how much Lisa told me this time. I do not remember exactly when it was in the session, but Lisa told me that she watches television when she feels bored. She said she experiences boredom in school too, even in subjects where she is capable like history. It would be easy to learn for her, but as you said, it does not make her feel happy. Although she has no practice speaking about herself,

Lisa seems to have a rich internal life, full of feelings that she keeps carefully available only to herself.

This last thought leads me back to the idea of depression and the lack of selfobject relationships. At this moment, reading Kohut, reading your letters over and over, and thinking about myself, it is difficult, even in German, to find the words for what is going on in me. Affect and empathy are the key words.

Yes, using the fax gives me the chance to have your response as quickly as possible and it diminishes the time that goes by while so much is happening. It's nearly like having supervision once a week and it's quite different. For instance, when I write I often think, "Will this be understandable to him?" If it is not understandable, I don't think I can do any better. Therefore I find myself being very careful with the words that I use. That's good. It gives me more time to think about what I really want to say. On the other hand, it seems to me that I can't express these things sufficiently. But this is not only because of the English translation but because there is more here than I can write. That isn't astonishing to you, is it? When I'm writing about something and think this is all too much I also think, "There will be time to discuss this too. It will not be lost."

I will never pass roses again without thinking of your ideas, meditating about grandiosity and trying to become relatively comfortable with incompetence. Thank you.

Sincerely,
Eva

Letter 4, Allen

Dear Eva,

It sounds as though Lisa and your work are both finding new lives. I am glad for you. Before I address your clinical material, however, I want to make a cautionary comment about theories in general and also about the battles people get into over their differing theories. I make these comments because I realize that, while you have not addressed this problem, I am certain that you have to live with it. It is a part of psychoanalytic life.

What I want to say is that the battles people get into over their theories are due to their narcissism, not to their theories. Some people forget that theories are merely the best attempts we have at a given moment to explain particular phenomena. Theories are temporary explanations. They will change with time. In your enthusiasm for the new ideas of self psychology it is crucial not to become wedded to these ideas, for they too will change with time. Twenty years from now we might laugh at how we thought a particular explanation was so important. At one time medical science asserted that the human body was composed of four humors. At one time all right thinking people were certain the earth was flat. All explanations are provisional. They simply represent the best way we have of understanding something at the present time. Kohut expresses this beautifully in the last three pages of *Restoration of the Self* when he suggests adopting the stance of the playful scientist, one who plays with ideas and is willing to change when better explanations come along. I can safely promise you that ideas within self psychology will eventually change.

In your last letter you sounded as though you are worrying about whether you are making yourself understood to me. Let me respond by saying that I have had no difficulty understanding what you have written. You are right in your thought that in time you will be able to articulate the ideas and experiences you are struggling with, even in English. It will not be lost.

Now to Lisa. I believe her changing posture reflects how she feels about coming to see you. She seems less withdrawn in this session. Clearly you are beginning to get the idea of allowing Lisa to talk without intruding your ideas so that she will have the opportunity to reveal her own experience. You mention the struggle you are having setting your old theories aside as you work. Your experience reminds me of a tennis player who learns a new serve or a pianist who is learning to hold her hands a new way. For a while the change is terribly uncomfortable and self-conscious. In time it will become natural.

Lisa presents a difficult problem because she is not yet very verbal. Because of this she needs help in giving voice to her internal life. At the same time it is essential to stay out of her way and not provide her with answers. Since she is a compliant child she probably will agree to many of the things you might say. The best stance is one of curiosity and naturalness. Try to leave your theories at the door when you enter the room with Lisa. Let "common sense" guide you at this point, rather than theories. When you feel stuck reflect upon what makes sense to ask Lisa at that moment. Often, when we speak directly from our theories, what we say in a clinical moment doesn't make much sense. At this point in your work with Lisa you are not in a position to apply any theory because theories provide explanations and we don't have enough data yet to formulate an explanation. We are in a data gathering phase, a period of evaluation. After we know Lisa better we will formulate theories to help explain who she is. For now let your natural curiosity, your interest and your nonintrusive warmth be your guide. By doing this, you will gather the information we need and Lisa will benefit from the interest of another person in her well-being. You will help her as she learns to talk about herself. All people have a deep wish to be listened to as we talk about our true selves. This is the case with Lisa and she will eventually respond to your efforts.

You are correct that Lisa's comment about hunger made you think too much. We haven't any idea what the comment meant. It might not have been symbolic. Her stomach rumbled. She was hungry. It could be that simple. In response you could ask her natural questions like: "What makes you hungry? Why are you hungry? What do you do when you are hungry? Do you like to snack?" These questions might open a path in the direction of Lisa's parents' attitude toward eating or snacking. If that path were to open we would learn about how they respond to Lisa and to her needs. In your work, I suggest that you adopt the attitude of the friendly detective. Find out as much as you can in your own nonintrusive way. Of course, I would not ask her so many questions all at one time. I want to be clear that when I list so many questions, as I often do in these letters, I am attempting to illustrate a few of the many possibilities. I am not suggesting that you bombard Lisa with a multitude of questions. That would be an assault.

When Lisa said, "It doesn't matter," I wonder if she was responding in a compliant way. I wonder if Lisa is accustomed to not mattering. If that is so, perhaps she has learned to pass over things that relate to her and to her needs. If I am correct in this speculation, then we are in agreement about how Lisa's parents respond to her. We will know this with time.

It would help me if you could describe the games you play with Lisa. Your description of Lisa becoming angry during the game tells me you are catching on to my way of working; however, you interrupted Lisa after she told you she was angry. I think you responded to her difficulty articulating what she felt when you offered her an explanation of why she had trouble talking about being angry. Your explanation came when you said, "One does not want others to know about one's feelings." In saying this you offered Lisa an explanation, and possibly a correct one, but it was not time for an explanation because, as I have implied, we do not yet know enough about her anger. My guess is that in the world outside the consultation room, if someone told you they were angry, your natural inclination would be to ask why they were angry. The same applies to Lisa. I would have asked her what made her angry. "What was it like to feel angry? When else did she feel angry? Does the way she feels now remind her of anything? Has she felt like this before? When?" Be a gentle detective of the internal world. Learn the facts for now; we'll formulate theories and explain meanings later.

Lisa revealed herself to you when you did function as a gentle detective and asked her what she meant by "Unfair!" She told you the story of the boy who was outnumbered by the hurtful people. Asking Lisa what she felt at that point was correct but you might have stayed with it a little longer even though Lisa was reluctant to talk about it. When you suggested that Lisa did not want you to ask her about it anymore, she complied with your idea. Instead, you might have gently encouraged her to talk by saying something like, "Try to tell me what you are feeling now. I know this is difficult, but give it a try." I might have asked Lisa what she thought it was like to be the black boy. How was it that she understood the boy's feelings? Did she ever feel ganged-up on like that? When? What was it like? By whom?

I understand that you are being careful with Lisa, as you should, but she has told us she wants to train and get strong. That comment is a communication that suggests to me that you can be more direct with her. Try it and see what happens. I think she will be encouraged by the chance to talk, even though it might be about things that frighten her. Good luck.

Sincerely,
Allen

Letter 6, Eva

Dear Allen,

Did you know what the next discovery would be? Doing treatment the new way I find my whole effort during the sessions goes to the question of how I can find a way to communicate with my patients so that they can speak about themselves. This leaves no time to formulate theoretical hypotheses.

Something is going on with me that is hard for me to describe. For instance, when I try to tell you about my feelings at the end of the last session with Lisa I find that I am unsure about myself. I try to find explanations for what is happening and I end up convinced that this is only a cognitive, rational task. Something else is coming up that I can't identify right now. I try and new ideas come up. It's as if I can't validate things and I end up not trusting myself anymore. At one moment I feel bad and deserted about this and at the next moment I could laugh. I know that there is no absolute truth, but everything seems to change every moment for me now and that's uncomfortable for me to feel. It seems that through this experience of change, sort of a cognitive dilemma that I am going through right now, I am able to understand the experience of fragmentation. It feels terrible and I run around in my head looking for some safe knowledge.

Now to Lisa and her mother. Monday morning Lisa's mother rang me up. She wanted to see me the very next day. I asked if something had happened. No, she said, but she wanted to discuss some things. I had time on Wednesday and we met. First she asked me if Lisa would be a good "co-worker" because it sounded to her like she would not. I asked if she had any doubts about her capacity to work and why she was asking. She then spoke about her sorrow that Lisa is too quiet and therefore she does not expect that she will achieve, not in school and not with me. I again asked her what gave her such proof that Lisa will fail and she told me that she had done better in English but she fears Latin. She never learns and then she doesn't want to go to school. In the morning she can't stand up and coming back from school she is always tired. Soon there were tears to be seen so I tried to find out her feelings about herself.

She told me that she recognizes painfully Lisa's separation from her. For example, she reported that she is not allowed to drink out of the same glass as Lisa anymore and when she took a piece of chocolate from her table Lisa threw the whole chocolate away. The mother very bravely said, "That is normal and I should learn not to do it anymore." Then she came to her feelings of guilt. She said that she often thinks, "What will Lisa say about her childhood when she is grown up? She has been ill so often and such an unhappy child." This was a very intense moment between us where we looked at each other quietly.

I don't remember how the next issue came up but she told me that she thinks Lisa is funny. Lisa can sing and make jokes, which the mother really enjoys. When the mother had to leave home for some days and when she called at night, Lisa had prepared some funny stories to read for her. Mother liked that very much. At the end of the session she said she wanted to come again and try to speak more about herself. I had the impression that it was helpful but difficult for her to speak about herself. Also, she was not used to being asked about herself and being listened to. She seems to be deeply depressed and in need of Lisa to stay her little girl. She suffers with Lisa going her own way but she is able to want Lisa to have her own life too.

Lisa's session. She began in quietness and with the barricade game. I tried to meet her quietness and how it feels. First it seemed empty, then, looking at her face, I noticed that she avoided looking at me. Every time she had the dice she returned it politely to me. I tried to meet her eyes but she avoided my gaze and looked to the ground. I decided to wait and see if there would be a chance to meet her. I felt alone at this time, like I think she might feel. Then she looked at me and meeting her glance I started with a very low voice.

Me: So quiet today?
Lisa: I'm always quiet.
Me: Aha . . . ?
Lisa: . . . Not always.
Me: (after some time:) When not?
Lisa: Playing dolls.
Me: With whom do you play?
Lisa: Schoolbus . . . friends.
Me: Oh yes . . .
Lisa: (Laughing cautiously.) With friends it's always good.
Me: Hmm . . . friends . . . ? (Lisa looks at the floor and I can feel her withdrawing again. I think she does not experience me as a friend right now. I can understand her hesitation. After some silent time, looking at each other, I tried to connect again.) What's the difference for you in being with friends or not? How do you feel about those situations?
Lisa: (Looking around a little helpless.)
Me: (Waiting:) Hmm?
Lisa: (Shrugs her shoulders.)
Me: How do you feel about being asked such questions?
Lisa: Sometimes good, sometimes bad.
Me: Could you explain that a little bit?
Lisa: Like in school, it's bad.
Me: What's happening in school?
Lisa: If I don't know, I wait for help from my friends.
Me: And they help you?
Lisa: (Smiling.) Yes, if they know.
Me: And if not?
Lisa: I sit down.
Me: And how do you feel then?
Lisa: Don't know.
Eva: Hm, how could that be . . . sitting down at such a moment?
Lisa: (Looking at the ground.) Normal. (She returns to the game and is winning at this moment. She immediately fetches another stone to build up a barricade.)
Me: You said "normal" and I wonder what normal means in your opinion.
Lisa: (Looks at me with small eyes and a wrinkled mouth.)
Eva: What's the matter now?
Lisa: Don't know what to say.
Eva: Oh . . .
Lisa: Sometimes it is better not to say.
Eva: When do you experience that?
Lisa: With Mom and Dad, school things, and what happens there.
Eva: What's your experience with Mom and Dad?
Lisa: *Looks around and shakes her head.*
Eva: Something you don't like to speak about right now?

Lisa: (Nods her head.)
Eva: I think about that and wonder if there are more things you don't like to speak about.
Lisa: Yes . . . secrets.
Me: Of course secrets . . . I don't want you to give them away. Instead, could you tell me how is it to live with secrets?
Lisa: Sometimes good, sometimes not . . . I should tell.
Me: And why don't you? What are your reasons not to do so?
Lisa: (Hesitates for a long time.) These are bad things.
Me: What's bad, in your opinion?
Lisa: (Seems to be astonished about this question. She shakes her head again and I continue.)
Me: Again, I don't want to know things you don't want me to know, right now, but what's the meaning of bad? One can never know what another thinks is bad.
Lisa: (Shaking her head and playing the game. Again we play without looking at each other. Lisa plays quickly and builds a real barricade. There are five minutes left so I start again, like talking to myself, not so much looking at her.)
Me: Now I think about you . . . sitting in school at your desk, not speaking but thinking for yourself. I wonder how that will be for you, how can one feel?
Lisa: (Speaking suddenly and quickly.) Misery!
Me: (I'll give you the German word for this because maybe it explains my astonishment at hearing her use this old fashioned word: Elend. I pick that up, cautiously in a low voice:) Misery. . .
Lisa: (Looking at me and I think seeing my serious face, eyes kind of sad and filled with consternation at this moment she smiles quickly.) Not so important . . .
Me: Not . . . ?
Lisa: This word is too strong I guess. (She hesitates but gives no new word.)
Me: Misery . . . good word . . . sometimes things are like that.
Lisa: (Nods her head and sighs.)
Me: . . . Nodding your head . . .
Lisa: Yeah . . .
(Our time is over and she looks at her watch. We didn't finish the game and I ask what she wants to do. Sometimes children wish to write up where we are so we can continue. Can't do anything more anyway. And she returns the game.

As you know, it is very hard for me to say nothing but we stand up and go to the door. I recognize now that this feeling of misery, whatever it is, is Lisa's own feeling and she has a right to feel it. I do not want to dissuade her anymore from such a feeling which possibly would give her the impression that I do not take seriously what she feels or do not want to listen to her experience, especially when she gives it to me in confidence. Lisa went to the door, gave me her hand, looked into my eyes directly and I felt her to be very near.

That's it for now. It's me who doesn't know how to leave. If you were present maybe I couldn't look into your eyes and I don't know how I would manage to leave without deep sadness. I wasn't aware how this would develop in our work.

Sincerely,
Eva

Letter 6, Allen

Dear Eva,

I read your letter with great interest and, before I respond, I want to tell you that it is absolutely natural and predictable that you would find yourself feeling upside-down as you try to do treatment in a way that is quite different from all that you have experienced previously. Everything that gave you a feeling of security when you entered the room with a patient is now called into question. I can understand that you would feel like Alice in Wonderland, finding nothing to be what it is supposed to be. As you said, your task now is to learn how to communicate so that your people can speak of who they truly are. If you can let yourself not worry about making formulations for now, you will find the task is not as difficult as you might believe. We will work on making formulations later. Our first task is to understand who this person is and to do what we have to do in order to help her tell us about *herself*. As I said before, we cannot develop a hypothesis about Lisa until we have sufficient data. We have plenty of time before we have to develop a formulation. In the meantime, Lisa is doing well with you and there is no rush. I certainly am not demanding that you formulate a theory about her. In fact, I'm suggesting the opposite. Take your time. We will learn a lot and Lisa will improve.

I'm not saying that we don't need a theory. We most certainly do. As I wrote earlier, all understanding is based on theories. One cannot listen without a theory to organize and make sense out of what is heard. In fact, my emphasis on helping Lisa talk about who she actually is represents the clinical application of a theory. It's a theory that suggests that before we can explain a person's psychology, we first must understand that person in a deep way. The kind of understanding I am speaking of requires that we inquire about the patient in a very precise and careful way so that we can immerse ourselves in the quality of her emotional experience. Actually I'm describing the empathic process, a tool that we use to help us gather information we will need to make our formulation. Only after we have spent sufficient time in this manner, with a given person, can we begin to fashion a meaningful explanation for why that person is the way she is.

What I am suggesting means that we enter the room without the armor of explanations. We enter the room in a state of not knowing and, yes, this task requires all of our creativity and it also requires that we be in good emotional balance ourselves. It requires our ability to live in a state of not knowing. It seems that as a result of your training you are accustomed to believe that the analyst "knows" and that she is supposed to "know" right from the start. I fear that in your training there was not enough space to be uncertain. Many analysts hide behind the "certainty" of their theories and use them to protect their personal vulnerabilities from being touched by the interactive analytic process.

Now to Lisa. The visit from Lisa's mother is quite interesting. The first thought that occurs to me is, "Why now?" What is she reacting to? My guess is that she is responding to something that is changing in Lisa. If I were pushed to say what I thought she was responding to I would say that she senses the positive feeling Lisa has with you. She senses something is different. I wonder if Lisa's "sickness" is an expression of her depression and I wonder if the depression is showing early signs of lifting in response to the new relationship in her life. We don't know, but these are tentative speculations.

It is clear that Lisa's mother has a need for Lisa to be a little girl. She has maintained a merged relationship with her that seems to be changing as Lisa lets it be known that she wants her own space. Perhaps Lisa's mother is responding to the loss of Lisa as she moves forward. Perhaps the mother has needed Lisa to be little so that she could have the comforting company of her "baby girl." Your initial description of Lisa was of a little girl who had an immaturity inconsistent with her age. Lisa's ability to make her mother laugh might serve a "sunshine" function, saving her mother from her depression. I would encourage you to see the mother for a session or two, if Lisa has no objection, in order to learn more about her and about their relationship. I would pay particular attention to the function Lisa has served for her mother since I believe Lisa has fulfilled some of her mother's unrequited selfobject needs. My guess here is that mother has a longstanding depression and also that her relationship with her husband is sterile at best. I have the hunch that the relationship might be more toxic than that, but time will tell us.

Regarding the session, I have little to say this time except that you have become a totally different therapist. You were able to listen to Lisa. You stayed with her affectively. You did not interrupt her. You were creative in your approach, you allowed her to feel what was within her and you made it possible for her to tell you more about herself than ever before. Well done! Her "misery" and her secrets are very interesting. I do not know the word Elend, but since it is such an old-fashioned word, one that you were surprised to hear from an adolescent, I wonder if it reflects something about her environment. Where did she get such a word? Does this reflect a quality of her home-life?

One technical suggestion. When Lisa told you that she had secrets, you moved very quickly to say, "Of course secrets . . . I don't want you to give them away . . . instead could you tell me how it is to live with secrets?" This is not true. We do want her to tell you her secrets and she knows that. Don't let her go so easily. I believe she can manage more than you think she can. I would have asked her if she could tell me her secrets. I am aware that she might not be able to do that right now. The fact that she told you she had secrets is remarkable in itself. If after I asked her whether she could tell me her secrets, and she was not able to do so, I then would have asked what you so correctly asked, "What is it like to live with secrets?" and "What is it about the secrets that make them hard to talk about?" She did say they were about her parents, which is no surprise to me. I think there is much about her family that we do not know. Hopefully, with time and with your sensitive approach to Lisa, she will eventually be able to tell us.

As Sherlock Holmes said to his colleague Dr. Watson when they began their detective work, "Watson, the game is afoot!" So it is with Lisa. "Eva, the game is afoot." Our work has begun.

Sincerely,
Allen

CONCLUSION

In our experiment we found that it is possible, even advantageous, to conduct an eSupervision. We offer our experience as a contribution to those who might wish to do the same. With no literature to serve as a reference and no colleagues to consult, we had no alternative but to tentatively follow the path that seemed to unfold before us.

Several surprises emerged from our experiment. We speculate that the letters themselves functioned cross-modally and replaced the stabilizing internal image that would have formed out of a face and voice. In a unique way they helped manage some of the affects that were stimulated in the course of the supervision.

The need for a visual image points to one of the major difficulties inherent in an eSupervision, namely the deprivation of the visual and auditory nonverbal elements of communication. Other users of the Internet, chatroom aficionados as well as those creating online study in virtual universities, have encountered this problem in email communications and what is referred to as the "digitally reconfigured world" (Essig, 2000). Slowly, a literature is beginning to develop in this field.

Interestingly, those working in the field of Internet communication are developing a language of visual symbols that communicate mood, affect state, rhythms of hesitation, surprise, or disgust and even explanations for silence. The most striking Internet symbol in relation to the problem of the missing face is the "smilie," the symbol of a smiling face. In fact, this symbolic replacement of the human face is so well integrated into electronic communication that when one types a colon followed by a parenthesis, MSWord 97® has been configured to automatically display ☺, a smilie.

The creation of a safe milieu between two participants is, in part, dependent upon the regulative need for immediate knowledge of the other's reaction, affect state, and emotional balance (Beebe and Lachmann, 1994). The absence of an immediate visual response once a message is sent into the dark silence of cyber-space creates a state in the sender that is reminiscent of the infant's experience in the "still-face" experiment. In that infant observation experiment, the infant is forced to cope with the frightening experience of a still face (Tronick et al., 1978). We speculate that Internet users are developing their visual symbolic language to compensate for the missing nonverbal communication of visual relatedness.

While we did not discuss the communicative deprivation inherent in an eSupervision at the time of our correspondence, both of us responded to it with an intense effort to be open, direct, precise, and clear in what we wrote. For Eva, precision and clarity meant being open with an unseen and unknown stranger. For Allen, eSupervision meant the assumption of responsibility for the treatment of a troubled child, using an unknown medium to work with an unknown and unseen analyst. It also meant teaching in a form that required precise articulation of both clinical and abstract theory, as well as tending to affect states expressed solely in written word.

In retrospect we see that open, explicit, precise, and expanded communication was essential in the creation of an ambiance that made learning possible in the face of the absent face. Allen responded to Eva's report of her clinical material and her emotional state with explicit support and encouragement. While not substitutes for the missing nonverbal elements, Allen's open support was a preconscious attempt to compensate for the visual reassurances that were absent in the eSupervision. Allen's encouragement was heartfelt and not gratuitous, for gratuitous support would most likely have been experienced as condescending and belittling. While appropriately supportive, he also was direct and unhesitating when he needed to identify and discuss miscues and misunderstandings. Another nonverbal element of our communication was the rhythmic pattern that developed in the timing of our letters. Without an explicit plan, an inadvertent pattern formed in which we anticipated the arrival of each other's letter, which began to arrive the same time each week. This unplanned patterning seemed to compensate for some of the missing, but anticipated, communicative expectancies. Retrospectively, we are able to see our preconscious attempts to overcome the deprivation of a communicative system that normally functions out of awareness. We now see how these preconscious attempts helped us establish the ambiance of concern and respectful collegiality that makes supervisory learning possible.

Another surprise emerged from Allen's perspective. Because the clinical material was entirely written, he, like Eva, was able to read the material as many times as he wished before crafting a response. This experience helped the patterns and responses of the therapeutic dyad emerge with greater than usual clarity and made it possible for Allen to formulate what he wanted to say with greater than usual precision. This opportunity, which enhanced both the supervisory and pedagogic experience for both, is an advantage of the eSupervisory experience.

In addition to the above, we found several other advantages of an eSupervision. One unique advantage is that, since all of the communication is written, the entire course of the work is available for microscopic study. Another unique aspect of eSupervision is the experience of working intensely with someone whom one has never seen or even heard. This experience magnifies the opportunities for transference elaboration by both supervisee and supervisor. We cannot explore this aspect of our experience at this time, but we certainly acknowledge its presence and suggest it as a matter for exploration by others who accept our recommendation to experiment with eSupervision.

In summary, we feel that the success of our experiment implies that geography no longer need be an obstacle to education. It is now possible to reach beyond one's geographical borders and seek supervision from specific people with whom one wants to study. This is especially important for today's expanding mental health community as professionals across the globe voice an interest in and a wish to learn the ideas embodied in the psychology of the self.

Eva's Epilogue

Four years have passed since we began our shared work, and I gratefully take this opportunity to describe the subsequent direction of my journey. During my deep involvement in the supervisory process,

I learned about narcissism and the empathic mode of observation from Heinz Kohut's perspective. In the process, to my surprise, I simultaneously recovered my appreciation for Freud! The new path also led to my current interest in the work of infant researchers and theorists such as Beatrice Beebe, Frank Lachmann, Edward Tronick, and many others. Their focus on the operation of an underlying, out of awareness, but inescapable presence of nonverbal and presymbolic aspects of "implicit procedural knowledge" within an "early interactive regulation" of communication became a valued and important addition to my work.

When I reflect upon my journey into the area of interactive regulation, I see that my interest in the coconstructed process began with the very first letter of the eSupervision. At that time I had clearly formed questions about the experience of narcissistic needs in the selfobject dimension and questions about motivational systems and attachment behavior. I realize now, however, that my first description of Lisa also contained elements of questions that I was not able to articulate at that time. These unarticulated questions addressed the problem of the "1/4-second response" (Pöppel, 1995) and all the dynamics of self- and mutual regulation that Beebe and Lachmann (1998) have described.

My current perspective assumes that human interaction depends upon the meanings that people have for one another. Meanings derive from continuous social interaction that, in turn, is modified through ongoing, dialectically organized interactive processes. As far as I can see for now, these interactive processes also make for change.

In summary, our eSupervision helped me find a path that has led toward the new and therapeutically useful perspective that I had hoped I would find. Proceeding from the interactive perspective made it possible for me to work with my "difficult to reach" young patient and I wish to thank all those who have helped this hope come alive.

REFERENCES

Beebe, B. & Lachmann, F. (1994), Representation and internalization in infancy: Three principles of salience. *Psychoanal. Psychol.*, 2:127–165.

——— ——— (1998), Co-constructing inner and relational processes, self and mutual regulation in infant research and adult treatment. *Psychoanal. Psychol.*, 15:481–516.

Dewald, P. (1987), *Learning Process in Psychoanalytic Supervision*. Madison, CT: International Universities Press.

Ekstein, R. & Wallerstein, R. (1959), *The Teaching and Learning of Psychotherapy*. New York: International Universities Press.

Essig, T. (2000), Disembodied intimacies. Unpublished paper delivered at meeting of American Psychological Association, Div. 39. San Francisco, CA.

Fosshage, J. (1997), Toward a model of psychoanalytic supervision from a self-psychological/intersubjective perspective. In: *Psychoanalytic Supervision,* ed. M. Rock. Northvale, NJ: Aronson, pp. 189–210.

Friedman, T. (1999), *The Lexus and the Olive Tree.* New York: Farrar, Straus, Giroux.

Fuqua, P. (1994), Teaching, learning, and supervision. In: *A Decade of Progress: Progress in Self Psychology, Vol. 10,* ed. A. Goldberg. Hillsdale, NJ: The Analytic Press, pp. 79–98.

Kohut, H. (1977), *Restoration of the Self.* New York: International Universities Press.

Levy, J. & Kindler, A. (1995), Prologue. *Psychoanal. Inq.,* 15:149–152.

Pöppel, E. (1995), *Lust Und Schmerz.* Munich: Wilhelm Goldman Verlag.

Rosbrow, T. (1997), From parallel process to developmental process: A developmental/plan formulation approach to supervision, In: *Psychodynamic Supervision,* ed. M. Rock. Northvale, NJ: Aronson, pp. 211–236.

Schindelheim, J. (1995), Learning to learn, learning to teach. *Psychoanal. Inq.,* 15:153–168.

Siegel, A., (1996), *Heinz Kohut and the Psychology of the Self.* London: Routledge.

Tronick, E., Als, H., Adamson, L., Wise, S. & Brazelton, T. B. (1978), The infant's response to entrapment between contradictory messages in face to face interaction. *Amer. Acad. Child Psychiat.,* 17:1–13.

Wolf, E. (1983), Empathy and countertransference. In: *The Future of Psychoanalysis,* ed. A. Goldberg. New York: Guilford, pp. 309–325.

——— (1988), *Treating the Self.* New York: Guilford.

——— (1993), Disruptions of the therapeutic relationship in psychoanalysis: A view from self psychology. *Internat. J. Psycho-Anal.,* 74:675–687.

——— (1995), How to supervise without doing harm: Comments on psychoanalytic supervision. *Psychoanal. Inq.,* 15:252–267.

Chapter 8

Bulimia as Metaphor: Twinship and Play in the Treatment of the Difficult Patient

James E. Gorney

Over the past several decades psychoanalysis has increasingly recognized the significance of the capacity for play as a central dimension of successful child development. Winnicott (1971) was perhaps the first to assert that the eventual real work of analysis was the liberation of a capacity to play. The implications of observationally based infant research further deepened the understanding of play as a primary intersubjective template for the subsequent capacity for self-cohesion (Lichtenberg 1983; Stern, 1985; Beebe and Lachmann, 1988). Most recently, Meares (1993) has made a systematic effort to expand the scope of self psychological theory and practice in regard to the treatment of severely character-disordered individuals by charting the vicissitudes of their incapacity for effective symbolic play.

My purpose here will be to elaborate upon some innovative technical implications of play in regard to patients manifesting severe forms of psychopathology. In particular, I will present material from the treatment of an extreme case of bulimia. According to Meares, early developmental failure to develop a fluid capacity for symbolic play implies manifold pathologic consequences for the self throughout development, often resulting in the crystallization of a borderline state or severe narcissistic disorder in adulthood. Incapacity for play may result in a breakdown in the self's sense of introspective consciousness and cohesive flow; it can adversely affect "hedonic tone," which is the heart of self-esteem; it can induce an experience of disjunction or alienation from self–selfobject experience, and it can negate any sense of inner life through pervasive, external stimulus entrapment. Ultimately, an incapacity for play will restrict and rigidify the self into a "hypertrophy of the real," inhibiting pleasure and forcing the individual into strictly linear thought and stereotypic behavior (Meares and Lichtenberg, 1995).

The challenge of analytic work with such severely impaired individuals is to find some technical means of facilitating entry into a zone of transitional play space. This is the critical step in order to put some play into the rigid pattern of transference/countertransference, which inevitably develops during the course of treatment with such patients, frequently resulting in impasse (Gorney, 1978). With patients with severe disorders of the self, it is the analyst who often must take full responsibility and provide all of the initiative for the provision of a play space. The fragmented patient generally does not know how to make play possible; indeed, all of his or her character armor may well be mobilized against it. Meares (1993) asserts, "Play takes place in a space that is created by the atmosphere of another" (p. 5). When confronted with a deadened or fragmented self, it is the analyst who must find the creative means of engendering a suitable atmosphere in which the play space may appear.

In extreme cases the analyst, even the self psychologically informed analyst, is pushed beyond the limits of his or her theory and technique. How does one address a self when a patient denies having one? How does one speak and interpret when a patient is organized at a preverbal level? How does one invite a patient into life when the patient is convinced that she is almost dead? In my experience, it is among patients with severe eating disorders that these profound technical challenges are perhaps presented most dramatically.

There is increasing agreement in the recent analytic literature that long-standing, serious eating disorders are in effect radical forms of self pathology. For example, Masterson (1995) asserts that bulimia is a form of narcissistic personality disorder; Kernberg (1995) observes that severe eating disorders represent a vicious attack upon the self's capacity for pleasure, and Feldman (1995), writing from a Jungian perspective, characterizes eating disordered patients as desperately attempting to forestall a disintegration of the self. The symptom structure of the eating disorder itself can be understood, in the words of Lacan (1977), as a "symbol written in the sand of the flesh" (p. 159). Bulimia, as metaphor, symbolizes the retreat from language into the body; the retreat from play into the hypertrophy of the real; and most essentially, the retreat from the viability of self–selfobject experience into a tomb of inner deadness and a concomitant solipsistic refusal of nourishment. Consequently, it may be claimed that the severely eating disordered patient stands beyond the limit of traditional self psychologically informed analytic theory and practice. She thereby has much to teach.

From the point of view of self psychology, Sands (1991) has located the genesis of bulimia within radical selfobject failure during the first year of life. Such failure undermines the development of a capacity for symbolic, verbal exchange; the deepest needs can be expressed only via somatization. Lewis (1997) has further developed this point of view and emphasized the "inner haziness," "externalized living," and "anonymity as identity," which characterizes the deadened self of the bulimic.

The question of how to initiate play, dialogue, and pleasurable selfobject experience in analytic work with a starving, dying self now becomes central. Toward addressing this technical quandary, I shall focus upon the actuality of an extreme case of bulimia, a case in which the possibility of relationship and of life itself, was tenuous in the extreme.

CLINICAL MATERIAL

Lisa stared across the room, away from me with her customary look of icy contempt. For what must have been the fiftieth time during only six months of treatment, she said again, acidly, "My life is totally absurd. There is no meaning to anything I do, to anything about me. I can't live because I'm dead—and you think that just talking to me will do something." With that she shrugged and grunted, "Huh!" This was her customary response to any of my words, and it is hard to convey the impact of this syllable. She emitted it with her chin raised and her nostrils dilated as if she detected a noxious odor—and it dug into me like an icepick in my craw.

On the day Lisa first arrived in my office, she had seemed an apparition from some other nightmarish world—Auchwitz, Cambodia, Somalia. Five foot four, 86 pounds, her long, limp brown hair framed a cadaverous face marked by sunken cheeks and dark-circled, bloodshot eyes. She moved without any wasted motion, on matchstick legs, and sat unmoving, silent and expressionless on the edge of the chair. It swiftly became clear that she was operating in a quasicomputerized mode and would speak only when spoken to and would provide data only in response to specific questions. Within this mode, the following bleak picture emerged—a thumbnail sketch of 34 years of thwarted living.

Lisa grew up in a large Victorian house in an affluent suburb. Surrounded by trappings of class, wealth, and privilege, she endured an extremely lonely childhood. Her mother was gripped by appearances, was a compulsive cleaner, and was hypercritical of any real or imagined flaw in her daughter, whether in habit, dress, grooming, or manners. Her father was often away on business; when at home, he hid behind the newspaper, puttered in the garden, or retreated for long naps. The family seemed to inhabit a neat, hermetically sealed bubble, with minimal contact with the outside world. Lisa did not recall ever having had a friend; she was baffled when other children would play at school, claiming that she had never learned to play. Instead, she spent endless hours in her room reading, vicariously searching for some indication of possible life out in the unreachable world.

Lisa endured a painfully shy adolescence, feeling throughout like an "outcast" and a "wallflower." In 34 years she had never recalled experiencing any sexual stirring or impulse; in 34 years she had never recalled daydreaming, fantasizing, or actively anticipating the future. Rather, she endured moment to moment, did her work at school and chores at home, and graduated valedictorian from high school as if on autopilot.

Whatever passion there was that burned within her, it fired only her intellect. Leading a monkish existence at a prestigious college, Lisa devoured Western Culture and compulsively gathered her A's, yet there was always a feeling of fraudulence, a sense of just regurgitating facts, without a quality of depth or feeling or any notion of what made herself or other people tick. Eventually, a metaphor was found, although it would be many years before Lisa herself would recognize it or be able to name it as such. This was the finding and making of a new hermetic circle consisting of shopping, hoarding, stuffing, puking, and emptiness. It came to fill her every waking moment when she was alone and in the absence of any external structure. She would delay returning to her room until as late in the evening as possible. Then, like an automaton, she would find herself carrying the bags of food into her room, only then to fall savagely upon them and rip them open, devouring their contents in a hand-to-mouth orgy, which forced her finally reeling to the toilet bowl. The feeding frenzy would repeat itself over and over again with undiminished fury until she passed out on the floor, several hours later, among the half-empty bags, into a deathlike, dreamless sleep. For Lisa the meaning of this unrecognized metaphor was that it had no meaning; she felt nothing, she understood nothing, she retained nothing except a bilious taste of shame and fraudulence upon awakening each morning to push herself compulsively again through the world.

Academic success led her to a predoctoral fellowship in a highly competitive graduate program. Increasingly, however, her academic achievements seemed overpoweringly fraudulent to her, and she developed the idea that she was playing a part from a script written by someone else whom she did not even know. By the time Lisa reached the point of writing her dissertation, she was frantic, unable to concentrate, and felt that all of her ideas were worthless. She became increasingly consumed by a vague sense of objectless rage. Her bulimia intensified to the point where it was devouring most of her waking hours, and this further filled her with a diffuse sentiment of criminality and self-loathing.

After shamefully dropping out of graduate school, Lisa moved into a roach-infested apartment on the edge of a slum and structured her days by working long hours as a computer programmer. She tried to read, but could not retain the text; she went to plays and concerts, but endured them without pleasure. Several abortive attempts at psychotherapy proved fruitless and she developed a keen sense of contempt and mistrust for the supposed "helping professions." Finally, she began to intersperse episodes of heavy drinking between the protracted bouts of bulimia, in order to tranquilize her disgust with herself, and took to wandering the streets of New York late at night, looking and feeling like a bag-lady. It was at this most unpromising juncture that she agreed to consult with me at the urging of her frightened and exasperated parents.

In our first meeting, Lisa herself was also exasperated—she felt that there was nothing more that she could do to improve her life and nothing that anyone could do for her—but she definitely did not feel frightened. Indeed, she had never felt frightened and did not feel anything at all except occasional objectless anger and an undercurrent of contempt toward herself and everyone around her. She claimed to have no interest in psychoanalysis, no belief that she could change in any way and, in fact, claimed that she was probably not even interested in changing one iota. All these declarations of utter alienation were not offered freely by her. Rather, I had to extract them from her with great effort as if I were rendering a few drops of juice from a shriveled up, old, hard lemon.

Yet when she asserted, "I have destroyed all the expectations that anyone has ever had in me—including my own." I sensed that there might be something to work with. What gave me this impression was that this statement was uttered with a discernible note of vindictiveness and perverse triumph—a definite sign of life, smoldering under her detached surface. When I told her this, I thought that I observed a faint smile, which flashed and disappeared swiftly across her face. So I continued: "If you are so inclined, I will try to engage in some form of psychoanalytic care with you. You are not required to have hope or belief—I will hold those for both of us. But the terms of treatment must be mine—five times a week for as long as in my judgment it is necessary. There must be thorough medical exams every 3 months, with the results sent to me. I will provide you with the name of my internist. If you agree, I know that you will fight the process at every turn, but you will find me a most worthy opponent." Somewhat to my amazement, she agreed. I ended the session by quoting her a line from Bob Dylan's "Like a Rolling Stone"—"When you ain't got nuttin', you ain't got nuttin' to lose."

Appalled by her almost total inability to form a viable human relationship, my first efforts were primarily directed at management and the establishment of a secure therapeutic frame. Yet I was able to hold her only through structure, not through relationship. I made focused and conscious efforts to differentiate myself from her as a defined and viable new object who might then assist her in defining herself through some larval experience of primal otherness or inchoate opposition. Yet Lisa could barely recognize my existence. After several weeks of providing me with a network of terse facts, which had to make do for my vain efforts at gathering a real history, there seemed nothing more to say. The terrain we had to traverse now became disturbingly clear; it was desert as far as the eye could see—lifeless without any notable features to break the endless monotony—no oasis in sight.

Lisa would arrive for her sessions with nothing to say; neither could she tolerate the silence. She denied any feelings; she did not have a life to contemplate because it consisted only of work and throwing up, and she claimed to have no memory session to session of anything that had previously transpired between us. I assessed her experience of emptiness as genuine and decided to respond to her actual need by providing her with something concrete to relate to at the outset of each session. I would begin by commenting on the previous session, on sharing some observation with her that had occurred to me during our time apart, yet she was unable to use these provisions. It was as if I kept trying to initiate Winnicott's (1971) squiggle game with an individual who was entirely unwilling and unable to squiggle back.

I gradually began to feel that I was losing my own sense of belief or conviction. My questions seemed feeble, I would fall silent, and my mind would go blank for long stretches. When she handed me her check each month, I could detect a half-buried feeling of fraudulence. While these fees were supposedly in payment for my performing the functions of a psychoanalyst, was I not really just enduring and participating in hours of apathy, emptiness, and boredom? My understanding that this was a process of projective identification and complimentary countertransference only partially assuaged my mounting feelings of uncertainty.

Lisa and I continued to wander lost in this desert, almost at impasse after only six months of treatment. She persisted in refusing to speak spontaneously and begin sessions on her own; she would not look at me; she would not even take off her coat. Finally, deciding to intervene again at the level of management, I insisted she take off her coat, stating, "This is not a bus trip or the subway station!" While she reluctantly hung up the coat and complied, she gave no other quarter. She found all of my questions and comments "meaningless" and "absurd"—particularly in regard to her continuing bulimia. She sat there expressionless, all 86 pounds of her, and said, "There is no *meaning* in vomit. And besides, I told you I died a long time ago." The paradoxical question that emerged was how to continue investigating her throwing up, even as she was regurgitating me and her psychoanalytic care.

The experience of offering sustenance, being swallowed up and then being spewed out and flushed away, left me feeling almost as hopeless and exhausted as Lisa herself, when she would crumple on the floor down among the empty bags. Every day she succeeded in erasing her memory of me and my words as rapidly and effectively as she expelled the food. For her there remained only a vague sense of absence, time out of time. Was it two hours or four hours that were spent last night savaging her body? She hadn't a clue. Could she remember what I had said to her yesterday? She claimed that it meant as much to her as her mother's "laundry list." I sensed that she was merging with me as she had with her parents and thus needed to recreate her own sense of futility *within me*, so I might hopefully find a way to solve it for both of us as her parents had never been able to.

Needless to say, interpretations, even when I could no longer bite my tongue and was foolhardy enough actually to suggest them, were to no avail. Proposals that she was warding me off as her intrusive mother or dismissing me as her ineffectual father were labeled as "talking from a textbook that has nothing to do with me." More pointed observations that she was spitting me out, that she was destroying all possibility of sustenance she might receive from my words, were greeted with, "I don't know what you are talking about." Then, after about one year of treatment, for the very first time, she began a session without waiting for me. "It is such a comfort to sit in a doctor's waiting room well-stocked with interesting magazines. Unfortunately, you have none." I stiffened and struggled to manage my rage. This attacked an area of culture and taste that had been vulnerable ever since my own childhood.

After all, did I not pride myself on my careful selection of periodicals—*The New Yorker*, *Opera News*, *Natural History*—nothing remotely mundane like *Time* or tacky like *Cosmopolitan*? With barely controlled anger, I stated, "You are like a large cloaca. You operate by a reflex that keeps turning nourishment into waste."

"I always found dissecting frogs *particularly* boring," she replied. We sat in silence for the rest of the session, both feeling acutely wounded by the other.

She arrived in my office the next day as if nothing had happened. I decided that I was left with no therapeutic choice but to wait and endure as patiently as possible until some new, authentic opportunity arose. This lasted several months.

It was not until well into the second year of treatment that there was a break and an opening in the grindingly repetitious pattern. One day, as usual, Lisa came in, sat down, looked away vacantly, and said nothing. Instead of trying to help her along with a question or comment as I customarily did, I just sat and stared. The tension between us built, and after several minutes she started tapping her foot impatiently and bitterly remarked, "Well, don't you have anything to say or are you just going to keep me waiting?" I felt acutely challenged, and after a dramatic pause, I replied, "There are exactly 13 perspectives from which we can understand the very powerful meaning and metaphor of your vomit. I am now going to enumerate in detail *all* of them—this will take several sessions. Listen carefully because at the end I shall quiz you on everything I have said to be sure that you have been listening. That shouldn't be too hard because you have an extraordinary mind and have always been a gifted student." She seemed mildly startled and perhaps even a bit less intransigently disinterested than usual.

On a roll, I decided that spontaneity was critical at this juncture. Thus, I allowed myself to "wing it" by assuming the role of a learned professor taking manic flight, not giving her breathing room to interrupt or negate me. In particular, for the next three sessions, I analyzed the meaning of her vomiting from the following 13 perspectives, improvising as I went along: developmental, interpersonal, intrapsychic, structural, self psychological, sociological, existential, literary, hermeneutic, feminist, behavioral, psysiological, and theological. I held nothing back and spoke didactically and intellectually, as well as passionately and directly to her life history and personal experience. It was only considerably later that I realized that the number 13, which had spontaneously occurred to me in the moment of the session, was exactly the number of years that had transpired between the onset of her bulimic symptoms and the day she had first entered my office.

As I lectured, I made every effort to link the ideas from each of the 13 perspectives to a possible meaning structure for her bulimia. I consciously tried to create an imaginative, transitional play space. Along the way I suggested readings and told her that, since after all, she was more simply human than otherwise, the results of 4000 years of human culture ought to have something relevant to say to her.

When I finished, Lisa seemed a bit stunned but dutifully complied with my request and repeated the essence of all 13 of my analyses. Her words were succinct, yet exacting, penetrating to the core of my, at times, long-winded discourse. When she finished, I saw my chance and said, "Up till now you have repeatedly told me that you are totally empty inside and can't remember from one session to the next anything that has been said. Who then is the Lisa that heard, remembered, and retained *all* of this—meaningless and irrelevant to you as it may be?" There was a long pause. She blushed slightly (a first!) and said, "She's very scared." At last our real work had begun.

DISCUSSION

The clinical picture that was presented by Lisa during the first phase of her treatment with me vividly exemplifies the catastrophic consequences of early foreclosure of the play space (Meares, 1993). Lisa's dying self obliterated introspective consciousness and self-state flow; it engendered massive disjunction from self–selfobject experience; it intensified pervasive false-self experience; and it rigidified stimulus entrapment. As in many instances of severe eating disorder, Lisa's near-delusional concerns in regard to nutrition and her repetitive assaults upon her body via food can be understood as a desperate primitive, preverbal effort to forestall a feared collapse into even deeper levels of self-fragmentation. At the same time, the eating disorder functions as a metaphor of a starving, dying self.

Given this clinical picture, I understood my task in the first phase of treatment with Lisa as twofold. First, it was clinically necessary to function as an auxiliary self (Kohut, 1977) or as a sort of exoskeleton. Consequently, I structured the treatment frame and held her in care, almost unilaterally. It is axiomatic that the interpretive processes of analysis are not relevant when the patient has not yet developed the verbal capacity to use the analyst or the analytic setting; it is likewise true that mutual, vitalizing self–selfobject experience is *not* a precondition for treatment to occur; rather, it is treatment's ultimate goal. Second, I needed to empathically understand and respect Lisa's need to enter into an aversive, adversarial relationship with me (Lachmann, 1986). This had to be understood not primarily as resistance but, rather, as a protection against further fragmentation.

In this context, it was critical that, for the most part, I maintained an essentially nonretaliatory stance (Kohut, 1984) in the face of persistent aggression and aversiveness. It is essential in the treatment of the dying self that the analyst and the analytic setting survive—and survive without undue retaliation. Through recognizing the patient's efforts at destruction as potentially growth facilitating, the analyst maintains an attitude of tolerance and forbearance, while at the same time maintaining himself as a real, strong, and bounded object that cannot and will not be ultimately destroyed (Winnicott, 1969). Thus, I maintained my dogged determination to offer care and meaning even when Lisa was almost entirely unable to allow me to function as an analyst. If such bounded holding can persist adequately over time, the patient will come to find a necessary personal limit in the very survival of the analyst. Grounded in its derivation from the Latin, the limits of the analyst and the setting become a *limes,* or boundary, which begins to precipitate a larval differentiation of the patient as a possible autonomous self. It is only at this juncture that a positive, vitalizing self–selfobject relationship becomes possible and analysis, as properly understood, may finally begin.

Becoming an auxiliary self, surviving destruction, and setting certain clear limits became the precondition for my efforts to facilitate play. For Lisa, who could not play or fantasize, this had to become my primary task. Thus, my three-session monologue designed to locate Lisa's bulimia within a context of meaning could be understood as an effort, calculated in intent yet spontaneous in style, finally to put some play into an overly rigidified, mutually enslaved interactional system. By virtue of having survived, I became able to *demonstrate* my survival to Lisa by opening up a potential play space, precisely in the area of her maximal line of development—the cognitive and the intellectual sphere. In retrospectively analyzing the how and why of my dramatic intervention/enactment, I believe that I seized upon it intuitively in order to facilitate what Meares (1993) terms *empathic "decentration."* That is to say, I made a radical effort to offer a series of different associational perspectives to the patient's own linear experience in order that she might begin to hear some melody of her own making.

When Lisa finally said to me "She's scared," in response to my question "Who is that Lisa. . . ?" she began her first experiment in analysis with creative living. She was not yet able to say, "I'm scared." That would only come much later. But she had finally become able to playfully respond and thus use the analyst and the analytic setting in order to begin creating a truly separate self.

The enactment of my three-session lecture arose spontaneously but at the same time was the product of two years of disciplined effort to locate a suitable point of intersubjective contact. The patient's maximal line of development had been in the intellectual and academic arena. Similarly, this area had always been a source of pride and achievement for me, even in the context of other areas of personal difficulty. Within this intersubjective context (Stolorow, Brandschaft, and Atwood, 1987) a point of fit finally became possible. For Lisa, vomit had been a metaphor of a meaningless, starving, dying self; now I was able to demonstrate to her that making meaning itself was a metaphor of being alive. In addition, I engaged her aversiveness with an insistent force-feeding of ideas, until she was finally able to hold some sustenance inside her. All of this constituted an effort to initiate self–selfobject experience through play via my *mirroring* of her unique selfhood, my representing myself as *idealizable* in a mode she could respect and initiating *twinship* relatedness at a point of fit and similarity.

Self psychologically informed work with patients who live within the metaphor of a dying self, such as many individuals with serious eating disorders, cannot proceed along traditional lines (Sands, 1991; Lewis, 1997). Verbal interpretation is most often experienced by the fragmented patient as a foreign, potentially persecutory intrusion, inhibiting the creative potential of the self. If the analyst cannot rely upon traditional interpretation for long stretches of the work with regressed patients, sometimes extending for several years, what then must this noninterpreting Zen analyst do? In the context of the patient's deadened self, the disciplined enactment of the analyst to initiate play itself functions as an action interpretation. The effort to forge a vitalizing twinship experience through relational play offers the patient a new metaphor that the self has a potential for life. In my judgment, this is consistent with the spirit of Kohut's (1977, 1984) entire project in regard to technique.

As Meares and Lichtenberg (1995) have observed: "A form of therapeutic engagement in which there is life, cannot be induced in a formulaic way. The therapist needs first of all to have a cast of mind that is reminiscent of playfulness, that is, relatively spontaneous and freely moving" (p. 57). With the deadened patient, the action that invites play must often come at the initiation of the analyst who is not afraid to be playful. If there is some degree of matching or "fit" and the analyst succeeds in opening the play space in a suitable manner for the patient, then well-being and the capacity for self–selfobject experience will be enhanced (Meares 1993, 1995). Anonymity will yield to self-declaration (Lewis, 1997). The resonant human connectedness necessary for two individuals to safely enter into and remain in the play space provides the basis for successful vitalizing twinship experience and the capacity for pleasure (Gorney, 1998). This phenomenon is well known to all who observe mothers and babies in the clinic or in the home. With advances in analytic technique, it is now also coming to be known by those who dare to go, without preconception and without precondition, to the place where the self still waits to come into life.

REFERENCES

Beebe, B. & Lachmann, F. (1988), Mother–infant influence and precursors of psychic structure. In: *Frontiers in Self Psychology: Progress in Self Psychology, Vol. 3,* ed. A. Goldberg. Hillsdale, NJ: The Analytic Press.

Feldman, B. (1995), Bulimia in adolescent women: An exploration of personal and archetypal dynamics in analysis. In: *Incest Fantasies and Self Destructive Acts: Jungian and Post-Jungian Psychotherapy in Adolescence,* ed. M. Sidoli & G. Boversiepen. New Brunswick, NJ: Transaction Publishers, pp. 173–186.

Gorney, J. E. (1978), The negative therapeutic interaction. *Contemp. Psychoanal.,* 14:246–276.

——— (1998), Twinship, vitality, pleasure. In: *The World of Self Psychology: Progress in Self Psychology, Vol. 14,* ed. A. Goldberg. Hillsdale, NJ: The Analytic Press, pp. 85–105.

Kernberg, O. (1995), Technical approach to eating disorders in patients with borderline personality organization. In: *Annual of Psychoanalysis, Vol. 23,* ed. J. Winer. Chicago, IL: Chicago Institute for Psychoanalysis, pp. 33–48.

Kohut, H. (1977), *The Restoration of the Self.* New York: International Universities Press.

——— (1984), *How Does Analysis Cure?* ed. A. Goldberg & P. Stepansky. Chicago: University of Chicago Press.

Lacan, J. (1977), The Freudian thing. In: *Ecrits,* trans. A. Sheridan. New York: Norton.

Lachmann, F. (1986), Interpretation of psychic conflict and adversarial relationships: A self psychological perspective. *Psychoanal. Psychol.,* 3:341–356.

Lewis, J. (1997), The treatment of eating disorders: Facilitating the shift from outer to inner life. Paper presented at the 20th International Conference on the Psychology of the Self November 15th, Chicago.

Lichtenberg, J. (1983), *Psychoanalysis and Infant Research.* Hillsdale, NJ: The Analytic Press.

Masterson, J. (1995), Paradise lost—bulimia, a closet narcissistic personality disorder: A developmental, self, and object relations approach. In: *Adolescent Psychiatry,* ed. R. Marohn & S. Feinstein. Hillsdale, NJ: The Analytic Press, pp. 253–266.

Meares, R. (1993), *The Metaphor of Play: Disruption and Restoration in the Borderline Experience.* Northvale, NJ: Aronson.

——— (1995), Episodic memory, trauma, and the narrative of self. *Contemp. Psychoanal.,* 31:541–556.

——— & Lichtenberg, J. (1995), The form of play in the shape and unity of the self. *Contemp. Psychoanal.,* 31:47–64.

Sands, S. (1991), Bulimia dissociation and empathy: A self-psychological view. In: *Psychodynamic Treatment of Anorexia and Bulimia,* ed. C. Johnson. New York: Guilford, pp. 34–49.

Stern, D. (1985), *The Interpersonal World of the Infant*. New York: Basic Books.
Stolorow, R., Brandschaft, B. & Atwood, G. (1987), *Psychoanalytic Treatment: An Intersubjective Approach*. Hillsdale, NJ: The Analytic Press.
Winnicott, D. W. (1969), The use of an object. *Internat. J. Psycho-Anal.*, 50:711–716.
——— (1971), *Playing and Reality*. London: Tavistock.

Chapter 9

Reflections on Selfobject Transferences and a Continuum of Responsiveness

Louisa R. Livingston

Recent debates within self psychology pit proponents of optimal frustration and those who wish to limit the analyst's role to empathic attunement and interpretation against advocates of optimal responsiveness, many of whom also emphasize the relational aspects of curative process. The goal of this chapter is to contribute to that dialogue.

My contribution is twofold: First, I propose that, rather than seeing writers as representing opposing camps, we view self psychologists as being on a *continuum* regarding their perspectives on the analyst's responsiveness. Second, we should address developmental strivings wherein the patient *needs* active responsiveness within a relationship in order for his experience with the analyst to be useable as a selfobject experience. I suggest that a patient's *requiring* this active responsiveness in order to maintain a selfobject transference results in additional types of selfobject transferences. Such responsiveness at those times is an essential part of the treatment rather than a parameter.

After introducing and defining two categories of selfobject transferences ("mirroring" and "twinning"), I shall define and discuss active

---

The author wishes to thank Martin Livingston, Ph.D. and Peter Zimmermann, Ph.D. for their help in clarifying and sharpening this chapter.

responsiveness. (Although I focus on those times when a patient *requires* active responsiveness to prevent trauma to his developing self, such responsiveness may also be used to *enhance* the patient's experience.) Next, I shall present Kohut's views on the analyst's responsiveness. Following that, the perspectives of other self psychological analysts concerning responsiveness and the analytic relationship will be delineated. A clinical discussion of work with one patient will then set forth two episodes—one involving a mirroring transference and one involving a twinning transference. I shall also describe the analyst's corresponding active responsiveness. In contrast, clinical work with another patient, for whom active responsiveness created empathic ruptures, will illustrate a mirror transference. In accord with those who argue that one of the analyst's essential aims is to be *optimally* responsive, I shall discuss when active responsiveness is optimal and when it is curative.

SELFOBJECT TRANSFERENCES

A selfobject serves a self-sustaining function. Kohut (1971) categorized selfobject *needs* into needs for mirroring, idealization, and twinship. His followers described other selfobject needs. Many analysts generally accept Kohut's (1979) succinct definition of a selfobject *transference:*

> If a patient whose self had been damaged enters psychoanalytic treatment, he reactivates the specific needs that had remained unresponded to by the specific faulty interactions between the nascent self and the selfobjects of early in life—a selfobject transference is established. . . . The psychoanalytic situation creates conditions in which the damaged self begins to strive to achieve or to reestablish a state of cohesion, vigor and inner harmony [p. 463].

Wolf (1988) explicitly included the *analyst* rather than the analytic situation per se. He wrote that the selfobject transference is "the displacement on to the analyst of the analysand's needs for a responsive selfobject matrix, derived in part from . . . selfobject needs mobilized in response to the analyst and the analytic situation" (p. 186). Bacal (1995) included *two* dimensions within the selfobject transference: "the reactivation of early yearnings and hopes as well as their associated fears and conflicts" (p. 362).

Stolorow and Atwood (1992), in essence, combined these views; they conceptualized transference as consisting of a selfobject dimension and a repetitive one. In the selfobject dimension of the transference, "the patient yearns for the analyst to provide selfobject experiences that were missing or insufficient during the formative years" while in the repetitive dimension, "the patient expects and fears a repetition with the analyst of early experiences of developmental failure" (p. 24). Culling from these definitions, I use *selfobject transference* to refer to the patient's needs for a responsive selfobject matrix and use *repetitive transference* as equivalent to Stolorow and Atwood's repetitive dimension.

The term *"mirror" transference* was coined by Kohut to denote the patient's need and longing to feel mirrored by the analyst—to be admired, understood, and seen for who he or she really was. This is especially important for those patients whose development was derailed at a time when they needed and failed to experience sufficiently what Kohut referred to as a "gleam in the mother's eye." This deficit then impedes the transformation of archaic grandiosity and leads to difficulty with self-esteem regulation. Kohut also coined the term *"twinship" transference,* which refers to the yearning to be like another, stemming from the developmental need of a child to be like a parent. Basch (1994) refined this transference as "the need to belong and feel accepted by one's cohort" (p. 4). Analysts later suggested other selfobject transferences, such as the adversarial (Wolf, 1988), self-delineating (Stolorow and Atwood, 1992), and undifferentiated (Rowe, 1998) transferences.

This chapter presents additional selfobject transferences in which the patient *requires* a relationship in which the analyst is *actively* responsive. At those moments, the patient is unable to sustain or regain a selfobject transference unless he receives active responsiveness. This longing and requirement for active responsiveness can be considered a type of selfobject transference since it expresses a selfobject need, albeit a transient one, in order for the self to be more cohesive and vital.

The post-Kohutian term *mirroring transference,* rather than Kohut's original *mirror transference,* is proposed for those times when active responsiveness is necessary for the patient to feel mirrored. Similarly, a twinning transference refers to those times when the patient cannot sustain or regain a selfobject twinship experience unless the analyst responds more actively to that selfobject need. (Within the mirroring and twinning transferences, the yearning and the *need* is for the analyst to *actively* mirror or twin, hence the "-ing" suffix.)

ACTIVE RESPONSIVENESS

Some writers limit analytic responses to listening, exploring, and interpreting. However, those in favor of optimal responsiveness hold that other responses belong within the analysis (Bacal, 1998). I hope to add to their perspective. *Everything* that an analyst does that strengthens the patient's self-structure, including nonverbal gestures, interpretations, an understanding tone, and approbation, can be seen both as offering a provision and as being responsive.

The *American College Dictionary* (Barnhart, 1965) defines *response* as an "answer or reply whether in words or some action" (p. 1034). Definitions of *responsive* include an "act of responding or answering, especially responding readily to influences, appeals, efforts" and "acting in response, as to some stimulus" (p. 1034). What I mean by an *active* responsiveness is a willingness to respond in ways not limited to listening, exploring, or interpreting. *Active* also conveys the analyst actively and overtly using his subjectivity as in mirroring, twinning, and the like, rather than remaining neutral.

Mermelstein (1998) echoes my contention that an analyst should consider modifying his behaviors based upon which of his behaviors enhance or diminish the patient's selfobject experience:

> The altering my behavior in accordance with what I perceived as necessary for the development of the selfobject dimension of the transference remains a controversial issue within self psychology. My goal was not on providing provisions or on providing a corrective emotional experience. My goal was to facilitate the unfolding of the selfobject dimension of the transference, which I saw as a prerequisite for productive treatment. I believe that had I not altered my stance, there would have been repeated empathic failures, and the selfobject dimension of the transference would not have been mobilized. In short, I believe that the repetitive dimension of the transference would have overshadowed the selfobject dimension and that active effort was required on my part to shift the balance in favor of the selfobject dimension [pp. 45–46].

This note justified his quietly nodding to his patient. His reasoning not only explains what I consider the necessity for other active responses but also reflects our field's discomfort about different analytic responses.

Being actively responsive refers not to a technique but to an authentic way of being within the range needed by the patient and with which the analyst is comfortable. It is informed by the analyst's feeling or experience derived from empathic resonance. Active responses encompass many verbal and nonverbal gestures, similar to responses one person offers another out of caring, such as expressing sadness or pleasure. Many (such as vocalizing "mmhuh") are so ordinary that the analyst may be unaware of their presence or impact.

Active responses appear in the literature. For example, Orange (1995) notes that, with certain patients, she leans forward. She sometimes responds "quite spontaneously to stories I am told with 'Oh, no!' or 'Ouch!'. . . I sometimes tell the patient what I or others have felt in similar situations" (p. 129). Bacal (1998) asserts that, when the smile of the analyst, the most common manifestation of his spontaneity, is in tune with the patient's selfobject need, it can be a more valuable therapeutic experience than words. Preston (1998) gave personal responses to a patient, such as "I am excited to hear about this" or "I miss you on Thursdays when I don't see you" (p. 212). This chapter mentions other examples.

A sampling of active responsiveness from my work and colleagues' work includes the following: (1) The analyst underlined a patient's insight, saying, "That's a very important idea." This enhanced the selfobject transference and validated and emphasized the patient's idea. (2) A patient was pleased that she sometimes successfully comforted herself when depressed, by telling herself she was not such a bad person. The analyst suggested the patient also try to imagine the analyst accompanying her and saying she was not a bad person. The patient brightened, revealing that she did that and it helped. This exchange heightened the selfobject transference and the bond with the analyst. (3) If the analyst interrupted a patient when he verbally described an upsetting incident, the patient felt that the analyst was not interested or was troubled by his affect. However, if the analyst was silent when the same patient spoke hesitatingly, he feared that the analyst was disinterested or displeased. The analyst modified his interventions accordingly, which helped maintain a selfobject transference.

Active responsiveness is an important element in the analysis. When this responsiveness supports the selfobject experience and enables the patient to feel understood, it facilitates treatment and builds structure. Bacal (1985) concluded that responsiveness is not a parameter:

> In my opinion, there is no such thing as a "parameter," an extraanalytic, or unanalytic, measure we adopt for a time in order ultimately to return to doing proper analysis in the traditional way. We must respond in ways that enable us to communicate understanding to the particular patient with whom we are working. That is analysis [p. 215].

In my view, this argument is applicable to active responsiveness. Later, Bacal (1990) recommended that the analyst take into account which aspects of his responsiveness will help the patient feel understood; these aspects were therapeutic for that patient rather than parameters. "*That is, the analyst's communications that are therapeutic are experienced by the patient as the provision of selfobject functions*" (p. 361).

The relationship between Bacal's concepts of selfobject experience and selfobject relationship, on the one hand, and my concepts of mirroring and twinning selfobject transferences, on the other hand, elucidates when active responsiveness is necessary. According to Bacal (1995), a selfobject *experience* is any experience that enhances the strength of the self, that is, where the patient feels his selfobject needs are being *met*. Bacal (1990, 1995) implied that, when the patient repeatedly has selfobject experiences and develops a *confident expectation* of the analyst's responsiveness to his selfobject needs, he is in a selfobject *relationship*. My use of selfobject *transference* includes both of these concepts.

Bacal (1990) discerned that, when a patient expected the analyst to be optimally responsive, he felt less urgency about his need for selfobjects and was less vulnerable to selfobject failures. From my point of view, this confident expectation implies that the patient will be able to sustain a selfobject transference or experience more easily. Similarly, he will less easily establish a self-state associated with a repetitive transference and will recover from that self-state more easily. Consequently, this patient has less necessity for active responsiveness in order to help him sustain or restore a selfobject transference.

Hopefully, the function served by active responsiveness will assist in anchoring it within our theory so that clinical practice will be more congruent with theory. Richer guidelines will be available to steer the analyst's choosing if and when to be actively responsive with a patient. Self psychological theory allows for a variety of responses, depending on the analyst's and the patient's needs.

KOHUT

Kohut fundamentally changed the course of psychoanalysis by focusing on what he called "selfobject needs." He used the selfobject transference by allowing it to blossom, accepting it, understanding the specific derivatives of this need in any particular patient, and eventually giving genetic and in-the-moment interpretations of the patient's experience. He believed that a significant task of the analyst was to be used as a selfobject in two ways: (1) permitting the patient to long for mirroring, idealizing, or twinship experiences from the analyst and (2) providing mirroring and more through an empathic understanding of the patient's experience. Kohut's concept of a selfobject transference stresses the patient's longing and developmental need for particular selfobject experiences but does not address those patients who require more than empathic understanding in order to feel or to sustain feeling understood.

Kohut was uncomfortable being more responsive than understanding and interpreting within the analysis, just as he was uneasy about the idea of gratifying the patient. Despite his misgivings, he was aware that sometimes it was desirable for an analyst to "reluctantly comply" with the patient's need/wish for him to be more responsive.

> At first hearing I might seem to be stating that, in instances of this type, the analyst must indulge a transference wish of the analysand. . . . There are indeed patients for whom this type of indulgence is not only a temporary tactical requirement during certain stressful phases of analysis. . . . And there is, furthermore, no doubt that, occasionally, the indulgence of an important childhood wish . . . can have lasting beneficial effects with regard to the relief of symptoms and behavioral change in the patient. . . . [F]or tactical reasons . . . the analyst might in such instances transitorily have to provide what one might call a reluctant compliance with the childhood wish, the true analytic aim is not indulgence but mastery based on insight, achieved in a setting of (tolerable) analytic abstinence [Kohut, 1971, pp. 290–292].

One instance of Kohut doing more than understanding and interpreting was when he offered two fingers to a deeply depressed patient. "I was deeply worried. So I . . . moved up a little bit in my chair, gave her two fingers. . . . She took a hold of them, and I immediately made a genetic interpretation to myself. . . . I reacted to it even there, to myself, as an analyst. . . . [I]t overcame a very, very difficult impasse at a given dangerous moment" (Kohut, 1981, p. 535).

A DUAL CONTINUUM OF FRUSTRATION TO RESPONSIVENESS AND OF RELATIONAL ASPECTS IN THE BACKGROUND TO THE FOREGROUND

Controversy currently exists within self psychology over which is more necessary to curative process—relational aspects of the analysis or the interpretation and working through of the unfolding selfobject transference (Doctors, 1998). Both camps believe in the importance of working through and interpretation but disagree on the priority of relational aspects and responsiveness. I find it more useful to place these differing views upon a continuum. At one end are self psychological analysts who advocate being as cautious as Kohut, theoretically refraining from providing any responses other than empathic listening or interpretation. Although these writers admit to the advisability under certain circumstances of offering more, they view such responses as parameters of treatment.

At the conservative end, MacIsaac and his coauthor unequivocally stated that the "mirroring and idealizing needs are understood and analyzed, not actively gratified through some verbal or nonverbal evaluative 'pat on the back'" (Rowe and MacIsaac, 1991, p. 304). From their point of view, although "feeling understood facilitates the treatment, active gratification . . . interferes with the understanding process and therefore the treatment" (p. 305).

MacIsaac (1996) defended Kohut's concept of optimal frustration and argued against viewing the analytic dyad as a relationship. He stated that "to direct attention to the discovery of an optimally responsive act switches the analyst's focus from this critical self-psychological stance [of empathic attunement] to an object-relational perspective, in which the focus is away from the patient's experience and toward the analyst as an object initiating and doing" (p. 15). It is as if he did not believe that a self psychologist can be both immersed in the patient's experience and also respond from the analyst's personhood. He acknowledged that an analyst could offer active provision as a parameter when patients underwent difficult periods or were unanalyzable.

MacIsaac (1996) presented a patient who demanded that he assuage her anxiety by providing answers and opinions. He steadfastly refused, instead continually attempting to immerse himself empathically in her experience. He did this partially so that he would not validate her core sense that she was powerless and crippled and also so that he would not send the message that intense affect should be avoided. He evidently did not sense that this patient was undergoing too difficult a period.

However, MacIsaac unintentionally described instances when he provided more than empathic understanding or explanation since he generously gave a vivid sense of what occurred in some sessions with this patient. The patient occasionally left notes outside his office door. I would argue that MacIsaac's accepting the notes was a provision beyond interpretation and was optimally responsive. Instead, he could have refused to read them and interpreted her need to leave the notes. Similarly, when the patient denigrated herself for being so angry with him, he told her that he "thought it was an important step ahead, and even a complement to our work that she was able to express her disappointment and anger openly" (MacIsaac, 1996, p. 11). I view this as active mirroring. Further, these provisions may have been crucial for the analytic process rather than incidental or nonanalytic, as he believed.

Paul Ornstein can be considered within the middle of the continuum. Like MacIsaac, he does not think of self psychology as a relational psychology. Ornstein (1995) stated:

> [Even] though . . . both the original "structure" formation and the subsequent maintenance of the integrity of these structures throughout life occur in a (descriptively) "relational" context . . . the self–selfobject concept brings external reality (the other in the relationship) [parentheses his] into the inner world of the self. Psychoanalytic focus, therefore, is *not* on what goes on *between* people, but on what goes on *inside* of them [p. 57].

However, unlike MacIsaac, Ornstein favored being responsive to a patient's specific needs. In conceptualizing the analysis of one of his patients, he and his coauthor (Ornstein and Ornstein, 1994) disclosed that he was initially reluctant to yield to the patient's demand that the analyst ask questions instead of giving statements. Ornstein then realized the function served for his patient of being asked questions. After Ornstein became aware that his countertransference "interfered with my responsiveness to Mr. K's archaic needs and demands," he asked questions in order to be useable to the patient (Ornstein and Ornstein, 1994, p. 983). He concluded that it "is only then, as the analyst's expanding capacity to respond in accordance with the patient's needs and his requirements for sustaining the analytic dialogue, that the working through could lead to structure-building and initiate the visible process of change in this analysis" (p. 992). I would use this same reasoning to include active responses in the analyst's repertoire.

Wolf occupies a different part of the middle of the continuum. His views on active responsiveness appear contradictory. As seen below, his agreeing with Goldberg indicates that he opposes active responsiveness, yet his definition of interpretation and his favoring optimal responsiveness indicates that he values the role of responsiveness. On the one hand, he emphatically agreed with a passage he quoted from Goldberg (1978, pp. 447–448):

> The analyst does not actively soothe; he interprets the analysand's yearning to be soothed. The analyst does not actively mirror; he interprets the need for confirming responses. . . . Of course, the analyst's mere presence, or the fact that he talks . . . all have soothing and self-confirming effects on the patient, *and they are so interpreted* [quoted in Wolf, 1988, p. 133].

Like MacIsaac, Wolf made exceptions, primarily for patients whom he regarded as nonanalyzable or very regressed during cohesion-threatening life crises who might need active advice or approval.

On the other hand, Wolf (1993) defined interpretation as "all those intentional activities of the analyst that in their totality bring about a modification of the analysand's psyche . . . (including) verbal statements and any other consciously directed interventions . . . including those apparent noninterventions" (p. 15). He supported the concepts of empathic responsiveness and optimal responsiveness "to replace the deprivation imposed by strict nongratification" (p. 17). Moreover, his upholding the value of the analytic ambiance, nonverbal gestures, and the selfobject bond implies the importance of the therapeutic relationship. "The availability of the therapist as a caring and understanding selfobject expedites the establishment of a selfobject bond with the therapist. . . . The role of interpretation now is to repair the selfobject tie and through it to restore the therapeutic process" (p. 29).

Other self psychological writers are at the more liberal end of the continuum regarding the analyst's moving beyond "reluctant compliance" to a more active and wholehearted responsiveness. They view such responsiveness as an integral component of the analytic process rather than a parameter. I shall name only a few writers. Bacal (1985) argued that "optimal responsiveness" rather than Kohut's "optimal frustration" built structure. He and other self psychologists have since expanded these ideas by eloquently reexamining views on provision and gratification. Lindon (1994), for example, advocated that the analyst respond with optimal provision; that is, "any provision which, by meeting a mobilized developmental longing, facilitates the uncovering, illuminating, and *transforming* of the subjective experiences of the patient" (p. 559; emphasis added). He further recommended that the analyst respond with optimal gratification to what he perceived as the patient's urgent desires.

Recent self psychological theorists view the analyst's subjectivity and the relationship between analyst and patient as essential elements in the therapeutic process in order to facilitate their developmental striving. They broadened Kohut's essentially one-person model to encompass a two-person model. For example, Orange (1995) proposed that emotional availability, "an active and responsive preparedness for empathic understanding," is *necessary* for the success of therapeutic relationships (p. 125). Preston (1998) and Brothers and Lewinberg (1999) shared vivid clinical illustrations of using their subjectivity as an integral aspect of the analysis. Many proponents of the analyst's subjectivity portray interactions that can be looked upon as unconventional and controversial. I admire their courage in attempting to move theory forward while sharing vulnerable aspects of themselves and risking disapproval from peers. However, many did not articulate whether their way of working applies to all patients or, if not, why not.

CLINICAL EXAMPLES

I shall now present portions of treatment with two patients. Work with one patient illustrates that active responsiveness sustained the selfobject transference. For the other patient, any active responsivity or sign that I was a separate person created a serious empathic rupture. During the periods described, both patients were in psychoanalytic therapy/analysis two to three times a week and were in the process of undergoing a reorganization of personality. My stance, adhering to Kohut's steps of understanding and explaining and focusing on the patient's self-experience, including empathic ruptures, was the same with each patient.

Development of a Mirroring Transference

For the first time, Ken, a 45-year-old magazine illustrator, wanted a relationship with his girlfriend to last. Because she suggested he try therapy and because she wanted him to talk about feelings, Ken felt some urgency to do so. He realized that he had difficulty knowing and communicating many of his feelings. What he most wanted from therapy was to feel like, and to be more of, a "grown up."

Ken, who usually dressed in jeans and a polo shirt, wanted to feel less like a "kid" *vis-à-vis* the adults he worked with. He also wished to feel more comfortable and confident when making calls to build up his business. He hoped to have a more stable career and afford a higher standard of living in order to offer more to his girlfriend. He dreaded feeling foolish, appearing stupid or angering others when he attempted to call strangers or relate to colleagues. As we shall see, these were related to feeling criticized and humiliated by his father, classmates, and teachers.

Ken's mother alternated between indiscriminately adoring him or talking constantly about herself, both of which felt as if she did not really see him. Ken's perception of his father was that he was critical toward him, did not give him much attention, and preferred Ken's brother. Most of the time when Ken was called on by a teacher, he felt too self-conscious to speak. The boys then teased him, which exacerbated his exquisite humiliation. Ken virtually dropped out of school from the last part of 4th grade through 11th grade, frozen by a mass of humiliation and shame. He experienced himself as different from others and therefore defective—initially with his father, later because he felt incapable of attending school and in the present since he did not fit into a salaried career and felt inferior to adults.

During the initial two years of weekly therapy, Ken presented me with pictures he had drawn. He also talked about his daily activities and plans for the future, hoping that I would be pleased but afraid I was bored. His fears of feeling foolish and humiliated kept painful or vulnerable feelings out of awareness just as he did not risk rejection or exposure outside of therapy. A mirror transference quickly became established. We increased his sessions to three times weekly as a way to deepen the unfolding of his yearnings and fears, to help him experience and communicate more affect. My approach with him was similar during the initial weekly sessions and the more intense analysis/psychoanalytic therapy. After the sessions were increased, Ken allowed himself to depend on me more and to feel more vulnerable. As a result, he felt retraumatized when he experienced a break in our empathic connection but was usually able to explore it.

Occasionally, my encouraging Ken to explore triggered a repetitive transference and its associated self-state. His mind went blank, and he became overwhelmed with the old confusion, panic, self-consciousness, and humiliation that he had experienced with his father, teachers, and colleagues. At those moments he ceased to be aware of his feelings and desires. I believed it was destructive to his developing self for him to remain in that self-state unnecessarily. Neither exploration, interpretation, nor nonverbal empathic communication were enough to reestablish a selfobject transference and further facilitate the therapeutic process. Active responsiveness often enabled him to overcome his retreat and denial of affect.

Ken's first dream after beginning the three times weekly sessions was as follows:

> I was on a platform or scaffolding. I was sculpting or something. I was naked. Then a young woman . . . motioned like to ask if it was OK to draw me. I didn't feel embarrassed or anything and I was struck by that. She was sketching as if she was a professional artist. Then she got partly undressed. Her top was unzipped. I was checking her out. Then she must've noticed it so she put it back on, then it slipped down again.

Ken thought that his being naked symbolized both his initial fear that he might be too exposed and, more importantly, his feeling of being seen and accepted for who he really was. Further exploration led to his realization that when he watched the woman:

> I felt good. Then when she put it back on I felt bad that it must not have been cool. When I looked at her it made her feel uncomfortable. Then when she let it go back down, I again felt it was cool. It reminded me that I now feel comfortable with women. I wasn't just hanging out but I was doing something. She was attracted to me because I was *interesting*. It feels much better to feel that I can do things.

One aspect of this dream concretized Ken's transition from manifesting a mirror transference to potentially establishing a *mirroring* transference. His dream and associations suggested triggers for two self-states: (1) confusion and humiliation (felt "uncool" and uncomfortable) when I hid myself and (2) more cohesiveness (felt comfortable, "cool" and "interesting") when my subjectivity was visible. Whether my subjectivity was visible or hidden affected his establishing a selfobject transference. Therefore, not only did he want to risk exposing his needs and himself to me, but he also *needed* me to actively respond by bringing my "person-ness" into our relationship in order for him to sustain a selfobject transference.

One instance of active responsiveness occurred when Ken discussed his fears of becoming more emotional, especially of crying. A mirror transference was established; he said he felt vulnerable talking about this with others, because if they were not responsive, he would feel very humiliated. Continuing, he said it was different talking with me because he knew I cared about him. In earlier sessions we had explored these feelings and how they were linked both to his critical, inattentive father and to his emotionally absent, self-absorbed mother. I listened silently, assuming that was enough. He repeated that, if no one responded, he would feel all alone, which would feel really awful.

His cloudy facial expression communicated that he was beginning to feel humiliated. If I limited my responses to exploration or interpretation, he would sink into the self-state of overwhelming humiliation because of the subjective meaning he would give to nonactive responsiveness. He was not yet able to regulate his affect at those times. Active responsiveness was required for him to feel understood and received. This responsiveness also validated his newfound sense of feeling entitled to his own feelings and needs. I responded to his mirroring transference because refraining from active responsivity seemed more destructive than neutral. I said that he would not be alone, that I would be with him. This simple verbal demonstrativeness visibly touched him. The mirror transference was restored, and he returned to the exploratory process.

Another instance of active responsiveness occurred when Ken manifested a twinship transference, which then shifted to a twinning transference. Ken began one session by fantasizing that I would cook tuna casserole for him like his mother had. He also described a dream in which he and a woman shed alligator skins. In his words, they "transformed into being human." After exclaiming that he had tuna casserole just last night, he wryly asked if I had tuna casserole last night. In exploring this, he said that he wanted to see if we were on the same wavelength.

His affect became flat. He no longer was aware of any thoughts or feelings, experiencing a moderate version of his familiar self-state of humiliation. A *twinning* transference entered the foreground. Neither understanding nor interpretation helped revitalize him. Truthfully, I replied that, instead of tuna casserole, I had made macaroni and cheese casserole, which I love. He was pleased that we had similar tastes, which reinstated a twinship connection. Active responsivity enabled him to regain the selfobject transference.

Development of a Mirror Transference

To further illustrate and differentiate the mirroring transference from the mirror transference, I shall now describe a very different patient. She resembled Kohut's (1971) Miss F. Kohut detailed that the narcissistic sustenance she needed could be given by his not going

> beyond what the patient herself had already said or discovered, even by a single step . . . , [she] would . . . accuse me . . . of undermining her. . . . [There] arose the renewed need for an archaic object (a precursor of psychological structure) that would be nothing more than the embodiment of a psychological function which the patient's psyche could not yet perform for itself: to respond empathically to her narcissistic display and to provide her with narcissistic sustenance through approval, mirroring, and echoing [pp. 285–287].

Donna, an intelligent, but colorless, 38-year-old, exemplified this need. Throughout the first year of her therapy, she required me to demonstrate my attunement only through deeply listening and remembering the specific content and details of her verbalizations. She entered therapy because she lacked confidence in herself and felt inferior to others. She oscillated between feeling quite anxious and feeling numb. She had a few acquaintances but no close relationships with men or women and had never had an overtly sexual relationship. She wished for, yet feared, intimacy. She expressed this ambivalence by spending most of her energy at home gathering information for her extensive genealogy logs and at work by tediously programming computers.

For as long as she could remember, her mother communicated to her verbally and nonverbally that all of her mother's unhappiness and any tension within the family was Donna's fault. Donna, who moved out of her parents' home at the age of 34, tried hard to please her mother. However, whenever she protested about her mother's accusations, her mother became upset and used Donna's complaints as further evidence that Donna was the one who created tension. In weekly phone calls, her mother insisted that Donna carry the conversation. She asked about her daily life, but before Donna could finish a sentence, her mother changed the subject. Consequently, Donna came to believe that no one would want to relate to her, that she was flawed, that she was doomed to a life of loneliness, and that any person upon whom she depended emotionally would eventually abandon her.

Donna saw me two or three times weekly because her daily life created so much anxiety and crisis. Her developmental deficits were pervasive. She quickly developed a *mirror* transference with me. When I listened to Donna, she maintained the fantasy that I understood her completely. If I displayed any affect, such as surprise or wondering, her anxiety increased because at those moments she experienced me as anxious, angry, or not omniscient. Slochower (1996) explained that some patients cannot afford to sense the analyst's subjectivity. They require a "holding experience . . . [where] *an illusion of absolute attunement* [is created, which] . . . centrally concerns the analyst's capacity to understand . . . the patient's needs or feeling states" (p. 326).

Understandably, if I attempted to explore an issue, Donna felt and believed that I, like her mother, did not understand or care about her at all. She then withdrew, feeling that I was unreliable. Each empathic break increased her anxiety. She felt as if she were falling apart, which was partially expressed with diarrhea and panic attacks. After about a year of my listening and nodding my head, she was occasionally able to tolerate brief exploration and interpretation; but she continued to fragment if I offered active responsiveness. She slowly became just noticeably livelier and more colorful.

DISCUSSION AND CONCLUSIONS

The mirroring and "twinning transferences point to the desire and selfobject need, at certain times in certain patients, for active responsiveness. Only then will that patient have a "good enough" experience of feeling understood and more cohesive. Those selfobject transferences more accurately describe Ken's transient selfobject need for active responsiveness than does Kohut's mirror and twinship transferences, since the latter deemphasize the patient's developmental need for a relationship with active responsiveness.

Some writers view active responsiveness as nonanalytic and as a potentially dangerous enactment. When they make exceptions, such as for a patient in crisis, this responsiveness is a parameter. Patients in a crisis sometimes require the analyst to make extra effort, such as active responsiveness, for them to shift from a repetitive transference to a selfobject transference. I argue that this holds true during the "mini-crisis" of a rupture as well. This chapter suggests that active responsiveness can be not only safe but also analytic. I join more liberal analysts in regarding provisions as essential elements in the curative process, whether or not they occur during a crisis.

I am not arguing that we should avoid all repetitive transferences. Rather, our theory, from Kohut's "selfobject transference" through Bacal's "optimal responsiveness," furnishes a conceptual formulation for a range of responses based upon our emotional comfort and our judgment about what would constitute a selfobject matrix for any specific patient. Ideally, theory allows for these interventions so that clinical practice is congruent with theory. A number of self psychologists have written that optimal responses, including empathic listening and active responsiveness, can be used in the service of empathically responding to the patient, depending on the specific selfobject needs reactivated. Moreover, other analysts (Ornstein and Ornstein, 1994; Mermelstein, 1998), who did not intentionally discuss optimal responsiveness, explained the value of changing their behavior in order for the patient to establish a selfobject transference enough of the time.

Active responsiveness can be seen as parallel to Kohut's original contribution of empathically listening to the patient. Kohut found that empathic listening was often experienced by self-disordered patients as a therapeutic experience compared to the more neutral Freudian interventions. In the same vein, refraining from offering authentic responsiveness to those patients whose selfobject needs include active responsiveness, for the sake of analytic neutrality, can erode newly built structure. The points made in this chapter hold for both psychoanalytic therapy and psychoanalysis. In those moments when patients like Ken *require* active responsiveness in order to sustain a selfobject transference, active responsiveness is optimal while its lack is traumatic.

Both of the patients I described fell toward opposite ends of a continuum. A narrow range of responsiveness was optimal for each, which will likely broaden as a patient becomes stronger and more resilient. Patients in the middle range of the continuum were not addressed. They might long for more active responsiveness and do not fragment when they receive such responsiveness. However, they do not developmentally *require* active responsiveness in order to sustain a selfobject experience.

In addition to assessing his personal comfort level, the clinician might find the following categories useful in deciding if active responsiveness would contribute to a selfobject matrix for a specific patient at a given moment, that is, whether it seems necessary or optional, will interfere with the patient's working through, or would be injurious. My reasoning assumes that mobilizing or enhancing a selfobject transference is curative, just as repairing an empathic break is.

In any moment, a patient's reaction to active responsiveness places him in one of the following four categories regarding whether or not active responsiveness is curative: (1) The patient *requires* active responsiveness in order to sustain or restore a selfobject transference, which was demonstrated with Ken. I have argued that active responsiveness in this circumstance is optimally responsive and curative. (2) The patient longs for active responsiveness but does not require it. On the one hand, active responsiveness will be curative if it enhances the selfobject transference; on the contrary, if it is not given and a rupture is repaired, this will also be curative. On the other hand, active responsiveness will *not* be curative if it is proffered yet does not impact the transference. (3) It will not be curative if it disrupts the selfobject transference. Neither will it be curative if it interrupts the patient's process of working through. (4) If active responsiveness is traumatic, as it was for Donna, then it could be destructive rather than curative.

Finally, it is important to mention a few cautions and pitfalls. Being actively responsive refers not to a technique but to an authentic way of being. The analyst's primary task is to be responsive to the patient's selfobject needs through empathic understanding, interpretation, and more active expressions within the overlap of the range needed by the patient and the range within which the analyst is comfortable. Any active responsiveness from the analyst should be to the patient's budding, genuine expressions of self in order to avoid reinforcing a manifestation of a false self.

In conclusion, the views of self psychological analysts regarding responsiveness and relational aspects of the analytic process fall on a continuum. Active responsiveness, that is, the analyst's active expression, is optimally responsive, builds structure for some patients at certain times and thus is curative. This occurs at the juncture when the analyst empathically senses that the patient requires it in order to restore a selfobject transference and when the analyst feels comfortable enough offering it. At other times or with other patients, more restrained responsiveness, such as empathic understanding alone, is optimal. The specificity of each analytic dyad calls for its own empathically informed responsiveness.

REFERENCES

Bacal, H. (1985), Optimal responsiveness and the therapeutic process. In: *Progress in Self Psychology*, Vol. 1, ed A. Goldberg. New York: Guilford, pp. 202–226.

——— (1990), The elements of a corrective selfobject experience. *Psychoanal. Inq.*, 3:347–372.

——— (1995), The essence of Kohut's work and the progress of self psychology. *Psychoanal. Dial.*, 5:353–366.

——— (1998), Is empathic attunement the only optimal response? In: *Optimal Responsiveness: How Therapists Heal Their Patients*, ed. H. Bacal. Northvale, NJ: Aronson, pp. 289–301.

Barnhart, C. L., ed. (1965), *American College Dictionary*. New York: Random House.

Basch, M. F. (1994), The selfobject concept: Clinical implications. In: *A Decade of Progress: Progress in Self Psychology, Vol. 10,* ed. A. Goldberg. Hillsdale, NJ: The Analytic Press, pp. 1–7.

Brothers, D. & Lewinberg, E. (1999), The therapeutic partnership: A developmental view of self psychological treatment as bilateral healing. In: *Pluralism in Self Psychology: Progress in Self Psychology, Vol. 15,* ed. A. Goldberg. Hillsdale, NJ: The Analytic Press, pp. 259–284.

Doctors, S. (1998), A controversial panel: The chairperson's view. *Newsletter,* 1:1–3.

Goldberg, A. (1978), *The Psychology of the Self: A Casebook*. New York: International Universities Press.

Kohut, H. (1971), *Analysis of the Self*. New York: International Universities Press.

——— (1979), Four basic concepts in self psychology. In: *The Search for the Self, Vol. 4,* ed. P. H. Ornstein. Madison, CT: International Universities Press, pp. 447–470.

——— (1981), On empathy. In: *The Search for the Self, Vol. 4,* ed. P. H. Ornstein. Madison, CT: International Universities Press, pp. 525–535.

Lindon, J. A. (1994), Gratification and provision in psychoanalysis: Should we get rid of the rule of abstinence? *Psychoanal. Dial.*, 4:549–582.

MacIsaac, D. S. (1996), Optimal frustration: An endangered concept. In: *Basic Ideas Reconsidered: Progress in Self Psychology, Vol. 12,* ed. A. Goldberg. Hillsdale, NJ, The Analytic Press, pp. 3–16.

Mermelstein, J. J. (1998), The figure–ground relationship of the selfobject and repetitive dimensions of the transference. In: *The World of Self Psychology: Progress in Self Psychology, Vol. 14,* ed. A. Goldberg. Hillsdale, NJ: The Analytic Press, pp. 33–62.

Orange, D. (1995), *Emotional Understanding*. New York: Guilford.

Ornstein, P. H. (1995), Critical reflections on a comparative analysis of "Self psychology and intersubjectivity theory." In: *The Impact of New Ideas: Progress in Self Psychology, Vol. 11,* ed. A. Goldberg. Hillsdale, NJ: The Analytic Press, pp. 47–77.

——— & Ornstein, A. (1994), On the conceptualization of clinical facts. *Internat. J. Psycho-Anal.*, 75:977–994.

Preston, L. (1998), Expressive relating: The intentional use of the analyst's subjectivity. In: *The World of Self Psychology: Progress in Self Psychology, Vol. 14,* ed. A. Goldberg. Hillsdale, NJ: The Analytic Press, pp. 203–218.

Rowe, C. E. (1998), The undifferentiated selfobject transference and its contribution to understanding suicidal pathology, repetition compulsion and fixations. Presented at the 21st Annual Conference on the Psychology of the Self. October, San Diego, CA.

——— & MacIsaac, D. S. (1991), *Empathic Attunement: The "Technique" of Psychoanalytic Self Psychology*. Northvale, NJ: Aronson.

Slochower, J. (1996), Holding and the fate of the analyst's subjectivity, *Psychoanal. Dial.*, 6:323–354.

Stolorow, R. D. & Atwood, G. E. (1992), *Contexts of Being*. Hillsdale, NJ: The Analytic Press.

Wolf, E. S. (1988), *Treating the Self*. New York: Guilford.

——— (1993) The role of interpretation in therapeutic change. In: *The Widening Scope of Self Psychology: Progress in Self Psychology, Vol. 9*, ed. A. Goldberg. Hillsdale, NJ: The Analytic Press, pp. 15–30.

Chapter 10

Easy Listening, Prolonged Empathic Immersion, and the Selfobject Needs of the Analyst

Jeffrey J. Mermelstein

Prolonged psychological immersion of the analyst in the patient's subjective experience has a profound effect on both the patient and the analyst and on the communication that occurs between them. The literature has tended to focus on prolonged psychological immersion as it is reflected in the listening process with difficult patients, emphasizing the communicative power that occurs with prolonged psychological immersion (Khan, 1979; McDougall, 1980; Kohut, 1981; Bromberg, 1998). In contrast, this chapter focuses on prolonged psychological immersion and the listening process when both occur in a relaxed and pleasurable manner with patients whom the analyst does not experience as difficult.

The listening process is always embedded in a relational matrix and is as complex as relationships themselves. Schwaber (1981) has pointed out how different psychoanalytic systems each provide a definition of the listening stance that is compatible with their own theoretical frame-

The author wishes to thank Fred Arensberg, Ph.D., Howard Bacal, M.D., James Fosshage, Ph.D., Robert Karen, Ph.D., Carol Munschauer, Ph.D., John Pagura, C.S.W., Robert Ruchames, C.S.W., and Peter Thomson, MBBS, FRCP(C), for their thoughtful responses to earlier versions of this chapter.

work. Theories of listening tend to reflect one's basic beliefs about human beings and about the analytic relationship. Freud viewed the analyst/listener as a neutral, passive recipient of the patient's communications, which ultimately reflect the patient's drives and defenses. The analyst was encouraged to be a blank screen whose neutrality was augmented by the technical injunction that the analyst should listen with evenly hovering attention (Freud, 1912, 1913). Using the structural model, Anna Freud (1936) defined the analyst's listening stance as occupying a neutral position equidistant from the id, ego, and superego. Greenson (1967) expanded upon this formulation, describing how: "From the evenly suspended, free-floating position, the analyst can oscillate and make blendings from among his free associations, empathy, intuition, introspection, problem-solving thinking, theoretical knowledge, etc." (p. 100). Reik (1949) emphasized that the patient's unconscious communications could best be understood through the analyst attending to the keen perceptual sensitivity of his or her own unconscious. Sullivan (1953, 1954) described the analyst as a participant–observer, which emphasized his belief that the analyst is not a neutral recipient of the patient's communications but is unavoidably actively engaged in a process with the patient. Beginning with Klein's (1929, 1946, 1975a, b) work on projective mechanisms, continuing with Bion's (1957) introduction of the container model and with contemporary approaches to projective identification (Grotstein, 1981; Ogden, 1982; Kernberg, 1987), object relations theorists have viewed the analyst as the receiver of projections, which emphasizes the analyst listening for the transmission of these self and object representations.

In an early paper that foreshadowed the birth of self psychology, Kohut (1959) reframed how the analyst should listen to the analysand. Defining empathy as vicarious introspection, Kohut emphasized the centrality of the introspective and empathic mode of observation as defining the main tool for clinical investigation, treatment, and psychoanalytic theorizing. Self psychology's emphasis on listening in an experience-near manner is a metaphor for the analyst's wish to remain as close as possible to the phenomenological experience of the patient.[1]

Current relational theories insist on a two-person model of listening and experiencing. These include Hoffman's (1983, 1991, 1998) social-constructivist perspective, which emphasizes how meaning is

---

[1] Although self psychological literature on listening has tended to focus almost exclusively on the empathic vantage point, one exception is the work of Fosshage (1995, 1997), who has suggested that the analyst's understanding of the patient can be enhanced by an "other-centered" listening perspective in which the analyst attends to his or her reactions to the patient from the vantage point of an "other."

coconstructed by each analytic dyad and the intersubjectivist perspective which emphasizes the analytic experience as a coming together of two subjectivities (Stolorow, Brandchaft, and Atwood, 1987; Stolorow and Atwood, 1992; Orange, Atwood, and Stolorow, 1997). The shift in psychoanalytic thinking toward a two-person model heightens our awareness of the listener as a central component in the listening process. Each analyst represents a somewhat different listener, based upon the totality of the analyst's history and personality, including the analyst's theoretical and personal organizing principles. Each analyst–patient dyad is unique; indeed, each and every session, if not each and every moment of every session, may be a somewhat different listening experience. It is difficult, if not impossible, for psychoanalytic theories of listening to capture the boundless complexity of the continually shifting listening process that is embedded in the analytic relationship. Reductionism for the purpose of simplicity and clarity is inevitable.

PSYCHOLOGICAL IMMERSION IN THE OTHER

Psychological immersion in the psychological life of the patient is at odds with the Freudian notion of neutrality; it is even at odds with current psychoanalytic sensibilities about maintaining clear psychological boundaries between analyst and patient. True immersion in the psychological life of a patient loosens the boundaries between analyst and patient. A window of opportunity for mutual interpenetration is created, crossing the usual ego boundaries and defensive barriers that enable us to maintain a clear sense of self and other. This psychic interpenetration of subjectivities leads to a certain degree of confusion about who is the owner or even the originator of a given feeling, thought, or enactment.

All listening involves some degree of boundary maintenance and some degree of boundary blurring by both participants. To speak and to listen involves the potential for significant mutual impact. Listening does not, however, always involve becoming deeply immersed in the other's subjectivity.[2] There is a continuum in the listening process: at one end being a more cognitive listening to the facts or details of a presentation with a fairly clear boundary between self and other, and

[2] When one is deeply immersed in listening to the other, one may have the experience of leaving one's own subjectivity behind and entering another's subjectivity. It is, however, not clear how one can ever truly abandon one's subjectivity. I prefer to think of psychological immersion in the subjectivity of the other as being deeply immersed in the listening process or deeply immersed in that aspect of one's own subjectivity that is most engaged (or "immersed") in the other's subjectivity.

clear defenses against being drawn too intensely into the emotional life of the other; at the other end of the continuum lies an emotional immersion in the other's life in which you are experiencing and being impacted by the other's subjective experience, not entirely as they are experiencing it, but as a mixture of how they experience their world and of how you, with a different subjectivity, experience their world. Bacal (1997), in his discussion of psychic distance, draws a distinction between empathic listening and a more total psychological immersion. Bacal suggests that

> Ordinary empathic listening entails neither total immersion in the patient's experience nor some kind of distant intellectual reflecting about the patient. It requires the maintenance of a certain degree of closeness or, if you will, of "psychic distance," which enables the analyst to be receptive to affects, states, and moods in the patient so that he may *sense* within himself what the analysand is going through without actually experiencing the patient's experience *in full* [p. 677].

Prolonged empathic immersion of the analyst in the patient's subjective experience can lead to complementary shifts in analyst and patient as they both move toward self-states that allow for a reduced sharpness of the boundary between self and other, greater interpenetration of selfobject functioning, greater permeability of affective experience, and the opportunity for greater mutual impact. Such a reduction in psychic distance can facilitate the expression and reception of primitive, unconscious communications, allowing the analyst to gain access to dissociated or otherwise lost aspects of the patient's experience that cannot be communicated directly and, instead, are communicated unconsciously through their impact upon the analyst and through enactments. Patients differ in the extent to which they benefit from such a reduction in psychic distance. Analysts differ in their beliefs about what amount of psychic distance is optimal for their patients and in the extent to which they are willing to become immersed in their patients' subjective experience. A reduction in the psychic distance between analyst and patient can be experienced as intimate and empathic or as a traumatic boundary violation, depending on the complex intersubjective field within which this reduction in psychic distance occurs.

EASY LISTENING

An understanding of prolonged empathic immersion and its impact on the analytic process must include a description of how the analyst approaches listening. I have come to use the term *easy listening* to refer to a method of listening and interacting that I gravitate to and enjoy in and out of the psychoanalytic treatment room. Easy listening is presented as a way of capturing the analyst's experience of prolonged empathic immersion in the listening process with certain patients with whom the selfobject transference develops and is maintained effortlessly and with whom the reduction in psychic distance between analyst and patient is experienced by both as empathic.

Easy listening tends to occur in dyads. The presence of a third person diverts from the kind of sustained gaze that is a quintessential ingredient of empathic immersion—and from the verbal equivalents of that gaze. With easy listening, communication occurs in a relaxed manner, and there is a basic mutual attunement that was easily acquired and expanded upon. When engaged in easy listening, the feeling of familiarity can be so great that the participants may feel as if they have known each other since childhood. I used to think that one needed to have the same personality type, be of similar ethnicity, or perhaps come from the same neighborhood to have such a feeling of familiarity. But similarity is not the issue, anymore than it is when one falls in love.

With easy listening, one never has to ask what the other is feeling. The other's feelings are obvious. The listener is freed to follow the content of what is being expressed. The listener enjoys the act of listening. He or she is not under any pressure, self-imposed or imposed by the other, to listen attentively or to read between the lines. Both participants are operating at the same level of depth. What makes the listening so effortless is that the speaker is communicating at a certain level of depth and the interaction is working at that level. The listener does not have to work to bring the conversation to a deeper level of intimacy. There is enough intimacy available in the interaction that is occurring that neither party is pushing to unilaterally bring the conversation somewhere else. Needless to say, if the listener is dissatisfied with the current level of intimacy or emotional relatedness that exists in his or her relationship to the speaker, he or she will not be able to listen easily. Easy listening requires a basic satisfaction and mutual pleasure taken in the listening process. If the listener wants some other form of engagement, be it deeper, more emotional, more cognitive, or more reflective, the rapport will suffer.

When I am seeing a couple for therapy, it is interesting to note which two of the three of us in the room have the easy listening. Sometimes, it is the couple coming for therapy, and sometimes the easy listening is between one of them and me. One of us will use the wrong word in the middle of a thought. The person who has easy listening with the one who made the slip of the tongue knows what was meant and continues to follow the material without distraction. He or she may not even recognize that a wrong word was used. Meanwhile, the person without the easy listening is totally thrown by the incorrectly chosen word or name. Similarly, the use of an ambiguous pronoun is rarely a problem when you have this kind of easy listening. The listener immediately knows to whom the pronoun was referring. When you have easy listening with someone, you tend to speak at the same pace.[3] You intuitively know which of their pauses are meant to be the launching pad for your associations or reactions and which are merely meant to be a moment to catch one's breath and regroup one's thoughts. And if you are mistaken and begin speaking when the other had meant to continue, it doesn't seem to matter. The relational process has a built-in self-corrective mechanism whereby you get back on track with a minimum of fuss or hurt feelings. When you have easy listening, there is hardly ever a struggle for control of the conversation. Both parties enjoy the dyadic development of the discourse. The whole is greater than the contribution of either participant.

There is a mutual surrender in easy listening. Both participants are sacrificing some of their individuality and competitiveness toward the greater good of the conversation and understanding that is being conjointly coauthored by the participants. The speaker tailors his or her presentation to facilitate accessibility and to enhance the other's grasp of what is being presented. The listener is suspending judgments that would only get in the way of the listening process. This mutual surrender is not the equivalent of submission (Ghent, 1990). Neither party feels trapped or held hostage by the other. This interchange must be entered into freely. People who desperately crave the experience of intimacy that is possible in mutual surrender tend to substitute submission or domination for surrender in their effort to acquire the attention of the other. This never brings about the wished for easy listening. Taking hostages breeds resentment, and resentment destroys the kind of easy listening that is being described.

When you have easy listening, you tend to quickly recognize when the speaker has shifted to humor or sarcasm. Although people differ in regard to what they find humorous, when you have easy listening, you tend to know that humor has been employed, even when you do not experience the joke or comment as particularly humorous. You may even find yourself laughing spontaneously in response to jokes

[3] Easy listening has much in common with mother–infant dyadic communication when there is a good fit between mother and infant (Beebe, Stern, and Jaffe, 1979; Beebe, Jaffe, and Lachmann, 1992).

that you have already heard. Laughter, especially when accompanied by relaxed giddiness, can be infectious. More generally, with easy listening, affect is contagious. Similarly, when you have easy listening, you never have to inform each other that a comment was meant to be sarcastic.

When immersed in easy listening, you may occasionally be distracted by the environment or by your inner thoughts, but the distraction does not derail the conversation. Even when you miss a sentence or two of the communication, you are usually able to resume listening, hardly missing a beat. The level of attuneness to the whole picture overshadows the importance of most details. When a missing detail is critical, the listener immediately recognizes that some confusion has disrupted the listening process and clarification is requested. Although the easy listening is momentarily disrupted, the relationship is not disrupted. There is a powerful attachment during easy listening that both participants wish to continue. Forgiveness over minor lapses of attention comes readily.

Attention during easy listening is effortless and does not require 100 percent of one's mental energy. The concept of total attentiveness is actually an oxymoron since such total focus is a psychological strain that compromises one's ability to be attentive. Easy listening does not require total attentiveness but, instead, relies on a relaxed dyadic interchange. Neither party is demanding the total focus of the other, yet each participant is more easily and freely giving a significant amount of attention to the other. Individuals who engage in monologues do not create the kind of easy listening that I am describing. Monologists may have the illusion that their partner is listening to them in a relaxed manner, but closer examination and feedback invariably contradicts this. Unfortunately, those who tend to monologue or lecture others usually do not seek out such feedback. It is difficult to engage in easy listening with individuals who treat each moment of life as a precious commodity that cannot be wasted on idle conversation or those who generally engage in every interaction with intense seriousness. Easy listening requires playfulness. Although I do succeed in developing intimate, often intense, relationships with patients and other individuals who are always serious, I would not describe these relationships as easy listening. When I have easy listening with someone, I find that our serious conversations are more relaxed—even though we are both aware and respectful of the seriousness of the topic. Easy listening contributes to an overall feeling of good rapport and mutual attunement, which impacts all aspects of the relationship.

When you are listening to someone with whom you have easy listening, you may anticipate the direction that their thoughts are going, but this does not create boredom. There is a mixture of the expected and the unexpected that keeps you interested but not confused. The speaker intuitively knows how much detail to provide the listener, and the listener knows how to ask for additional details without disrupting the speaker. Easy listening has much in common with being totally absorbed in a good book. Writers generally know how to keep the reader's interest with the right level of detail. Although there are times when writers provide laborious details to the reader, there are other times when the reader is expected to fill in the details with his or her imagination. Such details are automatically filled in by the mind, which detests a vacuum. The forces of entropy fill in the vacuum with projections from a wide range of related prior experience. And it generally does not matter that the details filled in by the reader or listener are "erroneous." When the rapport is going well and especially when it occurs easily, mismatched details do not distract from the overall feeling of attunement.

Communication always involves reading between the lines. When I have had the opportunity to listen to a tape recording of an analytic session in which a therapist and a patient had easy listening with one another, I have frequently been surprised to find that the two of them seem to have understood each other at moments when much of the content or nuance was ambiguous or confusing. I've had this feeling even when I was the therapist in the earlier recorded session. While I was totally immersed in the session, the patient's communication seemed absolutely crystal clear. As I later listened to the tape recording, I heard more ambiguity. I realized that I must have either projected my own thoughts into the ambiguity or been reading the mind of the person to whom I was listening. As I listened further to the recorded session, it appeared that whatever I was projecting into the ambiguity was an accurate or at least empathic reading of the intended meaning of the patient. As I listened to this tape recording, I was impressed with my own telepathic powers. I generally explain this telepathy by reminding myself that communication is a complex multimodal, here-and-now dyadic experience that cannot be recreated in a laboratory or accurately analyzed from a tape recording at a later time. The grandiosity I felt in response to my successful mind reading was short-lived. As I listened to a session with another patient, it was apparent that I had filled in all of the ambiguity in a misbegotten manner, which led the conversation astray and left the patient feeling misunderstood. With patients with whom I do not have easy listening, I am more successful as an analyst when I remind myself that I need them to dot their i's and cross their t's. The alternative is communications pandemonium.

Easy listening can feel a little like reading the mind of the other. You anticipate the ends of sentences, but you do not feel impatient. Occasionally, you may complete a thought for the other or at least add onto one during a pause, which demonstrates your attentiveness, and generally, your addition is experienced as empathic and connected, not as an interruption.[4] Although some people seem to maintain easy listening without adding onto each other's thoughts, I have generally found that the rapport and connection is strengthened through the occasional cross-fertilization of your thoughts into theirs.[5]

As we listen to others, we are always engaged in some degree of anticipation as to where the speaker's train of thought, as well as particular sentences, are going. Such anticipation sets us up for humor and a sense of irony. As we are listening, if we are feeling defensive, our anticipation is used in the service of helping us to prepare a retort (or an interpretation if we are in the role of analyst), though this always detracts from the listening process and generally does not lead to effective retorts or interpretations. In contrast, the anticipation of the speaker's thoughts plays a positive role in easy listening. The listener is moving at the same pace as the speaker. No one particular word or shift in thought derails the listening. Each sentence acts as a setup for the next. Indeed, the sentences and thoughts blur into one another. The speaker is directing the listener in a manner that holds the interest of the listener and gently guides him or her to a general vicinity before moving to more specific locales. Although the listener may have had no idea where he or she was heading just minutes before, by the time the speaker completes the thought process, there are

---

[4] Frank (1997), in discussing inadvertent self-revelations, presented clinical material in which, during a patient's pause "to find the words to characterize a particular exchange" (p. 296), the analyst decided to offer a phrase that might fit the patient's experience. Although Frank described his adding onto the patient's material as often being experienced as empathic, he does appear to be apologetic in describing his behavior. My sense is that this type of interacting in which the analyst adds onto a patient's material during a pause may well be construed by the analytic community as being too intrusive, perhaps the result of the analyst being too psychologically immersed in or not distant enough from the patient. I view this type of interaction as an expression of the mutual interpenetration that occurs during easy listening.

[5] Adding onto each other's thoughts contributes to and results from the blurring of boundaries that occurs with regard to who is the owner or originator of particular aspects of the thought process. With some patients, I experience a clear message not to intrude on their thought process. Others welcome such "intrusions"; indeed the intrusion is experienced as an intimate gesture. I find that there is significant variation in the frequency and degree of cross-fertilization (i.e., my additions to their thoughts and theirs to mine) that occurs with different patients. When working with patients on the couch, for example, I rarely add onto patient's thoughts in progress. Without face-to-face contact, I am less likely to comfortably and intuitively know when such an addition is welcome.

no sudden surprises, not unless the intention of the communication was to surprise the listener. The speaker has carried the listener along, and the listener arrives just where the speaker intended, sometimes getting there moments ahead of the speaker.

I suspect that this tendency to fill in blanks is what helps listeners when they are briefly distracted. Whatever is missed is embedded in a more complex, seamless communication and can usually be filled in rather handily by someone who has been following and understanding the entire communication. When I am engaged in easy listening, my mind may drift temporarily to related associations. Such associations are my own personal recollections and reactions triggered by and in resonance with the conversation (Searles, 1979; Jacobs, 1991). These associations tend to illuminate or expand upon the communication just received and are usually quickly woven into the ongoing dialogue. When I am listening to someone with whom I do not have easy listening, my mind is more likely to drift to associations that do not resonate with and are not easily woven into the conversation. Indeed, these associations are more connected to how I'm not engaged in the conversation, to why I'm not engaged in the conversation, or to someplace where I'd rather be. I am being engaged by the conversation in the sense that I am being impacted by what is being said, but I am not being engaged in a relaxed easy listening mode.

How do we read the mind of another? Reading the mind of another involves a profound and deep empathy, the kind of empathy that requires a merging and resonating of psyches. The precondition for reading the mind of another is that you are listening so effortlessly that you have actually turned your mind over to the other or to the experience. Although you have given over your mind to the other, you do not feel controlled by the other. Instead, you feel that you are engaging in a highly pleasurable intimacy. As the two of you are formulating your thoughts in resonance with one another, there is a seemingly telepathic connection between you. Psychotherapists of all persuasions tend to agree on the importance of open, honest, and clear communication and tend to react negatively to mind reading. Mature communication is viewed as requiring that each individual take responsibility for verbalizing his or her wishes, needs, and thoughts. Wishing to have your mind read is viewed as regressive, indicative of an infantile wish for a more primitive communication process, pathogenic of a young child's wish for an all-attentive parent. I would contend that human communication, especially intimate affective communication, frequently involves reading between the lines and thus involves some degree of mind reading. Survival requires it. The alternative would be incredibly time-consuming. When you have fairly consistent rapport with someone, you may not realize the extent to which you are both frequently reading between the lines of each other's communications. It is only when the communication process fails that it becomes apparent how ambiguous the communication had been. Mind reading, though a necessary aspect of communication, is obviously quite fallible.

EASY LISTENING AND SELFOBJECT EXPERIENCE

There is a magical quality to easy listening that provides both participants with a sense of specialness. Sexuality also has this magical quality, as does humor. Perhaps this is because easy listening, sexuality, and humor are all propelled by unconscious processes and all tend to involve a shift in self-state from the responsible adult who is governed by judgments and censors to the playful child who is more capable of relaxation, spontaneity, and magical thinking. The kind of relaxed, easy listening discussed in this chapter creates a magnetic field around its participants. Once immersed in easy listening, the participants resist pulling away from such a conversation or experience. One can easily lose one's sense of time. Easy listening has the kind of magical, healing power that one wants to hold onto, indeed needs to hold onto. An abrupt break in easy listening can feel like an assault on the entire (magical) relational experience. In order to maintain the intimacy (and selfobject enhancement) of the easy listening experience, each of the participants is likely to engage in defensive operations aimed at fostering the continuation of the easy listening. This contributes to why empathic disruptions in psychoanalytic treatment are frequently experienced as occurring abruptly. Both participants often ignore the precursors of whatever conflict is developing in the hope that the interaction will continue without interruption. Finally, the intersubjective problems cross a threshold and the dismissal of the conflict is no longer a viable option. Both participants may be shaken by the power and abruptness of the disruption while also quickly realizing that there was a history to the intersubjective experience that was not being adequately attended to. The wish to continue easy listening organizes our attention and keeps certain aspects of experience out of awareness.

I have described easy listening in an attempt to capture my experience of a consistent selfobject transference with certain patients with whom the selfobject transference was developed and maintained rather easily. When I am engaged in easy listening, the selfobject transference is operating so well that it requires virtually no attention. Analyst and patient generally focus upon the patient's life, past and present, including whatever is going on in the transference, but this discussion does not disrupt the easy listening or the selfobject transference. Regardless of what content is being addressed, when easy listening is maintained, this is because of the *process,* namely, patient and analyst are experiencing consistent selfobject enhancement through their interaction with one another. It is the consistency of the selfobject experience that enables the easy listening to proceed without disruption. This includes the consistency of both the selfobject experience of the patient and the selfobject experience of the analyst.

THE SELFOBJECT NEEDS OF THE ANALYST

Recent literature on countertransference from a self psychological perspective has emphasized the importance of the selfobject needs of the analyst. Bacal and Thomson (1996) have written:

> When a patient becomes seriously disrupted, the analyst's selfobject needs may become significantly frustrated; in particular, the analyst may experience a loss of the sense of efficacy. He may also experience dysphoric affects such as anger, inadequacy, disappointment in himself, and shame [p. 23].

In an earlier paper, Thomson (1991) wrote:

> In psychoanalytic therapy, the empathic bond functions (or fails to function) in both directions. Each partner is continually organizing and being organized by the other. There is thus a mutual process that results in the perpetual formation of new intersubjective fields. The analyst, whether aware of it or not from his vantage point, is expecting the patient to contribute to his own self-regulation via self-object ties [p. 84].

The idea that the patient contributes to the analyst's selfobject functioning has also been commented on by Wolf (1979), Lee (1988), and Stolorow (1995). If the analyst is acquiring selfobject experience through his or her work as an analyst, then the analyst is also vulnerable to disruption as a result of his or her interactions with patients. Schwaber (1983, 1986, 1992) has written extensively about defensive processes utilized by analysts to avoid potential disruptions in their own functioning. Schwaber has described in detail how the patient's perceptions, especially when the patient's functioning has been disrupted, can be extremely ego-dystonic and disruptive to the analyst. The analyst, however immersed he or she may be in the patient's psychological world, often opts to quickly distance himself from the patient's perceptions, striving to anchor himself in his own alternative view of reality. The patient is often disrupted by an unconscious communication or behavior from the analyst, which the analyst needs to quickly deny in order to continue feeling secure in his or her role as the good, caring provider. Stolorow and Atwood (1992) have also emphasized that many therapists have a strong need to maintain their view of themselves as good, caring analysts.

Perhaps the best model for the interaction of the selfobject experience of patient and analyst comes from the work of Beebe, Jaffe, and Lachmann (1992) on the reciprocal mutual influence that occurs between caregiver and infant as it has been applied to the analytic setting (Lachmann and Beebe, 1996). Reciprocity and mutual influence have also been discussed by Slavin and Kriegman (1992, 1998), Aron (1996), and Aron and Bushra (1998) and are integrated into theories of intersubjectivity (Stolorow et al., 1987; Stolorow and Atwood, 1992; Orange et al., 1997) and motivational systems (Lichtenberg, Lachmann, Fosshage, 1992, 1996). The selfobject needs of patient and analyst exist in an intersubjective field of reciprocal mutual influence in which patient and analyst are both being directly affected by fluctuations in the other's self experience.

CASE MATERIAL: A CLINICAL VIGNETTE

In my experience, with each particular patient, I am drawn into his or her psychological world with some degree of immersion and some degree of separateness, or to use Bacal's (1997) term, there is a varying degree of psychic distance. The ebb and flow in psychic distance that occurs from session to session and within each session is a function of a wide range of transference and countertransference issues that impact the immersion and the separateness. The totality of the analyst's prior relational experience, including the history and patterning of his or her selfobject experiences, impacts the extent to which he or she becomes immersed or remains separate from each particular patient at any given moment during the analytic enterprise. In order to illustrate the analyst's experience of easy listening, I will now describe a case in which I tended to become highly immersed in a patient's psychological life, including some of my countertransference experiences during the easy listening and during a disruption.

Jane, a 30-year-old attractive female, entered twice-a-week psychoanalytic treatment as a result of an impending divorce and recurring career problems. From the beginning of treatment, I found that I could rather easily and consistently understand her and that my responses were experienced by her as emotionally attuned and mirroring. A selfobject transference developed fairly quickly with both mirroring and idealizing aspects (Kohut, 1971, 1977, 1984). With the development of a selfobject transference, not only was she strengthened, but I also experienced an elevation in my self-esteem. She is the kind of patient who validates me as a good listener and as an overall empathic human being.

Over the course of the first few months of treatment, I became increasingly immersed in her psychological world. I would often find that I was deeply immersed within moments of a session beginning. In general, she did not have to tell me what she was feeling. Her feelings were obvious. She is the kind of patient with whom emotional attunement comes so easily that the analyst is free to follow his or her own associations without being particularly concerned about missing part of the patient's presentation. The entire listening process is relaxed when rapport and empathy come so easily. Jane developed an idealizing transference, which facilitated selfobject experience for both patient and analyst. Jane was strengthened through her idealization of me, and I received significant mirroring through being idealized. Jane helped me to feel like the analyst that I wanted to be. Her mood was elevated on the days of her sessions, and so was mine.[6] During this process of easy listening, there was a significant amount of intimate emotional contact between us in which Jane felt known by me and I felt that I knew her. Although the manifest content of the analytic sessions had been almost exclusively focused on Jane's subjectivity, analyst and patient were both having a positive impact upon each other's psychic functioning.

Six months into treatment, Jane came to her session more upset than I had previously seen her. Jane was upset about a conflict that she was having with her husband. While trying to explain all of the reasons why she was upset, she became increasingly intellectualized. In response to her diminished affect, I said, "I think that the most important thing is for you to just let yourself be upset. The understanding or explaining of it can come later." Jane began to sob. Within a few minutes, her sobbing stopped. She then began to talk through her tears, providing more information that helped to clarify how and why she had been so upset. I experienced the session as productive, not only because more emotion was expressed than usual, but also

[6] There is a significant difference in the power of the selfobject experience for the patient and for the analyst. This patient, for example, reported that her sessions strengthened her and that this "carried over" until the next session, which was 3 or 4 days later. The elevated self-esteem that I experienced was short-lived as I entered my next session and found my sense of self subject to additional impact. By the end of the day, however, her impact upon me carried a very positive weight when the cumulative effect of my day's work was tabulated.

because I had the sense that new possibilities were created, namely, that there was a freeing of spontaneous expression and a lessening of intellectual control. This shift continued into subsequent sessions. Meanwhile, the selfobject transference was deepening.

Three months later, I discovered additional meaning and importance of this session. Jane was upset in session about a friend of hers at work who had just been passed over for promotion. I asked her whether she felt an identification with her friend and was afraid that she would also be passed over. She replied, "Not really," but her response seemed stilted. The session continued and seemed to be productive, but I began to realize that the session was moving at a slower pace than usual. I also found myself with a sinking feeling, which usually indicates a shift in the intersubjective field. Such a feeling, which tends to impact me on a visceral level, is often my first experience that something is off in a session. My sense of self was being impacted, signaling to me that there was a disruption in the patient's selfobject experience. Something was not right, but I did not have a handle on it. Was it my question? When she was describing her friend working so hard at work and not being appreciated, was she also making a reference to our relationship? My ability to listen so easily to her while feeling immersed in her subjective experience had been disrupted. Was there something in what Jane was saying about her friend that threw me? I could not determine whether I had moved away from her and stopped understanding her or whether I had upset her, causing her to move away from me and leaving me feeling that I didn't understand her. I was all over the place. I was also aware that I had become more subdued. I had lost my ability to be empathic, or so it seemed. Within moments, Jane became quiet. I could not decide who was affecting who. Even such a question indicates that my functioning has been significantly disrupted. In a better state, it is unlikely that I would have been so concerned about differentiating what is me and what is the patient or with questions as to whose behavior came first. Finally, I said to her, "Is there something in the session that upset you?" Jane paused and then responded, "Yes. I think so. I think I was thrown by your question about whether I was identifying with Sally. It just came from nowhere. It seemed out of character. One of the things that I love about being here is that you usually encourage me to stick with my feelings and not focus so much on understanding. Your question really threw me. It was in direct contradiction to how you usually are. I answered your question because I thought it was a simple question deserving a simple answer. The whole experience was weird. Your question struck me as odd, but I assumed you must have had a reason for asking it. I think it upset me more than I realized at the time. I found myself thinking too much about what I was saying. It became a chore to talk. That's probably why I became quiet."

As Jane spoke, I felt calmer and more grounded. She had provided some clarification of my distress, which helped me to restore my sense of self. My thoughts then turned to the session 3 months ago when I had encouraged her to express her feelings without undue concern for processing them and to an article that I had just read by Jacobs (1996) in which he discussed the issue of analytic candidates being accused of being "too therapeutic" when they did not maintain the "appropriate" therapeutic distance. As I listened to Jane, I wondered whether I had been "too therapeutic" during that session 3 months earlier. Was it a mistake to be so encouraging of feelings? Did I intend to give her the message (3 months ago) that understanding was secondary to emotional expression? In any case, that was the message that she had received. I wondered whether such a message was a good message for her analysis. Although some degree of self-doubt may be useful, especially when confronted with a disruption in the therapeutic relationship, the barrage of questions that I was asking myself indicated that the recovery of my selfobject functioning had been only partial. Later, when I had fully recovered from the disruption, these same questions were less overwhelming. No, I had not been "too therapeutic." Yes, it was therapeutically correct (from my vantage point) to encourage affect, even if this occurs at the expense of understanding. And furthermore, I remind myself that empathic failures and therapeutic disruptions are inevitable, even with a patient such as Jane with whom I have such an easy and stable rapport.[7]

Prior to the disruption, Jane's treatment had focused almost exclusively on the present. Although the past would be referenced, her childhood had not been brought into the analysis in a meaningful way. As a result of this disruption, a window was opened into aspects of Jane's childhood that had not been previously verbalized or explored. Jane was the only child of two parents (both academics) who spoke to her as an adult from an early age and expected her to respond as an adult. This pattern intensified after her parents divorced in her pre-teens and she became each of their best friends. In her treatment, Jane had felt

---

[7] It is interesting that I had to remind myself that empathic failures are inevitable. With a patient such as Jane with whom empathy comes "easily," empathic immersion can potentially be deep and sustained. When deeply immersed in easy listening, one does not conceive of empathic failures. Although the empathic failures will be infrequent, when they do occur, they are more likely to cut to the core of my selfobject functioning. Jane was idealizing me, and when I was deeply immersed in her subjectivity, I felt like a wonderful idealized version of myself. Consequently, the disruption of the selfobject transference (even such a "manageable" disruption) had a major jarring impact on my selfobject functioning.

relieved when I suggested that she did not have to try to understand her feelings, that it was okay to just have her feelings, and that understanding would follow. To be allowed to just feel was equivalent to being allowed to be a child. To have to explain was to reenact her adult position with her parents. This pattern, as it had been woven into her character structure, became a central issue in her treatment. I have also come to realize that one of the reasons why I have been able to have such easy listening with Jane is that she had learned from an early age how to be a good listener. You can only have easy listening with someone who is also a good listener. Easy listening requires a mutual (mostly unconscious) attentiveness to each other's process. In her sessions, Jane was trying to be my best friend even as I was listening to her (and thinking that I was being the good parent). For Jane, being the best friend of her parents (and analyst) was a gratifying position, even though it contributed to a premature loss of childhood. Together, we were reenacting Jane's childhood. Thus, easy listening, like all aspects of character structure, is shaped by healthy strivings and pathological adaptations.

DISCUSSION, SUMMARY, AND CONCLUSIONS

Listening is a relational experience that can only be understood within the context of the relationship within which it is occurring. A lengthy description of easy listening was provided as a vehicle for exploring my experience with nondifficult patients of extensive empathic immersion, including the impact that this immersion has on how selfobject disruptions occur and are experienced by the analyst. During easy listening, analyst and patient allow themselves to gravitate toward a relaxed intimacy with a blurring of the boundaries between self and other, but neither participant seems to be concerned about this blurring, at least not while the easy listening is flourishing. A patient was presented with whom there had been a significant amount of sustained easy listening and with whom empathic failures were infrequent. With such a patient, the analyst experienced significant pleasurable psychological immersion. Such a case was presented in order to explore the impact of a stable selfobject transference upon the analyst's sense of self. A disruption in the selfobject transference was described, and the impact of this disruption on the functioning of the analyst was explored. I now wish to highlight certain observations.

Easy Listening and Selfobject Experience

Easy listening involves recognizing and enjoying the relaxed intimacy that is possible in human relationships, including the analytic relationship. Easy listening tends to rely on concordant identifications between analyst and patient (Racker, 1968), which follows self psychology's emphasis on empathy and similarity (Mermelstein, in press). Easy listening evolves in tandem with the development of a selfobject transference. Although all aspects of the intersubjective field and interpersonal interactions impact how and when a selfobject transference develops, when a selfobject transference unfolds effortlessly, there may not be much reflection about the patient's or the analyst's selfobject needs that are being attended to. We often only become aware of certain aspects of a selfobject transference or of the underlying relational matrix after an empathic failure occurs as we begin to more consciously attend to aspects of the relational matrix that had previously been neglected or avoided.

Easy listening and the relaxed relational context within which it occurs have much in common with play, more specifically, dyadic play. The creation of a relaxed easy rapport between analyst and analysand parallels the creation of a playspace, or *Spielraum,* as described by Meares (1990). When there is a rupture in the analytic relationship, there is a shift, often an abrupt shift to hard listening, that is, work.[8] As Meares points out, "Play ends as a consequence of alerting stimuli" (p. 86). When the shift occurs from play to work, the other becomes an object, attention is directed outward, and the child becomes more goal-directed in his or her engagement with the world.

Curative Factors in Psychoanalytic Treatment

Within self psychology, there is an ongoing debate surrounding the relative importance of the following three curative factors that are placed in juxtaposition with one another: the curative power of sustained selfobject experience; the curative power of the disruption-restoration process and the "transmuting internalization" that occurs as a result of this process being worked through; and the curative power of increased self awareness or insight, which Kohut subdivided into the "understanding only" and the "explaining" phases of treatment. Although this chapter highlights and explores the power of sustained selfobject experience, the clinical material that was presented emphasizes how these curative factors are interrelated and mutually

---

[8] By hard listening, I am referring to the wide range of listening that I must do with patients with whom I do not have easy listening and with patients when easy listening is disrupted. Hard listening requires more *consciously* focused attention. From the analyst's vantage point, the difference between easy and hard listening is primarily a difference in the analyst's self-state.

reinforcing. A prolonged selfobject transference strengthens the analytic relationship and strengthens the patient. This in turn facilitates the working through of the disruption–restoration process. Conversely, each time that the disruption–restoration process is successful in repairing the patient's self–selfobject bond with the analyst, there is an expansion and strengthening of selfobject usage. The strengthening of the analytic relationship also facilitates greater analytic exploration and understanding. And when the analytic dyad is successful at achieving greater understanding, this in turn validates and strengthens the selfobject transference and the analytic relationship. Thus, all three curative aspects of self psychological analytic treatment work in synchrony to strengthen the analytic relationship and facilitate analytic understanding.

Easy listening involves the creation of a relaxed dyadic interchange that reduces the psychic distance between self and other. The case material suggests that the relaxation of boundaries between patient and analyst contributed to the creation of an analytic *Spielraum,* which ultimately facilitated all three curative factors: the selfobject transference was strengthened; disruptions occurred and were worked on successfully; psychoanalytic reflection and insight were occurring throughout the easy listening and during the disruption–restoration process. Although this reduction in psychic distance was useful in this analysis, I am not recommending that analysts opt for such extensive psychological immersion with all of their patients. I believe that for each patient–analyst dyad, there is an optimal psychic distance, or a range of distances that are optimal, and that this distance is negotiated and renegotiated throughout analytic treatment.[9]

The Selfobject Functioning of the Analyst

The selfobject functioning of patient and analyst are intertwined. A disruption in the selfobject functioning of either impacts the selfobject functioning of the other. The greater the degree of empathic immersion by the analyst into the psychological life of the patient, the greater the potential for the analyst's selfobject functioning to be disrupted. The clinical material focused on how the selfobject functioning of the analyst is impacted by the self-state of the patient and how the analyst's

---

[9] I do not wish to imply that the analyst can simply make a judgment about how much psychic distance is optimal and that it is in the analyst's control to create this distance. The issue of how psychic distance is cocreated is complex, touching upon issues of psychoanalytic technique, enactments, and the entire relational matrix of the cotransference, much of which is unconscious.

awareness of a disruption in his or her own selfobject experience is often the first communication available to the analyst, signaling that there has been a disruption in the patient's selfobject experience. These signals included the analyst's experience of the session moving more slowly than usual, his "sinking feeling," and his overall feeling that the ambiance in the room had changed.

The shift from easy listening to hard listening (and the concomitant selfobject disruption) was experienced by the analyst as an abrupt shift. In retrospect, it is fairly easy to find precursors to the abrupt shift and conclude that patient and analyst were colluding to avoid dealing with problems that were developing in their relationship. Such an analysis pathologizes the intimacy and mutual psychological immersion that existed within the analytic relationship. Analyst and patient were benefiting from, indeed enjoying, the analytic relationship during the easy listening. Insofar as experience is organized affectively (Socarides and Stolorow, 1984/85; Spezzano, 1993), whatever material was ignored while the easy listening was flourishing was ignored because it did not fit into the patient's and analyst's dominant affective experience. Such material only becomes relevant when it is so profound that it shifts the dominant affective organization of the patient or the analyst (Mermelstein, 1998). After the dominant affective organization shifts, material that had previously been relegated to the background may now be highlighted within the new organization. Easy listening creates significant potential for surprise. During easy listening, the primary therapeutic work is occurring through the selfobject transference. Disruptions are not anticipated. Indeed, the precursors may be totally dismissed, with both participants wishing to continue the easy listening. There is time for the analysis of disruptions when they occur and in their aftermath. During the easy listening, the relationship is strengthened and the possibility of working collaboratively on future therapeutic conflicts is enhanced.

REFERENCES

Aron, L. (1996), *A Meeting of Minds: Mutuality in Psychoanalysis*. Hillsdale, NJ: The Analytic Press.

——— & Bushra, A. (1998), Mutual regression: Altered states in the psychoanalytic situation. *J. Amer. Psychoanal. Assn.*, 46:389–412.

Bacal, H. (1997), The analyst's subjectivity—how it can illuminate the analysand's experience: Commentary on Susan Sands's paper. *Psychoanal. Dial.*, 7:669–681.

——— & Thomson, P. (1996), The psychoanalyst's selfobject needs and the effect of their frustration on the treatment: A new view of countertransference. In: *Basic Ideas Reconsidered: Progress in Self Psychology, Vol. 12,* ed. A. Goldberg. Hillsdale, NJ: The Analytic Press, pp. 17–35.

Beebe, B, Jaffe, J. & Lachmann, F. (1992), A dyadic systems view of communication. In: *Relational Perspectives in Psychoanalysis,* ed. N. Skolnick & S. Warshaw. Hillsdale, NJ: The Analytic Press, pp. 61–81.

——— Stern, D. & Jaffe, J. (1979), The kinesic rhythm of mother–infant interactions. In: *Of Speech and Time: Temporal Patterns in Interpersonal Contexts,* ed. A. W. Siegman & S. Felstein. Hillsdale, NJ: Lawrence Erlbaum, pp. 23–34.

Bion, W. (1957), Differentiation of the psychotic from the non-psychotic personalities. In: *Second Thoughts.* New York: Aronson, 1967, pp. 43–64.

Bromberg, P. M. (1998), *Standing in the Spaces.* Hillsdale, NJ: The Analytic Press.

Fosshage, J. L. (1995), Countertransference as the analyst's experience of the analysand: Influence of listening perspectives. *Psychoanal. Psychol.,* 12:375–391.

——— (1997), Listening/experiencing perspectives and the quest for a facilitating responsiveness. In: *Conversations in Self Psychology: Progress in Self Psychology, Vol. 13,* ed. A. Goldberg. Hillsdale, NJ: The Analytic Press, pp. 33–55.

Frank, K. A. (1997), The analyst's inadvertent self-revelations. *Psychoanal. Dial.,* 7:281–314.

Freud, A. (1936), *The Ego and the Mechanisms of Defense.* New York: International Universities Press, 1946.

Freud, S. (1912), Recommendations to physicians practising psycho-analysis. *Standard Edition,* 12:109–120. London: Hogarth Press, 1958.

——— (1913), On beginning the treatment (Further recommendations on the technique of psycho-analysis: I). *Standard Edition,* 12:121–144. London: Hogarth Press, 1958.

Ghent, E. (1990), Masochism, submission, surrender. *Contemp. Psychoanal.,* 26:108–136.

Greenson, R. R. (1967), *The Technique and Practice of Psychoanalysis, Vol. 1.* New York: International Universities Press.

Grotstein, J. (1981), *Splitting and Projective Identification.* New York: Aronson.

Hoffman, I. Z. (1983), The patient as interpreter of the analyst's experience. *Contemp. Psychoanal.,* 19:389–422.

——— (1991), Discussion: Toward a social-constructivist view of the psychoanalytic situation. *Psychoanal. Dial.,* 1:74–105.

——— (1998), *Ritual and Spontaneity in the Psychoanalytic Process.* Hillsdale, NJ: The Analytic Press.

Jacobs, T. J. (1991), *The Use of the Self.* Madison, CT: International Universities Press.

——— (1996), On therapeutic interventions in the analysis of certain "unanalyzable" patients: Lessons from child and adolescent technique. *Contemp. Psychoanal.,* 32:215–235.

Kernberg, O. F. (1987), Projection and projective identification: Developmental and clinical aspects. In: *Projection, Identification, and Projective Identification,* ed. J. Sandler. Madison, CT: International Universities Press, pp. 93–116.

Khan, M. (1979), *Alienation in Perversions.* New York: International Universities Press.

Klein, M. (1929), Personification in the play of children. In: *Love, Guilt and Reparation and Other Works: 1921–1945,* London: Hogarth Press, 1975, pp. 248–257.

——— (1946), Notes on some schizoid mechanisms. *Internat. J. Psycho-Anal.*, 27:99–110.

——— (1975a), *Envy and Gratitude and Other Works, 1946–1963*. London: Hogarth Press.

——— (1975b), *Love, Guilt, and Reparation and Other Works, 1921–1945*. London: Hogarth Press.

Kohut, H. (1959), Introspection, empathy, and psychoanalysis. *J. Amer. Psychoanal. Assn.*, 7:459–483.

——— (1971), *The Analysis of the Self*. New York: International Universities Press.

——— (1977), *The Restoration of the Self*. New York: International Universities Press.

——— (1981), On empathy. In: *The Search for the Self, Vol. 4,* ed. P. H. Ornstein. Madison, CT: International Universities Press, pp. 525–535.

——— (1984), *How Does Analysis Cure?* Hillsdale, NJ: The Analytic Press.

Lachmann, F. M. & Beebe, B. (1996), The contribution of self- and mutual regulation to therapeutic action. In: *Basic Ideas Reconsidered: Progress in Self Psychology, Vol. 12,* ed. A. Goldberg. Hillsdale, NJ: The Analytic Press, pp. 123–140.

Lee, R. (1988), Reverse selfobject experience. *Amer. J. Psychother.*, 42:416–424.

Lichtenberg, J. D., Lachmann, F. M. & Fosshage, J. (1992), *Self and Motivational Systems: Towards a Theory of Technique*. Hillsdale, NJ: The Analytic Press.

——— ——— & ——— (1996), *The Clinical Exchange: Techniques Derived from Self and Motivational Systems*. Hillsdale, NJ: The Analytic Press.

McDougall, J. (1980), *Plea for a Measure of Abnormality*. New York: International Universities Press.

Meares, R. (1990), The fragile "Spielraum": An approach to transmuting internalization. In: *The Realities of Transference: Progress in Self Psychology, Vol. 6,* ed. A. Goldberg. Hillsdale, NJ: The Analytic Press, pp. 69–89.

Mermelstein, J. J. (1998), The figure–ground relationship of the selfobject and repetitive dimensions of the transference. In: *The World of Self Psychology: Progress in Self Psychology, Vol. 14,* ed. A. Goldberg. Hillsdale, NJ: The Analytic Press, pp. 33–62.

——— (in press), The role of concordance and complementarity in psychoanalytic treatment. *Psychoanal. Psychol.*

Ogden, T. H. (1982), *Projective Identification and Psychotherapeutic Technique*. New York: Aronson.

Orange, D. M., Atwood, G. E. & Stolorow, R. D. (1997), *Working Intersubjectively*. Hillsdale, NJ: The Analytic Press.

Racker, H. (1968), *Transference and Countertransference*. New York: International Universities Press.

Reik, T. (1949), *Listening with the Third Ear: The Inner Experience of a Psychoanalyst*. New York: Farrar, Straus and Co.

Schwaber, E. A. (1981), Empathy: A mode of analytic listening. *Psychoanal. Inq.*, 1:357–392.

——— (1983), Psychoanalytic listening and psychic reality. *Internat. Rev. Psycho-Anal.*, 10:379–392.

——— (1992), Countertransference: The analyst's retreat from the patient's vantage point. *Internat. J. Psycho-Anal.*, 73:349–361.

Searles, H. (1979), *Countertransference and Related Subjects.* New York: International Universities Press.

Slavin, M. O. & Kriegman, D. (1992), *The Adaptive Design of the Human Psyche.* New York: Guilford.

——— & ——— (1998), Why the analyst needs to change: Toward a theory of conflict, negotiation and mutual influence in the therapeutic process. *Psychoanal. Dial.*, 8:247–284.

Socarides, D. D. & Stolorow, R. (1984/85), Affects and selfobjects. *The Annual of Psychoanalysis,* 12/13:105–119. Madison, CT: International Universities Press.

Spezzano, C. (1993), *Affect in Psychoanalysis: A Clinical Synthesis.* Hillsdale, NJ: The Analytic Press.

Stolorow, R. D. (1995), An intersubjective view of self psychology, *Psychoanal. Dial.*, 5:393–399.

——— & Atwood, G. E. (1992), *Contexts of Being: The Intersubjective Foundations of Psychological Life.* Hillsdale, NJ: The Analytic Press.

——— Brandchaft, B. & Atwood, G. E. (1987), *Psychoanalytic Treatment: An Intersubjective Approach.* Hillsdale, NJ: The Analytic Press.

Sullivan, H. S. (1953), *The Interpersonal Theory of Psychiatry.* New York: Norton.

——— (1954), *The Psychiatric Interview.* New York: Norton.

Thomson, P. G. (1991), Countertransference in an intersubjective perspective: An experiment. In: *The Evolution of Self Psychology: Progress in Self Psychology, Vol. 7,* ed. A. Goldberg. Hillsdale, NJ: The Analytic Press, pp. 75–92.

Wolf, E. S. (1979), Transference and countertransference in the analysis of the disorders of the self. *Contemp. Psychoanal.,* 15:577–594.

Chapter 11

Dimensions of Experience in Relationship Seeking

Mary E. Connors

The concept of the selfobject holds a central place in self psychological theory. Bacal (1994) stated that it is generally agreed that the selfobject concept is "the cornerstone of the self-psychological perspective in psychoanalysis" (p. 21). Ornstein (1991) characterized the selfobject concept as the single element of decisive difference between self psychology and other psychoanalytic models. Basch (1994) noted that thinking in terms of selfobject needs furnished a much-needed corrective to instinct theory and enabled the psychoanalytic method to be applied with much greater success to many more patients. He regarded the concept of the selfobject as the most important contribution to our understanding and treatment of psychological issues since Freud's discovery of the psychoanalytic method and the transference. Goldberg (1998) similarly portrayed the selfobject concept as Kohut's major theoretical contribution and the idea of the selfobject transference as Kohut's central contribution to clinical work.

Much has been written about this exceptionally important construct since Kohut's (1971) early description of providing a function for a patient rather than being viewed as an object of love and hate. Kohut's final book (1984) defined selfobject as "that dimension of our experience of another person that relates to this person's functions in shoring up our self" (pp. 49–50). Similarly, Wolf (1988) stressed that the selfobject is neither self nor object, but a subjective experience in which a more cohesive self is evoked or maintained. This emphasis on intrapsychic experience relating to self-cohesion as the essential element of the selfobject concept has been repeatedly stressed.

However, as Goldberg (1998) noted, there has been continuing controversy within self psychology concerning whether any concepts of selfobject or object are needed that do not center exclusively on the self's internal experience. Some self psychologists have argued strongly against any such addition. Ornstein (1991) stated that self psychology is not an object-relations theory and that it does not require any concept of the object other than the selfobject. This selfobject may be archaic or mature, but Ornstein stressed that, from the vantage point of self-experience, the other is always a selfobject. Ornstein further emphasized that self psychology is distinguished by its focus on sustained empathic immersion in the patient's subjective experience, which includes the experience of the other as a selfobject. He points out that, as self psychologists, we are concerned with the structural integrity of the self, meaning that our focus has moved beyond relationships per se to self-structures on which all relationships depend.

Rowe (1994) similarly cautioned against what he termed an "object-related focus" (p. 16), which shifts Kohut's original stress on the experience of the self-sustaining functions provided by another to an emphasis on the object as provider of the functions. He suggested that this change limits access to experience-near data and moves self psychology away from Kohut's original concept of the experience-near mode of observation as the path to further theory development.

This traditional self psychological emphasis on the self and its selfobjects has been critiqued by psychoanalytic theorists outside of self psychology, as well as those working within it. Greenberg and Mitchell (1983) characterized self psychology as having a narrow interpretive focus, stating that in Kohut's published case material developmentally significant persons appeared sketchy and shadowy and that the complexity of the parent–child relationship was reduced to a limited categorical scheme. Similarly, Gill (1994) posited that in self psychology the subject construes the object "in only a limited sector of subject–object interaction, namely, that of the selfobject" (p. 201).

Various self psychologists have dealt with what they perceived as the limitations in the traditional selfobject concept in diverse and creative ways. Basch (1991) raised the question of whether selfobjects are the only objects, suggesting that Kohut's original idea of the selfobject referred to a situation in which an experience with another compensated for a deficit in the self-structure. Basch suggested that the term *selfobject experience* be reserved for situations in which an endangered self is strengthened by the intervention of another but that use of the terms *object* or *object experience* better characterizes those occasions in which a cohesive self acting as a center of initiative is expressing itself affectively.

Bacal (1991) questioned whether we are always accurately describing our empathic experience of another by using the selfobject concept. He suggested that in our emphasis on the experience of selfobject functioning, we have lost sight of the object that provides it and the importance of that relationship. Drawing on the work of Bowlby about the importance of a particular other, Bacal proposed that we add to our concept of the selfobject the idea that this experience is embodied in a significant object. He further suggested (1994) that a selfobject relationship is best conceptualized as the intrapsychic experience of another who can be counted on to provide essential selfobject functions and one in which a relatively stable sense of the other's availability as a selfobject exists. He stressed that, since the beginning of self psychology, the selfobject concept has implied not merely need, but also the experience of a relationship.

Bacal (1995) further noted that one aspect of Kohut's formulations currently under revision is the view that the patient is looking for the impersonal function of the therapist as selfobject. He suggests that it typically is the function of a particular other that is sought. In contrast to Ornstein (1991), Bacal and Newman (1990) state that self psychology is in fact an object-relations theory, although they commented that self psychology's emphasis on intrapsychic experience has served to minimize the actions and the specificity of the object.

Stolorow (1992) described his concept of the intersubjective field, which he conceptualizes as possessing a higher level of generality than the notion of a self–selfobject relationship. This intersubjective field includes dimensions of experience other than the selfobject dimension, which refers to a specific bond being required for positively affecting an individual's sense of selfhood. Stolorow (1995) stresses that selfobject longings are one of several types of principles that unconsciously organize subjective worlds and suggests that selfobject and other dimensions of experience oscillate between figure and ground in a constantly shifting intersubjective context.

Lachmann and Beebe (1992) have postulated the concept of "representational configurations" to describe the themes that organize a patient's representations of past experiences or those transferences traditionally described in psychoanalytic writings as "object-related." They described these representational configurations as affectively laden descriptions of self and other, referring to qualities of self and other and their interrelationships. Lachmann and Beebe suggest that, in the treatment relationship, representations of experience exist along the dimension of representational configurations in addition to the selfobject dimension. They speculate that representational configurations provide the context for selfobject experiences, and in addition, selfobject experiences enable access to representational configurations.

Several authors have thus proposed revisions or additions to the traditional concept of the selfobject that focus more on the actual or perceived qualities of the object. In this chapter, I shall similarly postulate that self psychology could benefit from additional conceptualization of the object. More specifically, I cite the example of a destructive relationship to illustrate a phenomenon for which, in my opinion, the traditional selfobject concept may not provide the most useful or parsimonious explanation. I further suggest that some current work from another area of study, attachment theory, has potential to illuminate some aspects of this issue in a fashion very compatible with self psychology.

PROBLEMATIC RELATIONSHIPS AND ATTACHMENT THEORY

Clinically, we often observe the fact that some patients seek relationships with others that may be quite painful and destructive. Individuals frequently select and choose to remain in relationships that offer a paucity of selfobject experiences and an abundance of negative and abusive experiences. How do we explain the fact that individuals may not simply gravitate toward relationships with the most prolific dispensors of mirroring, idealizing, etc.? Or as the editors of *Psychoanalytic Dialogues* (Mitchell, 1995) articulated this issue to a group of self psychologists, how are we to understand the regeneration of painful experience in relationships? Many self psychologists may hold implicit ideas about transferences to new objects based on various earlier experiences, but as Fosshage has suggested (1995), our self psychological emphasis on developmental strivings and the needed dimension in relationships may have led us to pay insufficient attention to the repetitive dimension of ties to bad objects.

Intersubjectivity theorists (Stolorow, Brandchaft, and Atwood, 1987; Brandchaft, 1988, 1994; Stolorow, 1995) have articulated the idea that individuals seek to maintain ties with others (often frustrating or depriving parental figures) who are experienced as indispensable. Brandchaft (1994) proposed that individuals develop "structures of pathological accommodation," or organizing principles that protect the tie to the object, even at great cost to the self. Lessem (1996) elaborated the idea that our hopes and desires for selfobject relatedness are configured by the types of relational patterns that originally resulted in painful experiences. Bacal and Newman (1990) coined the term *bad selfobject* to denote a situation in which a selfobject stimulates a child's needs for responsiveness but fails to meet them.

Recent contributions have thus recognized that there may be dimensions of relatedness not thoroughly accounted for by traditional selfobject theory, including a propensity to maintain connection with important others despite the painful nature of the relationship. Although controversy exists over whether to classify such phenomena under the heading of selfobject experiences, self psychological theory increasingly has attended to what Mitchell (1988) termed the "adhesiveness" of bad object relationships, yet our understanding of such experiences is only beginning to be articulated. I propose that an existing compendium of research and theory on attachment may illuminate this area.

Bowlby's attachment theory (1969) centers around the idea of a bond between infant and caregiver that promotes the protection, survival, and felt-security of the infant. Bowlby proposed that inherent motivation exists for seeking proximity to a parent or parent-substitute who can serve as a source of security. The infant uses the attachment figure as a secure base from which to explore and will seek greater proximity under conditions of danger, stress, or novelty; the goal of the attachment system is maintaining the caregiver's accessibility and responsiveness (Kobak, 1999). Because attachment represents the infant's chief mechanism for ensuring survival, the attachment system is viewed as continually operating; at some level (which may be out of awareness) the relative balance of safety versus threat in the current situation is being monitored (Main, 1995). The infant or child actively organizes information concerning the attachment figure's availability, both in terms of physical proximity and typical responses, and regulates her or his behavior accordingly in order to maximize security.

I believe that a good deal of overlap exists between Bowlby's concept of attachment needs and self psychological conceptualizations of idealizing needs, in that both stress the requirement for connection with another who is seen as stronger, wiser, and more competent than the self and who can provide soothing and comfort. However, criteria for an attachment relationship (Ainsworth, 1989) include the following: the bond is persistent, emotionally significant, involves wishes for proximity to the other, and takes place in a very specific fashion with a particular individual. Moreover, the individual seeks security and comfort in the relationship and suffers distress at involuntary separation when proximity is desired. Thus, attachment theory places more emphasis on the provision of a sense of safety and security and the need for a particular attachment figure. The dimension of experience depicted in attachment theory might be seen as most similar to some self psychological descriptions of archaic selfobject needs.

Attachment theory would postulate, however, that this "archaic" need for safety and security is not limited to early childhood, but remains vital throughout life, similar to self psychological concepts of selfobject needs across the life span. This affirmation of the importance of attachment security "from the cradle to the grave" (Bowlby, 1969, p. 208) is a major tenet of attachment theory. An additional important feature of attachment theory is its exploration of individual differences in attachment patterns in childhood and the implications of this for later life.

PATTERNS OF ATTACHMENT

Individual differences in attachment patterns are thought to develop primarily from different sorts of experiences with attachment figures rather than from child temperament or other factors (Ainsworth et al., 1978). As Bowlby (1973) put it, individuals develop varied expectations of the availability and responsiveness of attachment figures that are "tolerably accurate reflections of the experiences those individuals have actually had" (p. 202). These expectations or internal representations (termed "internal working models" by Bowlby) guide future behavior. Attachment researchers have identified some relatively stable configurations of behavior in children that are associated with varying types of behaviors in parents, although as Belsky (1999) has noted, maternal sensitivity is an important, but not an exclusive, factor in the development of attachment security.

Securely attached children seem to have parents who are consistently available, sensitive, and responsive. These children show distress upon separation from an attachment figure but are quickly comforted upon reunion (Ainsworth et al., 1978) and seem to be able to use the caregiver as a safe base from which to explore. Psychologically healthier parents are more likely than parents who are less emotionally robust to have children who are securely attached to them (Belsky, 1999).

Researchers have also identified patterns of attachment that they termed insecure. One group of infants seemed to have mothers who were inconsistent, unpredictable, discouraging of autonomy, and insensitive, although they did display warmth at times (Ainsworth et al., 1978). These infants were observed to be preoccupied with their mothers when they were present and unable to focus on exploration. These infants exhibited great distress at a brief separation and at reunion alternated intense proximity seeking with displays of anger, including temper tantrums. This group has been termed ambivalent or resistant. They seem to be organized around having a single attentional focus on the attachment figure (Main, 1995).

Another group of insecure infants displays a very different pattern. Infants termed avoidant have been observed to have mothers who are consistently rejecting and rebuffing of their infants' bids for contact with them. These mothers seemed to avoid physical contact with their infants and withdrew from them when the infants showed distress (Ainsworth et al., 1978; Grossmann and Grossmann, 1991). In laboratory playroom settings these infants showed no response to brief separations from the mothers, interacted as readily with a stranger as with their mothers, and ignored their mothers upon reunion, often busying themselves with toys. Attachment behavior was absent, replaced with active avoidance of the attachment figure and a focus on the environment, but high levels of physiological arousal suggested that these infants were indeed stressed by separation (Main, 1995).

Recent research has identified another group of insecurely attached infants whose behavior does not seem to fit any organized pattern, but the complexities of the findings on this "disorganized/disoriented" group (Main and Solomon, 1986) across the life span are such that my focus in this chapter will be on the three "organized" groups.

Securely attached infants are able to utilize the attachment figure to help them regulate distress. They turn to the attachment figure, are comforted, and may resume exploration. The insecurely attached infants, however, must find a way to modulate affect in the absence of a secure bond to a regulating other. They have to evolve conditional strategies that enable them to preserve some degree of proximity to a problematic attachment figure (Main, 1995). Ambivalent infants attempt to manage this situation by constant activation of the attachment system; they are hypervigilant in attending to the caregiver's whereabouts and state of mind. Since these parents do respond to their children at times, the children seem to engage in intense displays of neediness and emotionality in attempts to obtain nurturance from inept or self-preoccupied caregivers. Avoidant infants, whose mothers are consistently rejecting, attempt to minimize distress by defocusing from the attachment figure whose rebuff is so expectable. They regulate the level of need that they display to an unavailable caregiver and distract themselves with attention to the nonrelational world.

Longitudinal studies of attachment patterns show significant continuity over time. Children who were rated as securely attached in infancy are socially competent, are able to concentrate on studies, show positive affect, and are resourceful (Egeland and Sroufe, 1981). Children observed to be insecure/ambivalent in infancy are described as needy, vulnerable, helpless, and likely to be victimized by other children (Troy and Sroufe, 1987). They continue to display exaggerated clinginess with parents coupled with overt displays of anger and at times lapse into infantile behavior (Main and Cassidy, 1988). Children rated as insecure/avoidant as infants are described as socially incompetent, hostile, withdrawn, noncompliant, and likely to victimize other children (Erickson, Sroufe, and Egeland, 1985; Troy and Sroufe, 1987). Differential responses among children from these three groups to a peer who had suffered a minor injury while playing were very telling: secure children tried to help the hurt child and/or summon the teacher, ambivalent children seemed to have difficulty differentiating between the hurt child's experience and their own, and avoidant children derogated the weeping child as a "crybaby" (Sroufe, cited in Karen, 1994).

Although Bowlby stressed the importance of attachment needs throughout life, few authors focused on attachment in adulthood until the 1980s, when Hazan and Shaver (1987) began a series of studies in which romantic love was conceptualized as an attachment process. Attachment in adults was thought to be similar to attachment in children in that adults also experience greater desire for proximity to their attachment figure when stressed, feel increased comfort in the presence of that person, and experience anxiety when the attachment figure is not available (Shaver, Hazan, and Bradshaw, 1988). These researchers postulated that variations in early experiences lead to fairly persistent differences in relational styles in adulthood and that the secure, ambivalent, and avoidant styles are manifested in adult romantic love.

These and similar studies have utilized self-report measures that attempt to assess attachment within a particular relationship. However, another approach was taken by Main and colleagues in their development of the Adult Attachment Interview (AAI; George, Kaplan, and Main, 1996). This extremely sophisticated interview is designed to assess a subject's state of mind regarding attachment by requiring him or her to produce and reflect upon attachment-related memories while simultaneously maintaining coherent and collaborative discourse with the interviewer (Hesse, 1999). Intriguing findings utilizing the AAI include indications of intergenerational transmission of attachment style; results from nearly 20 studies involving the AAI have found significant correspondence between a parent's attachment status and that parent's infant's attachment status, including studies in which parents were interviewed prior to the birth of their child (Hesse, 1999).

Adults rated as secure seem comfortable with their own emotions and with intimacy, can discuss relationships with significant others in a coherent fashion, and generally report satisfaction with their work life (Hazan and Shaver, 1990; Main, 1995). Adults classified as insecure/ambivalent are termed preoccupied in adulthood because they display excessive preoccupation and entanglement with parents and may be overtly angry or passive (Main, 1995). This group also reports that their intimate love relationships are characterized by idealization, jealousy, dependence, and intense reliance on partners (Feeney and Noller, 1990). Avoidant adults are also termed dismissive because they minimize the importance of relationship, are uncomfortable with intimacy, and become very involved with work pursuits (Feeney and Noller, 1990; Hazan and Shaver, 1990). They report that they do not remember much about their childhoods, assert their normality, and minimize the impact of relational experiences (Main, 1995).

INTEGRATION OF SELF PSYCHOLOGY AND ATTACHMENT FINDINGS

The implications of different attachment patterns for the development of the self are profound, since the attachment literature suggests that attachment-related experiences become internalized both in the form of personality functioning and in styles of relating. It is probable that a great deal of overlap exists between parental capacity to engender secure attachment and the ability to provide adequate selfobject experiences for the developing child, because they similarly require parental sensitivity and attunement. Securely attached adults seem most likely to have a cohesive and healthy self that can actualize its ambitions and goals and at the same time participate in close relationships. Securely attached adults are sensitive to their relational partners (Kobak and Hazan, 1991) and to their children (Hesse, 1999). Theoretically, one might predict that this group would have minimal vulnerability to fragmentation and the development of psychopathology, and in fact securely attached adults (as measured by the AAI) comprise a very small percentage of clinical samples (e.g., Fonagy et al., 1996).

Preoccupied adults are likely to be quite fragmentation-prone. Their parents seem to have been so embroiled in their own emotional difficulties that they were not able to serve as idealizable objects, resulting in deficits in self-soothing capacities. Some mirroring might have been provided in response to emotional caretaking of the fragile parents, but probably little positive reaction ensued for any independent competencies or the development of one's own self-agenda. As adults, these individuals struggle with intense affect states and experiences of need and dependency on others that are not likely to be met to their satisfaction. Preoccupied individuals feel unable to cope with life on their own, and "anything goes" in their efforts to secure the care from others that they experience as desperately needed. Preoccupied attachment status has been strongly associated with borderline personality disorder (Fonagy et al., 1996) and with suicidal behavior (Adam, Sheldon-Keller, and West, 1996). Preoccupied adults might be likely to choose relational partners who, like their parents, are impaired and inconsistent but occasionally respond, fostering hope that at last all of their needs will be met.

The avoidant or dismissive group is organized to avoid fragmentation by eschewing relational needs. Overt displays of need resulted in parental rejection, although some mirroring might have been provided in response to autonomous play and the development of nonrelational competencies. As adults, these individuals might be seen as having a vertical split and disavowing most of their painful experiences and unacceptable longings for nurturance. They learned that only such suppression of need (and of anger about unmet needs) enabled them to avoid further rejection and withdrawal in the relationship with the attachment figure. In the wake of consistent rejection, dismissive individuals are organized around believing that relationships are useless at best and dangerous at worst (Connors, 1997). Their access to affect is much more attenuated than is the case for the previous two groups. Dismissive status has been linked to a variety of psychological disorders, including substance abuse, eating disorders, and anxiety disorders (see Dozier, Stovall, and Albus, 1999, for a review).

CLINICAL IMPLICATIONS OF ATTACHMENT THEORY

The utility of embracing attachment concepts stems in part from their explanatory value in helping us understand relational phenomena. I believe that the inclusion of attachment processes can aid in conceptualization of a variety of situations in which individuals seem overly detached from or excessively preoccupied with relational matters, but my emphasis here will be on the painful bond with a "bad object." Clinicians frequently treat patients who select relational partners who are abusive, impaired, addicted, and so on, and we may experience great concern about the potentially deleterious impact upon the patient's emotional well-being. Physical safety is threatened as well in the case of battering relationships. However we may try to maintain our empathic immersion in the patient's subjective experience, actions that seem inexplicable, as well as destructive, render attunement more difficult. A further impediment to empathic appreciation of the meaning of the relationship is the fact that patients frequently have difficulty articulating the nature and depth of their ties to abusive or inadequate partners, instead focusing on their conscious misery. My patients have often expressed confusion and concern about their own behavior in such relationships, aware as we explore the topic that they experience panic at the prospect of loss of the relationship but with little understanding for why this might be so.

For instance, a female patient of mine whose father had been close to psychotic developed a relationship with a homeless man whom she invited to move in with her after knowing him for just a few weeks. After my patient began living with this man, she was puzzled by many aspects of his behavior, including long absences, moodiness, and lack of interest in sex. Several months into the relationship, she discovered that he was a heroin addict with a habit of many years duration. This news did not suggest to my patient that she had chosen poorly; instead, she felt even more sorry for him and was determined to help and support him. The appeal of this situation for her is difficult to understand, with our usual ideas about what people "get" in relationships, including selfobject experiences; this man stole and sold most of her possessions, was verbally abusive, was physically unkempt and unaffectionate, had been unemployed for many years and contributed nothing to the household, and provided little companionship because he spent all of his time searching for drugs or getting high. Nonetheless, my patient imagined a future with him and soon felt that she would literally die without him.

My patient's family had been dominated by her father, who was physically and emotionally abusive to her and her siblings. Both parents were extremely self-preoccupied and impaired, and the children were neglected unless the housekeeper was present. The father terrorized the children, and their depressed mother seemed powerless to help them. However, the father was warm and loving at times. He was also extremely emotionally needy, could not tolerate being alone, and would order my patient to keep him company rather than be involved with peers. My patient's role in the family was to be his primary emotional caretaker. She felt responsible for alleviating his pain (and this was a man who did not suffer in silence; he would loudly moan and groan for hours if he had a headache or other ailment). She derived some sense of security in being needed by him, and this provided a degree of safety from his more frightening behaviors. Her most positive contact with a parent occurred in the context of caring for her father's needs; when not doing this, she was neglected, abandoned, or abused. Given the alternatives, it is not surprising that my patient learned to focus on another person with great intensity, regardless of the level of harm caused to the self. Survival in this family required self-neglect with hypervigilance to the needs of an impaired other, a pattern my patient continued to reenact in adult relationships.

Use of self psychological concepts enables us to understand that this patient's self-structure was fragile and fragmentation-prone, resulting from the gross deficiencies in her selfobject matrix while growing up. This patient's idealizing needs had rarely been met, leading to insufficient self-soothing and self-calming capacities. The self–selfobject relationship with her father was reversed, necessitating her provision of cohesion-enhancing experiences for him, with little emphasis on her own self-development. Lachmann and Beebe's (1992) idea that representational configurations may provide the context for selfobject experience further enlarges our understanding that any mirroring this patient received was in the framework of ministering to another and that she might repeat this familiar pattern in adult relationships.

These conceptualizations are immensely helpful; however, I believe that they do not fully capture the "life and death" quality that this patient has experienced concerning the presence of this partner. Deciding whether she wished to remain in this relationship was not very possible for her as an adult deliberation; the prospect of loss of this partner seemed to reduce her to feeling like a small, helpless, and terrified child. And although psychoanalytic clinicians, including self psychologists, might explain this relationship as a "father transference," self psychological theory has not focused on explicating the dynamics of reenacted early relationships. Clearly, selfobject needs, rarely met in childhood and hoped for in adulthood, are important here, but the utterly compelling nature of my patient's tie with her partner, including the equating of the potential dissolution of this bond with death, suggests to me that perhaps something more primal than even the most archaic selfobject experience is operating.

The attachment system is designed to ensure survival, and it is this most basic issue that seems to be evoked here. Attachment research suggests that objects are not interchangeable, that it is responsiveness from a particular other that is desperately sought, and that historically one's very survival depended upon securing it. This patient certainly might be described as having a "father transference," but I believe that attachment theory can help us understand this more specifically as a manifestation of a preoccupied attachment style carried forward from childhood via internal representations of self and other in relationships. The hypervigilant and caretaking relationship with her impaired father was the primary source of any sense of safety and security available in childhood, compromised as it was, and the powerful template that it created for how one might survive in the world led my patient to a familiar scenario with a similarly limited partner as an adult.

POSSIBILITIES FOR INTEGRATIVE THEORIZING

Stolorow (1995) commented upon the conflict within self psychology about whether it is preferable to consider Kohut's work to be the authoritative and final statement or to integrate into self psychology ideas from other sources. There is currently much interest in the potential of expanding self psychology by integrating concepts from other areas, including attachment, as exemplified by the overall theme of the 21st Annual International Conference on the Psychology of the Self (1998). I believe that self psychology would benefit from a more comprehensive developmental framework, which attachment theory and research offers. Lessem and Orange (1993) and Shane, Shane, and Gales (1997) have similarly suggested the utility of including concepts from attachment theory in our understanding of development and psychopathology.

Self psychology and attachment theory have essentially focused on different, though very related, phenomena. Self psychology's supraordinate emphasis on the development of the self, although vital, might lead to a somewhat generic view of the myriad of experiences occurring in relationships. Case descriptions and analyses in self psychological writings often convey a vivid sense of the unique nature of an individual's family experiences and subsequent relationships, but as noted earlier, theory has remained focused on the selfobject concept. I am in agreement with the group of authors that Goldberg (1998) has termed "relational self psychologists" who believe that self psychology would benefit from better delineation of the object as separate.

Attachment theory, with many of its roots in the study of children rather than adult analysands, has always been a "two-person" psychology with a primary focus on relationship. Although self-development and the development of relational styles and competencies are inextricably intertwined, as the self develops only within relationships, attachment theory has focused more upon the process of relating itself than has self psychology. However, I see nothing incompatible in these different foci; rather, there seems great potential for integration. Both theories stress the potentially pathogenic impact of real, rather than fantasied, experiences; the importance of parental sensitivity; and the continuation of needs for others throughout the life span.

If self psychology does incorporate attachment concepts, much work remains to be done in integrating them in a coherent fashion. Stolorow (1988) has proposed that integration of theories is possible if the discourse remains on an experience-near plane and if units of analysis that are more general and inclusive than those of either theory alone are employed. Regarding Stolorow's first point, attachment theory, like self psychology, eschews complex abstractions and focuses on core concepts such as safety and security that are quite experience-near. I have found that my theoretical explanations for graduate students and clinical interpretations for patients utilizing attachment theory have resonated with salient subjective experiences.

One method of utilizing the larger units of analysis that Stolorow regards as necessary for integrative theorizing is to employ his concept of the intersubjective field (Stolorow, 1992), which includes other dimensions of experience in addition to the selfobject dimension. The exact relationship of selfobject needs and attachment needs is probably quite complex, but we might speculate that they comprise two separate but overlapping dimensions of experience. Because the attachment system functions to ensure survival, a more primary motivation is unlikely. If survival is experienced as threatened on some level, for instance, when the attachment figure is unavailable or unresponsive, needs for various selfobject experiences and self-development will probably remain subordinate until a greater degree of security concerning survival is restored. This "pathological accommodation" (Brandchaft, 1994), which prioritizes the tie to the other and may require self-abnegation, is probably responsible for much self-pathology. Yet the experiences of mirroring, idealizing, twinship, and so on, vital as they are, may only be useable if a reasonable level of attachment security exists. In secure attachment, attachment needs may remain in the background, with selfobject experiences assuming the paramount position when safety is not threatened.

Fosshage (1992) points out that the selfobject dimension of experiencing is always present; our vitality and sense of self are continually changing as they are affected by all of our experiences. I would add to this the notion from attachment theorists (e.g., Main, 1995) that the attachment dimension of experiencing is always present as well and that on some level we are monitoring and being affected by potential threats or enhancements to our sense of safety and security. Kohut (1984) stated that the experience of the availability of empathic resonance is "the major constituent of the sense of security in adult life" (p. 77). The attachment perspective would specify that this resonance must be available from particular others, but the quote beautifully captures Kohut's profound understanding of the interrelationship between empathy and security. This connection might be elucidated further by integrative theorizing.

Over the last century psychoanalytic thought has been heavily influenced by various ideas about child development, some of which have been shown to be inaccurate as knowledge has progressed. Attachment concepts have the advantage of being grounded in empirical research on infants and children that represents the most current thinking among developmentalists. Self psychologists must continue to construct theory that accounts for behavior in relationships, including destructive behavior. Within current psychoanalytic thinking, interpersonalists and object-relations theorists have become much more influential in recent years. Concepts they utilize to explain interpersonal behavior such as projective identification may or may not be correct, but I suspect these theories are increasingly popular because they address issues of concern to clinicians and patients alike who want to understand relationships.

Self psychology must offer a convincing alternative model of relational events that retains what Fosshage (1995) terms a subject-centered listening perspective, in which the vantage point of the patient is primary. Although I disagree with Ornstein (1991) that self psychology requires no concept of the object other than the selfobject, I share his view that self psychology's focus on sustained empathic immersion in the patient's experience should not be abrogated. However, as Fosshage (1992) stated, we can retain our self psychological focus on the patient's subjective experience and at the same time utilize "two-person" models of development and psychopathology. I have found that my ability to maintain empathy with my patients' subjective experiences has been strengthened rather than diluted by my inclusion of attachment processes in my understanding and explanation, and I suggest that such integration has potential to contribute to the evolution of self psychology.

REFERENCES

Adam, K., Sheldon-Keller, A. & West, S. (1996), Attachment organization and vulnerability to loss, separation, and abuse in disturbed adolescents. In: *Attachment Theory: Social, Developmental, and Clinical Perspectives,* ed. S. Goldberg, R. Muir, & J Kerr. Hillsdale, NJ: The Analytic Press, pp. 309–343.

Ainsworth, M. (1989), Attachments beyond infancy. *Amer. Psycholog.,* 44:709–716.

——— Blehar, M., Waters, E. & Wall, S. (1978), *Patterns of Attachment.* Hillsdale, NJ: Erlbaum.

Bacal, H. (1991), Notes on the relationship between object relations theory and self psychology. In: *The Evolution of Self Psychology: Progress in Self Psychology, Vol. 7,* ed. A. Goldberg. Hillsdale, NJ: The Analytic Press, pp. 36–44.

——— (1994), The selfobject relationship in psychoanalytic treatment. In: *A Decade of Progress: Progress in Self Psychology, Vol. 10,* ed. A. Goldberg. Hillsdale, NJ: The Analytic Press, pp. 21–30.

——— (1995), The essence of Kohut's work and the progress of self psychology. *Psychoanal. Dial.*, 5:353–366.

——— & Newman, K. (1990), *Theories of Object Relations: Bridges to Self Psychology.* New York: Columbia University Press.

Basch, M. (1991), Are selfobjects the only objects? Implications for psychoanalytic technique. In: *The Evolution of Self Psychology: Progress in Self Psychology, Vol. 7,* ed. A. Goldberg. Hillsdale, NJ: The Analytic Press, pp. 3–15.

——— (1994), The selfobject concept: Clinical implications. In: *A Decade of Progress: Progress in Self Psychology, Vol. 10,* ed. A. Goldberg. Hillsdale, NJ: The Analytic Press, pp. 1–7.

Belsky, J. (1999), Interactional and contextual determinants of attachment security. In: *Handbook of Attachment,* ed. J. Cassidy & P. Shaver. New York: Guilford, pp. 249–264.

Bowlby, J. (1969), *Attachment and Loss: Vol. 1. Attachment.* New York: Basic Books, 1982.

——— (1973), *Attachment and Loss: Vol. 2. Separation.* New York: Basic Books.

Brandchaft, B. (1988), A case of intractable depression. In: *Learning from Kohut: Progress in Self Psychology, Vol. 4,* ed. A. Goldberg. Hillsdale, NJ: The Analytic Press, pp. 133–154.

——— (1994), Structures of pathologic accommodation and change in psychoanalysis. Presented at the Association for Psychoanalytic Self Psychology, March.

Connors, M. E. (1997), The renunciation of love: Dismissive attachment and its treatment. *Psychoanal. Psychol.*, 14:475–493.

Dozier, M., Stovall, K. & Albus, K. (1999), Attachment and psychopathology in adulthood. In: *Handbook of Attachment,* ed. J. Cassidy & P. Shaver. New York: Guilford, pp. 497–519.

Egeland, B. & Sroufe, L. A. (1981), Developmental sequelae of maltreatment in infancy. In: *Developmental Perspectives in Child Maltreatment,* ed. R. Rinzley & D. Cicchetti. San Francisco: Jossey-Bass, pp. 72–92.

Erickson, M., Sroufe, L.A. & Egeland, B. (1985), The relationship between quality of attachment and behavior problems in preschool in a high-risk sample. In: Growing Points of Attachment Theory and Research. *Monographs of the Society for Research in Child Development*, ed. I. Bretherton & E. Waters. 50 (1–2, Serial No. 209), pp. 147–166.

Feeney, J. & Noller, P. (1990), Attachment style as a predictor of adult romantic relationships. *J. Personal. Soc. Psychol.*, 58:281–291.

Fonagy, P., Leigh, T., Steele, M., Steele, H., Kennedy, G., Mattoon, M., Target, M. & Gerber, A. (1996), The relation of attachment status, psychiatric classification, and response to psychotherapy. *J. Consult. & Clin. Psychol.*, 64:22–31.

Fosshage, J. (1992), The selfobject concept: A further discussion of three authors. In: *New Therapeutic Visions: Progress in Self Psychology, Vol. 8,* ed. A. Goldberg. Hillsdale, NJ: The Analytic Press, pp. 229–239.

——— (1995), Interaction in psychoanalysis: A broadening horizon. *Psychoanal. Dial.*, 5:459–478.

George, C., Kaplan, N. & Main, M. (1996), Adult Attachment Interview Protocol (3rd ed.). Unpublished manuscript, University of California at Berkeley.

Gill, M. (1994), Heinz Kohut's self psychology. In: *A Decade of Progress: Progress in Self Psycho,* pp. 197–211.

Goldberg, A. (1998), Self psychology since Kohut. *Psychoanal. Quart.*, 67:240–255.

Greenberg, J. & Mitchell, S. (1983), *Object Relations in Psychoanalytic Theory.* Cambridge, MA: Harvard University Press.

Grossmann, K. E. & Grossmann, K. (1991), Attachment quality as an organizer of emotional and behavioral responses in a longitudinal perspective. In: *Attachment Across the Life Cycle*, ed. C. M. Parkes, J. Stevenson-Hinde & P. Marris. New York: Tavistock/Routledge, pp. 30–40.

Hazan, C. & Shaver, P. (1987), Romantic love conceptualized as an attachment process. *J. Personal. Soc. Psychol.,* 52:511–524.

——— & ——— (1990), Love and work: An attachment-theoretical perspective. *J. Personal. Soc. Psychol.*, 59:270–280.

Hesse, E. (1999), The Adult Attachment Interview: Historical and current perspectives. In: *Handbook of Attachment,* ed. J. Cassidy & P. Shaver. New York: Guilford, pp. 395–433.

Karen, R. (1994), *Becoming Attached.* New York: Warner Books.

Kobak, R. (1999), The emotional dynamics of disruptions in attachment relationships: Implications for theory, research, and clinical intervention. In: *Handbook of Attachment,* ed. J. Cassidy & P. Shaver. New York: Guilford, pp. 21–43.

——— & Hazan, C. (1991), Attachment in marriage: The effects of security and accuracy of working models. *J. Personal. Soc. Psychol.,* 60:861–869.

Kohut, H. (1971), *The Analysis of the Self.* New York: International Universities Press.

——— (1984), *How Does Analysis Cure?* Chicago, IL: University of Chicago Press.

Lachmann, F. & Beebe, B. (1992), Representational and selfobject transferences: A developmental perspective. In: *New Therapeutic Visions: Progress in Self Psychology, Vol. 8,* ed. A. Goldberg. Hillsdale, NJ: The Analytic Press, pp. 3–15.

Lessem, P. (1996), Hope, the fear of change, and the repetition of painful experience: A self psychological perspective. Presented at the 19th International Conference on the Psychology of the Self, October.

——— & Orange, D. (1993), Self psychology and attachment: The importance of the particular other. Presented at the 16th Annual International Conference on the Psychology of the Self, October.

Main, M. (1995), Recent studies in attachment. In: *Attachment Theory,* ed. S. Goldberg, R. Muir, & J. Kerr. Hillsdale, NJ: The Analytic Press, pp. 407–474.

——— & Cassidy, J. (1988), Categories of response to reunion with the parent at age six: Predicted from attachment classifications and stable over a one-month period. *Dev. Psychol.,* 24:415–426.

——— & Solomon, J. (1986), Discovery of an insecure-disorganized/disoriented attachment pattern. In: *Affective Development in Infancy,* ed. T. B. Brazelton & M. W. Yogman. Norwood, NJ: Ablex Publishing, pp. 95–124.

Mitchell, S. (1988), *Relational Concepts in Psychoanalysis.* New York: Basic Books.

——— (1995). Follow-up Questions. *Psychoanal. Dial.,* 5:401–402.

Ornstein, P. (1991), Why self psychology is not an object relations theory: Clinical and theoretical considerations. In: *The Evolution of Self Psychology: Progress* in *Self Psychology, Vol. 7,* ed. A. Goldberg. Hillsdale, NJ: The Analytic Press, pp. 17–29.

Rowe, C. (1994), Reformulations of the concept of selfobject: A misalliance of self psychology with object relations theory. In: *A Decade of Progress: Progress in Self Psychology, Vol. 10,* ed. A. Goldberg. Hillsdale, NJ: The Analytic Press, pp. 9–20.

Shane, M., Shane, E. & Gales, M. (1997), *Intimate Attachments.* New York: Guilford.

Shaver, P., Hazan, C. & Bradshaw, D. (1988), Love as attachment: The integration of three behavioral systems. In: *The Psychology of Love,* ed. R. Sternberg & M. Barnes. New Haven, CT: Yale University Press, pp. 68–99.

Stolorow, R. (1988), Integrating self psychology and classical psychoanalysis: An experience-near approach. In: *Learning from Kohut: Progress in Self Psychology, Vol. 4,* ed. A. Goldberg. Hillsdale, NJ: The Analytic Press, pp. 63–70.

——— (1992), Subjectivity and self psychology: A personal odyssey. In: *New Therapeutic Visions: Progress in Self Psychology, Vol. 8,* ed. A. Goldberg. Hillsdale, NJ: The Analytic Press, pp. 241–250.

——— (1995), Loyalism and expansionism in self psychology. *Psychoanal. Dial.,* 5:427–430.

——— Brandchaft, B. & Atwood, G. (1987), *Psychoanalytic Treatment: An Intersubjective Approach.* Hillsdale, NJ: The Analytic Press.

Troy, M. & Sroufe, L.A. (1987), Victimization among preschoolers: The role of attachment relationship history. *J. Amer. Acad. Child Psychiat.,* 26:166–172.

Wolf, E. (1988), *Treating the Self.* New York: Guilford.

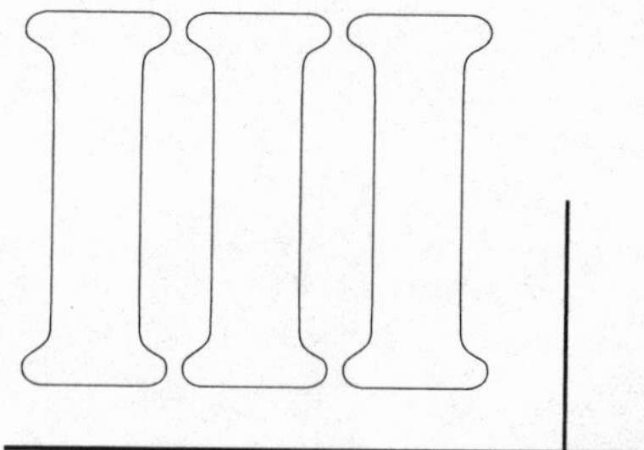

III Applied

Chapter 12

Using Self Psychology in Brief Psychotherapy

Jill R. Gardner

Brief or time-limited psychotherapy is not usually thought of as the province of self psychology. Yet, as described previously (Gardner, 1991), I believe that brief psychotherapy is an eminently appropriate and fertile domain for the application of self psychology and that self psychology, in turn, can greatly enhance the effectiveness of brief treatment.

In this form of treatment, the therapist attends centrally to the state of the patient's self and the establishment of a selfobject bond with the therapist as a matrix for change. The core mutative process occurs through empathic interpretations, which articulate and legitimize the patient's subjective experience, particularly his or her frustrated selfobject needs and longings. This process strengthens the self, leading to a reorganization of experience and reinstating a process of development, repair, and structure building. All of these events can and do occur even in the context of very time-limited therapeutic encounters.

The goal of this chapter is to elaborate on some of the practical steps involved in the application of this theoretical perspective. I address this goal primarily by providing a set of questions and organizing frameworks intended to help clinicians conceptualize brief treatment from a self psychological point of view. Before turning to

---

An expanded version of this chapter was published in *Psychoanalytic Social Work*, Vol. 6, 1999.

this material, I offer a summary of the literature on self psychology and brief treatment.

BRIEF TREATMENT AND SELF PSYCHOLOGY: A SUMMARY OF THE LITERATURE

The rather extensive literature on short-term, dynamic psychotherapy contains relatively few articles written explicitly from a self psychological perspective. Books by Basch (1980, 1988, 1992), Kohut (1987), and Elson (1986) and an article by Ornstein and Ornstein (1996b), though not about short-term psychotherapy per se, do include a number of brief treatment cases that were informed by the authors' self psychological perspective. They provide, for this reason, useful illustrative material.

Although he did not explicitly write about short-term therapy, Kohut (1987) saw his ideas as very relevant for brief treatment. He felt that a little bit of help, emanating from the borrowed strength of the therapist's support, could accomplish a great deal.

Goldberg (1973) offered perhaps the earliest explicit attempt to apply the evolving insights of self psychology to short-term psychotherapy. Discussing the psychotherapeutic treatment of narcissistic injuries, he described a need for the patient to be able to use the therapist as a source of selfobject functions in order to restore self-esteem. It was specifically in the understanding and interpretation of the patient's frustrated selfobject longings that repair of the injured self was seen to occur.

Like Goldberg, Lazarus (1980) conceptualized the goal of brief therapy with narcissistic disturbances as one of reestablishing the patient's feelings of self-esteem and self-cohesion by allowing the patient to use the therapist as a source of selfobject experience. He saw the reinstatement of the patient's premorbid level of functioning as the primary outcome in most cases. However, he also believed that in some cases the patient might begin to internalize the therapist's functions, leading to an accretion of psychic structure and further working through of narcissistic problems after termination.

In a later paper, Lazarus (1988) described the use of self psychological principles to conduct brief psychotherapy with elderly patients whose entry into treatment was precipitated by a narcissistic injury or other selfobject loss. Lazarus again described how the relationship with the empathic therapist may serve as a bridge to restore self-esteem and enable the patient to reestablish a supportive selfobject milieu outside of the treatment context.

Chernus (1983) described the use of focal psychotherapy (a close precursor of this model) to treat a structural deficit in the self, thus expanding the terrain previously described by others. In the case she reported, the *primary* therapeutic goals were structure building and internalization of the therapist's selfobject functions, rather than the repair of the self and return to premorbid levels of functioning that had been emphasized by previous authors. (For an extended description of this case, see the report later published by the therapist, P. Ornstein [1988].)

Chernus (1983) also suggested that the briefer the treatment, the more likely it was that the weight of the working-through process would occur in the context of the patient's external relationships and experiences, rather than in the transference to the therapist. Ornstein and Ornstein (1972) similarly found that working through occurred in meaningful ways outside of the therapeutic relationship.

In a detailed case report, Gardner (1991) also described a process of structural change occurring through brief, self psychological treatment. Baker (1991) published a paper around the same time, which similarly summarized how self psychological principles could guide brief psychotherapy.

Taking a different approach, Ringstrom (1995) used a combination of intersubjectivity theory (Stolorow, Brandchaft, and Atwood, 1987) and motivational systems theory (Lichtenberg, 1989) to suggest a new model of brief treatment. His focus was on the uncovering and modification of unconscious organizing principles, emerging in the intersubjective context of the transference relationship and illuminated through the analysis of paradigmatic model scenes (Lichtenberg, Lachmann, and Fosshage, 1992). He also emphasized the importance of self-state assessment, a concept that is elaborated on at length later in the present chapter.

A major addition to the literature appeared with the publication of Basch's (1995) book on brief psychotherapy. One of Kohut's closest original collaborators, Basch integrated, applied, and extended the major developments in self psychology, creating a developmental model that emphasized affect while integrating cognition and information processing. Major emphasis was placed on the mobilization of the patient's strengths to facilitate brief treatment.

Finally, Seruya (1997) offered a model of "empathic brief psychotherapy" that integrated self psychology with cognitive–behavioral theory. While not exclusively self psychological in approach, her model draws on self psychology extensively, provides an excellent summary of the theory, and extends the model to brief work with couples.

Although the literature on self psychology and brief psychotherapy is not extensive, it is encouraging that it is increasing. As stated earlier, I believe that brief psychotherapy is fertile ground for the application of self psychological concepts, which, in turn, can make brief psychotherapy more effective.

It is important to note that there is not one approach to brief treatment within self psychology, but many. Like theories of therapeutic action or criteria for optimal response (Bacal, 1985, 1998), the literature just reviewed provides a variety of viewpoints regarding what we do, how we do it, and why it works. My own approach draws most heavily on the contributions of Basch and the Ornsteins, along with my experience doing and supervising brief treatment in the settings of a hospital-based, community mental health center and private practice. The model I describe is not a particular technique but, rather, a series of components that, when put together, make treatment more efficient.

While we have a conceptual roadmap for self psychologically informed brief treatment, the exact way these concepts are applied is not always clear to those who seek to practice this model. In the sections below, I address this issue by describing some pragmatic steps to assist clinicians in making the translation from theory to practice.

PATIENT SELECTION

Most approaches to brief therapy prescribe selection criteria. It is certainly logical to begin by trying to determine whether a given patient is a suitable candidate for self psychologically informed brief treatment, yet this begs the question that most clinicians face. In some settings patients can indeed be directed to brief or open-ended treatment tracks at an intake level. In most cases, however, it is not the therapist, but rather clinic policies, third party reimbursers, or the patient's own financial, time, and emotional limitations, that dictate how long the patient and therapist will have to work together. When the length of the treatment is set arbitrarily by these extrinsic factors, the question becomes less one of who is appropriate and more one of how to use whatever time one has. Bellak (Bellak and Small,1978) reflected this reality when he suggested that what we select, essentially, is problems and goals, not patients.

Another stumbling block to using well-established selection criteria is the lack of empirical data upon which to base them. Early models of brief dynamic treatment did have good outcome studies (see Messer and Warren, 1995, for a comprehensive review) but were criticized for using selection criteria that were so narrow as to exclude a majority of the patients who applied. A more recent approach (Basch, 1995), taking the opposite stance, suggests that we consider all patients as potentially suitable candidates for brief dynamic treatment until proven otherwise. How do we prove otherwise? Are there prognostic clues we can rely on? Fortunately, the lack of systematic outcome studies has not kept theorists from offering some suggestions.

Ornstein and Ornstein (1997) saw their capacity to formulate a focus early on as a key determinant for successful brief treatment. For the Ornsteins, a focus is not the presenting problem but a formulation that explains the presenting problem. Whether or not the therapist can arrive quickly at such an organizing formulation and focus the treatment around it is seen as a crucial prognostic indicator.

Ringstrom (1995) believed that the rapidity with which someone has a positive response to the therapist's empathy may be a good predictor of the efficacy of brief treatment. Drawing on Lichtenberg et al.'s (1992) observation that the state of the self depends on a person's responsiveness to empathy and vulnerability to lack of empathy, he urged therapists to consider questions such as: How restorative or fragmenting are the first sessions? How responsive is the patient to the therapist's attunement?

Most clinicians have had the experience of offering an empathic connection that is like water to a wilted plant for one patient and water off a duck's back to another. The former seems to grow firmer before our eyes, while the latter stares at us blankly, seeming to ignore whatever we say. Others respond aversively, with antagonism, withdrawal, or anxiety.

Basch (1995) emphasized the presence of an idealizing transference, stating that the success of brief treatment may depend on whether a positive (idealizing) transference is in place or can quickly be mobilized.

> the question of whether or not short term therapy can be effective or whether lengthier treatment is needed depends often not so much on the nature of the problem per se, but on how soon patients can permit themselves to feel safe, supported, and enhanced in the therapeutic relationship [p. 94].

When Basch used the term *idealization,* he was referring to the patient's capacity to rely on the therapist's guidance and support.[1] This is a necessary prerequisite for both trust and credibility: if the patient can't

---

[1] In his final book, Basch (1995) actually dropped the term *idealization* and began using the word *reliance* to denote this aspect of the patient's needs and transference.

idealize or rely on the therapist, validation or mirroring from that therapist won't have any impact. Validation that is useful to us has to come from credible sources whom we can look up to in some fashion.

Basch also underscored how patients who are highly defended or resistant often require longer treatment to work through their shame over needing to rely on the therapist before any progress can be made. Because shame interferes with letting needs arise in therapy, it must be sufficiently resolved before the patient can tolerate both the therapeutic relationship and the underlying painful affects that have been protectively warded off (Kohut, 1984; Basch, 1988, 1995). It is through the vicissitudes and analysis of the transference that such patients' problems eventually become manifest and are resolved.

There were two other groups of people whom Basch defined as usually not good candidates for brief treatment: people who need to make up for substantial developmental deficits and those needing prolonged support in order to function. He didn't believe that brief therapy could be a substitute for dealing with these problems in more open-ended treatment. At the same time, he saw people needing long-term psychoanalysis or long-term support as being at the ends of the bell curve, leaving a lot of people in the middle. He was fond of saying, "When all you have is a hammer, everything looks like a nail" (Basch, 1995, p. xii). By this he meant that it was our attachment to psychoanalysis and lack of alternative methodologies that led to our reluctance to realize that brief treatment might be the treatment of choice for many of our patients.

My own experience is that many people can work in circumscribed problem areas, leave major domains of character pathology untouched, and derive considerable benefit from relatively brief treatment. Others can reinstate a process of structural growth and change, impacting long-standing patterns. (For case illustrations of the latter, see Chernus [1983] and Gardner [1991], in addition to Basch [1995].)

The more conventional clinical indicators we usually consider in evaluating patients for brief treatment remain important: how pervasive the problems are, how limited, how long they have been going on, the presence of clear precipitants, the extent of substance abuse, and the degree of other internal resources and external supports, to name a few. But having been both surprised and wrong often enough, I have come to believe that it is more useful to begin with the assumption that the patient in front of us could potentially benefit from brief treatment and then look for what, if anything, would lead us to disconfirm that assumption. It might be severe, uncontrolled substance abuse; it might be massive defenses against enough idealization to make at least some use of what the therapist has to offer. It might become obvious in the first 10 minutes, or it might take several sessions to determine.

Self psychologists, warning against the dangers of selectively perceiving or molding data to fit our preconceived conceptual schemata, have begun to suggest that we should "hold our theories lightly" (Orange, 1995). When we approach the task of determining which patients might benefit from brief treatment, we would do well to hold our assumptions lightly as well.

TREATMENT PLANNING AS A CLINICAL PROCESS AND COLLABORATIVE ACTIVITY

For many clinicians, the words *treatment planning* signify onerous forms and administrative intrusion into the treatment process, yet treatment planning is crucial to the success of brief treatment. What we need is another way to think about it.

I see treatment planning as a clinical process, not an administrative one. It evolves out of the clinical exploration of problems and goals and provides a way of establishing an explicit understanding, with the patient, of the nature of why he or she is there and what's to be done. Engaging the patient this way as an active collaborator in defining the purpose of therapy promotes ownership and patient responsibility, helps to prioritize problems, and facilitates the establishment of a focus. Problems are not equivalent to goals. Basch (1995) noted that "the process of establishing what the patient is there to accomplish is in itself therapeutic" (p. 52).

The material that follows addresses, from several different perspectives, the issue of focusing the treatment, starting on a broadly conceptual level and then moving through some very specific ways of determining the issues to be worked on.

CENTRAL FOCUS ON SELF-EXPERIENCE AND SELFOBJECT RELATIONSHIP WITH THERAPIST

In any kind of brief or time-limited treatment, the therapist must decide where to put his or her therapeutic energy, given limited resources. All forms of brief therapy address the issue of focus in one way or another. From a self psychological perspective, the therapist's central focus must be on the self-experience of the patient and on the relationship between the patient and therapist as a new self–selfobject unit. This selfobject bond is the matrix in which change takes place. In brief treatment, as in longer term treatment, the emphasis is on strengthening the self (Wolf, 1988). When there has been a weakening or disorganization of self-experience caused by changes and losses in the selfobject surround, then the selfobject relationship with the therapist functions as a bridge to restore the self to its previous healthier state.

Ornstein (1986) suggested that concern with the state of the self should be the primary focus in the treatment of all patients, regardless of the nature of the pathology or form of the treatment. In any duration of treatment, feeling understood can lead to an increase in self-cohesion, which allows an exploration of previously repressed or disavowed affects, wishes, fears, and fantasies. The emergence of these previously unavailable aspects of the patient's experience into awareness provides an opportunity to understand their meaning and, in so doing, to use the therapy relationship to strengthen the self.

Elson (1986) stated it eloquently:

> Self psychology clarifies the universal striving to secure a response to one's potential for individuality and significance. In even the most seriously deprived individual, underneath abrasive and cynical behavior, a vestige of the need to be confirmed remains alive to be rekindled. The very presence of the [therapist] may quicken this need. Many methods and approaches have been devised for responding to and controlling the relationship which ensues, but, regardless of method, how one orders what one sees and experiences, how one uses oneself on behalf of the individual, becomes more vivid through an explanatory system of human behavior that places the self of the individual at the center of one's observations and views the new self/selfobject unit as the medium for treatment [p. 136].

With the state of the self[2] as a point of departure, assessment can be facilitated by a series of organizing questions that help both to conceptualize the clinical material and to establish a focus for treatment. This self-state assessment is described below under four broad headings: symptoms and deficits, adaptations, strengths, and transference.

SYMPTOMS AND DEFICITS

There are two lenses through which a self psychologist might look at symptoms. The first asks: How do the patient's presenting symptoms express a deficit in or loss of the self's cohesion or vitality?

---

[2] For the sake of convenience, I use the term *the self* in the remainder of this chapter to refer to the subjective sense of self and to the organization of self experience. I do not mean to imply, by this term, an entity, agent, or fixed structure.

Patients who exhibit agitation, anxiety, disorganized behavior, or a deterioration in appearance often signal through these symptoms a problem in the cohesiveness of their self-experience. Debilitating disintegration anxiety often accompanies incipient states of fragmentation. One patient, usually meticulously groomed, arrived for her appointment in an agitated and disheveled state, saying that she felt "like Humpty-dumpty," a quintessentially apt metaphor for the subjective experience of fragmentation.

The patient suffering from a lack or loss of vitality, in contrast, sags rather than splinters. When we see symptoms that cluster around a lack of energy, motivation, and ambition and the affect is melancholy, we think in terms of a devitalized or depleted self.

Through the second lens on symptoms, we ask the question: In what ways do the patient's symptoms reflect attempts to restore or reorganize the weakened self? Substance abuse, eating disorders, and sexual acting out may be used to stimulate and enliven someone with a sense of deadness or depletion. Any of these symptoms might also be employed to calm or reverse an anxious state of fragmentation. Some people get high to feel alive; others drink to calm their nerves. Some people binge when they're anxious, others when they're bored and lonely. When we see an increase in any of these symptomatic behaviors, we can begin to think in terms of how the behavior reflects an attempt to alter the underlying self-state the patient is experiencing. Attending specifically to the patient's subjective experience of the symptomatic behavior and its sequelae will usually clarify what that underlying self-state is.

For example, a man who often felt slighted by his boss and coworkers would regularly go cruising in bars for sex on days he suffered such narcissistic injuries. Although his dangerous promiscuity created other problems for him, the affirmation he found in being sexually desired helped restore his self-esteem and sense of vitality.

Another patient was driving her family and coworkers to distraction with her angry, irritable, and controlling behavior. Her unreasonable attempts to force everyone to fulfill her most minute wishes could be understood as an effort to maintain eroding self-esteem and control over her selfobject world, as serious medical problems and job changes combined to make her feel totally out of control. This pattern of symptoms quite often is secondary to the sense of helplessness caused by illness, parenting problems, or job-related stress.

Self psychologists generally view symptoms as the patient's best available means of protecting a fragile, vulnerable self against retraumatization or of revitalizing and reorganizing a depleted or fragmented self. Keeping these purposes in mind, we can ask the question:

To what problem is this symptomatic behavior a solution? The answers help us make the translation from symptom to self-state, an important step in determining the focus of treatment. It is a shift in understanding from the level of behavior (e.g., this person abuses cocaine) to the level of dynamics (e.g., this person has a crushing sense of deadness and he is devoid of other [internal] resources to counteract it). Symptoms reflect efforts to achieve both a reintegration on the level of self-organization and a shift in the subjective experience of self.

When we evaluate problematic affect, cognition, and behavior, we also need to determine whether we are dealing with transient symptoms or ongoing deficits. Again, a series of questions is helpful: What deficits are apparent in the patient's self-experience? Are they acute? chronic? In other words, has this individual ever acquired the self-soothing and regulating functions needed to maintain self-esteem and regulate affect? To judge this, it would be helpful to know how prone the patient is to fragmentation or depletion experiences. Is the current upset less than, as bad as, or worse than what the person has felt before? Is this a pretty typical way of feeling or is it unusual? As always, subjective experience is crucial. What one person considers an alarming sign of impending breakdown may for another be an everyday experience of self, albeit a painful or distressing one. To evaluate symptoms of anxiety or absent-mindedness, for example, it matters whether one is a person who is generally unflappable or one who is always worried, one who never misplaces things or one who can lose their keys while holding them in hand.

In a sense, I am discussing the pervasiveness and chronicity of presenting problems. Generally speaking, the more symptoms reflect a loss of cohesion or vitality rather than a lack of them, the more likely it is that brief intervention may help the individual get back on course.

ADAPTATIONS

In conjunction with deficits, we also need to know: How, typically, has the person tried to compensate for these deficits? Here I am referring to the range of defensive adaptations, compensatory structures, and characterological solutions that people devise, over the course of development, to deal with whatever trauma and selfobject failures they have experienced.

Most people have characteristic ways of coping, that is, maintaining cohesion, competence, or adaptive functioning and avoiding anxiety. These ways of dealing with trouble and maintaining a viable sense of self include both internal mechanisms (functional capacities) and external supports (sources of needed selfobject experience).

The search for treatment is often precipitated by something that triggers an inability to cope. Usually the trigger is a loss or a new challenge. The situation then exposes what we might think of as "fault lines." These are structural deficits, which are exposed when the usual defenses are overwhelmed. Precipitating stresses disrupt the previous adaptations and strain them to the point where they cannot hold. Although this development is often preceded by an initial redoubling of usual defensive efforts, these emergency measures eventually fail as well. It is at this point that the underlying problems may come more into view and can therefore become a focus of treatment.

For example, some people protect themselves against unbearable feelings of dependency by developing a pattern of defensive self-sufficiency. When external events, such as an accident, illness, or job loss, necessitate requesting or accepting help from others, they become acutely anxious. The anxiety is associated with the memory of previous traumatic failures in the face of needs. It is the inability to employ the usual solution that reveals the underlying vulnerability. A more obvious example is phobic avoidance. As long as the object of one's phobia can be avoided, the patient appears asymptomatic. If the defense of avoidance is precluded or fails, however, the underlying anxiety immediately becomes apparent.

A similar problem can be observed in patients who rely on defensive isolation or distance to regulate their anxiety about intimacy. They often become symptomatic when external events necessitate more closeness than they are used to or comfortable with. Obvious examples are signs of increased commitment to a relationship, such as moving in with a partner, getting engaged, or getting married. These are common times for us to see symptoms emerge. This problem can also be precipitated, however, by a change as innocuous-seeming as needing to share an office at work. The loss of the physical wall or partition may subjectively constitute the loss of a psychological wall, which enabled the person to function within a range of acceptable emotional distance.

One patient became increasingly anxious as her pregnancy progressed. Exploration revealed her ever-expanding abdomen as the focus of her distress. As we explored the meaning of this concern, she described her father's bitter disappointment in not having a son and his disdain for his two daughters. Desperately needing an antidote to her depressed mother, she managed to evoke some affirmation from her father by becoming a star athlete, winning a place on the national team in her sport. What her advancing pregnancy made clear to us was how her flat stomach had always been not only a source of pride, but a crucial symbol of the one thing that she felt made her valuable in the eyes of her father, securing the selfobject bond with him she desperately needed to maintain her self-esteem.

Sports and physical activity are often used to regulate tension, as well as self-esteem. It is not uncommon to see patients who rely on this outlet become both depressed and anxious when an injury prevents them from their usual routine. While others may simply become irritable or feel less energetic when they can't run or work out, for this kind of person more extensive underlying deficits in self-regulation become apparent.

The pressures in many workplaces brought about by downsizing and other cost-cutting measures create particular difficulty for people whose compulsivity and perfectionism are defensively tied to their psychological security. When one now has three jobs to cover, it is impossible to cover all the bases as thoroughly.

Finally, there is the patient who relies on the suppression of affect to maintain his or her psychological equilibrium. It seems to matter less which particular defenses are used than it does that unmanageable (usually dysphoric) affect is kept at bay. When precipitating events mobilize too much affect to suppress, the person experiences emotional flooding, anxiety, and symptoms. The characterological defenses against affect simply can't handle the emotions that have been stimulated.

Such patients often say things like, "I'm a coper," "I'm a minimizer," or "I'm a control freak." When something then happens that the person can't cope with, minimize, or control, he develops symptoms. It is often then not the presenting symptoms or even the defenses but, rather, the meaning of the need to minimize or control in the first place that becomes the focus of treatment. As the patient's usual means of sequestering his or her underlying anxieties and affects fail, these experiences can be brought to light, understood, and explained.

The conception of treatment I am elaborating here is very close to the model of focal psychotherapy developed by Balint and the Ornsteins (Balint, Ornstein, and Balint, 1972; Ornstein and Ornstein, 1972). As defined by Chernus (1983), focal psychotherapy involves the exploration and working through of a focal conflict precipitated by a recent event that has overwhelmed the patient's characterological defense mechanisms. That characterological weakness becomes the focus of treatment. In contrast to the goal of crisis intervention, which is a return to the previous homeostasis, the goal of focal psychotherapy is a modification of the maladaptive defensive structures.

More recently, the Ornsteins (1997) have updated their description of brief focal psychotherapy in ways that clarify how the examination of symptoms, deficits, and adaptations can create a focus in brief treatment. They suggest that, rather than trying to examine the whole personality, we should look at a slice or sector of the personality in depth, cutting across the levels of surface or presenting problems, attempts to cope with the problems, and core or nuclear problems. In other words, the therapist must establish the dynamic connection between the current problem, precipitated by some kind of stress, and what has gone on in the person's life before. When such a formulation can be expressed in terms of an interpretive comment to the patient, it creates a focus for the treatment. As stated earlier, for the Ornsteins the focus is not the presenting problem but, rather, a formulation that explains the presenting problem. Also, if the focus provides an explanation for the current problem, while at the same time touching on the patient's character pathology, then work on the immediate problem includes working on the chronic problems.

My own experience has been that successful cases of brief treatment often conform to these models. A woman referred by her employer because of the irritability and stress she was exhibiting at work reported a history of several recent medical problems, all quite serious. While she was aware of sadness and anger in connection with these problems, she was not in touch with her considerable anxiety. She only knew she was snapping at everyone around her. As she described her situation, she revealed herself to be a high-functioning, very competent person, who characteristically downplayed both needs and dysphoric feelings. She said she was a "minimizer" who had "no tolerance for self-pity." However, as her sense of choice and control was being rapidly eroded by her health problems, she was confronted with feelings she could not successfully minimize, and her previous defenses no longer served to protect her from the anxiety such feelings created in her. Successful treatment focused on increasing her affect awareness and tolerance. When she could experience and express her feelings more directly, feeling entitled to them as legitimate, she regained her equilibrium and was able to terminate the treatment. I saw her a total of six times.

In another case, the patient came requesting help to manage better the tension associated with several external stresses in both his family and work life. His presenting complaint was depression. What quickly became apparent was his great difficulty in asserting himself effectively with a disabled relative who was making enormous demands on him. Although massively frustrated, he was trying very hard to be compassionate, understanding, tolerant, and helpful. His history revealed that he had responded to a very critical and guilt-inducing parental environment with a combination of compliance, resentment, and withdrawal. This was a man who had learned to sit on feelings until they reached a boiling point, at which point they felt too dangerous to express, leading him to retreat and become depressed. Treatment focused on his long-standing fears regarding self-assertion. As with the previous case, effective treatment involved enabling him to identify and express his own needs and feelings more directly, even in the face of significant others in his life whose needs seemed to him much greater. It was this change in relation to his internal life that enabled him to achieve his original goal of managing the external stresses more effectively.

In both cases, it was a focus on the underlying problem in the self that was exposed by the failure of characteristic defenses that led to successful brief treatment. These cases also underscore Socarides and Stolorow's (1984–1985) emphasis on the central role of the selfobject transference bond in the "articulation, integration and developmental transformation of the patient's affectivity" (p. 112).

STRENGTHS

When working with people in brief treatment, attention to their strengths becomes pivotal. We need to ask: What has the patient used in the past to maintain or restore vitality and cohesion? In what areas does the person continue to exhibit strength now?

Basch, in particular, emphasized the need to elicit and foster strengths and to focus on how the strengths no longer serve the patient, rather than focusing on the origins of problems in childhood. In his view, the patient is seen as possessing the resources to cope with his or her problem; the therapist's job is to mobilize them. He described the patient as an agent for change in the present rather than simply a victim of the past and saw patients' strengths as the leverage to help them do something about their problems (Basch, 1995).

> When we work successfully, we are not solving patients' problems per se; rather we are helping them to use or enhance what they have on the plus side to minimize, offset, and occasionally eradicate what is on the minus side. We are helping them to right themselves so that they will be in a position to solve the problems that brought them to us in the first place (pp. 6–7).

Basch felt that people come to therapy because their strengths are no longer working. The fostering of self-righting, which he is describing above as a goal of treatment, has been emphasized by other self psychologists as well (Tolpin, 1983; Lichtenberg et al., 1992). Kohut actually talked 20 years earlier about mobilizing the patient's strengths. In a 1975 lecture he stated:

> In those cases in which the essential task is the analysis of a disturbed core self, the crucial work deal[s] predominantly with opening up the possibility of new choices . . . with the freeing of sources of strength that were not present before. . . . The primary analytic task is understood to be an effort that will enable the patient to use something that is in him by freeing it or putting it in working order. . . . It is not that one is finally able to see that he has an unacceptable drive that has to be discarded, but that he has a central source of strength that was not available before [Kohut, 1975, pp. 370–371].

One man came to treatment with a crisis of confidence as he stood on the threshold of his professional career. He believed that only regaining a previously felt (and defensively held) sense of invincibility would cure his anxiety, inhibition, and fear of competing in the marketplace. Hearing that he had been a soccer player, I asked him what he did when he was playing a game and fell down. With great emphasis, he replied, "I got up and got back in the game! If I gave up a goal, I was embarrassed, but then I tried even harder." This allowed me to suggest that perhaps what he had lost confidence in was not his invincibility, but his resiliency. Drawing on his history, I pointed out how over and over he had been able to turn an initial disappointment to advantage and move his life forward. Looking at this pattern helped him realize that, even when he hadn't been invincible, he had nevertheless been successful. Armed with a new sense of confidence in his own resiliency, he became able to accept the much more attainable goal of "getting back in the game" following whatever setbacks might occur. With this shift, it took only a few sessions for him to come out of the malaise that had overtaken him and feel more secure about launching his career.

Consistent with Kohut's, and later Basch's, emphasis on potentials for strength and growth, we need to emphasize what the person is doing right and support it. The orientation in our training toward pathology often interferes with this focus on strengths. A simple inquiry regarding what patients feel they need from us can be useful in supporting their capacities to define their own resources and limitations, reinforcing our view of them as active collaborators in the therapeutic endeavor. On a practical level, Basch (1995) also suggested that we note the content associated with shifts from negative to positive affect as the patient tells his or her story. He felt that such shifts toward brighter affect signal hidden strengths and adaptive coping mechanisms one hopes to mobilize.

Sometimes the mobilization of strengths involves less reconnecting with previous experiences than reframing them. Basch was particularly effective at doing this. With one man who took his children's rather minor misconduct as disrespectful insults and challenges to his authority, complaining that he never behaved that way as a child, Basch (1995) replied that the man never had a chance to be a child, behaving in all the ways that are typical of children and frustrating to adults. The fact that his kids could afford to do this was a compliment to what he had achieved psychologically for them. In contrast to his own anxiety-filled childhood, his children had a basic confidence and trust that he would be there to take care of them, whether they responsibly performed every chore or not. Basch noted that this interpretation validates the patient's achievement, while protecting his fragile self-esteem. Reframing weakness to strength is a familiar process to self psychologists, who emphasize the adaptive and protective functions of behavior generally.

TRANSFERENCE MANIFESTATIONS OF SELFOBJECT NEEDS

Manifestations of selfobject needs in the relationship with the therapist provide another way to understand the organization of self-experience and state of the self. Insufficiently met selfobject needs lead to vulnerabilities in the self and defenses that are erected to protect the precariously organized self from retraumatization. When a patient enters therapy, the needs, vulnerabilities, and defenses all become manifest in the transference. The unmet developmental needs are reflected in the "selfobject dimension" of the transference, while the vulnerabilities and defenses are reflected in the "repetitive/conflictual dimension" (Stolorow et al., 1987). Therefore, it is helpful to ask ourselves: What needs of the self are being expressed in the patient's behavior towards the therapist? How are these manifested (or defended against)?

The patient who provides detailed descriptions of his activities and accomplishments, for example, may be seeking mirroring and validation through which to bolster self-esteem. The patient who clamors for advice and direction may be appealing to the therapist to be a source of idealizing selfobject experiences and functions that would organize and make sense out of his or her experience. On the other hand, the patient who engages in hostile, provocative behavior toward the therapist may be trying to protect a vulnerable self from being retraumatized, by rejection or misunderstanding. Through behaviors that create distance and mask underlying vulnerabilities, the patient prevents exposure of previously thwarted selfobject needs. Self psychologists understand this protective function as the fundamental goal of all defenses. When the therapist recognizes and affirms the legitimacy of whatever selfobject needs are evident in the transference, the self is strengthened. When the therapist fails to do so, the self is threatened and symptoms may worsen.

Careful attention to the selfobject dimension of the transference may also clarify the specific nature of underlying deficits or recent injuries, since patients tend to reactivate in the transference those selfobject needs that have been thwarted. In an early paper, Goldberg (1973) described two brief treatment cases who presented in nearly opposite ways to the therapist. The first patient "entered the hour as a storm-tossed and agitated man who wanted smoothing of his ruffled feathers and agreement and reflection of his outrage" (p. 724). The therapist was implicitly beseeched to admire the patient (his "charm, wit, and presence") and to refrain from any kind of criticism. In the second case, the patient immediately assigned the therapist the role of an expert, whom he expected to tell him what was wrong with him and what to do about it.

These obvious bids to meet mirroring and idealizing needs, respectively, paralleled the internal meaning of the narcissistic injuries that had brought these patients to treatment. In the first case, the man became symptomatic after a group of students whom he had hoped to impress called him pompous; in the second, the patient's symptoms were triggered by his boss's failure to be the omnipotent protector for whom he longed.

By recognizing a patient's appeal in the transference for the therapist to be a source of reparative selfobject experiences, the therapist is alerted to the nature of the underlying difficulty. The specific problems that emerge through this process clarify deficits in the self and point to a potential focus for treatment. An analogous process for exploring precipitating events is described below.

As a final note regarding transference, it is important to reiterate the need to evaluate the extent to which a positive transference is either in place or is able to be mobilized quickly (cf. Basch, 1995). When deeply entrenched defenses prevent such engagement, brief treatment may not be possible.

SUBJECTIVE (INTERNAL) MEANING OF PRECIPITATING EVENTS

All therapists seek to understand the role of precipitating events in the patient's presenting problems and search for treatment. This is the familiar question, "What brings you in now?" A self psychologically informed version of this question would ask: What is the meaning of the precipitating events in terms of their impact on the patient's self-experience and selfobject surround? More specifically, how do the stresses that led the person to seek therapy involve the loss of important selfobject experiences? Which kinds of selfobject experiences were lost or became less available? And finally, what role did these experiences play in sustaining an inner sense of vitality and cohesion? All of these questions aim to clarify the nature of the internal problem that has to be addressed. As therapists, we respond not to external events, but to the subjective experience of those events. An empathic mode of inquiry is used to determine what the subjective experience is.

The internal loss might be precipitated by a loss or rupture in a relationship, leading to a temporary loss of cohesion, depletion, or fragmentation. Or it may be precipitated by the loss of a role that was affirming, like a job or parenting.

When the normal process of psychic structure building is incomplete, an individual is more vulnerable to a loss of needed selfobject experiences. If a relationship is disrupted or ends, the selfobject loss is then more pronounced. For example, if the mirroring functions of a relationship were necessary to stabilize and maintain self esteem, then with the other person could go the capacity to feel good about oneself. One patient, struggling with feelings about her physical appearance after breaking up with her boyfriend, expressed this very concretely: "I miss the feedback I got from Perry. He always told me I looked good and made me feel attractive. Now I look in the mirror and I don't know what to think. I can't tell. I feel like I have to go to such effort to make myself look good and I don't always feel like it. But I would feel terrible if I went out and people saw me looking awful. With Perry, he just told me I looked good no matter what and I felt OK." This description underscores the difficulty she is having regulating her self-esteem in the absence of her boyfriend's mirroring affirmation.

If, on the other hand, the calming and soothing functions of an idealized other are needed because of deficits in the person's own capacity for self-soothing, then with the loss of this selfobject dimension of the relationship may go the capacity for affect regulation and the ability to calm down. Increased anxiety and decreased cohesion usually follow. This is a very common pattern in patients with borderline personality disorders because of the extremely tenuous nature of their underlying self-organization (Tolpin, 1984). It becomes easier to understand how people stay in apparently destructive relationships when we consider these selfobject functions being served by them.

Focusing on the selfobject dimension of precipitating events sheds light on the state of the self, the state of the patient's selfobject world, and the connection between the two. There is generally an inverse relationship between the strength of the internal psychic structure and the strength of the external selfobject surround. When less has been organized internally, more is needed externally. Thus the individual is more vulnerable to disruptions in those externally stimulated selfobject experiences. Conversely, the more cohesively organized one's internal experience is, the less vulnerable the individual is to the vicissitudes of the selfobject surround or to debilitating narcissistic injury in the face of selfobject failure.

In other words, one person's wobble is another person's earthquake. One person can shrug off the boss's scowl as reflecting a bad mood, while a coworker is devastated by even a hint of criticism. This is why a knowledge of external events tells us nothing without a corresponding understanding of their meaning to the patient.

That meaning has to be understood with a great deal of specificity. For example, one patient reported that Marine boot camp was one of the best periods of his life. Surprised by this statement, I encouraged him to elaborate. He described how competent he felt at doing what was required of him physically and how much he enjoyed the sameness of uniforms and haircuts. It became clear that he loved boot camp for its structure, discipline, and challenge. These qualities, which had been sorely lacking in his family growing up, helped him with self-regulation, self-esteem, and a sense of belonging.

Basch (1992, 1995) constantly urged therapists to get examples when a patient described a problem, believing that it was the specific details that would clarify the meaning of the events and issues the patient reported.

When someone reports difficulty getting over a relationship, I've found it particularly helpful to ask, "What do you think about when you think about him (or her)?" Does the person describe missing the affirmation of an admirer, the company of a playmate, or the solace of being held in the dark of the night? These point to differing internal experiences and needs.

In describing her boyfriend, one patient said, "Don is amazing . . . when he holds me his strength just seems to flow into me, wrapping around me and keeping me safe." When she later broke up with Don, the lost selfobject experience for her was very different from the woman described earlier who struggled with her appearance after her boyfriend left.

This question of what the patient thinks about is relevant to any loss, whether of a relationship, a job, or one's health and faculties.

It is equally relevant to new challenges. Moving away from home, starting a new school or job, getting married, having a baby, and retiring are all life changes that have highly subjective, personal meanings.

For one patient, struggling with feelings of depletion after leaving her large and chaotic family, the significance of the change was in the loss of stimulation provided by all the commotion and activity at home. Suddenly on her own, her underlying emptiness became apparent. The appropriate focus of treatment was not anxiety about either separation or the new challenges she faced but, rather, the need for external stimulation in order to mobilize or sustain any sense of vitality.

For another woman, who spent years nursing a failing spouse, her husband's death triggered a loss of structure and meaning. Her sense of self had become organized around the caregiving role, a pattern not uncommon for people in her situation. Treating this only as a problem of grief and mourning would miss what in fact became a more relevant concern for the treatment: finding a new basis for a sense of purpose in order to restore her self-esteem. Finding new ways to sustain self-esteem constitutes a very different focus for treatment than resolution of an object loss or grief reaction.

Sometimes what is lost is a hope or fantasy, for example, the losses and challenges involved when a woman closes the door on unsuccessful fertility treatment (Bergart, 1997) or the loss of dreams when a parent gives birth to a disabled child (Fajardo, 1987).

The question of what comes to mind when the patient thinks about the presenting problem is helpful when dealing with trauma as well as loss. The specifics of traumatic memories provide clues to the nature of the underlying problem and/or continuing difficulties. This is true of a wide range of situations, including assaults, accidents, and abuse.

When a hospital chaplain told me she was stymied by a patient who seemed unable to resolve the death of his wife, I asked her what he talked about when he talked about his spouse. In fact, the man always returned to exactly the same point, the experience of discovering her in the bathroom, dead of cardiac arrest, shortly after bringing her home from the hospital. Rather than suffering from an unresolved grief reaction, he was suffering from an acute anxiety reaction, more specifically posttraumatic stress, triggered by the way in which he discovered his wife's death. What he needed was help in integrating the shock, sense of helplessness, and other affects connected with this traumatic memory. This is, again, a very different focus from his grief over his lost partner.

These last few examples bring to mind what I consider the quintessential story for brief treatment.[3] As the story goes, an army general, very frustrated when his men are unable to fix his broken jeep in a foreign land, calls for a local mechanic. After looking under the hood for a bit, the mechanic asks for a hammer and gives the engine a bang. To the general's amazement, the car starts right up. Impressed and grateful, the happy general asks how much he owes. The mechanic says, "That will be $100." Taken aback, the general responds, "$100? For one bang?" "No," said the mechanic. "$1 for the bang, and $99 for knowing where to bang."

For treatment to be brief, we need to avoid wasting time either trying to address the wrong problem or trying to solve a problem on the wrong level. Using an empathic mode of observation to investigate the patient's subjective experience of precipitating events and problems helps us know "where to bang," that is, where the internal problem in the self is.

Ultimately, our inquiry always comes back to understanding the ways in which the self is vulnerable or disrupted and to establishing a selfobject relationship that will strengthen vitality and cohesion. The more rapidly we can translate the precipitants, symptoms, deficits, strengths, and transferences into statements about the organization of self-experience, the more readily we will be able to do this.

It is through an empathic mode of observation, facilitated by the questions described above, that we are able to understand the selfobject dimension and subjective meaning of the patient's experience. It is through empathic interpretations that we communicate that understanding to the patient.

ADDRESSING SELFOBJECT EXPERIENCE THROUGH EMPATHIC INTERPRETATIONS

Empathic interpretations accept, understand, and explain the meaning of the patient's experiences (Ornstein, 1986), including their frustrated selfobject needs or longings. Understanding phenomena from the point of view of the patient's subjective experience allows the therapist to offer the selfobject responsiveness needed to restore cohesion and enable symptoms to abate.

To illustrate, using an empathic interpretation to capture his patient's experience of losing his girlfriend, one therapist declared, "When she

---

[3] I don't know who originated this story, but credit Leo Bellak with bringing it into the domain of brief dynamic treatment.

left it was like all your good feelings about yourself walked out with her." Another therapist, responding to a young man who was upset by the cold water his father had thrown on his ideas, replied, "You wanted support for your plan and an expression of confidence in you, not 20 questions about how you'd get it to work." When the patient's older brother offered a similarly disappointing response to an accomplishment, the therapist said, "You wanted him to take pride and pleasure in your achievement, not be competitive and resentful about it."

Such interpretations belatedly legitimize underlying needs or wishes. We are accustomed to reflecting the feelings that are reactive to needs not getting met, usually feelings of hurt, anger, sadness, or disappointment. But when we go beyond these reactive affects to the underlying longings and fantasies, our interpretations can have a powerful mutative effect. As Goldberg (1973) observed:

> Behind the sadness of the adolescent who is rejected for a date is the image of a dashing and irresistible hero whom no one can resist. His anger at the girl who turns him down is secondary to feeling injured. Relief comes when someone can understand the hidden image of himself without ridicule or condemnation. Behind the disabling depression of the chronically ill is the fantasy of the perfect body that is intact and beautiful and cannot be damaged [p. 726].

A cancer patient, successfully treated in brief psychotherapy for problems stimulated by her illness, described feeling enraged when people told her that the way she felt was "normal" when it was anything but normal for her. What she wanted was understanding, not reassurance that couldn't really be offered. When the doors closed behind the people leaving the room where she received radiation, she wanted someone to simply appreciate the fear she felt at that moment, to understand her sense of aloneness and helplessness. She needed this experience accepted and confirmed.

An elderly man home alone recovering from major surgery complained that the physical therapist wasn't showing up and his home-delivered meals weren't coming on time. Looking at the internal meaning of his situation, we could understand that he was upset at being failed by those who were supposed to take care of him, adding salt to the injury that he couldn't take care of himself. He missed his strong, capable body and was disappointed and furious with the idealized caregivers who were not coming through for him.

He railed at the therapist, "I'm still waiting for my meals, can you believe it? I am so upset, I don't know what to do! I can't get well. I want to get strong, so I can go out. Do you understand?" She replied, "I do. I understand that you are trying to get better, stronger, how you used to be. You want to recover from the surgery, so that you can get back to doing all these things like cooking meals for yourself, so you won't have to wait for a delivery. And the fact that you have to wait, sometimes not getting meals, is standing right in the way of your getting better, getting back to where you want to be. It's frustrating you in reaching your goal." With a huge sigh and great sense of relief, he replied, "Yes, exactly, that's it." He wanted her to appreciate his destination, not just his frustration.

The use of empathic interpretations to clarify and legitimize needs, affect, and experience is a crucial mutative tool in any self psychologically informed treatment. In brief treatment, it occupies center stage. We constantly articulate our understanding of what events and experiences mean to the patient, and we do so in a very active, explicit, and ongoing way.

In addition to its general mutative power, using an empathic mode of observation to focus on internal experience and specific meanings also saves time because of its power to mitigate defensiveness and resistance. Consider, for example, this excerpt from the second session of a brief treatment case:

Pt: I don't understand why I am here with you; you're just going to send me home after we talk. Maybe I should leave now.

Th: You're worried that what we do here won't be enough. You're wondering if it's even worth it.

Pt: Sometimes I think I'd be better off in the hospital for a while. Then I could try to deal with everything that has happened to me. I wouldn't have to worry about being strong and responsible or taking care of everyone else.

Th: Although you're feeling a lot of your own pain, you don't feel you have time to deal with that because you're too busy taking care of everyone else. Perhaps you see the hospital as a place where you'd have permission to stop worrying about everyone else and just take care of you for a while.

Pt: Yes. Even when I'm here with you, I'm thinking about everything else I have to do. I can't let myself focus on all my problems or let you push me to talk about them, because when I go home I have to be strong and pretend like everything is okay. No one would know what to do if I fell apart. Who would take care of me?

Th: You want to know that someone cares about you and would take care of you if you fell apart.

Pt: You don't care about me. You're only here because it's your job, picking people apart! You're supposed to open me up so you can see what's wrong with me, explain it to me, and then leave me to deal with it. You know, just when the going gets tough, you get going!

Th: So you expect that I'll open you up and then just leave you all alone to deal with what's wrong, right when you most need my help. From what you've said, this is something you have experienced before. You've gotten used to people getting inside you and then rejecting what they see. You're afraid that I will do the same thing, and you don't want to be hurt like that again.

At this point the patient began to cry. The therapist's empathic attunement and understanding, of both her wishes and her fears (i.e., the protective functions of her anger and defensiveness) enabled her to feel understood. Her affect changed markedly as she began to talk about her earlier experiences of rejection, expressing painful feelings in a way she had previously been unable to do.

In describing the profound effect on the state of the self that this kind of empathic understanding has, Ornstein and Ornstein (1996a) explained: "Feeling understood is the adult equivalent of being held, which on the level of self-experience results in firming up or consolidating the self" (p. 94). The underlying feelings and needs made available by the ensuing suspension of defense are then integrated and transformed through the therapist's empathic interpretations.

To summarize, empathic interpretations constitute the therapist's most powerful tool for communicating understanding, clarifying experience, legitimizing affect and needs, mitigating defensiveness, facilitating the reorganization of affective experience, and strengthening the self. In addition, for most patients the experience of being responded to in this way constitutes a new relational experience, which is in itself a potent aspect of the mutative process.

ADDRESSING SOMETHING WITHOUT ADDRESSING EVERYTHING

With brief treatment our goal is less to get something finished than to get something started. We're aiming for a correction in course. Whether what gets started is a process of understanding, of stabilization, or of change, we're trying to strengthen the self, to help the patient develop more internal and external resources for dealing with life. This process does not need to be completed at the time of termination for continued working through and growth to occur afterwards. In other words, in brief treatment, we can address something without addressing everything.

Yet a little bit can go a long way. Sometimes what the patient emerges with is a new experience of what is possible, both in relation to themselves and to others. One patient, faced with the need to end treatment because her therapist was moving away, said, "All my life I was waiting for someone who could understand me. You came along and now you're leaving and I won't have that anymore." After reflecting the patient's feelings of loss, the therapist added, "So you'll never again have the experience of feeling that there's no one who could ever understand you." "Right," the patient responded, "it makes me feel like less of a freak."

The therapist's response to this isolated and disconnected woman underscored that there was some experience in her of the relationship that would remain with her, whatever else might be lost in their termination. Once she has felt understood in this way, she can no longer go back to seeing herself as incomprehensible or the world as a place where such an empathic connection would never be possible. She might believe that it will never happen again. However, much as the task of clearing a path in the woods that has become overgrown is much less difficult than the task of carving it out the first time, finding one's way back to an experience is usually easier than getting there initially. This patient's experience with her therapist opens the door to her being able to seek out and find similar experiences with others.

Experiences like those of the woman just described are powerful events, which can permanently change the internal landscape. Elson (1995), encouraging therapists doing brief treatment to appreciate the enormous potential of even brief encounters, drew on an experience of Dostoevsky's to illustrate:

> We not infrequently despair over the brevity of our work with the individuals who come to us or are mandated for treatment. I would like to share an illustration of the manner in which a weakened and endangered self can be sustained by the brief experience of a selfobject function which becomes transformed into psychic structure capable of restoring cohesion and strength to that self.
>
> When Dostoevsky was but twenty four, he spent more than a year revising and editing a work of fiction called Poor Folk. Finally he read it to a friend, who in turn showed it to other friends, who woke him in the middle of the night to give him hugs and congratulations. One friend took it to a much feared and revered Russian critic, urging him to read the manuscript and likening its author to a new Gogol. Skeptical at first, he roared, "Bring him to me!" His enthusiasm and praise were unstinting. And Dostoevsky left him in a daze, wondering, "Am I really such a great man?"
>
> Many years later he wrote, "This was the most blissful moment of my life. Every time I remembered this moment when I was in Siberia [where

> his wrists and ankles were shackled for four years, leaving permanent scars] I found new courage and strength. Still today I remember it with joy.' (Geir Kjetsa, Fyodor Dostoevsky: A Writer's Life, 1987, p. 45.)
>
> Our clients and patients perhaps do not have the genius of a Dostoevsky, yet the experience of being the center and focus of our empathic attention, the experience of being understood, does not go away. It remains as a beacon and may assist an individual in his lifelong quest for meaningful goals and relationships.

As therapists, we can reflect on moments both in our own lives and in our own treatment when this kind of powerful experience left a lasting impression. We might think of our appreciation of small gestures of understanding when grief-stricken, our swelling with pride when affirmed by someone we particularly admire, or our deep sense of connection and well-being when someone responds to us by sharing their own experience in a way that makes us feel known and understood in the depth of our being. It is not the duration, but the affective intensity of such experiences, that gives them their tremendous mutative power.

TERMINATION: OBJECT LOSS AND SELFOBJECT LOSS

When termination occurs before the therapist or patient feels the work is fully "done," which is often the case in brief treatment, there can be concern about what will be lost by stopping. It is helpful here to distinguish between object loss, which concerns the therapist as a separate, valued person who might be missed or mourned, and selfobject loss, which has to do with sustaining functions or experiences of which the therapist has been the source. When selfobject loss is a concern, there is a fear that with the loss of the therapist will come a loss, for example, of the capacity to be self-regulating, the ability to calm or motivate oneself, or (like the patient above) the opportunity to be understood and appreciated.

When we evaluate how people might do after termination, this selfobject dimension of the relationship is important to examine. It is helpful to ask ourselves what the patient will be able to sustain internally without us, either because there has been an increase in self-esteem or self-regulating capacities and the self is more firmly structured or because there has been an expansion of the selfobject milieu and the person is better able to find others who can be a source of sustaining selfobject experiences. These are connected: one has to believe a feeling or need is legitimate before one dares to express or seek to meet it. Being validated in therapy leads to more ability to assert one's needs outside of therapy.

It is useful to talk to people directly about these issues. One patient, announcing she no longer felt the need for me, stated, "I can validate myself now." Some people have described how they imagined writing in a journal or turning more to other people to sort out their feelings once they stopped coming to therapy. Others described recalling specific words I'd said or concepts we'd discussed to help them stay calm or hopeful when anxiety or despair threatened to overwhelm them.

Keeping in mind that brief treatment often ends at a time when the structure-building process and reorganization of self-experience have been set in motion but not completed, it is appropriate to help patients think through the consequences of leaving the selfobject matrix of the therapy relationship. This can best be accomplished by exploring together the current state of the patient's internal and external resources for sustaining a cohesive and vital sense of self.

SUMMARY: COMPONENTS OF A MODEL TO FACILITATE BRIEFER TREATMENT

Earlier I stated that the model I describe is less a particular technique than a series of components, whose combined use can make treatment more efficient. These components include

1. Eliciting patient expectations and active collaboration in defining the goals of treatment, reinforcing the patient as a center of initiative in the process;
2. Emphasizing and using the patient's strengths;
3. Illuminating and addressing underlying vulnerabilities that are exposed when usual defenses and solutions are overwhelmed;
4. Using an empathic mode of observation to focus on the selfobject dimension (internal meaning) of precipitating events; and
5. Using empathic interpretations to clarify and validate subjective experience, needs, and frustrated longings.

There is nothing new in these activities per se or different from what one might do in long-term treatment. But any one of them might be less emphasized in longer term therapy. That is not the case here. It is the combined and active use of all of these steps that makes the difference.

Focus is crucial, in both assessment and intervention. We are constantly looking for specific things, through particular lenses, for example, looking not simply at precipitating events, but at the selfobject dimension of those events. By utilizing strengths and clarifying vulnerabilities, we can move rapidly to the interpretation of focal issues.

Careful assessment of changes in the state of the self and associated selfobject surround, using the frameworks described above to determine how self-experience is vulnerable to disruption, enables the therapist to understand what must be addressed in order to enhance the self's vitality and cohesion. When we then communicate our understanding of the patient's subjective experience through empathic interpretations, we strengthen the self, mitigate defensiveness, facilitate the formation of a selfobject bond, and provide a new relational experience, all of which advance the therapeutic process.

Once this process has been mobilized, it may well continue on its own momentum after the treatment relationship ends. Thus a correction in course, rather than a completed journey, may be sufficient to produce benefit from brief treatment.

Although developed in the context of long-term, intensive psychotherapy and psychoanalysis, the conceptual framework provided by self psychology is ideally suited to facilitate treatment of any duration, no matter how brief. When translated from theory to practice, this framework provides a roadmap that can help us use whatever time we have to maximally help our patients.

ACKNOWLEDGMENTS

I would like to express my appreciation to my patients, students, and supervisees, who were sources of clinical examples incorporated in this chapter, and to Ernest Wolf and Carla Leone, who offered valuable suggestions on earlier drafts. I am also very grateful for the wisdom, support, and editorial comments of Miriam Elson and for the legacy left to us all through the work of Michael Franz Basch.

REFERENCES

Baker, H. (1991), Shorter-term psychotherapy: A self psychological approach. In: *Handbook of Short-Term Dynamic Psychotherapy,* ed. P. Crits-Christoph & J. Barber. New York: Basic Books, pp. 287–322.

Balint, M., Ornstein, P. & Balint, E. (1972), *Focal Psychotherapy: An Example of Applied Psychoanalysis.* London: Tavistock.

Basch, M. F. (1980), *Doing Psychotherapy.* New York: Basic Books.

——— (1988), *Understanding Psychotherapy: The Science Behind the Art.* New York: Basic Books.

——— (1992), *Practicing Psychotherapy: A Casebook.* New York: Basic Books.

——— (1995), *Doing Brief Psychotherapy.* New York: Basic Books.

Bellak, L. & Small, L. (1978), *Emergency Psychotherapy and Brief Psychotherapy,* 2nd ed. New York: Grune & Stratton.

Bergart, A. (1997), Women's views of their lives after infertility treatment fails. Doctoral Dissertation. University of Chicago.

Chernus, L. (1983), Focal psychotherapy and self pathology: A clinical illustration. *Clin. Soc. Work J.,* 11:215–227.

Elson, M. (1986), *Self Psychology in Clinical Social Work.* New York: Norton.

——— (1995), Pathways to health in self psychology. Seventy-Second Annual Meeting, American Orthopsychiatric Association, Chicago, Illinois, April 26, 1995.

Fajardo, B. (1987), Parenting a damaged child: Mourning, regression, and disappointment. *Psychoanal. Rev.,* 74:19–43.

Gardner, J. (1991), The application of self psychology to brief psychotherapy. *Psychoanal. Psychol.,* 8:477–500.

Goldberg, A. (1973), Psychotherapy of narcissistic injuries. *Arch. Gen. Psychiat.,* 28:722–726.

Kohut, H. (1975), Technique, termination, trial internalizations. In: *The Chicago Institute Lectures,* ed. P. Tolpin & M. Tolpin. Hillsdale, NJ: The Analytic Press, 1996, pp. 365–379.

Kohut, H. (1984), *How Does Analysis Cure?* ed. A. Goldberg & P. Stepansky. Chicago: University of Chicago Press.

——— (1987), *The Kohut Seminars on Self Psychology and Psychotherapy With Adolescents and Young Adults,* ed. M. Elson. New York: Norton.

Lazarus, L. (1980), Brief psychotherapy of narcissistic disturbances. *Psychother.: Theory, Res. & Prac.,* 19:228–236.

——— (1988), Self psychology: Its application to brief psychotherapy with the elderly. *J. Geriatric Psychiat.,* 21:109–125.

Lichtenberg, J. (1989), *Psychoanalysis and Motivation.* Hillsdale, NJ: The Analytic Press.

——— Lachmann, F. & Fosshage, J. (1992), *Self and Motivational Systems: Toward a Theory of Psychoanalytic Technique.* Hillsdale, NJ: The Analytic Press.

Messer, S. & Warren, C. (1995). *Models of Brief Psychodynamic Therapy:* A *Comparative Approach.* New York: Guilford.

Orange, D. (1995), *Emotional Understanding: Studies in Psychoanalytic Epistemology.* New York: Guilford.

Ornstein, A. (1986), "Supportive" psychotherapy: A contemporary view. *Clin. Soc. Work J.,* 14:14–30.

——— & ——— (1996b), II. Speaking in the interpretive mode and feeling understood: Crucial aspects of the therapeutic action in psychotherapy. In: *Understanding Therapeutic Action: Psychodynamic Concepts of Cure,* ed. L. Lifson. Hillsdale, NJ: The Analytic Press, pp. 103–125.

——— & ——— (1997), Brief but deep: Finding the focus in "focal psychotherapy." Twentieth Annual International Conference on the Psychology of the Self, Chicago, Illinois, November 13, 1997.

Ornstein, P. (1988), Multiple curative factors and processes in the psychoanalytic psychotherapies. In: *How Does Treatment Help?* (Workshop Series of the American Psychoanalytic Association, Monograph 4, ed. A. Rothstein. Madison, CT: International Universities Press, pp. 105–126.

——— & Ornstein, A. (1972), Focal psychotherapy: Its potential impact on psychotherapeutic practice in medicine. *J. Psychiat. Med.*, 3:311–325.

——— & Ornstein, A. (1996a), I. Some general principles of psychoanalytic psychotherapy: A self-psychological perspective. In: *Understanding Therapeutic Action: Psychodynamic Concepts of Cure,* ed. L. Lifson. Hillsdale, NJ: The Analytic Press, pp. 87–101.

Ringstrom, P. (1995), Exploring the model scene: Finding the focus in an intersubjective approach to brief psychotherapy. *Psychoanal. Inq.*, 15:493–513.

Seruya, B. (1997), *Empathic Brief Psychotherapy.* Northvale, NJ: Aronson.

Socarides, D. & Stolorow, R. (1984–1985), Affects and selfobjects. *The Annual of Psychoanalysis,* 12/13:105–119. Madison, Ct: International Universities Press.

Stolorow, R., Brandchaft, B. & Atwood, G. (1987), *Psychoanalytic Treatment: An Intersubjective Approach.* Hillsdale, NJ: The Analytic Press.

Tolpin, M. (1983), Corrective emotional experience: A self psychological reevaluation. In: *The Future of Psychoanalysis,* ed. A. Goldberg. New York: International Universities Press, pp. 363–380.

Tolpin, P. (1984), Discussion of "A current perspective on difficult patients" by B. Brandchaft and R. D. Stolorow, and "Issues in the treatment of the borderline patient" by G. Adler. In: *Kohut's Legacy,* ed. A. Goldberg & P. Stepansky. Hillsdale, NJ: Analytic Press, pp. 138–142.

Wolf, E. S. (1988), *Treating the Self: Elements of Clinical Self Psychology.* New York: Guilford.

Chapter 13

Discussion of Jill Gardner's "Using Self Psychology in Brief Psychotherapy"

Linda A. Chernus

Dr. Gardner has eloquently presented an overview of brief psychotherapy utilizing a self psychological approach. She rightly emphasizes that this approach is not a technique but, rather, a mode of listening and understanding and suggests a series of components to enhance the effectiveness of what can be accomplished psychotherapeutically in a relatively brief and finite time period. In so doing, Dr. Gardner maintains the self psychological emphasis on the empathic mode of listening, in contrast to other psychodynamic approaches to brief psychotherapy, which tend to be technique-based (see, for example, Budman and Gurman, 1988; Piper et al., 1991; Davanloo, 1995). As in the case of the longer psychoanalytic psychotherapies, including psychoanalysis, Dr. Gardner's approach to psychoanalytic self psychology in a time-limited modality is rooted in a particular mode of listening, understanding, and communication of our understanding, which is ideally the *antithesis* of a technique-based brief psychotherapy.

Probably Dr. Gardner's most overarching contribution today is the idea that brief psychotherapy and a self psychological approach to treatment are highly compatible and, in fact, make possible a very productive brief treatment precisely *because* the use of the empathic mode enables the focus to be depth psychological, rather than superficial and behavioral. This is of the utmost importance because I believe that brief psychotherapy cannot be successful without a focus, and use of the empathic mode leads to a psychological focus rather than a preoccupation with external events. The reason for this is because attention to the state of the self, as well as to the external precipitants leading to self-state disruption, in conjunction with an effort to understand the selfobject functions we serve, allows a subjective and internal focus to emerge quickly. Since the treatment is by definition time-limited, rapid engagement and identification of an affectivity significant focal issue facilitates the process by providing more opportunity for the working through and termination phases.

The essence of this process is structure building, as is the case in the longer term treatment modalities; however, focal psychotherapy requires even more finely tuned skills because of the impact of the time limit on the treatment process. Though the therapist attempts to identify an internal focus whose exploration, through the empathic mode, will lead to a strengthening of the self, this understanding must be even clearer and more immediate if he and the patient are to do some working through of the issue in a limited period of time. In contrast, a more technique-based brief treatment, even one that is psychodynamic both in its treatment process and in its understanding of the patient, does not tend to become depth psychological because it is not grounded in the empathic mode but, rather, in a more superficial understanding of the symptoms and presenting problems. This limits the degree to which a genuine process of internal structural growth can be initiated.

The idea of a depth psychological brief treatment is also enormously relevant at this time, because in the managed care climate it is frequently assumed that brief is equal to superficial, cognitive, behavioral, or some combination thereof. These diametrically opposed mindsets are illustrated by Dr. Gardner's discussion of treatment planning as being a *clinical,* rather than an *administrative,* process. From this vantage point, *genuine* treatment planning involves a natural process of engagement, identification of a focal issue that is internal to the patient and manifested in the selfobject dimensions of the relationship, and discussing this focus actively with the patient. We hope to achieve some sort of lasting internal change, which may, to a greater or lesser extent, be manifested externally and behaviorally.

By contrast, in a managed care model the treatment is conceptualized as leading to measurable, behavioral goals, so that the treatment planning is *administrative* rather than emerging naturally from an understanding of the issues bringing the patient to treatment. Since the goal is quantifiable, so too is the treatment planning, which in this frame of reference has little to do with the patient's specific psychological and therapeutic needs but, rather, with the minimum number of sessions estimated to achieve the measurable outcomes.

In my opinion, not only does a self psychological approach enhance the effectiveness of time-limited psychotherapy, but furthermore, the importance of recognizing that brief psychotherapy can be depth psychological refutes the pre-self psychological polarization of "supportive" versus "insight" psychotherapy. If brief is generally intended to be "supportive," the best support we can provide in times of crisis consists of trying to communicate our understanding of what the patient is experiencing and why. This is very different from a superficially "supportive" treatment predicated on reassurance and, in my experience, much more therapeutically viable both in understanding the factors contributing to the current internal crisis and in promoting self-cohesion.

There exists, in fact, a long tradition of brief psychotherapy being interwoven with the evolution of self psychology, beginning with the Balints and the Ornsteins (Balint, Ornstein, and Balint, 1972; Ornstein and Ornstein, 1972, 1997), Elson (1986), Basch (1992,1995), and others (Chernus, 1983; Gardner, 1991). The term *focal psychotherapy* has been frequently utilized in this tradition to refer to a time-limited, in-depth therapy utilizing the empathic mode. In contrast with many other brief psychotherapy models, focal psychotherapy, like the longer term modalities, has generally not excluded patients with more chronic fragmentation states. I believe that this is because use of the empathic mode promotes cohesion and integration, so that patients can be treated within a self psychological framework who would be "too sick" to tolerate a more experience-distant analytic approach.

If diagnosis in and of itself is not the crucial variable in patient selection for focal psychotherapy, what is? First, I agree with Dr. Gardner that a focal issue must emerge early in the treatment. It is important to note, however, that the emergence of an internal focus is not simply related to the patient, but equally or more so to the *therapist's* capacity to understand the state of the patient's self, including why and how it has been disrupted. The therapist in a sense helps to "shape" the focal issue, based on his immersion in the patient's subjective experience and the patient's emerging selfobject needs.

A second important factor in successful focal psychotherapy is a capacity to engage fairly quickly, which we also previously saw as primarily a patient variable. Most of us now recognize, however, that the therapist is an important ingredient in promoting a rapid therapeutic engagement, because the very process of assessing the state of the patient's self promotes a feeling of being understood, which simultaneously leads to a deepening of the therapeutic relationship and to the emergence of a focus for the treatment. Diagnosis and treatment are, in fact, inseparable, with both processes beginning at the first contact and remaining ongoing throughout the entire treatment process. Our understanding of the patient generally becomes deeper and more comprehensive the longer we know him, so that our diagnostic understanding is continually being revised. Consequently, the briefer the therapeutic contact, the more difficult it is to understand the patient "diagnostically."

It probably won't come as any surprise that I believe a third factor related to successful outcome, the capacity to terminate without malignant regression and/or other severe symptomatology, is once again a variable of *both* patient and therapist. In deciding on focal psychotherapy as a treatment of choice, the clinician must attempt to predict whether the patient, in the context of a solid engagement based on empathic understanding, will be capable of utilizing the termination phase to grow in his or her capacity to tolerate loss and to respond more adaptively to it. If it appears that this is likely to be the case, the termination phase can further add to the internal process of structural change and growth, rather than becoming a repetition of previous painful losses, which were experienced as an assault on the self. Perhaps the most important variable related to outcome, however, is the motivation of both patient and therapist to work intensively on the patient's issues. If this motivation is strong and solid, the process is more powerfully fueled and can withstand the ravages of, in this instance, too *little* time.

I would now like to emphasize what I feel are some of Dr. Gardner's most salient points. First, by looking at the selfobject dimensions of the precipitating event and why the patient's usual defenses failed to sufficiently contain painful affective states, a focus emerges. This in turn reveals the underlying problems or characterological vulnerabilities resulting in the recent psychological disequilibrium and internal crisis. In this process, it is essential that the therapist also attempt to understand the "selfobject dimension" of the precipitating event(s), because this helps him see how dependent the patient's self is on his particular selfobject milieu for regulation and stability. Like a thermostat regulating the temperature within a building or a warm-blooded animal's body, the greater the efficiency of the furnace, the structural organization of the heating system, and the building's insulation, the more readily it can maintain a constant and steady state, despite fluctuations in the outside environment. Under ideal conditions, the thermostat is not required to work intensively to regulate the internal state, and the "self" is less vulnerable to changes and disruptions in its selfobject environment. It is for this reason that a knowledge of the external events or precipitants leading the patient into treatment is relatively meaningless unless we understand how the patient experiences them (i.e., the impact of these events on the patient's psychological regulatory system), which can vary greatly depending on what the patient brings to the situation. The more self-regulating and flexible the self, the less powerful will be the impact of external fluctuations, and the psychological thermostat will not be as easily overloaded by the demands of the system.

As a result of understanding the selfobject dimensions of both the precipitating event and the developing therapeutic relationship, a degree of specificity becomes possible, which I have rarely observed in clinical work not utilizing a self psychological approach. Generally, when patients come to treatment following a loss, the therapist conceptualizes the problem as a grief reaction, though he or she may specify whether it is "relatively uncomplicated," complicated by characterological features, delayed, or for other reasons unresolved. Dr. Gardner's two clinical examples of patients coming to treatment following losses, however, eloquently illustrate how the specificity of understanding resulting from the empathic mode led to two very different treatment processes with both patients seemingly experiencing "unresolved grief reactions."

The first patient, a woman who had spent years nursing her ill husband, came to treatment with symptoms similar to those of a grief reaction. However, by recognizing how her sense of self was organized around her role as caregiver, Dr. Gardner was able to understand this patient as needing to find a new sense of meaning through other selfobject relationships in order to restore her self-esteem. This is very different from treating someone for a "simple" grief reaction. Actually, I believe that probably most patients who present with so-called "simple" grief reactions are in fact experiencing some fragmentation of the self related to subtle or obvious changes in their selfobject milieu subsequent to the loss. To return to my thermostat metaphor, the self has been unable to adequately self-regulate, so that the therapist and the selfobject transference dimensions of the therapeutic relationship are needed to provide a thermostat that will achieve some regulation, though not necessarily at the same temperature as was previously maintained. A fine-tuning of the furnace and duct system, as well as higher quality or more efficiently packed insulation, may also be provided by the therapist's selfobject functions. None of this would be possible, however, were it not for attention to the selfobject dimensions of both the precipitant and the therapeutic relationship, which promotes this specificity and adds to the positive impact of the treatment.

Dr. Gardner's next clinical vignette, of a man who was seemingly unable to resolve his wife's death, also further illustrates the specificity achieved through an empathic assessment of the patient's self-state and selfobject needs. The therapist realized that this patient was not simply experiencing an unresolved grief reaction, but rather one that was complicated by a posttraumatic stress reaction to the way in which he discovered his wife's death. Thus the "treatment plan" involved "integrating the affects connected with this traumatic memory," a very different focus from either resolving "simple" grief or from Dr. Gardner's work with the previous patient.

I also want to emphasize Dr. Gardner's conceptualization of psychological symptoms as both expressing deficits in the cohesion, strength, or vitality of the self and as reflective of "attempts to restore or reorganize the weakened self." Though this is always the case, I believe it is especially important that we attend to the structure and function of symptoms in a time-limited therapy, because it is tempting, in view of our time constraints, to try to simply "take away" symptoms. Instead of doing so, however, our role is to understand and communicate our understanding of the attempted functions symptoms are meant to serve, including why and how they are not working well enough to regulate the system. In the treatment process, we hope to replace the attempted functions of the symptoms with functions provided through the selfobject transferences, so that the fragmented self can be restored to prior functioning and ideally become even more adaptive and flexible when future external disruptions threaten its integration. In a sense, then, understanding the meaning and functions of the patient's presenting symptoms becomes the essence of the treatment process.

Also worthy of emphasis is Dr. Gardner's discussion of "legitimization," a concept that is frequently misunderstood by critics of self psychology. Use of the empathic mode of understanding involves legitimizing the patient's feelings, including defensive feelings of denial or even psychotic-like symptoms such as delusions. To say, based on our empathy, that it makes sense in light of all that we know about the patient that he might feel or behave in a certain manner, not only leads to a strengthening of the self, but deepens the therapeutic process and enables the patient to at times be integrated enough to begin to question for himself the functions of his behavior. Though perhaps the term is misleading in its tone, such legitimization is in no way experienced by the patient or intended by the therapist as a collusion with or sanctioning of the patient's feelings, behaviors, and symptoms. We are simply attempting to communicate our understanding of the psychological reasons for the patient's current and past subjective experiences. More often than not, the strengthening of the self that this process promotes leads to changes in the patient's coping mechanisms, which are initiated by him through self-awareness, rather than by the therapist. Perhaps, ironically, it is difficult for *me* to empathically understand how such misconceptions about the meaning of legitimization in this context can occur, since it seems clear that empathic understanding, as opposed to confrontation from an external vantage point, promotes self-cohesion and subsequently a greater capacity for self-reflection.

Dr. Gardner also presents clinical illustrations demonstrating how a focus on the underlying problem in the self, which is exposed by the failure of characterological defenses, leads to a successful therapeutic outcome. In one instance, a woman whose characterological defense was her competency and her independence became symptomatic when her medical problems were such that she could not successfully minimize her lack of control and helplessness. When the therapist was able to legitimize the reasons for the failure of her usual defenses, she could understand her anxiety as reasonable in light of the situation and regain her psychological equilibrium. I believe this is in part because the communication of our understanding serves a selfobject function that increases integration and substitutes for the previous, more poorly functioning defenses.

Though other clinical examples are presented, Dr. Gardner's final clinical example, including an excerpt from the second session of a brief psychotherapy, is perhaps most meaningful because it illustrates the role of empathic understanding and communication in engaging a patient who is initially defensive and resistant. By empathically accepting and trying to understand her initial resentment, the therapist was able to engage her in a process exploring the meaning of this resentment, which stemmed from a feeling that she must take care of everyone else, even at the expense of dealing with her own problems. This led to an amazingly rapid engagement and to the emergence of intense affect that became therapeutically viable, resulting in at least a new experience of allowing herself to express pain and feel that it was accepted and understood. I would expect that this would have further resulted in some genuine internal growth in this woman's capacity to use others to serve soothing and integrating selfobject functions for her.

Perhaps the essence of Dr. Gardner's treatment is most effectively stated when she says, "Empathic interpretations constitute the therapist's most powerful tool for communicating understanding, legitimizing affect and needs, reducing defensiveness, facilitating the reorganization of affective experience, and strengthening the self. In addition, for most patients the experience of being responded to in this way constitutes a new relational experience, which is in itself a potent aspect of the mutative process."

Finally, I want to underscore with Dr. Gardner that the treatment process need not be completed by the termination of the therapy, because once set in motion, it can lead to further and deeper changes both in the focal area and in other aspects of the personality. Furthermore, it makes sense, if our goal is strengthening the self, to enable the patient to do as much of the therapeutic work as possible by himself, with the certain knowledge that he can return for brief periods of treatment when he needs the selfobject functions of the therapist in order to continue the process of change.

REFERENCES

Balint, M., Ornstein, P. & Balint, E. (1972), *Focal Psychotherapy: An Example of Applied Psychoanalysis*. London: Tavistock.

Basch, M. F. (1992), *Practicing Psychotherapy: A Casebook*. New York: Basic Books.

——— (1995), *Doing Brief Psychotherapy*. New York: Basic Books.

Budman, S. & Gurman, A. (1988), *Theory and Practice of Brief Therapy*. New York: Guilford.

Chernus, L. (1983), Focal psychotherapy and self pathology: A clinical illustration. *Clin. Soc. Work J.*, 11:215–227.

Davanloo, H. (1995), *Unlocking the Unconscious*. Somerset, NJ: Wiley.

Elson, M. (1986), *Self Psychology and Clinical Social Work*. New York: Norton.

Gardner, J. (1991), The application of self psychology to brief psychotherapy. *Psychoanal. Psychol.*, 8:477–500.

Ornstein, A. & Ornstein, P. (1997), Brief but deep: Finding the focus in "focal psychotherapy." Presented at the Twentieth Annual International Conference on the Psychology of the Self, Chicago, Illinois, November 13.

Ornstein, P. & Ornstein, A. (1972), Focal psychotherapy: Its potential impact on psychotherapeutic practice in medicine. *J. Psychiat. Med.*, 3:311–325.

Piper, W., Hassan, F., Azim, A., Joyce, A. & McCallum, M. (1991), Transference interpretation, therapeutic alliance and outcome in short-term individual psychotherapy. *Arch. Gen. Psychiat.*, 4:946–953.

Chapter 14

Developmental Aspects of the Twinship Selfobject Need and Religious Experience

Lallene J. Rector

"If thou sorrow, he will weep; if thou wake, he cannot sleep; thus of every grief in heart he with thee *doth bear a part.*" (Shakespeare, *Passionate Pilgrim)*

Many clinicians have difficulty in determining how to deal with the religiosity of some patients (Goldberg, 1996). In the history of psychoanalytic endeavor, the experience of belief in and relation to a sacred Other, often called "God," has been variously understood, and contradictory views have emerged on a spectrum of two extremes (Freud, 1927, 1930; Winnicott, 1971; Meissner, 1984). At one end, religious experience is seen as a pathological expression of intrapsychic conflict or psychosis; at the other, religion is viewed as a necessity for mental health. More moderate views understand religious belief as serving psychological functions, either to the benefit and/or to the detriment of an individual's sense of well-being. The psychology of the self represents such a position in its interpretation of religion and suggests, in contrast to the previous extremes, that religious experience, belief, and practice may be understood as an expression of the state of the self and the life-long need for self-esteem–enhancing selfobjects. Kohut recognized that religion could serve any of the selfobject functions he had described (1971, 1984).

This chapter begins with a review of both Kohut's definition of the twinship selfobject function and the subsequent discussion of it in self psychology literature. Second, it is noted that Kohut did not as fully elaborate the twinship selfobject concept as he did the mirroring and idealizing selfobject concepts. A developmental continuum of the twinship trajectory is suggested with a movement from early childhood manifestations of more imitative behavior to a mature capacity to experience essential alikeness and belonging on the broadened basis of feeling oneself to be a human being among other human beings. Third, the role of gender is considered as a dimension of the twinship selfobject need. And finally, the ways in which certain aspects of religious experience and belief may be motivated by twinship longings is explored with particular attention to how the twinship selfobject need may function in ideas about the nature of God, the concept of *imago dei* (the claim that human beings are made in the image of God), the nature of gendered God-images, and the incarnational beliefs of some religions (i.e., the belief that God is/was manifested in human form). The chapter concludes with a discussion of a brief clinical vignette and the significance of these ideas for the clinical setting.

DEFINITION OF TWINSHIP AND ITS PSYCHOLOGICAL FUNCTIONS

Kohut (1971) originally defined the twinship selfobject need as the middle stage of a developmental process encompassed by the mirroring selfobject. Preceded by an earlier merger stage in which the other was experienced as an extension of the self, twinship recognized a greater degree of separateness from the other who was experienced as just like oneself. Mirroring in the narrow sense described the experience of the other as important only in the enthusiastic confirmation of the self. Later, Kohut introduced the term *alter ego* and concluded in *How Does Analysis Cure?* (1984) that the alter ego transference was a "selfobject transference *sui generis* and not [as] a subgroup of the mirror transference" (p. 193). Here, he offered the definition of an alter ego selfobject as "a selfobject that will make itself available for the reassuring experience of essential alikeness (twinship or alter ego transference)" (p. 193). Describing the experience at greater length, it is a "confirmation of the feeling that one is a human among other human beings" (p. 200) and

> something human beings have in common: an overall alikeness in the capacity for good and evil, in emotionality, in gesture and voice. These aspects of our basic alikeness are signposts of the human world that we

need without knowing we need them so long as they are available to us (p. 200).

Since Kohut's writing, a number of discussions have emerged that offer further elaboration and alternative definitions of this basic concept. Of particular note is the work of Detrick (1985, 1986) and Brothers (1993). Detrick suggested that twinship and alter ego should not be used synonymously. He (1986) offered the following distinctions: "Twinship phenomena are those in which an experience of sameness and alikeness serves the central function in the acquisition of skill" (p. 304), and, "Alter ego phenomena are experiences of sameness or alikeness that anchor the individual in a group process" (p. 304). While Detrick maintains the essence of Kohut's definition, these distinctions seem somewhat arbitrary. Similarly, Brothers (1993) agrees with a twinship definition as the experience of alikeness, but suggests a different definition for alter ego: "the need to experience the presence of essential sameness or alikeness with disavowed or hidden aspects of the self" (p. 192).

The focus of this chapter is delimited to the concept of twinship and the experience of belonging, based on a feeling of alikeness, as one dimension of this selfobject function. While the concept of twinship does not exhaust the complexity of the belonging phenomenon and while there may be aspects of mirroring and idealizing selfobject experiences that also relate to belonging, Kohut (1984) did confine his discussion of belonging to the twinship selfobject:

> The mere presence of people in a child's surroundings—their voices and body odors, the emotions they express, the noises they produce as they engage in human activities, the specific aroma of the foods they prepare and eat—creates a security in the child, *a sense of belonging* and participating, that cannot be explained in terms of a mirroring response or a merger with ideals [p. 200; emphasis mine].

Also relevant to this examination are the contributions of Basch and the characterizations of Goldberg (1988, 1990). In Basch's (1988, 1992) later work, he began to use the term *kinship* to refer to Kohut's earlier understanding of twinship. Basch (1992) agreed with Detrick (1986) that this was the most basic of the three selfobject functions Kohut described:[1]

---

[1] Basch (1992) described a "hierarchy of selfobject needs" with kinship being the most fundamental and basic to the emergence of idealizing selfobject needs. The capacity for idealization was regarded as a prerequisite for the fulfillment of mirroring.

> I prefer to call this the "kinship experience" because it asserts and strengthens the sense of being a member of a group—the acceptance that comes from "being like" the other. It is the appreciation of and resonance with, another's affect [p. 17].

Interestingly, Basch tended to speak of kinship in terms of belonging to the human race, a very broad casting of the basis for a feeling of belonging. Goldberg (1990) characterized the "healthy embodiment" of the twinship need as "the adult's feeling of belonging" (p. 11).

In the psychological functions of the twinship experience that Kohut did articulate (i.e., that the needs for the experience of essential alikeness and belonging are fundamental to human nature), they are similar to those of all selfobject motivations in their universality and thus constitute part of Kohut's psychological anthropology. When these needs are adequately met, self-esteem is enhanced, and narcissistic vulnerability is reduced. A sense of cohesion is strengthened, and the self is less likely to be derailed in the face of disappointment and narcissistic injury.

THE DEVELOPMENTAL CONTINUUM OF THE TWINSHIP SELFOBJECT NEED

There is very little elaboration in Kohut's work of the developmental trajectory for the twinship selfobject need, and he acknowledged this as a research agenda for future work (1984). In his earliest thinking, when twinship was the middle stage of development on the way to a mirroring function proper, Kohut (1971) thought twinship experiences began as preverbal experiences—similar to merger experiences (p. 124) and that they were the most nascent experiences of being human.

In childhood, twinship experiences are observed in what appear to be very ordinary circumstances, such as a little girl standing beside her grandmother in the kitchen, both kneading bread dough or a little boy pretending to shave next to his father and helping him with tools in the basement (Kohut, 1984, p. 197). In these examples, the child does not assume that the father is like him or the grandmother is like her, but rather, the child imitates the behavior of the selfobject or participates through imitative action in order to establish an experience of essential alikeness and belonging. Kohut regarded twinship support as especially critical during the oedipal phase when masculine and feminine identifications are becoming more solidified and when more conscious feelings about one's gender begin to emerge. Solomon (1991) extended this with her claim that twinship experiences with both parents help pre-oedipal girls sort out "anatomical realities" and the associated meanings.

In latency and beyond, twinship relationships with peers and with adults are critical for learning and for the acquisition of skills. In adolescence, peers may serve as twinship selfobjects that provide

> 1) confirming reflections and extensions of the endangered self;
> 2) increasing security through contact with sameness;
> 3) an increasing feeling of cohesion through maintenance of empathic contact with others; and
> 4) an increasing feeling of cohesion in the sharing of common ideals [Kohut, 1972, p. 661].

In adulthood, "twinship support" continues to supply major maintenance of the self throughout life and can be found in friendships, partnerships, and marriages; membership in civic organizations, clubs, congregations; and in professional identity shared with colleagues. Twinship selfobjects are also very significant during periods of great creativity (Kohut, 1976).

In Kohut's discussion of the experience of returning from a foreign country, he suggested that negative or difficult experiences of alikeness may be preferable to more positive experiences of support from those who are experienced as too different.[2] Support of the self is derived as much (and sometimes exclusively) from "nonverbalizable experiences of sameness, of identity" (1984, p. 227) as from the receipt of actual help. This feeling of support for the self can happen even if one is moving from "benevolent non-alter egos" to "inimical alter egos."

To more fully explicate a developmental trajectory of twinship, I am suggesting that the early end of the continuum could be viewed as an archaic or unmodified form of twinship that is characterized by an inclination to imitate the other as an attempt to establish the experience of alikeness that may in turn contribute to a sense of belonging.[3] This can take the form of seeking a kind of literal match. For example, a psychoanalytic patient reported a dream in which she was putting up pictures in the analyst's kitchen that she had drawn. When she heard the analyst coming into the house, she quickly began to take them down. When in the session she was asked to tell about the pictures, the patient described one as being bright yellow. As the patient

---

[2] See Gehrie (1996) for a discussion of negative selfobject experience.

[3] Earlier discussions with colleagues highlighted the importance of making a distinction between the child's experience of finding something alike in the other ("matching") that resonates with his or her own self versus a literal imitation in order to establish a sense of alikeness and belonging.

explored the significance of the color yellow, she began to cry, saying it had been her favorite color as a child because it was her mother's favorite color. She was concerned that the analyst not see the pictures because they represented her feelings of love for the analyst, and she was quite anxious about letting the analyst know this. In the negative dimension of the maternal transference, the patient expected the analyst to reject her wish to be alike. This would have constituted a retraumatization of the humiliation suffered when her older siblings mocked the patient's attempts to be like her mother. In her childhood, other imitations, or archaic twinship experiences, were expressed by wearing dresses made of the same material as her mother's and by later joining the mother in her diets.

A significant theme in the treatment of this patient dealt with the longing for a twinship selfobject experience that allowed the patient greater flexibility in experiencing herself and the analyst as alike and, more importantly, the possibility of establishing a twinship experience "in harmony with the preformed outline of the patient's preanalytic self" (Kohut, 1984, pp. 100–101). The fact that the patient's favorite color as an adult is purple and that she developed her own sense of fashion suggests a capacity to experience alikeness without regressing to archaic forms of twinship requiring literal imitation of the mother or the analyst.

As noted, Kohut's examples of the little girl kneading bread or the little boy shaving also suggest that early twinship selfobject experiences are essentially imitative and create an experience of being alike. As such, a certain phase appropriateness can be granted, but if adults engage in this imitative behavior in order to experience alikeness or belonging, as if there is no deeper sense of self guiding one's activities and allowing for the recognition of similarity in the other, then this may indicate a developmental arrest.[4] Such imitative behavior may be more indicative of a pseudo-identification rather than an archaic form of twinship.

In a similar vein, Goldberg (1988) addressed the "nature of the misfit" from a developmental perspective. He observed a certain universality in the experience of being unable to fit in or of not belonging. However, the misfit has a more chronic sense of feeling alien, the extent of which constitutes character pathology. Although Goldberg did not speak of a twinship trajectory per se, he did offer the idea of a

---

[4] Winnicott's (1960) concept of the true self/false self is a relevant concept. However, within the framework of self psychology, the phenomenon of imitation is more consistently understood as the attempt to find a needed selfobject responsiveness that provides an experience of alikeness and perhaps functions as a basis for the experience of belonging.

continuum from "primitive relationships to mature selfobjects," representative of Kohut's developmental perspective, and from "absolute conformity to bizarre outsider" (chapter 1). The latter continuum seems to address disturbed twinship needs at both ends of the continuum.

Kohut did not develop in any depth what constituted a mature or health-enhancing twinship selfobject experience but believed normal adult twinship experiences would at least be emotionally analogous to the experiences of latency he had already described (shaving with the father or kneading dough with the grandmother). At the very least, a more mature formation of the self recognizes how others may be like oneself and vice versa, in addition to having a capacity to benefit from twinship experience. Given these assumptions, as one develops with adequately empathic experiences of being essentially alike and adequate experiences of belonging, the potential for experiencing difference without undue anxiety and for valuing diversity would increase.

As in the developmental trajectories of the mirroring and idealizing selfobject functions, a broadened base of experience evolves, which may serve the twinship need, perhaps contributing to a more deeply felt sense of kinship with the human species of which Basch (1992) speaks. One is a human being among other human beings despite the particularities of difference (e.g., sex, race, religious affiliation, sexual orientation, etc.). This capacity depends heavily in childhood upon having had one's own distinctiveness valued and affirmed, or mirrored, the very characteristics that might, in a different context, constitute an experience of twinship and provide some basis for a sense of belonging. The experience of diversity and difference can be viewed as the other side of sameness and is unavoidably influenced by one's experiences of alikeness.

Identification and Twinship

Identification is generally regarded as a form of internalization and its concept is sometimes appealed to in the explanation of self–selfobject dynamics. While it has relevance to the discussion of experiencing a shared likeness with an other, it is to be distinguished in self psychology by the experience of mutuality between self and selfobject and by the shift from a process of internal representation of the selfobject to a transmuting internalization of the selfobject function (Goldberg, 1988).

> The process of establishing, enhancing, and making enduring the self–selfobject relationship can also be seen as one of identification. This is not a case of merger between self and object or selfobject, but rather

> one of mutuality. Similar aims and values permit the stabilization of the self–selfobject linkage whereas differences breed disruption [Goldberg, 1988, p. 210].

The consideration of developmental perspectives does allow for a differentiation between archaic and mature selfobjects, so that while some might view Kohut's descriptions of archaic twinship experiences as early forms of imitative identification or even as pseudo-identification, the experience of something similarly shared is motivated not by loss (Freud, 1917), but by the need for selfobject sustenance, which is experienced as mutual and which enhances cohesion and esteem. Goldberg (1988) offers certain dimensions that can be considered in ascertaining the developmental level of self–selfobject linkage: "physical presence, intensity of attachment, interchangeability with similar relationships, and so forth" (p. 206).[5]

Kohut did not directly address the concept of identification in terms of its role in the twinship selfobject experience. Kohut (1971) spoke of gross or massive identifications with the analyst as a common response to the misguided efforts of some clinicians to induce change in the patient through the means of education and suggestion. The effect was ephemeral and did not result in the laying down of enduring structures in harmony with "the outline of the patient's preanalytic self" (1984, p. 101). In contrast, he noted the results of more selective identifications with "features or qualities of which are indeed compatible with the analysand's personality and enhance (up to now dormant) talents of the patient himself" (1971, p. 167). These are assimilated "in the identificatory process" and may constitute the acquisition of "solid nuclei of autonomous function and initiative" (1971, p. 167).

Though the latter reference to identificatory process seems to resemble the outcome of transmuting internalizations, that is, the acquisition of enduring structures or functions, the two may be distinguished again in that identification relates to the recognition of some shared quality between the self and the other (Freud, 1921) whereas transmuting internalizations refer to the (mutual) process, whereby following a disruption in the empathic connection between self and selfobject through "optimal frustration," the tie is reestablished via empathy and results in the incremental accrual of psychological structure. Anna

---

[5] Though Goldberg is not explicitly addressing twinship experience, he does allude to the difficulty in cleanly separating the three major selfobject needs from each other when he observes, "The self may share the same contents as that of the other (i.e., superego or selfobject) but unless these are idealized, that is, suffused with narcissistic libido or charged with emotional value, then there is no real relationship of meaning" (1988, p. 211).

Ornstein (1983) offered a further consideration of gross identifications. She concluded that, when there is a gross identification with the same-sex parent in the oedipal phase, this is evidence of a selfobject failure, that is, the failure of a twinship experience.

In the psychoanalytic situation, Kohut (1971) suggested that gross identification with the analyst, as seen with regard to behavior, mode of speaking, attitudes, and tastes, occurs frequently in the early phases. These identifications should be welcomed as a first step toward permitting structure building and working through and could be viewed as precursors to transmuting internalizations. The appearance of such identifications late in treatment was regarded as a possible harbinger of the termination phase.

DEVELOPMENTAL DISTURBANCE IN THE TWINSHIP TRAJECTORY

In considering the effects of any selfobject need that is frustrated and inadequately met during early development, the concept of empathy is crucial. Kohut (1978) defined empathy as "vicarious introspection" (pp. 205–232) and later as "the capacity to think and feel oneself into the inner life of another person. It is our lifelong ability to experience what another person experiences, though usually, and appropriately, to an attenuated degree" (1984, p. 82). He regarded it as the central feature of human experience that could mediate affirmation, support, and potential transformation where needed.

Without appropriate empathy for the twinship selfobject need during childhood, a self may develop feelings of not belonging, a chronic sense of not fitting in or of being marginalized, and/or a related difficulty in the capacity to experience alikeness without regressing to archaic literal imitations or to the gross identifications Ornstein observed (1983). This can result in creating "twins" through imitative efforts, often quite unconscious, in order to avoid the painful feeling of not belonging. An empathic environment, on the other hand, provides an acceptance of the longing to experience oneself as essentially similar to an other. Gehrie (1976) discussed a related issue, the experience of prejudice predicated upon the feeling that one is not like the other. He suggested the narcissistic injuries sustained by being the target of prejudice can be understood as based upon an inner experience of differentness that is painfully highlighted and whose etiology derived, in his sample, from early caregiving that emphasized the need to fit in, perhaps through a contrived twinship based on denial or disavowal, at the expense of valuing one's distinctiveness (i.e., an absence of positive twinship experience). More optimally, the parent allows the child to imitate him or her and does not humiliate or mock the child for these efforts to be alike or to establish a sense of belonging on this basis.[6] Inadequate empathy for the twinship selfobject need results in an "alter ego hungry personality" (Kohut and Wolf, 1978). "Alter ego hungry personalities need confirmation by being associated with another self whose appearance, opinions, and values they share" (Wolf, 1988, p. 73). One replacement after another will be sought, each time with the inevitable discovery that the other is not like oneself.

Having earlier theorized that imaginary playmates may be created by the child as a compensation for the absence of adequate twinship experiences (1971), Kohut reported the case of a female patient who described a protracted loneliness in childhood (1984). At one point in the treatment, he informed the woman of his summer vacation plans. Her reaction to the impending "loneliness" was to revisit her childhood fantasies of what she called "the genie in a bottle." At first, Kohut thought the genie originally represented a beloved grandmother and now represented him. It was the patient's attempt to control him for herself and to retain some of his presence. However, as they discussed the fantasy, it emerged that the genie was really an imaginary playmate, a little girl just like herself, a "twin to keep her company" (1984, p. 196). This patient created a twin when faced with the absence of the grandmother's selfobject responsiveness. Another characteristic of this alter ego experience was the need for a silent presence, a presence to whom the patient could talk, but from whom no response was required. The experience of being in the presence of a God whom one understands to be like oneself in some fundamental way may also function as a silent twinship.

TWINSHIP, GENDER, AND RELIGIOUS EXPERIENCE

One of the central features of twinship selfobject needs in early development is the experience of gender. Lang (1984) was one of the first to suggest that the experience of selfobject needs in childhood and throughout life may, in fact, be affected by one's experience of gender. What is mirrored or validated for little girls and for little boys often differs according to gender. Similarly, what are deemed idealizeable or

[6] Obviously, this has technical implications in psychoanalytic treatment for how the analyst responds to and interprets the patient's longing to experience the analyst as a twin. Kohut warns that the use of educational and suggestive means (versus interpretive means) forces a reliance on gross identifications with the analyst rather than the incremental building up of structure through transmuting internalizations—structure which is more consonant with the patient's own nuclear program (Kohut, 1971, pp. 320, 327).

admirable traits of personhood may also divide along the gender lines of femininity and masculinity. With regard to twinship, the challenge is to identify what kind of experiences in development support positive feelings about one's sex and gender identity, as well as positive twinship with other persons of one's own sex. Lang concluded that gender theory must include an accounting of how sociocultural role definitions are transferred into psychic structures.

Kohut (1984) observed difficulties where there was an absence of appropriate twinship experiences "to give support when a proud feminine [or masculine] self should have established itself" (p. 21). In his study of selfobject failures and gender disorders, Lothstein (1988) hypothesized that (1) the early organization of self-experience must involve a male or female imprint; (2) that the gender self-images that the primary caretaker has adopted become the child's gender self-images; and (3) finally, with Lang (1984), that "an awareness of one's gender [ought to] occupy a central place in one's sense of self" (p. 231). Gender imprint is in place before and/or during the consolidation of a cohesive self, so that gender is a central dimension of the self's experience. Thus, it should be addressed as a dimension of each selfobject need. Gardiner (1987) endorsed these ideas in calling for a recognition of gender differences in the formation of self-esteem.

These arguments for how masculinities and femininities are acquired can be extended to the experience of sexual orientation and represent another dimension of twinship need.[7] Persons with homosexual, bisexual, or transgendered orientations often describe, beginning in childhood, internalized feelings of strangeness and the experience of being socially marginalized. These experiences intensify archaic twinship selfobject needs, which, in turn, may contribute to more literal expressions, for example, seeking friendships only with those who are alike in these ways or rejecting others who are different. Considerations being given to gender in self psychology (Ornstein, 1983; Martinez, 1993; Shane and Shane, 1993) and in the work of Fast (1984) and Benjamin (1988, 1995) merit much more extensive discussion in terms of the developmental fate of the experience of difference.[8]

---

[7] See Goldberg's (1988, chapter 1) discussion of the case of a young homosexual man who despised his sexual orientation, but could not identify with a heterosexual orientation.

[8] Fast (1984) addressed the necessity of the child eventually coming to grips with the realization that he or she does not possess both sets of sex characteristics, but only one, and that the other is to be valued. Benjamin (1988, 1995) proposed a fascinating argument for the role of differentiation as an early point on the developmental continuum of gender experience and then described a more encompassing point of development in which oedipal complimentarity is transcended, that is, that feminine and masculine attributes, as these have been culturally and symbolically represented have a both/and quality in every human personality, rather than being treated dichotomously.

Participation in religion may meet any of the selfobject needs, though the mere presence of religion does not automatically convey the meaning, function, or derivation of religious interest within the personality. The role of gender in experiences of alikeness may inform and motivate interest in certain aspects of religion (Rector, 1996). Contemporary theology movements often emphasize aspects of a group of people that distinguish it from other groups. For example, when constructions about the nature of God, the nature of human beings, and concepts of salvation resonate with something experienced as similar to the members of a particular group, the appeal of these ideas may be understood in terms of the twinship need. With regard to a developmental continuum, the attempts to meet this need through religion may be more or less healthy, or religion may serve a compensatory function in the repair of earlier inadequate twinship experiences.

In the Judeo-Christian traditions, the concept of *imago dei* (i.e., the claim that humanity is created in the image of God) derives from the book of Genesis and can be regarded as one of the most fundamental claims to being God-like. Phyllis Bird, a Hebrew scripture scholar, suggests that, in "Sexual differentiation and the divine image in the Genesis creation texts" (1991), God-likeness is "the defining attribute of humanity" (p. 19). In addition to this God-likeness in image, Bird also observes a problem in the story of Adam and Eve, regarding Adam's need for

> a companion and helper. The resolution of the problem [she says] is accordingly signaled by the man's response, in his recognition that the one who confronts him [woman] is truly like him, not merely in appearance, but in substance—"of the same bone and flesh" [p. 14].

While her analysis of the text is quite complex, the centrality of being created in the image of God and of substantive human alikeness between man and woman is emphasized. Connection with the sacred other is appealed to, at least partially, on the basis of some alikeness in image.

The recognition of essential alikeness between man and woman is interpreted as a prototypical experience. From the view of self psychology, an affectively intense and concretized insistence on fundamental differences between the sexes accompanied by a rigid and exclusive preference to be only with "one's own," as this is sometimes expressed in liturgical practices and other social arrangements, may, in fact be indicative of disturbance in earlier developmental experiences of twinship, whether discovered or created. This stands in contrast to a capacity to feel alikeness based on broader, less concrete aspects of shared human experience.

In theological literature, gendered images of God are addressed by Sallie McFague's (1982, 1987) work on metaphorical theology. She suggests that all language is metaphorical and that there are images and understandings of God that seem more useful at different times in history. "The question we must ask is not whether one is true and the other false, but which one is a better portrait of . . . faith for our day" (1987, p. xiii). Further, there is a range of feminist interest calling for maternal images of God, or at least including the possibility of a feminine aspect of God. This can be seen in the feminine Hebrew concepts of Shekinah (light) and Sophia (wisdom) and in feminist theologians who speak of goddess, or God, as mother, lover, and friend (McFague, 1982, 1987; Ruether, 1983; Saussy, 1991).

In any of these instances, from a psychological perspective, part of the issue of God image and inclusive language has to do precisely with the basic need to feel some essential alikeness and the way in which that feeling contributes to a sense of belonging. Carol Saussy addresses this in *God Images and Self Esteem* (1991). She notes:

> When women image Deity in exclusively male terms, they relate to God (that is, male Deity) as "like the other but not like me." The symbols used of this Jewish and Christian male Deity or God are often symbols of power and authority: Father, Lord, Ruler, and King. When women image Deity in female terms, however, they relate to Goddess as "like me." Symbols that speak of the Goddess are also powerful symbols but are more likely representative of nurturing and relational power and are perhaps more serene: Earth Mother, Life Giver, Comforter, Wisdom. . . . Evoking the Goddess can be enormously creative, challenging, and energizing. However, replacing male imagery of Deity with female images is not a long term solution [p. 17].

Saussy proposed the word *God/dess* as an inclusive term, and similar to Bird, she did not recommend using only feminine pronouns for God. Instead, she called for a greater capacity to feel alikeness broadly on the basis of shared humanity, using imagery that is not gender-exclusive.

Kohut (early 1970s) referred, inadvertently, in his observation of the tragic figure's "incarnations in the myths of organized religion" (p. 214) to theological concepts of incarnation and suggested these beliefs are directly related to twinship needs. God takes on a human form, becomes like, and as a result knows what human beings experience. For some Christians, Jesus, the incarnation of God, becomes a companion, one who suffered as a human being and who identified with the lowly and the oppressed. In each of these theologies—Black theology, womanist theology (African American female), mujerista theology (Latina), and minjung theology (Korean)—there is an appeal to a human messiah figure who is alike in color, race, experience, and/or gender. Believers of these perspectives derive a heightened sense of well-being based in part on the experience of alikeness. They also are able to temper painful feelings of being marginalized and may feel encouraged to participate in the larger religious community, by virtue of having a place, of belonging. That these theologies have developed around concrete particularities with which persons experience alikeness does not automatically convey archaic twinship need. It seems, rather, that it is the degree of exclusivity that gives an indication of the developmental level of expression.

CLINICAL VIGNETTE AND DISCUSSION

The clinical vignette that follows is intended to illustrate how a twinship selfobject dimension can be expressed through a patient's religious experience and through dimensions of the transference (though in this case not as the dominant selfobject transference). The presentation pertains primarily to the religious content of Ms. F's treatment, to some related transference expressions, and is suggestive of how religious material may be understood and analyzed in terms of its selfobject function(s).

Ms. F was a religious woman pursuing professional ministry as a career when she entered intensive, twice-weekly psychotherapy. She had experienced certain relational difficulties and related anxieties as she tried to pursue her life ambitions. Ms. F was familiar with feminist theologies when she began the psychotherapy and during the period of our work together, she became even more immersed in this literature and began to prefer, rather exclusively, feminine images of God. She surrounded her environment with pictures of significant women in her life and in history, and at one point she excised all the male pronouns from her devotional literature and replaced them with feminine pronouns. It soon became clear that the complexity of Ms. F's religious involvement was related to a shame-filled, at times enraged, and esteem-depleted self who sought responsiveness in all three selfobject arenas. Her focus on a feminine image of God and the attempt to surround herself with various images of admirable femininity pointed to twinship (as well as idealizing) needs.

Ms. F described her childhood as dominated by feelings of loneliness and fear of her angry and critical parents. She felt both parents were controlling and that her father was especially authoritarian, as well as disappointed at not having a son. Her mother was experienced as emotionally and physically intrusive. Ms. F was subject, as well, to the beautification ministrations of her mother and interpreted this as an indication that her own distinctive femininity was not adequate and needed improvement. Twinship experience, at least in the realm of being a woman, depended more on a semiliteral imitation of the mother. Feeling she was not successful here, Ms. F removed herself from these pressures by pursuing a more typically masculine profession. Twinship support experienced in this work situation depended more safely on her subjective sense of alikeness in a shared profession rather than on the basis of her gender.

Ms. F's religious history was typical for a mainstream Protestant family. Her parents were reasonably active church members, attending worship services regularly. She was confirmed and baptized as a youth. During latency and adolescence, Ms. F was part of a girl's group at the church sponsored by one of the young adult women in the congregation. The group was involved in religious education, recreation, and charitable activities. Ms. F felt this group had been particularly important to her because it had provided much needed positive emotional engagement with an older sister/maternal figure and because it, along with her Girl Scout membership, provided an experience of shared interests and values with her peers. These experiences were interpreted as significant, at least in part, because of the sense of alikeness and, therefore, the sense of belonging that resulted.

During the beginning of the treatment, Ms. F quickly developed a positive attachment to me. Though the dominant transference was organized around a mirroring selfobject need, archaic twinship dimensions became evident and were interpreted in the observation that she often tried to be like others as a way of protecting herself from the more painful feelings of not fitting in, of being a "misfit."[9] It was difficult to determine what Ms. F's nuclear self-proclivities and ambitions were because she so readily engaged in imitative responses as efforts to establish a needed twinship experience. Yet, when she became anxious or was narcissistically injured, Ms. F retreated behind angry tirades against the offending persons, feeling herself to be an outcast. Some of this dynamic was manifested in the transference in her oscillations between imitating my style of dress (or at least experimenting with it) and then telling me, rather angrily, that she was not like me.

---

[9] Perhaps this inclination to resort to more imitative behavior is related to the kind of developmental organization based on "negative" selfobject experience that Gehrie (1996) describes.

Repeated interpretations of the negative maternal transference were made with attention to Ms. F's longings to feel we shared some things in common and, at the same time, her fear of an intrusive merger resulting from the expression of this twinship selfobject need.

It was revealed relatively late in the treatment, as we sought more deeply to understand her interest in professional ministry, that the most important influence on Ms. F's adult religious interests had been her paternal grandmother, a devout practitioner of the faith. To see her grandmother reading the Bible daily and to be exposed to her grandmother's love of the church had a major impact on Ms. F. Her own latency and adolescent involvement in religious activities may have been the expression of a silent twinship experience. During this period, I interpreted the development of Ms. F's exclusive preference for female God imagery as reflecting her need for a positive experience of female alikeness, perhaps modeled on the experience with her grandmother, but one that she had been unable to achieve with her mother. The goddess functioned to reassure her of having a place (belonging), as well as validating her own sense of femininity. This twinship dimension of her religious experience, albeit with elements of idealization and mirroring, was essentially based on the gendered aspect of the deity. Though there were ways in which this female God was experienced as validating and admirable, the exclusiveness and thoroughness of the feminine imagery was understood as a manifestation of an earlier developmental form of twinship based on the sense that she and the goddess were alike in a fundamental way; they shared femininity.

Ms. F felt support for some of these expressions in the twinship aspects of the selfobject transference, feeling that we both had feminist commitments and that we were both interested in teaching. Toward the end of the treatment, Ms. F had developed a personal style that was more conventional and that counteracted some of her feelings of not fitting in. We understood that her difficulty in not allowing herself to "fit in" and her inclinations to try and become like the other had been protective measures in response to the fear of merger, that is, a defense against the anticipation of retraumatization at the hands of an intrusive mother.

Once this was understood in the context of the selfobject experience with me and the merger anxiety worked through, Ms. F was freer to pursue her own inclinations. Though she retained a commitment to feminine images of God rather exclusively and was still vulnerable in some ways, Ms. F terminated treatment, pursuing her own "nuclear program" and experiencing alikeness based less on imitative efforts and more on an increasingly cohesive and vital self.

CONCLUSION

In summary, I have suggested that clinicians may find useful principles in the theoretical framework of self psychology for understanding the psychological function of religion in their patients. One motivation operative in certain dimensions of religious experience is the twinship selfobject need; however, diagnostic attention to the developmental continuum of the twinship need provides a deeper understanding of the psychodynamic underpinnings in adherence to certain religious beliefs and in the experience of relating to gendered images of God.

Twinship experience of alikeness forms a basis for the experience of belonging and has its own developmental trajectory. When twinship experiences are not adequately provided early in life, individuals are left with certain vulnerabilities and may seek experiences of alikeness through imitation of others or may suffer feelings of alienation and of being a misfit. These alter ego hungry personalities seek "twins" or may try to create twins in a more intense way as an attempt to repair low self-esteem and to manage proclivities toward fragmentation. This can result in experiences of not fitting in and in a lack of tolerance for difference and diversity. Archaic or compensatory needs for sameness may be indicated when there is a reliance on concretized forms of alikeness. More mature expressions of the need for sameness are seen in a preference, at times, to be with "one's own," but not exclusively. In healthier religious beliefs and practices, twinship can be seen operating in the emphasis on ways in which God, saviour, and neighbor are similar to oneself, especially with reference to gender, and yet not appealed to exclusively.

REFERENCES

Basch, M. F. (1988), *Understanding Psychotherapy: The Science Behind the Art.* New York: Basic Books.

——— (1992), *Practicing Psychotherapy: A Casebook.* New York: Basic Books.

Benjamin, J. (1988), *The Bonds of Love: Psychoanalysis, Feminism and the Problem of Domination.* New York: Pantheon Books.

——— (1995), *Like Subjects, Love Objects: Essays on Recognition and Sexual Difference.* New Haven: Yale University Press.

Bird, P. (1991), Sexual differentiation and divine image in the Genesis creation texts. In *The Image of God: Gender Models in Judaeo-Christian Tradition,* ed. K. E. Borresen. Minneapolis, MN: Fortress Press, pp. 5-28.

Brothers, D. (1993), The search for the hidden self: A fresh look at alter ego transferences. In: *The Widening Scope of Self Psychology: Progress in Self Psychology,* Vol. 9, ed. A. Goldberg. Hillsdale, NJ: The Analytic Press, pp. 191–207.

Detrick, D. (1985), Alterego phenomena and the alterego transferences. In: *Progress in Self Psychology, Vol. 1,* ed. A. Goldberg. New York: Guilford, pp. 240–256.

——— (1986), Alterego phenomena and the alterego transferences: Some further considerations. In: *Progress in Self Psychology, Vol. 2,* ed. A. Goldberg. New York: Guilford, pp. 299–304.

Fast, I. (1984), *Gender Identity: A Differentiated Model.* Hillsdale, NJ: The Analytic Press.

Freud, S. (1917 [1915]), Mourning and melancholia. *Standard Edition,* 14:243–258. London: Hogarth Press, 1957.

——— (1921), Group psychology and the analysis of the ego. *Standard Edition,* 18:69–143. London: Hogarth Press, 1955.

——— (1927), The future of an illusion. *Standard Edition,* 21:5–56. London: Hogarth Press, 1961.

——— (1930 [1929]), Civilization and its discontents. *Standard Edition,* 21:64–145. London: Hogarth Press, 1961.

Gardiner, J. K. (1987), Self psychology as feminist theory. *Signs,* 12:761–780.

Gehrie, M. (1976), Aspects of the dynamics of prejudice. In: *The Annual of Psychoanalysis, Vol. 4,* ed. G. Pollack. New York: International Universities Press, pp. 423–443.

——— (1996), Empathy in broader perspective: A technical approach to the consequences of the negative selfobject in early character formation. In: *Basic Ideas Reconsidered: Progress in Self Psychology, Vol. 12,* ed. A. Goldberg. Hillsdale, NJ: The Analytic Press, pp. 159–179.

Goldberg, A. (1988), *A Fresh Look at Psychoanalysis: The View from Self Psychology.* Hillsdale, NJ: The Analytic Press, pp. 143–156.

——— (1990), *The Prisonhouse of Psychoanalysis.* Hillsdale, NJ: The Analytic Press.

Goldberg, C. (1996), The privileged position of religion in the clinical dialogue. *Clin. Soc. Work J.,* 24:125–136.

Kohut, H. (1971), *The Analysis of the Self: A Systematic Approach in the Psychoanalytic Treatment of Narcissistic Personality Disorders.* New York: International Universities Press.

——— (1972), Discussion of "On the adolescent process as a transformation of the self" by E. S. Wolf, J. E. Gedo & D. M. Terman. In: *The Search for the Self: Selected Writings of Heinz Kohut: 1978–1981. Vol. II,* ed. P. H. Ornstein. Madison, CT: International Universities Press, 1978, pp. 659–662.

——— (early 1970s), From the analysis of Mr. R. In: *The Search for the Self: Selected Writings of Heinz Kohut: 1978–1981, Vol. III,* ed. P. H. Ornstein. Madison, CT: International Universities Press, 1990, pp. 183–222.

——— (1976), Creativeness, charisma, group psychology: Reflections on the self-analysis of Freud. In: *The Search for the Self: Selected Writings of Heinz Kohut: 1978–1981. Vol II,* ed. P. H. Ornstein. Madison, CT: International Universities Press, 1978, pp. 793–843.

——— (1978), *The Search for the Self: Selected Writings of Heinz Kohut: 1978-1981, Vols. I and II,* ed. P. H. Ornstein. Madison, CT: International Universities Press

——— & Wolf, E. (1978), The disorders of the self and their treatment: An outline. In: *The Search for the Self: Selected Writings of Heinz Kohut: 1978–1981, Vol. III,* ed. P. H. Ornstein. Madison, CT: International Universities Press, 1990, pp. 359–385.

——— (1984), *How Does Analysis Cure?* ed. A. Goldberg & P. Stepansky. Chicago: University of Chicago Press.

Lang, J. (1984), Notes toward a psychology of a feminine self. In: *Kohut's Legacy: Contributions to Self Psychology.* ed. P. E. Stepansky & A. Goldberg. Hillsdale, NJ: The Analytic Press, pp. 51–70.

Lothstein, L. (1988), Selfobject failure and gender identity. In: *Frontiers in Self Psychology: Progress in Self Psychology, Vol. 3,* ed. A. Goldberg. Hillsdale, NJ: The Analytic Press, pp. 213–235.

Martinez, D. (1993), The bad girl, the good girl, their mothers, and the analyst: The role of the twin ship selfobject in female oedipal development. In: *The Widening Scope of Self Psychology: Progress in Self Psychology, Vol. 9,* ed. A. Goldberg. Hillsdale, NJ: The Analytic Press, pp. 87–107.

McFague, S. (1982), *Metaphorical Theology: Models of God in Religious Language.* Philadelphia, PA: Fortress Press.

——— (1987), *Models of God: Theology for an Ecological, Nuclear Age.* Philadelphia, PA: Fortress Press.

Meissner, W. (1984), *Psychoanalysis and Religious Experience.* New Haven, CT: Yale University Press.

Ornstein, A. (1983), An idealizing transference of the oedipal phase. In: *Reflections on Self Psychology.* ed. J. Lichtenberg & S. Kaplan. Hillsdale, NJ: The Analytic Press, pp. 135–148.

Rector, L. (1996), The function of early selfobject experiences in gendered representations of God. In: *Basic Ideas Reconsidered: Progress in Self Psychology, Vol. 12,* ed. A. Goldberg. Hillsdale, NJ: The Analytic Press, pp. 249-268.

Ruether, R. (1983), *Sexism and God-Talk: Toward a Feminist Theology.* Boston: Beacon Press.

Shane, E. & Shane, M. (1993), Sex, gender, and sexualization: A case study. In: *The Widening Scope of Self Psychology: Progress in Self Psychology, Vol. 9,* ed. A. Goldberg. Hillsdale, NJ: The Analytic Press, pp. 61–74.

Saussy, C. (1991), *God Images and Self Esteem: Empowering Women in a Patriarchal Society.* Louisville, KY: Westminster/John Knox Press.

Solomon, B. (1991), Self psychology may offer new way to understand how penis envy functions. *Psychodynamic Letter,* 1:1–4.

Winnicott, D. W. (1971), Ego distortion in terms of true and false self. In: *Maturational Process and the Facilitating Environment.* London: Hogarth, 1965.

——— (1960), *Playing and Reality.* New York: Basic Books.

Wolf, E. S. (1988), *Treating the Self: Elements of Clinical Self Psychology.* New York: Guilford.

Chapter 15

The Creative Process

George Hagman

The perceiving and the forming are the same. The self has gone into what it perceives and what it perceives is, in this sense, itself. So the object becomes the subject and the subject the object. [Coleridge on Creativity, quoted in Richards, 1935, p. 57].

Since Freud's early writings on the subject (Freud, 1908), art and artists have fascinated psychoanalysts. The analytic literature on art is large and varied, and each school of psychoanalytic thought has attempted to develop its own understanding of the artist and his audience (for example, Freud, 1908, 1910, 1925; Klein, 1929; Rank, 1932; Sachs, 1942; Kris, 1952; Stokes, 1963; Freiberg, 1965; Ehrenzweig, 1967; Winnicott, 1971; Noy, 1979; Segal, 1991; Rose, 1992). One crucial area of the psychology of art, which has continually challenged and eluded analytic theorists, is the psychodynamics of the creative process itself. In this regard, Freud complained that although his theory helped him understand the unconscious meanings of art, he despaired at unlocking the secrets of the creative act (Freud, 1925a). In fact, subsequent analytic theories of creativity, while offering interesting observations, also failed to develop an adequate model of the psychological process, which makes artistic creativity unique (Noy, 1979). In this chapter I will show how self psychology offers just such a model of the creative process.

I have developed the ideas in this chapter from several sources: first, my own experience as an artist, a vocation I pursued for 10 years intensively and have continued to be involved with for the past 20 years; second, my knowledge of the experience of other artists, as patients and friends; third, a study of the writings of artists regarding their creativity; and forth, a review of the psychoanalytic literature on the creative process.

For purposes of this chapter, my definition of the creative process is the following: the psychological processes of the artist that result in the creation of new, aesthetically legitimate works of art. I will not be discussing the concept of creativity as a general psychological principle or as an aspect of our relationship to the world. It is not that I do not consider creativity in the broad sense important or unrelated to the issue at hand; rather, I wish to focus on the creation of art works. Is there a fundamental process that can account for the artist's ability to produce the extraordinary and sublime creations that we call "fine" art? Throughout I will use the painter as my prototype of the artist for purposes of discussion and illustration; however, the perspective that I am taking is, I believe, applicable to most forms of art and, perhaps, other forms of creative endeavors.

SELF PSYCHOLOGY'S CONTRIBUTION TO UNDERSTANDING THE CREATIVE PROCESS

Self psychology has tried to identify the special role of self-experience in the creative process. Heinz Kohut felt that the creative person possesses a more fluid self-structure characterized by dynamically active archaic modes of psychological organization. Kohut believed that the artist's relationship to the world was narcissistically driven and that the boundaries between self and object were less rigid. He wrote (1966):

> In creative work narcissistic energies are employed which have been changed into a form to which I referred earlier as idealizing libido. The creative individual is less separated from his surroundings than the non-creative one; the "I-You" barrier is not as clearly defined. The creative individual is keenly aware of these aspects of his surroundings that are of significance to his work and he invests them with narcissistic-idealizing libido [p. 112].

At the heart of creativity Kohut believed that the artist was seeking an experience of perfection or, rather, a reexperiencing of a lost, ideal self-state. He (1985) wrote:

> Creative artists may be attached to their work with the intensity of an addiction and they try to control and shape it with forces and for purposes which belong to narcissistically experienced world. They are attempting to re-create a perfection that formerly was directly an attribute of their own [p. 115].

Kohut envisioned a form of psychological process, which characterized the internal psychological life of the artist. This process involves movement between states of self-cohesion, to fragmentation and depletion, to periods where the self is able to reinvest the work with renewed energy. He (1978) wrote:

> The psychic organization of some creative people is characterized by a fluidity of the basic narcissistic configurations, i.e., that periods of narcissistic equilibrium (stable self-esteem and securely idealized internal values; steady, persevering work characterized by attention to details) are followed by (precreative) periods of emptiness and restlessness (decathexis of values and low self-esteem; addictive or perverse yearnings: no work), and that these, in turn, are followed by creative periods (the unattached narcissistic cathexis which had been withdrawn from the ideals and from the self are now employed in the service of the creative activity: original thought; intense passionate work. A phase of frantic creativity (original thought) is followed by a phase of quiet work (the original ideas of the preceding phase are checked, ordered and put into communicative form, e.g., written down), and that this phase of quiet work is in turn interrupted by a fallow period of precreative narcissistic tension, which ushers in a phase of renewed creativity, and so on [p. 815].

At the present time we understand this process as an unfolding experience of self-cohesion, selfobject failure, restoration, and renewed self-experience. As we will discuss, Kohut's model of creativity stresses the relationship between selfobject failure and restoration. Later I will develop this idea further.

Charles Kligerman was the first to devote an entire paper to the development of a self psychology of creativity. Essentially in agreement with Kohut, Kligerman (1980) described four characteristics of creativity:

> 1) An intrinsic joy in creating. This is perhaps the most important factor, but the one we know least about.
> 2) The exhibitionistic grandiose ecstasy of being regarded as the acme of beauty and perfection and the nearly insatiable need to repeat and confirm this feeling.
> 3) The need to regain a lost paradise—the original bliss of perfection—to overcome the empty feeling of self depletion and to recover self-esteem. In the metapsychology of the self this would amount to healing the threatened fragmentation and restoring firm self-cohesion through a merger with the self-object—the work of art—and a bid for mirroring approval of the world.
> 4) We can also add a fourth current to the creative drive—the need to regain perfection by merging with the ideals of the powerful selfobjects, first the parents, then later revered models who represent the highest standards of some great artistic tradition [pp. 387–388].

Kligerman's paper opened the way to a new perspective on creativity in which the artist actively seeks to bring about an experience in which his or her sense of self is confirmed and/or repaired. Rather than being a regressive phenomena, creativity is a complex, high-level psychological activity that attempts to create an experience in which a fragile or precarious self is linked to an ideal object, idealized relationships, and ideal values. As a result of the successful creative effort, the artist experiences him- or herself as renewed, confirmed, and vitalized. Kligerman's psychology of the artist is based on a model of developmental psychopathology; however, he does suggest that the drive to create may occur without serious self-pathology and be engaged in as an end in itself.

In 1988, Carl Rotenberg sought to develop a more elaborate self psychological model of creativity. Rather than viewing art from a purely clinical perspective, Rotenberg recognized the "powerful organizing influence that visual arts have for the self" (p. 195). Focusing primarily on the viewer of art, he argues for the important role of creativity and art appreciation in normal human psychology. For example, consistent with Kohut's viewpoint that selfobjects play a role, not just in an archaic developmental sense, but throughout life, even in the psychological lives of psychologically healthy adults, Rotenberg described how both artists and viewer seek out the confirming, vitalizing, and tranformative functions of the aesthetic selfobject experience. He believed that they do this not just to cope with pathology, but as a healthy, affirmative, and vital experience in and of itself. In addition, he saw the selfobject function of art as embedded in a *shared experiential space* between the subjectivity of the viewer and the artist. The point at which these multiple subjectivities come together, of course, is the experience of the artwork itself. The question is: In what sense does the artwork contain or reflect the subjectivity of the artist? In this regard, Rotenberg has something quite interesting to say:

> In the area of interaction between the artist and his own work, he puts his own puzzles and mental ambiguities outside of himself and then reacts to them as if they were other than his. In a sense, once the artist begins a work, he surrenders to it as though the work were dominating him, demanding the solution of its own ambiguities, and requiring completion. The artist experiences the selfobject functioning of the artwork as alive, active, interpretive and eventually having transformational capabilities, to the extent that inner puzzles of the artist are worked out through this externalization [p. 209].

In the above quote Rotenberg began to identify the internal dynamics of the creative process but not in the traditional terms of intrapsychic life; rather, he was talking about the dialectical relationship between the artist and evolving artwork, in which aspects of the artist's subjectivity are externalized as artistic form. In this chapter I would like to elaborate on Rotenberg's model. Rather than seeing the artist as surrendering to the work, I believe the artist engages in a process in which internal and externalized aspects of self-experience enter into a dialectical relationship that transforms both. Successful creation is determined by the symbolic articulation of feeling, of the vital experience of living made manifest through the completed artwork. To begin, I will introduce the reader to the aesthetic theory of Suzanne Langer. I believe that Langer's model is highly compatible with self psychology through her view of art as the externalization of subjective experience. This will allow us to see more clearly the unique nature of the aesthetic selfobject experience wherein the artist is linked, not to another object per se, but to externalized aspects of their own subjective life.

CREATIVITY AND SELFOBJECT EXPERIENCE

> Art brings together the real and the perfect [Stokes, 1963, p. 26].

> Although art is fundamentally everywhere and always the same, nevertheless two main human inclinations appear in its many and varied expressions. One aims at the direct creation of universal beauty, the other at the aesthetic expression of oneself, in other words, of that which one thinks and experiences [Mondrian, 1937, p. 561].

In the development of a self psychological model of the creative process, it is important to understand just how the artwork (both in process as well as in completed form) is linked to the artist's self-experience. Kohut, Kligerman, and Rotenberg all stated that the artwork functioned as a selfobject, and this is fundamental to any self psychological model. However, what I would like to explore is the question: "If the artwork exists in a borderland, or transitional area between the artist's inner world and reality, what is the nature of their relationship?" I think that part of the answer can be found in the philosopher Suzanne Langer's work on creativity and symbolism where she argues that art is a type of language of human experience, of human feeling.

Langer developed a remarkable and influential theory of art in which a new view of symbolization could explain the nature of artistic expression. She suggested that art symbolizes "forms of feeling" and that there is a parallel between different arts and common forms of human feeling. However, for Langer feeling means far more than emotion. The following quotations are from *The Problem of Art* (Langer, 1957). Here Langer argued that art is fundamentally different from discursive forms of symbolism, such as written language. Art, she believed, is the means by which artists capture and communicate lived experience. She wrote:

> An artist expresses feeling, but not in the way a politician blows off steam or a baby laughs and cries. He formulates that elusive aspect of reality that is commonly taken to be amorphous and chaotic; that is, he objectifies the subjective realm. A work of art expresses a conception of life, emotion, and inward reality. But it is neither a confessional, nor a frozen tantrum; it is a developed metaphor, a non-discursive symbol that articulates what is verbally ineffable—the logic of consciousness itself [p. 26].

> What does it mean to express one's idea of some inward or "subjective" process? It means to make an outward image of this inward process for oneself and others to see; that is, to give the subjective events an objective symbol. It is an outward showing of inward nature, an objective presentation of subjective reality. It is the created image that has elements and patterns like the life of feeling. But this image, though it is a created apparition, a pure appearance, is objective; it seems to be charged with feeling because its form expresses the very nature of feeling. Therefore, it is an *objectification* of subjective life [p. 9].

Langer believed that the articulation of feeling was not the same as emotional expression, affect, or cathartic, although these components of experience may be used as raw material for the creation of artistic form. In artistic creation the artist attempts to objectify by means of symbolization the fullness of lived experience, the feeling, not simply of emotion or affect, but of life itself. The following quote from the nonrepresentational artist Robert Motherwell expresses some of what Langer was trying to say:

> I never think of my paintings as "abstract" nor do those who live with them day by day. I happen to think primarily in paint—this is the nature of the painter—just as musicians think in music. And nothing can be more concrete to a man than his own felt thought, his own thought feeling. I feel most real to myself in the studio, and resent any description of what transpires there as "abstract," something remote from reality [Motherwell, in Protter, 1997, p. 256].

For Motherwell and Langer the artist's self-experience is made real to him or her through the creative process. This experience is only partly affective. Langer argued that those emotions that we commonly identify as anger, sadness, or joy are only the most obvious and socially delimited aspects of inner life. The life of feeling, the experience of self in the world, was, according to Langer, largely ineffable and incommunicable—in logical forms—in language discourse. However, self-experience can be contained and communicated through the formal relations of art, through space, movement, and/or the dynamic relations of interacting forms and colors.

The artist, through the process of creation, seeks to find objective expression of the experience of living, in other words, his or her subjectivity. The artist attempts to articulate the fullness of self-experience. In this sense self-experience is not found in a momentary experience of joy or grief or anger (although these affects may have their role). Art does not simply capture how we feel; it articulates who we are, a living person with an inner life with its rhythms and connections, crises and breaks, complexity and richness. However, more importantly, art expresses subjectivity through formal perfection and the realization of ideal values. Kohut (1985) saw this as an important aspect of the creative process: "A leading part of the psychological equipment of creative people has been shaped through the extensive elaboration of a transitional point in libido development: idealization" (p.114).

Through art, what is temporary and ineffable is expressed in terms that are permanent (even eternal), vivid, and beautiful. What is common becomes sublime. What is incomplete becomes whole. This is crucial to our understanding of creativity: the artist does not simply express feeling; rather, feeling must be expressed in an ideal form. It is the accomplishment of an idealized formal organization that gives the cohesion, vitality, and continuity to the aesthetic experience and thus the self-experience of the artist and, by extension, the experience of his or her audience.

What we have been discussing regarding creativity, Kohut also described in more general terms in his psychology of the self. For example, for Kohut optimal self-experience involved feelings of self-cohesion, self-continuity, and vitality, but he did not mean a bland uniformity but a vital, dynamic inner world of feeling and fantasy. The sense of self-continuity is not just of ongoing sameness, but of the meaningful flow of lived experience. And vitality is not just excitement, but the experience of being fully and clearly alive to oneself, other people, and the world. Kohut described how this cohesive, continuous, and vital experience of a person's self originated, was maintained, and/or repaired through selfobject experiences. Put simply, selfobject experience arises as a result of engagement with another, the experience of that engagement resulting in a psychological state of greater self-cohesion, continuity, and/or vitality. In most instances, selfobject experience is associated with relationships with other people, but Kohut was also clear that other objects, institutions, and even ideas could serve the same function. However, the selfobject experience is most importantly a transcendent one. The self is felt to be grand, the other ideal, and the companionship of the twin sublime.

Aesthetic creativity is motivated by the desire for selfobject experience through artistic activity. In this regard, artistic creation is a unique form of relatedness. The artist creates an object, which, as we noted above, is a formal embodiment of his or her deepest experience of being in the world. The artist's relationship to the art object is in actuality a relationship with his or her own subjectivity. Not only does the artist create an ideal object, which mirrors the grandiosity of the artist's self-experience, but more importantly, the artist seeks that perfection through a dialectical process between self-experience and the experience of the art object, which are merged as well as separate and in which split aspects of self-experience alternately blend and differentiate. For the artist it is never enough to sit and enjoy the fruit of their labors; this for most artists is rarely satisfying. The artist is compelled again and again to recreate a process of self-experiencing in which he or she seeks an elusive, yet powerful, affective event. Once the object is finished, possessing a fully separate life, the artist must return to the process, the continuing search.

Although the artist seeks to express self-experience in ideal form through his artwork, the idealization must authentically reflect the artist's inner life. Art often depicts forms of idealization that are shallow and inauthentic, pretty pictures that defend against or avoid the articulation of true experience. On the other hand, many great artists seek to portray in the ideal forms of their art the most ugly and grotesque aspects of their fantasy life. In these instances the creative process involves the creation of a sublime and organized image, which paradoxically articulates the actual, threatened, or imagined fragmentation, distortion, or depletion of the artist's self-experience. This is similar to the healing empathic resonance of the analyst wherein the analyst mirrors the complex, often disturbed, inner experience of the patient. The great work of art must be idealized but true, expressing in objective form the depth and breadth of the artist's inner life.

The source of the creative impulse is the fantasy life of the artist. These fantasies are not simply conscious, but include multiple levels of self-organization, including the most hidden levels of the unconscious. On the other hand, unlike psychological fantasy, the evolving artwork quickly takes on its own nature, which compels the artist to work to express inner fantasy in external forms. Once a mark is put to the canvas, inner fantasy is changed in response to the external image; this is followed by further action to express fantasy through increasing manipulation of the image. At this point the distinction between inner processes and outer art object breaks down and is replaced by dialectic in which inner and outer processes seek a state of conjunction. Creativity from this perspective is intersubjective, however paradoxically the two subjectivities are aspects of the same self-experience—one aspect concrete and alterable as a medium and formal structure, the other psychical, both immersed in a fantastic and imaginative dialogue with each other, out of which there is an increasing articulation of experience.

The creative process involves three stages, which are described below; however, creativity is not linear, and the stages do not necessarily unfold in a neat progression. In fact, as the artist develops a work of art, the stages may recycle many times until it is completed. Nonetheless, I do believe that the following stages generally do fall into the sequence described and that it is heuristically useful to delineate the components of the creative process in this way. As an introduction, here is a quote from Mark Rothko regarding the earliest phase of a painting:

> It begins as an unknown adventure in an unknown space. It is at the moment of completion that in a flash of recognition they are seen to have the quantity and function which was intended. Ideas and plans that existed in the mind at the start were simply the doorway through which one left the world in which they occurred [Rothko, in Protter, 1997, p. 239].

Inspiration and Self-Crisis

Following upon the desire to create an ideal image of inner life, the artist begins to put brush to canvas. During this phase the artwork remains fragmentary and incomplete. The artist is in what Kris referred to an the *inspirational phase* in which unconscious fantasy and primary process thinking predominate. Beginning a piece of work is experienced as an opportunity and a risk. This is when the artist focuses on the *primary structure* of the work, that is, the archaic fragmentary elements that compose the initial phase of the work's development. During this phase the artist tries to access every aspect of conscious and unconscious subjectivity. Doubt, uncertainty, and confusion may trouble the artist, alternating with joy and exhilaration. Kohut (1976) describes the psychological state of the artist: "During creative periods the self is at the mercy of powerful forces it cannot control. It feels itself hopelessly exposed to extreme mood swings, which range from severe precreative depression to dangerous hypomanic overstimulation" (p. 818).

The artist assesses each mark on the canvas and responds with an internal adjustment of fantasy. As Kohut noted, he or she experiences this phase primarily in affective terms; anxiety is followed by pleasure and, hopefully, confidence. In most cases the experience of crisis occurs on an optimal level. Rather than being derailed or immobilized in the face of an aesthetic challenge, the artist experiences a heightening of attention, a sense of tension and discomfort that leads to a deepening responsiveness to the work. In some cases, the artist's self-experience is often precarious and at times threatened by the fragmented and ill-defined nature of the artwork. The work during this phase involves the manipulation of the medium and image in order to sustain and formally articulate a particular self-state.

> A picture is not thought out and settled beforehand. While it is being done it changes as one's thoughts change. And when it is finished, it still goes on changing, according to the state of mind of whoever is looking at it. A picture lives a life like a living creature, undergoing the changes imposed on us by our life from day to day. This is natural enough, as the picture lives only through the man who is looking at it. [Picasso, cited in Protter, 1977, p. 202].

The foregoing quote captures the dialectic between the inner subjectivity of the artist and the external subjectivity of the artwork. Both seem to have a life of their own, but they are also profoundly and ineluctably linked. The artwork is like a growing, changing, living thing, but it lives only through the man who is looking at it. As Coleridge said, "The perceiving and forming are the same"(cited in Richards, 1935). However, the man is also altered by the work. At a certain point in the creative process, the artist begins to experience a state of aesthetic resonance with his or her creation.

Aesthetic Resonance

Once the artist begins to experience a growing conjunction of feeling and image, the second phase begins. During this phase the feeling that the artwork is beginning to take form excites the artist. There is an increased experience of self-cohesion, effectiveness, and vitality. The artist feels in sync with the artwork, and there is a sense of resonance in which the artwork seems to become the perfect reflection of the artist's inner fantasy life. I use the term *aesthetic resonance* in this context to describe the intensification of feeling that the artist experiences both internally and externally because of the conjunction between self and work. This is the most affectively charged moment of the creative selfobject experience in which the artist feels both in the presence of the sublime and confirmed in his grandiosity. Jackson Pollock tells how he unrolls his canvas on the floor and uses unconventional tools, in order to experience himself as "literally in" the painting. He wrote:

> What I am in my painting, I'm not aware of what I am doing. It is only after a sort of "getting acquainted" period that I see what I have been about. I have no fears about making changes, destroying the image etc. because the painting has a life of its own. I try to let it come through. It is only when I lose contact with the painting that the result is a mess. Otherwise there is pure harmony, an easy give and take, and the painting comes out well [Pollock, cited in Protter, 1997, p. 253].

During the creative process the experience of merger with the artwork is necessary, and it is not only the object that is experienced as part of the self, but also the self as part of the object. The artist feels at one with the artwork. In fact he or she is. It is not an illusion. Yet for an artwork to be new it must also exist on its own terms, "out in the world," a creation of the artist's subjectivity. To bring this about, the artist must remain aware of the reality and physical nature of the evolving artwork—continuing recognition of the unique qualities of the artwork is essential. At the same time, the artist's self-experience is powerfully linked to this "other," which is a part of him or her, while remaining profoundly separate. If this differentiation were collapsed, if a full experience of merger occurred and persisted, the creative process would cease, and the artist would be reduced to the status of a common dreamer.

From the first moment of creation, the artist engages in dialectic with the selfobject/artwork. This dialectic is the engine of creativity. The artist extends his subjectivity outward and alters the medium. From this point on there is something new, which has been created out of a merger between the self-experience of the artist and the world. The work in progress exists. The artist observes the work, appraises it, and there is a dialectic between that which has been created and the subjectivity and judgment of the artist. The important thing is that the dialectic occurs between two realms of self-experience, that which is internal/subjective and that which is external/objective. Each influences the other (the imaginary and the manifest), and the result is further creation. Thus there is an increasing elaboration of the artwork toward a level of refinement—in other words the artist finds in creativity an opportunity to give form to subjective experience in an increasingly articulate and formally refined manner. There is an output, feedback, response/output, dialectic within the realm of the artist's subjectivity. The measure and guide for this process is the delicate sense of resonance that the artist experiences with his or her developing artwork. Mondrian (1937) uses the term *intensification* to describe this process in which the artist creates "successively profound planes." Through *intensification*, rather than simply repeating cultural or natural forms, the artist elaborates something truly new and emotionally stirring.

> The most important tool the artist fashions through constant practice is faith in his ability to produce miracles when they are needed [Rothko, in Protter, 1997, p. 239].

Transmuting Externalization

The experience of aesthetic resonance, while essential to the elaborative phase of creativity discussed above, is not the only important factor in successful creativity. Inevitably, there is an experience of failure in resonance, of selfobject failure. Kohut put it this way: "Creative people tend to alternate during periods of productivity between phases when they think extremely highly of their work and phases when they are convinced that it has no value" (Kohut, 1985, p. 114). It is the artist's response to this sense of failure that further intensifies the creative effort, compelling the artist to elaborate ever more radical formal organizations. In most cases, this stage begins when the artist's feeling of certainty gives way to sober reflection and reassessment. The artist may come to doubt the perfection, and the artwork no longer seems to perfectly reflect the feelings that the artist wishes to capture. (Ehrenzweig [1967] describes this experience as the "grayness of the morning after" when the artist must confront the flawed reality of what was felt to be sublime just the day before.) This phase is characterized by selfobject failures in which the resonance breaks down and the artist must use all of his or her skill and resourcefulness to reassess the image and rework it to restore the selfobject tie. The selfobject experience is restored when the artwork is felt once again to capture the ideal and grandiose components of fantasy. As described in phase 1, the experience of selfobject failure during this phase should be within certain limits of intensity. As with the optimal frustrations described by Kohut, the selfobject failure, which is experienced at this point in the creative process, should not be traumatic in most cases. There may be some heightened anxiety and even depression, but as with optimal frustration the artist should be able to rally and address the aesthetic problems that he or she is faced with. The process that occurs at this point I refer to as *transmuting externalization,* in which the artist attempts to restore the selfobject tie, not through the accrual of self-structure, but through alteration of the artwork. During this phase preconscious and conscious processes play a part in organizing and clarifying the elements in the artwork as the artist attempts to bring the work into harmony with self-experience. I call this activity working on the *secondary structure* of the artwork, that is, rather than relying on inspiration and primary process thinking, the artist approaches the work more synthetically with an eye toward the total organization of the work and the relationship between its formal components. This is similar to Kris's (1952) notion of the elaboration phase. However, while Kris stressed the use of secondary process thinking during this phase, I believe that the artist must continue to respond to the work on multiple psychical levels. Similar to transmuting internalization the response to a break in the selfobject tie is the accrual of structure; in this case the artist refines and strengthens the artwork's formal organization in order to be more resonant with fantasy. At the same time the artist's inner experience changes in response to the artwork as well. The end result of transmuting externalization is the restoration of the selfobject tie between artist and artwork.

> When you begin a picture, you often make some pretty discoveries. You must be on your guard against these. Destroy the thing, do it over several times. In each distorting of a beautiful discovery, the artist does not really suppress it, but rather transforms it, condenses it, makes it more substantial. What comes in the end is the result of discarded finds. Otherwise, you become your own connoisseur. I sell myself nothing [Picasso, cited in Protter, 1997, p. 203].

Kohut compared creativity to addiction (Kohut, 1966, p. 115), and in a sense the comparison is an apt one. I would, however, change this somewhat and say that the artist's addiction is to the process of selfobject failure and restoration. The artist is driven to seek out again and again the experience of heightened, lost, and regained self-experience. Central to the "addiction-like" nature of this process is the artist's experience of "doing it himself." This may be what Rank referred to as the artist's quest for "self-begetting" and "self-rebirth." As Stolorow and Atwood (1993) stated in their analysis of Rank: "The artist's own self-created differentiated self is his first creative work and throughout his life 'remains fundamentally his chief work'" (p. 143). Rank argued that the artist seeks to transcend reality and mortality. Albert Pinkham Ryder expressed this motivation about his work:

> When I stood before my easel with its square of stretched canvas, I realized that I had in my possession the wherewith to create a masterpiece that would live throughout the coming ages. I at once proceeded to study the works of the great to discover how best to achieve immortality with a square of canvas and a box of colors [Ryder, cited in Protter, 1997, p. 150].

I would argue that the artist repeatedly seeks to transcend the experience of selfobject failure and that by means of creative effort the artist experiences his own power in bringing about the restoration of self-experience. In most cases the aesthetic resonance with the completed artwork will fade, and although the work may always hold some positive meaning for the artist, the search for transcendence and renewal must be reengaged.

It is this complex dialectic between artist and artwork, between selfobject experience and selfobject failure followed by restoration, that drives the artist to seek increasingly refined and sophisticated formal means to express subjectivity. The artist who engages in this process is driven to repeatedly seek out the wonder of the aesthetic selfobject experience; therefore, he or she must continually work to articulate and perfect a formally organized and ideal representation of lived experience. The skillful and talented artist can feel the potential for this experience in artistic activity; this is perhaps the source of the feeling of joy, which Kligerman described, in the earlier quote. In a sense the successful artist is possessed, even driven to seek to restore this experience until he or she reaches a point at which there is a conjunction between inner experience and outer image. Matisse stated this quite simply when he was asked when he knew that a piece was finished. He explained: When it expresses emotion as completely as possible. It is at that point when the sense of resonance is enduring and durable. The artist assessing the work does not experience anxiety, depression, or fragmentation but sureness and calm. The artist no longer feels compelled to change the work because it feels balanced and complete. The work is done. It exists as a thing in itself. Mark Rothko describes the artist's relationship to the completed work:

> Pictures must be miraculous: the instant one is completed, the intimacy between the creation and the creator is ended. He is an outsider. The picture must be for him, as for anyone experiencing it later, a revelation, an unexpected and unprecedented resolution of an eternally familiar need [Rothko, cited in Protter, 1997, p. 239].

In summary, I have in this section made the following points about the creative process:

1. Art is the externalization of self-experience, what the philosopher Suzanne Langer calls *objectification of subjectivity* or, more simply, the symbolization of "feeling."
2. The motivation to create can be characterized as a desire for an experience of idealization of self-experience.
3. As a result, during the creative process the artist engages in dialectic with her own idealized subjectivity in the objectified form of the developing artwork.
4. The feeling of harmony (aesthetic resonance) that the artist experiences with the work in progress is a form of selfobject experience. The artist longs to establish this form of selfobject tie.
5. However, in the course of creating a particular artwork, the artist inevitably experiences the selfobject tie as elusive, precarious, or broken. The artist is repeatedly disillusioned regarding the work's perfection.
6. The artist seeks to strengthen or restore the selfobject tie through its gradual refinement. By this means, the artwork is moved closer to a formal ideal.
7. The repeated experience of self-restoration and the creation (and recreation) of a truly ideal object out of one's self explains the addiction-like quality of creativity. Through creation the artist triumphs over the ineluctability of selfobject failure and the vulnerability of self-experience.
8. In the end, the artist's fantasy is that he or she will surmount personal mortality through art.

In the next section I will discuss the treatment of a young artist, which illustrates some typical disturbances that can occur in the creative process. The case illustration was chosen for the way that this man experienced transitory problems during each phase of creativity. The childhood sources of his self-vulnerability will be touched on.

CLINICAL EXAMPLE

Several years ago I saw a young painter in psychoanalytic psychotherapy. Rob had been working as an artist for some time and was on the verge of receiving some much-deserved recognition. Initially he had come to treatment after the breakup of a six-year relationship with a woman upon whom he was extremely dependent. He continued to be despondent for several months, but his motivation to paint (he was actually doing pastels at the time) remained high. In fact, he seemed to use his artwork to express his despair and loneliness. For a time his work became dominated by varieties of grays and dark earthtones.

About six months into the treatment Rob received an invitation to hold a one-man show at a downtown gallery. Although he had exhibited in group shows frequently, this was his first solo exhibition. He was elated. Having viewed himself as a struggling, junior artist for some years now, he saw this as his chance to "break out" and "make it big." He worked day and night for a number of weeks, and when the show opened, the reviews were generally positive and in some case laudatory. However, Rob was literally paralyzed with self-doubt.

It is not uncommon to encounter artists with this type of response to success. The state of vulnerability that is experienced during exhibitions (especially early on in the artist's career) can lead to hard-to-manage excitement and profound disappointment. However, for the purpose of this chapter what interested me was the subsequent impact of Rob's success on his creative process. In general up to this point, Rob had been free of work inhibitions or other creative conflicts. He produced a large amount of work with a reasonable amount of effort until several weeks after the show, when he began to work on a series of dramatic and very ambitious pastels. He came to sessions in a state of panic.

"I can't seem to get a handle on things. I know basically what I want to do. I can almost taste it. I feel like I'm on the verge of something really different, but it's all just a mess. I can't seem to pull it together. I just sit and stare at these blotches of color. It's as if all the talent is just gone, just gone. I don't know what to do."

As we talked, it became clear that Rob's expectations had become extremely high, and his need to prove his talent led to anxiety as he struggled with the early, inchoate phase of his new work.

"Before, I used to be able to just go with it. I'd sit back and say to myself. *Stay calm, just wait a bit, and it will come together.* But now, it's like the stakes are so high. I feel like so much is expected of me. I'm no longer just a struggling artist, but I also feel I have not really made it. It could all fall apart so easily."

In fact, Rob had begun to feel that it had fallen apart. As he struggled with each new drawing, he was unable to sustain his confidence and focus during the confusing early phases of his creative process. His need for a sense of confirmation, which resulted from his sense of vulnerability to selfobject failure, made the challenge of each new drawing into proof of his fundamental, and now undeniable, failure.

Rob was gradually able to recover his self-confidence, but his sense of vulnerability and precarious self-cohesion remained a problem throughout all phases of his work. For example, when he was finally able to move beyond the early phase of a work in progress and had developed a sense of rhythm and renewed excitement, he would wake up in the morning in a state of dread. A particular piece of work, which he had been inspired by the day before, would appear to him like a "trainwreck." That image captured his self-experience perfectly.

"It's like I am just cruising along and everything is coming together, and then the first bump in the road, wham, out of control and than crash! Then I feel like it's all gone and is never coming back again."

Most artists reach a point where the sense of harmony and perfect fit becomes disrupted. The challenge then is to recover and solve the problem through a reassessment and, often times, a reworking of the piece. The capacity to sustain self-experience enough to repair the sense of disruption is crucial. Even the worst "trainwreck" may be a necessary stage leading to a creative advancement. Rob's sense of self was so tenuous that the selfobject failure typical of this phase resulted in collapse and a sense of fragmentation.

A crucial part of Rob's recovery from success was his experience of me as both consistent and confident in him. He saw me as "having my feet on the ground," and he explained how, when he was in session, he was able to "retool" himself and get a handle on his work. Eventually, he was able to struggle through and create some interesting work, but he became afraid to show his completed work even to close friends. It was as if he saw every flaw and imperfection. He felt ashamed of his self-doubts. He remembered when he was a child and his father criticized him for being a "big shot."

"That's it. That's it." Rob seemed almost elated. "I feel like I have been paying the price for being a *big shot*. I never felt with my dad that it was all right to be a big shot. I don't even think I was, but he would always criticize me as if I was doing something wrong. The show, that was my undoing. I was acting like a big shot when I am really just a kid trying to please my dad. But I never could. I don't remember any time when I really felt like I did anything good. One time when I was in high school I had just won a big race and I was all excited. He comes up to me and all he says (in front of my friends) is *'Put your sweater on.'* I was pissed off. Suddenly my excitement was gone. All I felt was anger."

Rob's long-anticipated success was followed by a period of self-crisis during which his experience of shame and selfobject failure impacted on every phase of his creative work. The precariousness of his self-experience resulted in an increased need for mirroring, as well as his craving for the presence of a reassuring idealized figure. As a result, he was unable to sustain confidence in the face of routine experience of doubt and confusion, which had always been a part of his creative process. Over time, Rob struggled with each instance of uncertainty as if it represented his ultimate unworthiness. His fragile capacity to sustain or recover self-experience led to extreme states of self-crisis, rather than a sense of challenge and opportunity. Gradually, through his growing awareness of the sources of his vulnerability in his relationship with his father and his experience of my availability and confidence in him, he was able to come to terms with the meaning of his success and move on with his career.

CONCLUSION

In closing I would like to say a word regarding the creative artist's challenge to conventions, which is frequently seen, at least in modern western art. It would seem from a cursory look at the lives of many modern artists that they exhibit what appears to be a driving need to challenge and provoke. Creativity has become synonymous with the different and new, and the image of the artist as an outsider and rebel has become a common cultural stereotype. At least superficially, it would appear that artists are more interested in disruption and conflict than cohesion, continuity, and vitality. If there is any truth to this view of the artist, how can it be reconciled with the notion of the artist's search for selfobject experience? The psychoanalyst Carl Rotenberg (1992) addressed this problem. He claimed that the creative artist is fundamentally driven by a desire to challenge conventional forms of thinking. He developed a special set of terms for this trait: *Optimal Operative Perversity*. He (1992) offered the following definition:

> *Perversity* is the expression of the artist who consistently, and with technical means, contradicts a previously held principle of organization (p. 171).
>
> The introduction of elements that are original or new results in perception whose implications have not yet been assimilated into the order-making structures of the self (p. 172).
>
> *Optimal* refers to the quality and degree of unusualness that also achieves integration with the rest of the pictorial field of which it is a part (p. 177).
>
> *Operative* refers to the enacted quality of the artwork and to the technical skill that makes it possible (p. 179).

Rotenberg believed that artists are driven to produce work with an unusual organization of meaning and form, which also achieve new levels of aesthetic integration. Once again, I believe that the desire to challenge convention is principally based on the artist's desire to truly express his or her self-experience. The ability of conventional or traditional forms of art to express the subjective experience of artists over time is limited. The artist seeks to challenge conventions in the process of discovering new, more powerful means to express self-experience. It would be useless for an artist to adopt another artist's style unless he or she believed that they could make use of the style or technique to convey their own experience. In addition, given the artist's search for selfobject experience, the underlying wish of the revolutionary artist is to be responded to as a unique and special person. The bottom line is that the challenge of modern art is the desire to convey more completely, accurately, and vividly the experience of living in the modern world. Jackson Pollock said that new times require new art forms, and this is true, but also, new times are populated by new people who require new forms of self-expression. The old will rarely do unless the artist is able to find new potentials or new facets in the old, which can be made relevant to current experience.

For example, one of the most influential revolutionary movements in the history of modern art was Abstract Expressionism. These artists were viewed by many at that time as wild radicals seeking only to undermine and damage artistic traditions. Once again, Jackson Pollock, a prominent member of that group was at one time referred to in print as "Jack the Dripper" because of his use of dripped or poured paint. It is certainly true that these artists sought to create a new, radical vision of art. However, when one looks closely at their statements and writings, it appears that their motive was not only to disrupt, but also to create new ways to express their self-experience. Not content with conflict, virtually all of them longed for professional and social recognition of their work. In fact it is interesting to see how, for many of these artists, the failure to receive the requisite mirroring in response to their work or the anticipation of selfobject failure led to disastrous, even suicidal, results. Once again behind the revolutionary movement of the Abstract Expressionists was a desire to express subjectivity more accurately, vividly, and powerfully. For these artists the experience of the modern self required a new, more dramatic form of expression. Each sought through the development of new approaches to technique and form to create a sense of aesthetic resonance, which would capture their sense of lived experience as truly as possible.

REFERENCES

Ehrenzweig, A. (1967), *The Hidden Order of Art.* Berkeley, CA: University of California Press.

Freiberg, L. (1965), New views of art and the creative process in psychoanalytical ego psychology. In: *The Creative Imagination,* ed. H. Ruitenbeek, Chicago, IL: Quadrangle Books, pp. 223–244.

Freud, S. (1908), Creative artists and day-dreaming. *Standard Edition,* 9:141–153. London: Hogarth Press, 1959.

——— (1910), Leonardo Da Vinci and a memory of childhood. *Standard Edition,* 11:63–137. London: Hogarth Press, 1957.

——— (1925), An autobiographical study. *Standard Edition,* 20:7–74. London: Hogarth Press, 1959.

Klein, M. (1929), Infantile anxiety situations reflected in a work of art and the creative impulse. In: *The Writings of Melanie Klein, Vol. 1,* London: Hogarth Press, 1975.

Kligerman, C. (1980), Art and the self of the artist. In: *Advances in Self Psychology,* ed. A. Goldberg. Madison, CT: New York University Press, pp. 383–391.

Kohut, H. (1966), Forms and transformations of narcissism. In: *Self Psychology and the Humanities,* ed. C. Strozier, New York: Norton, 1985, pp. 97–123.

——— (1976), Creativeness, charisma, and group psychology. In: *Self Psychology and the Humanities,* ed. C. Strozier. New York: Norton, 1985, pp. 793–843.

——— (1978), Creativeness, charisma, group psychology: Reflections on the self-analysis of Freud. In: *The Search for the Self: Selected Writings of Heinz Kohut: 1950–1994, Vol. 2,* ed. P. Ornstein. New York: International Universities Press, pp. 793–843.

——— (1985), *Self Psychology and the Humanities.* ed. C. Strozier. New York: Norton.

Kris, E. (1952), *Psychoanalytic Explorations on Art.* Madison, CT: International University Press.

Langer, S. (1957), *Problems of Art.* New York: Charles Scribner's Sons.

Mondrian, P. (1937), Plastic art and pure plastic art. In: *Art and Its Significance: An Anthology of Aesthetic Theory,* ed. S. D. Ross. Albany, NY: SUNY, 1984, pp. 554–567.

Noy, P. (1979), Form creation in art: An ego psychological approach to creativity. *Psychoanal. Quart.,* 48:229–256.

Protter, E. (1997), *Painters on Painting.* Mineola, NY: Dover Publications.

Rank, O. (1932), *Art and Artist.* New York: Knopf.

Richards, I. A. (1935), *Coleridge on Imagination.* New York: Harcourt, Brace, 1969.

Rose, G. (1992), *The Power of Form: A Psychoanalytic Approach to Aesthetic Form.* Madison, CT: International Universities Press.

Rotenberg, C. (1988), Selfobject theory and the artistic process. In: *Learning from Kohut: Progress in Self Psychology, Vol. 4,* ed. A. Goldberg. Hillsdale, NJ: The Analytic Press, pp. 193—213.

———(1992), Optimal operative perversity: A contribution to the theory of creativity. In: *New Therapeutic Visions: Progress in Self Psychology, Vol. 8,* ed. A. Goldberg. The Analytic Press: Hillsdale, NJ, pp. 167-188.

Sachs, H. (1942), *The Creative Unconscious*. Boston, MA: SCI-ART Publishers.
Segal, H. (1991), *Dream, Phantasy and Art*. London: Routledge.
Stokes, A. (1963), *Painting and the Inner World*. London: Tavistock Publications.
Stolorow, R. & Atwood, G. (1993), *Faces in a Cloud: Intersubjectivity in Personality Theory*. Northvale, NJ: Aronson.
Winnicott, D. W. (1971), *Playing and Reality*. New York: Basic Books.

Chapter 16

Restoration of the Past: A Guide to Therapy With Placed Children

Marilyn W. Silin

Children referred for therapy from foster homes or residential settings typically have experienced multiple placements and losses of caretaking adults. These early disruptions lead to expectations of further discontinuity and impermanence. Placed children are especially vulnerable to severe pathology because of unresolved mourning and unfavorable life conditions preexistent to subsequent placements (Samuels, 1995, p. 309). Deficits in development, restriction of cognitive capacity, and underlying depression may lead to symptomatic behavior that interferes with attachment to new caretakers. Without psychodynamic psychotherapy, placed children rarely sustain more than superficial, conflictual relationships to the outside world.

A major thesis of this chapter is that effective psychotherapy needs to focus on the child's understanding of his/her past experiences, in order to give meaning to them and to build a sense of coherency within the framework of the child's developmental stage and cultural surround.

This approach is derived from narrative theory as formulated by Joseph Palombo (1992). He postulates that overwhelming experiences that have not been integrated into one's understanding of oneself prevent the establishment of a coherent sense of meaning. In this framework therapists "function as historians who have an understanding of human nature who are entrusted with the task of constructing a plausible coherent narrative of the patient's life" (p. 265). Palombo continues, "We are privy to the schisms to which their lives have been exposed. We are in the presence of a stirring struggle to make coherent what was formerly meaningless. By empathically indwelling with the patients in their experiences, we glean clues about their deficits and strengths. They thus begin building their autobiography" (p. 265).

The youngster described in this chapter is illustrative of children who experience multiple losses in early childhood without the benefit of empathic, attuned caregivers who respond to their needs age appropriately. Palombo (1992) states, "Failures in the interaction of experiences result from the exposure to emotions that are overwhelming and that cannot be made meaningful for the person. It is in the nature of trauma that the person is overwhelmed by the intensity of the feelings stirred by the experience and cannot make the experience sufficiently meaningful as to integrate it with the rest of his/her experiences" (p. 262).

This view is supported by Anna Ornstein in her article, "Trauma, Memory, and Psychic Continuity" (1994). She states, "The integration of traumatic memories into the flow of one's life narrative depends on the healing of the split between experiences as they are lived and as they are remembered. This process is the function of therapeutic dialogue in which the articulation of images and reconstruction of memory fragments are undertaken jointly by patient and therapist . . . everything that is remembered is the product of mutual integration of the past with the present" (p. 139).

A therapeutic dialogue with children is multidimensional, rarely a two-person verbal interaction. Dramatic play, stories, art, and behavior itself become the vehicles through which the child weaves fragmentary themes, alone, or by assigning roles to the therapist. As the therapist immerses herself in the material and begins to identify the threads of the child's story, meanings evolve, which can be pieced together with the facts from the child's known history. In this process the therapist begins to verbalize her understandings explicitly or within the metaphors of the child's creations. Thus, the child's experiences begin to be affirmed, and new shared meanings develop.

Although a therapist may try to contain this process in the treatment office, it inevitably spreads to the living situation where the foster parents, child care staff, or adoptive parents become recipients of the child's vacillating transference and the reenactment of earlier trauma. Outbreaks of disruptive or regressive behavior upset the adults who are trying to nurture, protect, and guide the children. Collaboration and frequent communication between the therapist and the caregivers is essential for the progress of the case.

CASE ILLUSTRATION

Sarah was a 10-year-old girl referred to a private agency group home by her adoptive father because of demanding and rebellious behavior at home, coupled with enuresis and poor school performance. Nothing was known about her biological parents. She had been adopted at birth although the adoptive mother was already suffering from a terminal illness. Sarah's earliest years were characterized by lack of consistent mothering, substitute caretakers, and a father preoccupied with the medical condition of his wife. The adoptive mother died when Sarah was four. After the death Sarah would run up to strangers and call them "Mommy." The relatives felt sorry for her, and her father told her to be a good girl.

A year and a half later the father married again, this time to a schizoid young woman recently discharged from a psychiatric hospital. She made it clear from the beginning that Sarah was perceived as an unnecessary burden on the marriage. She openly rejected Sarah and within two years she and the father had two babies of their own. During the intake study the stepmother said to a social worker, "When I look at Sarah, I see an ugly, smelly ape who lays in bed in a stupor sucking her thumb. She makes me sick."

The father felt that he had to move Sarah out of the house in order to save the marriage, but he appeared ready to cooperate with the agency and agreed to see a case worker. The author treated Sarah.

I met Sarah when her father brought her to the agency for her first appointment. She was tall with dark curly hair and a dark complexion. When I invited her to come into the office, she looked back at her father, who urged her to go along with me. In the office she told me how her stepmother made her ride in the back of the car and would get so mad at Sarah that she would hide under the seat. I told Sarah that her father had told me how difficult things were for her at home and described the apartment house where we thought she might like to live, with five other girls, on one floor. I told her the names of the childcare workers. She then spontaneously told me a story. "There were two little boys outside on the school playground. They found a baby bat," she said, "that had fallen out of its nest and was hurt. The boys yelled up to the teacher to ask what they should do with it. The teacher told the boys to bring it up to the school room where it would be taken care of." It was not difficult to connect her story with her own situation and I felt optimistic about the treatment.

After two preplacement visits Sarah moved into the group home. In the beginning she seemed shy and curious and the childcare workers found her appealing.

The therapy lasted 19 months. In the first phase, which I call "the Garden of Eden," Sarah developed themes using monkey and tiger hand puppets, one on her hand, the other placed on mine. The puppets hugged and kissed when she started the sessions. They rolled around together and played in a swimming pool (a section of the desk), and ate "German chocolate candy." (Sarah herself ate real chocolate in my office, dubbing the candy in honor of Wilma, her favorite childcare worker, whose birthplace was Germany.) Sarah had begun to become attached to Wilma, an active, warm young woman. Clearly, Wilma was becoming an idealized selfobject for Sarah. Wilma could enjoy her, protect, and feed her, thus offering qualities of strength and power with which Sarah began to merge. The childcare staff appeared to welcome her fantasies of merger.

While Sarah created the story of the monkey and tiger swimming and taking sun baths in fantasy play in my office, the staff in the group home observed that she had begun to eat voraciously and to become babyish and demanding of undivided attention from Wilma. Any change in routine created a crisis. Wilma's days off were very hard for Sarah. Shopping trips outside were frightening, even with Wilma at her side. One day after a brief camping trip with the group, Sarah walked into my office as if she were about to collapse, and I felt she wanted me to pick her up and hold her.

Discussion of the First Phase

Without details of her earlier history, we postulated that Sarah had held herself together with "Scotch Tape" defenses, afraid to express her fears and rage at the two mothers who had been unable to provide age-appropriate selfobject functions for her. Their lack of attunement and their conflictual connections with her left her with an enfeebled sense of self. One might speculate that one person, perhaps the father or the adoptive mother prior to her illness, had partially fulfilled some of her early object needs. Evidence for this might be seen in her calling strangers "Mommy" with expectations of a positive response. Her story about the injured, abandoned baby bat supports this thinking.

By the time she was referred to the agency, Sarah had been straining her emotional resources to cover up her basic needs for nurturance and self-regulation. Eruptions of rage, clingy behavior, and disorderliness further alienated the caregiving adults from her. Furthermore, difficulties in learning ensued, possibly because she had never developed a capacity to soothe herself so she could focus on the tasks of learning.

Reality testing was still intact, however, as Sarah began to observe the actions of the staff and children in the home and realized that here the adults were different. They tried to listen to the children; no one was rejected or abandoned because of bad behavior. Food was always available; the adults affirmed age-appropriate behavior. They cared about the kids. They offered structure and models for self-regulatory functions. Thus, at the age of 10, Sarah found herself in a selfobject surround, which in a short time ushered in a major depression.

Second Stage: Regression

The second stage of therapy, the regression, lasted three months. While Sarah continued to play out the monkey and tiger themes with me, her affect began to fade, and she seemed more artificial in the office. At the same time, her daytime behavior in the group home was becoming erratic, irrational, and psychotic-like. At night she woke up frightened but unable to talk about anything. In the special school, also administered by the agency, she lost all motivation to work and ran out of the room when frustrated. Team meetings were held frequently to discuss how to handle her as we saw her fragmenting in front of our eyes, helpless to soothe her.

She still came to the downtown office to see me but sat wordlessly sucking her thumb and twirling her hair. Her wordless depression filled the room. I said little. One day, however, she started to tell a story about her mother (which one?) who went to the hospital to have babies or to die. This seemed painfully real, and I responded by saying softly that she got her mother mixed up with her stepmother. Her mother had really been in the hospital many times and then died. Her stepmother went to the hospital twice, each time for a few days, to have a baby. Sarah seemed to listen while she absently twiddled a dish on my desk. In a subsequent session she talked about the funeral for her mother and confused this with scary memories of a funeral for her grandfather.

In the group home she became so anxious with the flooding of these memories that her behavior totally vacillated between wild activity or almost total withdrawal. Soon she did not want to get out of bed at all, and we decided to accept that. We made a conscious treatment decision to let her stay in bed, hoping that with appropriate therapeutic management she would be able to regain an earlier level of integration, perhaps this time with greater capacity for self-regulation and beginning growth of a cohesive self.

Accordingly, we reformulated the treatment plan to support her regression, withdrawing demands to go to school and to participate in activities, with the exception of having meals in the dining room with the others. (Thankfully, she never gave up her interest in food.) A mild sedative was prescribed for the night time so that she and the childcare staff could get some sleep. Above all, she would not be encouraged to talk about her memories or her bad dreams. We hoped she would temporarily repress the feelings associated with grief, mourning and abandonment, until her self was sufficiently strengthened to deal with them.

It was decided that I would go to the group home and be with her for our usual treatment time, in the place and the manner she chose.

Discussion of the Second Phase

As Sarah started to feel safe and protected in the group home, she began to reexperience the affects connected with the psychic pain that had been pushed away for so long. The anger, grief, and sorrow that followed the death of the first mother and rejection by the second reemerged in confusing fragmentary memories that overwhelmed Sarah's enfeebled self. Her attempts to disavow them depleted the energy she had available for fulfilling the expectations of everyday life so she just shut down, so to speak. At night, however, fearful memories returned, and she suffered night terrors.

The staff's therapeutic decision to let Sarah retreat from the demands of the real world was taken with the hope that the fulfillment of their caretaking functions would set into motion a process of growth of new psychic structure. Elson (1986) states, "Those who perform caretaking functions for the child in tune with his needs are selfobjects: they are prestructural selfobjects whose functions, through transmuting internalization, become uniquely his own" (p. 11).

Third Phase: Convalescence

At first when I arrived at the home I would find Sarah curled up in bed, silent. I sat near the bed. Within a few weeks I found her in the living room snuggled in a big soft chair near the TV, sucking her thumb, watching a program. We watched together. I would comment on what we were seeing, but when I tried to direct a remark to her, she got angry. It was easier to discuss the "Beverly Hillbillies." Her psyche, I felt, was still too raw.

After a few weeks she was able to move from the safety of the living room to a therapy office on another floor of the building. However, she came down wearing a large old shirt of Wilma's, a transitional object, which, I felt, comforted and protected her in those first steps away from Wilma herself. This stage stretched over 3 months, where she was unable to go outside the house, but related to me away from her floor. In the fourth month she felt strong enough to take the trip with an escort to see me in the downtown office.

During that phase I followed Sarah's lead in doing whatever she wished. The first activity she initiated with me was in the area of painting by number. She wanted to paint the head of a horse, and I had to help her. Repeatedly, we painted other animal figures together, carefully and slowly, with intense concentration, but little joy. I felt Sarah was returning to the world buttressed by compulsive, rigid lines that were symbolically enclosing her anxieties in the presence of my soothing self. After completing several animal figures, she asked for blank paper and painted tiny colored lines triangular to each corner. "It's finished," she said. The rest of the paper was left blank. Was she offering us a blank slate, which the new selfobject would begin to fill in?

Recovery Phase

The staff dated Sarah's return to more adequate functioning the day she started to imitate the teenage behavior of two girls in her group. They were "cool" and "groovy" and were hysterically in love with the Beatles and the Monkees (popular groups of the 1960s). Renouncing her infantile wishes, Sarah suddenly became a teenager, although in an artificial fashion, an "as if" preteen girl expressing wishes to grow up. She asked me to bring paint-by-number Beatles books. I did and I listened to expressions of exaggerated distress when one of the Beatles announced his marriage plans. Sarah was furious with him. "How could he do this to me?"

She talked with me dramatically as if she, Sarah, personally had been left at the altar. Significant is the fact that she had begun to talk to me again, in the metaphor of the Beatles, about the basic history of her life. No one suffering from the loss of a Beatle, however, fell apart. On the contrary, the girls banded together, supporting each other in screaming reactions whenever the Beatles appeared on TV.

Slowly Sarah was able to return to her own past and ask questions about her adoption, the illness of her first mother and why she hadn't had babies of her own. We talked about her dad, whom she saw monthly on visits, and her grandfather who had died. The anxieties surrounding these sessions were contained in the office and she could leave without trying to prolong the hour or to appear to lose all functions as she walked away from me.

In the group home she began to write letters to me when she was angry at a childcare worker. She would draw endless connected circles on the paper in which she wrote the letter, which looked to me like embryos tied together. When a session had to be cancelled due to a holiday she sent me a note asking for a make-up.

During this period we held two supervised visits with the father for Sarah to ask him questions about the past, in my presence. His caseworker had prepared him for these visits, and I met with the father and Sarah together.

The first of these took place right after the death and televised funeral of Martin Luther King, Jr. Sarah had watched all the proceedings with the other girls. We were afraid that experience might revive frightening memories, but she did not become upset. When Sarah and I met with the father, he spontaneously spoke of Mrs. King and the three King children. "You know," he said with genuine warmth, turning directly to Sarah, "Dr. King was a great man to the world, but he was the husband and father of his children, and they will miss him more than anyone else." I was very moved and felt that the father and Sarah were talking symbolically about the emotional effect of the mother's death for the first time.

Having received her father's and my permission to express grief for her mother (mothers?), Sarah began to work through the fantasies of an all-giving or all-punishing mother. It became possible for her to develop new understandings from her individual distorted memories of the first years of her life. She began to interact with members of her extended family. In the next several months she developed an active interest in her other relatives, her stepmother and the stepsiblings. Learning took on new meaning in school, and she came to sessions eager to show me her papers in science and math.

Along with this development Sarah began to perceive me as a real person who worked with other children. Her rivalry with another girl in the group home was expressed by Sarah's attempt to imitate her, which I interpreted as Sarah's opinion that I would then like *her* more. I told her how much I enjoyed her for herself and for her special talents. We took out the folder with all her drawings and we appreciated them together.

In the nineteenth month after therapy had begun, I told Sarah of my forthcoming resignation from the agency. At first she was very angry but cried with Wilma later that day. In the following session she became very clingy and sad and would not hear of another therapist. She was able to say that the next one would be cruel like her stepmother. She added, in response to my benign statement of how much she had grown, "I did not grow up to go to my three mothers' funerals."

During the last two weeks Sarah repeated in condensed fashion much of the behavior observed in the course of treatment, but with less intense affect. The tiger and monkey puppets had become teenagers and were being prepared to move to the new therapist's office. I was also directed to tell the new therapist about her past.

In the last hour she brought a card she had purchased for me. Printed on the card was the line, "You're in my thoughts." To this she added in her own handwriting, "and always will be, and I'll write to you every day even though you'll be far away. Love, Sarah." On the other side of the card she wrote, "I'll miss you very very very very very much," and she drew four drops labeled, "Tear Drops."

DISCUSSION

We have seen how a 10-year-old who suffered from losses and emotional deprivation before the age of 4 achieved a new sense of self, more cohesive and age-appropriate. The absence of predictably available selfobjects in her earliest years led to disturbances in cohesion reflected in the child's free-floating anxiety, states of depletion, and empty depression.

Miriam Elson (1986), in her book *Self Psychology in Clinical Social Work,* writes: "These states are expressed in rage, clinging, demanding behavior, in functional impairment or inhibition in the capacity for new steps in learning, motor skills, socialization. Injured cohesion or failure to achieve cohesion is also expressed symbolically in fears of the dark, witches, goblins, abandonment, and annihilation" (p. 80).

"The psychological functions and capacities that are normally heir to the multiple functions of childhood selfobjects have failed to 'go inside.' And such children suffer deficits in the normal workings of the mind, perception, delay, reflection, planning, the capacity to fantasy action and its consequences" (Elson, 1986, p. 80).

How did healing take place? The comfort, protection, and availability of concerned caregivers allowed Sarah to relax the defenses that for so long had protected her from further trauma. She could afford to access painful affects because of the fantasied merger with the strength of Wilma. While the disavowal had been self-preservative in the nonempathic environment, now it was possible to bring her two lives together.

Anna Ornstein (1994) writes, "The integration of traumatic memories into the flow of one's life narrative depends on the healing of the split between experiences as they are lived and as they are remembered" (p. 138). The undertaking of the therapeutic dialogue with Sarah could only commence after she was sure that telling her story, even in symbolic forms, would not retraumatize her. Before she could begin, she had to experience the staff as neither unemphatic nor indifferent to her. On the contrary, the childcare workers responded with exquisite sensitivity to her verbal and nonverbal clues while remaining attuned to signs that might indicate that she was ready to take tiny steps outward.

The treatment in the group home led to a strengthened sense of self with continuity and resilience, which allowed Sarah to participate in the therapeutic dialogue "in which the articulation of images and the reconstruction of memory fragments are undertaken jointly by patient and therapist" (Ornstein, 1994, p. 139).

Palombo's exposition of narrative theory adds a dimension to Ornstein's contribution. He (1992) writes,

> The therapist's empathy provides an experience that is affirming and reinforcing to a patient that may lead to a spontaneous resumption of growth through the integration of experiences that may have remained dissociated from the rest of the person's narrative. . . . The essential component in this experience is the comfort derived by the patient from having been able to share, within the dialogue, what may have been private, and may never have been exposed to anyone before. The therapist's understanding of the meaning to the patient of these experiences is a major curative factor [p. 267].

Narrative theory postulates that pathology may be conceived as

> the failures in the integration of personal and shared meanings. It also may be understood in terms of the disharmonies within the person's narrative. It is the malaise that results from unfulfilled longings, or from the tensions between irreconcilable motifs in one's personal and shared systems of meanings. It may represent the discomfort that results from the failures to integrate overwhelming experience that leads to incoherence that are experienced as feelings of meaninglessness. It is these that create the human suffering that we may identify as "psychopathology" [Palombo, 1992, p. 261].

The unique, individual manner in which Sarah recalled the old experiences and tried to integrate them into her psyche was determined by her own constitutional make-up and the culture of the group home. The therapist's challenge was to recognize Sarah's struggle to experience the affects evoked by the traumatic memories and her fear of doing so. After she presented the therapist with the "blank slate" and began to fill in her own story with new meanings, the need for disavowal diminished. Relevant to this observation is Ornstein's (1994) statement, "Though the healing of the vertical split, the undoing of disavowal, may never be complete, patients may become relatively free of nightmares and other trauma related symptoms as the traumatic memories become gradually transformed into episodic though forever painful memories" (p. 140).

Sarah was treated before self psychology and narrative theories were constructs available to clinicians. Their usefulness in understanding the genesis and treatment of Sarah's disturbance throws significant light on our basic comprehension of childhood and child pathology. It is hoped that this chapter will stimulate research and publication of similar cases to adapt and refine our understandings of this most disturbed sector of our child population.

REFERENCES

Elson, M. (1986), *Self Psychology in Clinical Social Work.* New York: Norton.

Ornstein, A. (1994), "Trauma, memory, and psychic continuity. In: *A Decade of Progress: Progress in Self Psychology, Vol. 10,* ed. A Goldberg. Hillsdale, NJ: The Analytic Press.

Palombo, J. (1992), Narratives, self-cohesion and the patient's search for meaning. *Clin. Soc. Work J.,* 20:261–268.

Samuels, S. (1995), Helping foster children to mourn past relationships. *The Psychoanalytic Study of the Child,* 50:309. New Haven, CT Yale University Press.

Chapter 17

A Disorder of the Self in an Adult With a Nonverbal Learning Disability

Joseph Palombo

Kohut (1971) stated that a disorder in which the deficit is clearly identified can be instructive in clarifying the function the missing element performs in healthy individuals. This construct, which appears to have been borrowed from neurological research, is applicable to the patient I am about to present. This patient suffers from a nonverbal learning disability (NVLD). NVLD is a neurologically based disability that manifests in, among other things, an impairment in the capacity to communicate nonverbally and also interferes with the capacity to form relationships with others. The deficits, which are in the visual–spatial area and in the area of processing social cues, interfere with the reception, expression, and processing of nonverbal signs. In many patients, a disruption occurs in the dialogue with caregivers during development resulting in a disorder of the self. The selfobject deficits that arise often lead to narcissistic personality disorders or to more pathological personality formations. Studying the dynamics of these patients can be instructive to clinicians in several important ways. They can shed light on the effects neuropsychological deficits have on the

I wish to acknowledge the contributions to this work made by my colleagues of the interdisciplinary NVLD/SLD study group at the Rush Neurobehavioral Center: John Bartok, Meryl Lipton, Karen Pierce, Pearl Rieger, and Warren Rosen. I also wish to thank Anne Berenberg whose insights have enriched my understanding of this disorder.

development process, they can clarify the dynamics of a broader set of disorders of the self, and they can assist in examining the role the learning disability plays in the way in which the patient presents in the clinical process.

In this chapter, I focus on the meaning of the impairment to the patient and her perceptions of how it affected her and her relationships. If we are to be truly empathic with our patients' experiences, it is necessary for us to take into account the ways in which such neurological deficits affect their lives from the earliest years. While empathizing with a patient who has such subtle neuropsychological deficits presents its own set of problems, the failure to take these deficits into account may lead to serious disjunctions or misinterpretations of what occurred to them historically. Furthermore, if an ongoing diagnostic focus is to be maintained during treatment, then assessing the effects of these deficits on the process and on the transference is imperative. This means that the treatment techniques we use are not fundamentally different from those used with any patient. However, the interventions and interpretations we make to explain the patient's problems are quite different from those we would make were the patient not affected by such a neuropsychological deficit.

I will begin with a brief definition of the construct of nonverbal learning disabilities. In presenting the case material, I limit myself to two essays that the patient wrote, which represent a sample of a voluminous set of materials she has given to me over the years. She often prefers to communicate in written form because she feels that her anxiety during sessions prevents her from being as open as she can be in the privacy of her home. The essay that I present first was written during the third year of treatment. The second essay she wrote after she had read one of my papers on nonverbal learning disabilities and had her diagnosis confirmed through neuropsychological testing. The significance of these documents is that they present this patient's experience of her disability both as she presents during a session and longitudinally. They clearly illustrate the impact her disability has had on her sense of self. Following these essays, I will discuss what we can learn from patients with this disorder about the impact of a nonverbal learning disability on the development of a disorder of the self.

NONVERBAL LEARNING DISABILITIES

Nonverbal learning disabilities (NVLD) are neurological conditions that occur in children or adults of at least average intelligence. These disorders are identified under a variety of labels including right-hemisphere deficits syndrome, right-hemisphere developmental learning disability, and social/emotional learning disability (Denckla, 1983; Weintraub, 1982; Semrud-Clikeman, 1990; Voeller, 1995). These labels are indicative of the belief among researchers that the etiology of the deficit is found in the right hemisphere. Most of the research has been done on children, although in my practice I have now seen several adults diagnosed with this disability. What is notable about patients with NVLD is that the language of nonverbal communication is largely unavailable to them. Consequently, like color-blind individuals, a segment of the world is largely overlooked. Another outstanding feature of patients with this disorder is the problems they have in initiating and maintaining social relationships. It is easy for clinicians to assume that they wish to isolate themselves from others and have no desire to connect with others. Sometimes the patients are diagnosed as schizoid or schizotypal. What these diagnostic labels overlook is the psychodynamics that have evolved resulting from the neuropsychological deficit. The patients have suffered repeated and multiple injuries in their inept attempts at connecting with others. Their withdrawal is therefore a result of these injuries rather than being motivated by a wish to avoid connecting with others.

Two researchers who have investigated this disorder are the neuropsychologists Rourke and Pennington. Rourke (1989) has done extensive research on this disorder. He describes a set of neuropsychological assets and deficits that he claims result from dysfunctions in right-hemisphere white matter. The assets are in the areas of simple motor functions, auditory perception, learning of rote material, attention, and speech and language. The deficits lie in the areas of tactile perception, visual perception, complex psychomotor functions, dealing with novel material, attention to tactile and visual input, exploratory behavior, memory for tactile and visual input, concept formation, and problem solving. For him, the children's socioemotional problems are part of the neuropsychological symptom constellation.

Pennington (1991), on the other hand, hypothesizes a more complex picture. He believes the syndrome may conflate two different populations. One set of children has problems in social cognition. These symptoms place the disorder within the "autism spectrum," along with high functioning autism and Asperger Syndrome. The characteristics of this population of children are deficits in social contact, imitation, emotional perception, intersubjectivity, pragmatics, and symbolic play, while the other set of children has right-hemisphere deficits in spatial cognition. The characteristics of children with this type of problem are deficits in object localization and identification, short- and long-term visual or spatial memory, deployment of attention to extra personal space, mental rotations and displacements, spatial imagery, and spatial construction. The socioemotional problems the children display are secondary to the neuropsychological problems. These symptoms find expression as shyness, depression, social isolation, deficits in eye contact, gestures, and prosody.

My colleagues and I see an even more complex clinical picture. Some, but not all, of our patients have problems in spatial cognition. Those who have these problems also appear to have problems in the areas of cognition, involving fluid reasoning, problem solving, difficulties with novel situations, and transitions. They also have socioemotional problems such as the misperception of social cues and problems with the regulation of affect states. But other patients do not have the problems in spatial cognition yet have similar cognitive and socioemotional problems. As with many disorders, the course a child's development takes and the symptoms they will manifest vary considerably. Few patients display all elements of the disorder, and even within a single symptom's manifestation a range of severity exists. Consequently, the description that follows should be understood as representing a list of the possible areas affected by this learning disability rather than a set of criteria to determine the presence or absence of the disorder. Each patient will be different from other patients, but essential similarities will remain.

DEVELOPMENTAL PROFILE OF CHILDREN WITH NONVERBAL LEARNING DISABILITIES

From a developmental perspective, caregivers report that as infants and toddlers these children are passive, fail to engage in exploratory play, and do not respond as expected. They are unable to put puzzles together and appear clumsy and ill-coordinated. They are slow to learn from their caregivers' limits and instructions and appear unable to understand causal relationships (Johnson, 1967, 1987). Caregivers find themselves having to intervene frequently to prevent them from harming themselves or getting into trouble. By the age of three, the children go through an initial stage when their speech is difficult to understand because of articulation problems. These problems dissipate as they become adept at verbal communication. This channel becomes reinforced by caregivers, who then become overreliant on it to relate to their children. By the time the children reach kindergarten or first grade, other problems emerge. They have difficulties with the classroom setting; some academic tasks are hard for them, and they are unable to form friendships or to sustain being with other children even for brief periods without eruptions resulting (Palombo, 1995, 1996; Palombo and Berenberg, 1997).

By latency, children with NVLD are generally referred for evaluation or treatment, boys usually because of behavioral problems, girls because of their social isolation. Both boys and girls often present with clinical signs of severe anxiety, depression, attentional problems, obsessional preoccupations, and self-esteem problems. They perform poorly in some academic areas, but not in all. As readers, they are good decoders, although their comprehension of abstract contents seems impaired. Tasks involving writing or arithmetic are usually difficult for them. Neuropsychological testing reveals their cognitive deficits, while their histories and the clinical impressions from diagnostic interviews disclose their social and emotional distress. They have difficulty with new situations and with transitions from one situation to another. They also find it difficult to deal with problem situations; each situation appears to them to be different from others they have encountered. Consequently, they cannot generalize what they have learned from prior experience. They either misapply the rules of conduct they are taught or are unable to solve the problem they confront.

The area of affective communication is problematic for patients with NVLD. Receptively, the patients appear unable to decode prosodic or vocal intonations, although their hearing is unimpaired. They also have difficulty reading facial expressions and reading bodily gestures, as though they suffer from "nonverbal dyslexia" (Badian, 1986, 1992). In the expressive area we see the counterpart of these problems. The patients do not use body gestures in speaking and so seem wooden and constricted. They do not use vocal intonations, speaking in a flat monotone or with a sing-song voice. Reading their mood from their facial expressions is difficult. We know very little about the ways in which they process affective information. It is not clear whether their problem lies in the area of decoding affective states or in the area of visual processing. They respond to affect-laden situations with anxiety, withdrawal, or sadness and appear to have problems modulating certain affects. When frustrated, they lose control and have temper tantrums. Their response to most feelings is one of generalized excitement that is unfocused and lacking in content. To adults these patients appear to have no compassion or empathy for others. They appear not to have the same feelings about events and people that their peers can have.

Finally, some children also exhibit psychiatric symptoms. They generally suffer from one or more of the following: high levels of anxiety, severe self-esteem problems, depression, obsessive–compulsive symptoms, and attentional problems. Often, they are diagnosed as having attention deficit disorder (AD/HD), which they may display, but the nonverbal deficits are not taken into consideration. Sometimes they are mistaken for children who suffer from Asperger's Syndrome or mild autism.

We are now realizing that a group of adults with similar problems exists. Many appear socially inept, seldom make solid eye contact, cannot decode prosodic or vocal intonations, and have difficulty reading facial expressions and bodily gestures or do not use appropriate body gestures; they seem wooden and constricted or use overly dramatic gestures that are not concordant with the context. Their moods are difficult to read from their facial expressions or posture. When frustrated, they lose control and have temper tantrums. As adults these patients are often misdiagnosed as schizoid or avoidant personality disorders.

What is impressive about these patients is their outstanding verbal fluency. Both children and adults often present as highly intelligent, articulate, and seemingly unimpaired by their learning disabilities. It is only as a relationship develops that the odd features in their behaviors emerge. These features, at first, are puzzling. The lack of eye contact, the absence of facial expression, the fidgety anxiety, and other traits contribute to a sense of discomfort in dialoging with them.

Relational Problems

Clinically, these patients' functioning is most impaired in their object relationships. Since their experiences are filtered through their neuropsychological deficits, the information they obtain about their interactions with others and of the world around them is incomplete. The conclusions they draw about the events they encounter are different from those most patients would draw under the same circumstances. Their inability to integrate into their understanding the meaning of other people's facial expressions, vocal intonations, gestures, and other nonverbal communications causes them to miss the significance of many affective messages these channels convey. It is not that they "distort" what they perceive so much as that they do not fully grasp or observe many cues that people convey. Consequently, their responses are based on incorrect or incomplete information. Simultaneously, they carry a conviction that their perceptions are correct and that they are justified in their responses. For them, negotiating interactions with others is as difficult as running an obstacle course at night with a flashlight. What is perceived is negotiable or avoidable; what is not observed trips up the runner, leading to bewilderment and frustration. NVLD patients are unaware that these failures are caused by their deficits and not obstacles placed in their path by others.

As a result, their experiences acquire personal, rather than shared, meanings, meanings that do not include elements of the communications with others that are highly significant. They develop patterns of interaction that are dysfunctional. These patterns are incorporated into themes or motifs that become organizing features of their self-narrative. When these motifs are concordant with others' responses, their view of reality appears similar to that of others. When they are not, the patient's construction of reality leads to relational problems. Since the patient is convinced that his or her self-narrative is coherent, there is little awareness of the dis-synchrony that exists between his or her view and that of others (Bruner, 1990).

Mitigating the effects of some of these deficits are the compensatory functions patients sometimes develop. Some patients learn to compensate through the "verbal mediation" of nonverbal tasks. They achieve the goal of completing a task by "talking their way" through the nonverbal steps. Some learn to structure their environment to reduce the reliance on visual cues. Others, with help, learn to rehearse verbally what is to occur in anticipation of an encounter with a new situation (Palombo, 1984, 1991, 1993, 1996).

What is of interest is the relationship between these social difficulties and the development of their capacity for attachment and for making use of selfobject functions. Traditionally, we have made the assumption that social difficulties reflect problems in object relatedness. Distinguishing between behaviors that are neurologically driven and those that are determined by the patient's deficits is essential to the proper understanding of these patients' dynamics. The issue of the relative weight to give to each of these components in assessing the patient's symptoms is a challenge to every therapist. Therapists must distinguish clearly between conduct that is "brain-driven" (hence, unmotivated) from conduct motivated by conscious or unconscious factors. We do not attribute a motive to an aphasic who either cannot express his/her thoughts or understand verbal communications and would not look for transference meanings to these responses in a treatment relationship. We simply recognize that the symptoms are directly related to the brain injury the person suffered. However, all people with such injuries continue to have motives that impel their behaviors; for example, they continue to desire closeness to others or defend against such wishes. These motives may also be entwined with unconscious desires that they themselves do not recognize. These will manifest within the transference. In such instances, it may difficult to sort out what is motivated from what is unmotivated. For patients with NVLD, the situation is as complex, if not more so, because their neuropsychological problems are not evident. It is therefore easy to confuse conduct that is unmotivated with conduct motivated by selfobject deficits. A patient's failure to make good eye contact may be mistaken for the patient having a poor capacity for object relatedness. A patient's disorientation in walking into a therapist's office that may lead him or her to sit in the therapist's chair, although this may by the second or third session, may be interpreted as a sign of grandiosity or of turning passive into active. A patient's failure to recognize the therapist outside the office may be mistaken for disavowal. The subtle ways in which the neuropsychological deficits manifest may not be fully appreciated for what they are and may result in being attributed to motives that may not be part of the patient's dynamics.

It is my belief that, in patients with nonverbal learning disabilities, their innate capacities for attachment and for making use of selfobject functions are intact but that they have erected defenses against making use of these capacities because of adverse life experiences. The failures in communication they experienced led them to perceive others as unresponsive, unemphatic, and unpredictable. Consequently, they defensively withdraw from social contacts to protect themselves against further injuries.

Adults with NVLD present as intelligent, highly verbal, somewhat successful people, who have been in a series of relationships, all of which have failed for unclear reasons. These patients seem unhappy with their isolation; they crave contact but seem totally inept at sustaining a connection with others. An important element is the vague or even garbled picture they relate regarding the occurrences in their lives. It is as though they are unable to narrate their story in a manner intelligible to others. They claim to be clear about what occurred, but that does not come across in the dialogue with therapists. Even if the attempt were made to clarify incidents, their responses are seldom enlightening. Their central problem is related to the fact that they do not speak the language of nonverbal communication. While they have an excellent grasp of verbal language, the code associated with nonverbal signs is mysterious or nonexistent to them.

Case Illustration

Pat[1] was referred to me by a colleague who had known her for some years. When I first saw her, she was a 40-year-old government employee who had never gone to college but had risen to a supervisory

[1] I wish to express my deep appreciation to my patient for her willingness to share her history. Her hope is that by so doing she will be helping others with similar problems.

position by virtue of hard work and good native intelligence. Although she had been in several relationships with men, she had never married. The presenting problem was a fear that her drinking was getting out of control. She had never thought of herself as having a drinking problem, having centered her social life around the people in a tavern she frequented. However, she now found herself drinking alone at home.

In the first session, she announced that she had decided to stop drinking and did not feel she would have a problem with that. Since this was her first experience in therapy, she did not know what else there might be to say. She agreed to once-a-week therapy.

Over the next year, we focused on what appeared to be an underlying depression, which she was medicating with the alcohol. She was unable to comply with her resolve not to drink and continued to drink but not immoderately. During that period, she discovered my interest in self psychology and on her own went out and bought Kohut's and Basch's books. She is an avid reader who was able to extract the essence of what she read as well as most social work graduate students. Eventually, a year after treatment began, she discovered that I had published papers, and she tracked down some of them. She read one of my papers on nonverbal learning disabilities and quickly recognized herself as having similar problems. She asked me to verify whether she was correct; I shared that I suspected that she did have such a learning disability but wanted her to be tested to have that suspicion confirmed. I referred her to a neuropsychologist[2] who is expert in this area, and he indeed confirmed the diagnosis.

In what follows, I first share some of her impressions of how she experienced coming to therapy for her sessions. She wrote this note to help me understand some of her difficulties in beginning each session. Second, I present a lengthy essay she wrote in an attempt at integrating her discovery that she had a learning disability with what she knew of herself and remembered of her past.

She writes:

> It's another Thursday morning. As I have done usually once a week for three years, I walk into the den that Joe uses as an office, pick up the throw pillow on the chair that is so obviously meant for the patient, sit, turn on the small recorder I carry with me to almost every session, slide off my shoes, and ask Joe how he is, as he sits down across from me. Every once in awhile, if he has been out of town or if I'm aware of something that has happened in his life since our last session, I can ask

[2] Warren Rosen, Ph.D. is the neuropsychologist at the Rush Neurobehavioral Center, of the Rush-Presbyterian-St. Luke's Medical Center, who diagnosed her condition.

a more precise question and be rewarded with a 2–3 sentence response, but generally he says "fine," and waits. This is usually the worst part of each session. I curl up in the chair and hug the pillow as I try to think of a meaningful way to begin.

I dread this moment so much, that often I have prepared a beginning before the session, like a good student preparing for class. Often I have even written it down. Sometimes I have mailed it to him so he has had time to read it, and I can begin the session by asking if he received the letter. Yet, even when I come prepared, there is almost always this uncomfortable silence as we first sit facing each other. I feel as though no matter what I say will sound trite and boring, or be repetitive. I wonder why I am here. I wonder why he keeps letting me come here. I wonder why the thought of not continuing to come here fills me with fear.

In the picture, he is sitting where he always sits and I took the picture from the chair I sit in. I am looking at the picture as I write this. He has the same expectant though calming look on his face as he does week after week when I sit across from him. I'm not sure how long ago it was when I asked him, but he told me that he was 65. His hair has receded and he has a small mustache. He's probably about 5' 10" tall. He always wears sports slacks and a long sleeve shirt, (I think) sometimes with a sweater vest. I don't believe I've ever seen him wear a tie. He also always wears sox and leather shoes. This seems peculiar to me. He is, after all, in his own house. To me, shoes are torture devices made to be rid of as soon as possible. But I suppose that he would feel naked in his stocking feet during a clinical session. One time, when he was going to vacation on an ocean beach, I asked him if he would walk barefoot in the sand. He said yes.

I need the picture in front of me to try to physically describe Joe. After 3 years I'm not certain if I would recognize him if I ever saw him out of context. One time, when I had an assignment for school that required a physical description and I spent hours torturing myself over it, Joe suggested that I emphasize the feelings I got when looking at what I was supposed to describe. For that assignment, his suggestion worked. I wonder if it could work for a description of Joe? This is probably the heart of where I feel as though I keep getting stuck in therapy. I can't find Joe. I can't feel Joe. I can't penetrate Joe. His eyes are kindly. When I am hurting, I believe that he hurts also. If I feel proud of an achievement, I know he is cheering for me. I believe he likes me. Maybe he even loves me a bit. But, at least lately, I can't reach him, I can't feel him. It hurts me. It seems that there was a time when I felt him. It seems there was a time when I let him closer. If there was, why can't I now. If I can't now, why are my eyes tearing as I write this, with the pain I feel for not letting him close?

Joe has a theory that I started pulling away from him when he advised me not to do something. Usually he has not been that directive, but he felt strongly that I was making a mistake. I listened to his reasons and they seemed logical, but they didn't seem applicable to me or the situation. I had a terrible feeling of "you just don't understand." I think that was almost six months ago. I did do what Joe advised against. I think that I had already done it before I spoke to him about it, although I don't think I told him that. After listening to his reasoning, I had a chance to at least partially undo what I had done, but I chose not to. I don't have any strong evidence even now, about whether the decision was "right" or "wrong." The point was that I felt Joe had completely misunderstood me. But that was months ago. Could it still be effecting [sic] my relationship with him today, as I grope for a beginning of what to talk about in this session? Or have I never let him get close to me?

In fact, by now, I have probably launched into a topic that is important to me, in order to end those uncomfortable early moments of anticipation. But no matter what degree of importance the subject has to me, only a part of me is with it. The rest of my mind is carrying on a now familiar conversation with the room around me. I look to see if things have changed, and if I recognize the change. Joe tends orchids in his basement. When they bloom, he often will bring one up and let it see daylight and be seen and admired for the period of it's [sic] blooming. Yet in the picture of Joe that sits in front of me, although there are flowers, I'm pretty sure they are not orchids. I don't remember them being in the den in real life. Usually the room doesn't change much, other than the flowers and weather outside of the big windows. But it never quite feels familiar. It took me a year to notice the room had a piano. I think that pictures sometimes change or new pieces are added to the room and maybe some taken away, but I'm never really sure. Sometimes as I talk or listen, my hand mentally reaches out to touch something. There is a sphere-shaped, shell-like thing that is even in the picture in front of me. Often I focus on it. I want to hold it. I want to see if it is hollow. I want to see if it is fragile. I want to squeeze it if it is not, because I think it is probably prickly and I want to feel the prickles dig into my hands. I don't think they would be sharp or deep enough to hurt, but they would cause a sensation. I think the shell has been there as long as I have. I have never asked to touch it.

About the only time that I was ever really certain that a change had been made in the room was when many of the books in the bookcase changed. An extra shelf or two of clinical journals replaced books that had been there and other books changed places. How many times has my mind idolly [sic] scanned the titles of his books, as I try to learn about him from them? Often the scanning oportunity comes when I give him something to read. While I wait, I avidly look for clues. But the books in this den are not the books that are still very meaningful to him. I doubt if any have been opened by him in years. This is his place of business. When a subject has come up and a book has been mentioned that seems important to both of us and I have asked to borrow it, he always goes upstairs to get it. The books in this room are gifts or books once loved but now relegated to decoration. I doubt if Joe could anymore throw out a book than I could. These are the orphans too dated for anyone else to want, but no longer belonging to the current library, wherever that is and whatever that holds.

The rest of the house is a mystery. I get a fleeting glance when I enter and leave. I am almost embarrassed by that glance, as though I am invading private property. Yet, just like I want to hold that shell, I want to see the orchids, the books, the cats who I know are there but I've only seen twice. I have never even asked to use the washroom, even though there have been times when I needed to and have left a session early to get to the train station's facilities just down the road. The most daring I have ever been, was to ask if I could look at his backyard on my way out one day.

Joe's house is my grandmother's house of my childhood. I know that Joe's house, just like my grandmother's is filled with treasures that I may not fully appreciate but would most certainly respect. It is on a very quiet street with several other large houses. There is an undeveloped treeful area across the street, just as there was behind my grandmother's house. Both his house and my grandmother's are made of brick and three stories. Both he and my grandmother love flowers and have beautiful gardens. Fairies could live in his backyard the same as they lived in my grandmother's. But when I went back to take a quick peak, I did not have time to meet Joe's fairies. Again, I did not feel as though I belonged. I had to leave quickly. What if another patient drove up as I searched for fairies? But at least I asked for, and was granted that glance. Do I really think that if I asked to hold the shell or use the washroom, he would turn me down? Of course not. But what if he did?

She subsequently wrote this extended "paper":

In response to Joseph Palombo's The Effect of Nonverbal Learning Disabilities on Children's Development: Theoretical & Diagnostic Considerations. By Pat J.

I have been in psychotherapy with Joseph Palombo for over two years. Recently I read his article "The Effect of Nonverbal Learning Disabilities on Children's Development: Theoretical & Diagnostic Considerations." In December of 1993, W. R. and J. G. administered a battery of 20 tests to me. Early this year, they returned a neuropsychological evaluation. I believe that the following phrase from the evaluation of me, sums up my interest in Mr. Palombo's paper: ". . . the cluster of visuo-spatial difficulties and affective processing deficits make up an entity known as non-verbal learning disability."

I am a 42 year old woman. I have never been married and have been physically and financially independent since I was 18. For most of that time, I've worked for the Postal Service. In the last three years I have accumulated almost a year of college credit, geared more towards my areas of interests, than a degree program. The therapy, the schooling and a recent emergence in creative writing are slowly pulling me out of wherever I spent the first 40 years of my life. The puzzle that Joe and I have been recently trying to solve, is how much of my prior (and present) difficulties were related to this non-verbal learning disability and how much to other factors.

When I first requested a referral to see a therapist, it was because I was feeling out of control from alcohol abuse. Immediately after I made the call, I stopped drinking. It was at least six weeks later before I met Joe. I now feel that the fifteen years that I spent abusing alcohol was more related to clouding over other issues in my life than an "addiction." I am not presently abstinent, though I don't feel conflicted over my alcohol use. The layer underneath the alcohol use, we labeled dysthymia. (In one of the first sessions with Joe, he explained that for insurance reasons, we needed a diagnosis. I was taking Psych 101, got my hands on a DSM-III-R, and diagnosed myself as having a schizoid personality disorder. He overruled me on that one.)

Dysthymia (once I learned what it meant) made sense. Although superficially functioning, I was withdrawn, unmotivated in any direction, energy-less and isolated. (Except, of course, when I was drinking in my friendly, neighborhood tavern.)

It also made sense diachronically. My mother was and is severely clinically depressed. My father probably *could* be diagnosed as having a schizoid personality disorder, in that he seems to be devoid of human empathy. They divorced when I was seven and both remarried volatile partners, with their own share of diagnosable symptoms. My childhood was spent continually moving, not only physically, but into almost completely different familial situations. (Kind of a "please pass the kids, syndrome.") My brother, at least until I was fourteen, was the only constant in these ever changing environments.

During the first year of treatment, Joe probably did little more than try to fill self-object functions for me. I couldn't say for sure, because I was only occasionally, emotionally with him. I don't know that this reaction could be labeled as resistance. I immediately liked and trusted him. I wanted to connect with him. But it has always seemed like there is a transparent barrier, perhaps made of Saran Wrap, which acts to mute connections between anyone and myself. Even now, in my relationship with Joe, the barrier is still there, though thankfully, ripped and shredded. Now, he evokes long latent emotions. I respond, with only quiet temper tantrums, in exactly the way he writes on p.11 about children with NVLD. "They respond to affect laden situations with anxiety, withdrawal or sadness. They appear to have problems in the modulation of certain affects. When frustrated, they lose control and have temper tantrums. Their response to most feelings is one of generalized excitement that is unfocused and lacking in content." Joe goes on to explain the effect this has on the adults around the child. I've probably learned to hide the disorientation I feel when I'm suddenly "attacked" by this sort of disembodied emotion. That's the closest that I could come to describing it, prior to reading Joe's explanation above. It's not a comfortable feeling!

So, first we have a layer of substance abuse. Then we have a layer of dysthymia. Then we have a layer of inadequately filled self-object functions. Now, we have a nonverbal learning disability. Which chicken laid which egg?

It was well over a year ago when I first brought up in therapy, a feeling of kinship to something Joe had written about a woman who he believed suffered from, among other things, a nonverbal learning disability (Palombo, 1993). (I was covertly reading his articles from the time I first learned that he was published. After I confided that, he made life easier for me and local librarians, by giving me copies.) It was the first time I considered that my inability to remember faces, places and things, might come from something other than disinterest, stupidity and/or laziness. It was the first time I considered that there might be a difference between my experience of the world and that of others. It had never come up in therapy before, because I thoroughly believed memory-aid masters who assert that everyone has the ability to develop a photographic memory if they only make an effort. I failed in my effort, so why keep trying, I knew that whenever I found myself in a different environment and with different people, I would only remember the most outstanding characteristics. I had learned to accept that. It wasn't something I would think to bring up in therapy. It was just the way it was. It wasn't something that most therapists would have understood, even if I had brought it up.

So, Joe began to explain some of the normal ramifications of a NVLD. Some fit, some didn't. My handwriting was terrible as a child, but so are most children's. I spent a lot of time working at it. It is now compulsively legible. I never learned arithmetic tables but I could get around it with a strong understanding of mathematics. (I have never known by rote what 8 × 7 =, but I could always figure it out.) I hated art and phys-ed, because they made me feel incompetent. I am only physically organized with efforts of will which soon deteriorate, so my apartment and my work space are frequently in shambles. I bought my condo six years ago. I have never felt capable of putting up a picture or decorating, because I fear that I would do it "wrong." I find visual entertainment frustrating. I never know "who is who" in movies. I prefer old westerns, where the good guys always wear white hats. I passionately avoid games such as "Trivial Pursuit." I hate puzzles. They underline what I feel are my inadequacies. Likewise, I don't want to engage in sports which require any kind of eye-hand coordination. (I do like to swim.)

These things contributed to my isolation. That brings us to the affective ramifications I've experienced, at least in part, because of this disability.

I remember at an early age, forcing myself to learn to make and retain eye contact with people, because someone told me that I should. The neuropsychological evaluation, included these observations: "She made clear efforts to engage the examiners appropriately, chatting and sustaining eye contact for long periods of time. Her continuous gaze and lack of non-verbal feedback, such as nodding and smiling during conversation, seemed a bit unnatural and might feel somewhat uncomfortable to others." It is unnatural! Although my gaze appears to be into the other's eyes, there is that Saran Wrap shield in between. I don't want either of us to see through "the windows of our souls." I probably won't even remember meeting you, the next time I see you.

Although nothing significant in the area was noted (or, I believe, tested for) in the evaluation, I also seem to have a poor oral memory of any affect laden situation. I tape my sessions with Joe. When I listen to them, even immediately afterwards, I often wonder where I was. In fact I've recently begun to tape anything that I truly care about, because I don't trust my memory in this area any more than I trust my visual memory. Perhaps Joe could figure out if there is a tie-in. It probably has to do with strong affect.

I'm presently enrolled in a creative writing course. Most of the work I've done has been slightly fictionalized, personal recounting. As I was re-reading some of it, I was struck by the number of times I alluded to going from one "world" to another or of being in a different "world." In many of Joe's papers, he refers to a feeling of fragmenting or incoherent self-narratives, both from a Self-Psychological perspective when self-object functions are not met, and in children with verbal or non-verbal disabilities, which cause them to see the world differently then their caretakers. I believe that I have maintained a reasonably coherent self-narrative because I have been able to fractionalize the world, instead of myself.

Each time that I moved, from depressed mother in a rented house, to self-involved father in a roach ridden apartment, to spending summers with my grandmother, to a house in the suburbs with a new obsessive-compulsive step-mother and younger step-brothers who I was expected to care for, to an apartment with my depressed mother and volatile step-father, I experienced "another" world.

Each school I was transplanted to (9, through highschool) apparently had different rules. I had nothing to take with me, each time life changed. It seemed that none of the previously learned behavior was applicable to the new situation. I was always starting from scratch.

Starting from scratch, meant almost complete initial withdrawal. I had to figure this new world out. I had to categorize the new cast of characters. After a time, I usually made one close friend who was also marked as "an outsider." These friends may have acted as buffers, by explaining the parts of the world I didn't understand. Their "outsideness" generally related to overt shyness, being "the fat kid," or coming from "the wrong side of the tracks." Since I never understood any of these concepts, I'm sure that I filled equal needs by just accepting them. Then it was time to move on. We would vow perpetual friendship. For a time, we'd write. But again, I was in a new world that had no connection with the older world. My energy was sapped in learning the new rules. I could not maintain a friendship.

Similar withdrawal accompanied new family situations. Actually, by the time I was ten I learned to build a barrier between myself and all new and old family members. In this arena, there was no one to explain the new rules. My brother was just as confused as I was, and four years older. He had the escape of highschool and after school work. I learned to love to read in my bedroom, with my door locked.

How does this apply to Joe's paper? I don't believe that in early childhood I had any sense of viewing the world "idiosyncratically", as he refers to. I believe that both my brother and my father share my nonverbal disability. Confusion as to which waitress was ours in a restaurant, which beach we had last been to, which bush bore black raspberries, was shared by all of us. Our responses, though perhaps confusing to those around us, seemed perfectly normal (from p. 9 of Joe's paper, it seems likely that he would not agree that this would be the expected outcome when people live together with shared NVLDs.) It was only at 10 years old, when my world changed to a completely "different world," that difficulties arose.

When my father remarried, he turned me over to my stepmother, and for all practical purposes, withdrew from my life. My brother began highschool. Suddenly, everything seemed "idiosyncratic." Looking back on the time, I always thought that it was my step-mother's emotional difficulties that started my own. In light of Joe's paper, it may have been that I was suddenly thrust into a world which was viewed completely differently, by those closest to me. Now, there was a lack of cohesion.

But however it came about, I had ten years of a reasonably coherent self-narrative built up. My aunt, Dodie taught psychological testing at the Western Michigan University in Kalamazoo. She used me as a "testing guinea pig for her class, when I was 10. I loved it—wonderful attention! Not only did I score a high I.Q., but I was also assessed to be abnormally well-adjusted, considering the trauma of living through a divorce, an infrequent phenomena at the time. When my father remarried, I did withdraw. I became hyper-vigilant. But I never disintegrated. It was the world that was different. Not me. All I had to do was keep learning new rules. Sure, it wore me out. Sure, I escaped into mild, chronic depression. Sure, the fifteen year sojourn in my local tavern gave me a feeling of belonging that I had never had. But, it seems that in many areas, I was able to compensate, without paying too high a price.

I have used two areas of compensation that Joe mentions (p. 18) for as long as I can remember. I almost always "verbally mediate" nonverbal tasks and "rehearse verbally what is to occur in anticipation of an encounter with a new function." Now, with the knowledge of the disability, I am further able to compensate by unashamedly questioning others in order to aid in the rehearsal. I'm more able to admit that I have no recall of previous meetings with people. (The conclusion that Joe has come to, that says NVLD people don't have a good sense of what is a socially acceptable confidence, is a great aid in this area. I just blurt out that I have this peculiar problem and they tell me who they are. Of course, they then may want to run!) Often I used to try to cleverly finesse my way through uncomfortable situations, or more frequently, just avoid them. This isn't uncommon for people, even without my visual memory deficits. The difference was that often I had met these people many times before, not just once. They knew me and things about me. It turned out that I had often had intimate prior conversations with them, but I had no recall. All my memory told me, was that given certain situations, it was probable that I should recognize them. In the last six months, now that I have an understanding of what is going on, I've learned to take notes, write down names with brief descriptions of a memorable peculiarity and rehearse the lists prior to entering a situation when I'm likely to see the same people again. I've learned not to expect to recognize another person as a gestalt until after many meetings. I didn't even recognize a picture of myself taken at a recent work-related meeting.

Joe also writes of caretaker's complementing these sorts of disabilities, or being unable to, because the child's behavior seems so foreign. When I first read Joe's paper, I wondered whether my impression of my mother's emotional absence could have something to do with my misreading her intentions and because of the disability, I reacted unusually towards her. Maybe so, however other sources do attest to her clinical depression. Likewise, I wondered about my father. If anything, until I was 10 he related more empathically with me than he probably ever has with anyone. After that, I think that I just emotionally outgrew him. Obviously, from this upbringing, there was no chance of someone else performing a complementary function, with the possible exception of the short term friends that I mentioned, nor any chance of a developing symbiosis.

Would it have helped me, if I had been diagnosed with a non-verbal learning disability at an early age, even with everything else remaining the same in my upbringing? I have no doubt that it would have, provided I was at an age where I could at least partially understand it. No caretaker could have, but at 10, I think that I would have. This would be where some of the negative affective results could have been avoided. Children born with other sorts of handicaps learn to understand them and are probably less likely to blame themselves for things beyond their control. In the range of possible handicaps, a non-verbal learning disability would certainly not rate highly in it's [sic] disabling features. Looking back on ways I adjusted to the world, the only truly harmful outcomes came from the elusiveness of the problem. As I said at the beginning, the world translates the effect as being caused from laziness, inattention, or stupidity. It is very similar to the way children with verbal disabilities were looked at, prior to the discoveries of such things as dyslexia. With the knowledge that there is a cause outside of my control, I could have learned at a much earlier age, to modulate the control that I do have, to fit the context.

Instead, I reacted by trying to hide my laziness, inattention and stupidity. I withdrew to the extent possible. And, although I'm not sure that Joe follows me on this one, I think that I divided the world rather than myself, thus maintaining a certain coherence. I conceptualize my moves from Chicago to Arlington Heights to Riverside to Evanston (all in the Chicogoland area) as being similar to an untraveled American who only understands English, going from Japan to Australia to Greece. In order to survive, I believed that each situation had to be treated as a "different" world. If, from early on, I had a better understanding of the dynamics of the disability that made this true, maybe I could have applied learning from the past to the present and the future and not forever have felt like "A Stranger in a Strange Land."

DISCUSSION

Many facets of these documents deserve comment. However, because the focus of this chapter is on the diagnostic relevance of the disorder to the treatment process, I will restrict my remarks to three sets of issues that bear on this area: the differentiation between etiology and dynamics, the meaning of failures in empathy in patients with neuropsychological deficits, and the symptom of withdrawal and isolation. Central to this discussion is the issue of the effect of the inability to understand the effects of a nonverbal learning disability on the development of a patient's sense of self and on the establishment of attachments to others.

Kohut (1971) suggested making a differentiation between etiology and dynamics. This differentiation embodies the duality between mind and body that separates the issues of causes and reasons or motives (Gill, 1977). In this case some of the causes for Pat's problems are found in her neuropsychological deficits, and some of the motives for her actions are found in the meanings she drew from her experiences. These meanings form part of a narrative she constructed to bring coherence to her experiences. This narrative embodies meanings encoded through both the nonverbal and the verbal language systems. In trying to understand her dynamics, we confront two sets of problems: one relates to the integration of the neuropsychological causes into our understanding of how her narrative evolved, and the other relates to her failure to integrate the meaning of her experiences within the nonverbal domain because of her impairment.

Cases such as that of Pat demonstrate that the division between causes and motives is clinically unworkable. The meanings she assigned to her experiences were always filtered through the neuropsychological capacities she brought to the events. Whether it was her ability to remember, the sensitivity of her sensory system, her capacity to conceptualize, the level of attention she gave to visual–spatial phenomena, or the affects aroused in her by events, each of these colored her experiences in a way that led her to perceive the world differently from others. In a sense her "reality" was different from that of others. The individual differences in her neuropsychological make-up contributed to the personal meanings she gave to events. To ignore the contributions of her endowment in the acquisition of meanings leads to an overemphasis on the contribution of environmental factors. It results in the view that she as a child did not contribute to the meanings she construed out of her experiences but was the passive recipient of what occurred.

Until her diagnosis was established, in the absence of any information about her neuropsychological deficits, Pat struggled to make sense of her life experiences. She felt she had a clear perspective on her past, one that attributed many of her difficulties to what had happened to her. Certainly, events in her history gave her ample reason to feel that her mother's depression, her father's coldness, the many moves to which she was subjected could all be responsible for her lack of success in forming long-term relationships, in being depressed, and medicating herself through alcohol. The problem we confronted in understanding her is that her narrative was incomplete. In her narrative she had "normalized" the events and her responses. The realization of her differences from others led her to modify her behaviors to make them conform to what others expected of her. She processed these differences as resulting from her not having learned to respond in the ways that others expected, unaware that the sources of her difficulties lay elsewhere. Yet she knew she could not remember faces or attach names to people's faces; she realized that she was not well coordinated, that her handwriting needed improving, and that she did not make good eye-to-eye contact. To all these shortcomings she responded by trying hard to find accommodations, having learned on her own that her verbal strength could help her compensate for her weaknesses. In all these areas she worked hard and succeeded in making up for many of her deficits. The area that remained problematic was the social area. Although she managed to develop one or two friendships on which she relies for contact with others, she had little awareness of the level of closeness that others could experience but that she could not.

While much in the environment could explain the form her personality eventually took, ignoring the neuropsychological leaves much unexplained. In particular, what often remains unexplained in such cases are the differences in children's responses to the same parental environment. Searching for reasons in the different responses that caregivers make to each of their children is often insufficient. One can speculate about the effect on Pat during her infancy of the inability to recognize faces and its influence on the attachment she formed to her mother or about the effect of her not making good eye contact on her mother's ability to respond to Pat as an infant. These and other factors can only have played a significant part in the interaction between her and her mother. I suggest that we cannot separate etiological factors from the dynamics. The two are inextricably entwined. The resulting meanings that people extract from their experiences are a result of the two sets of factors.

The second issue I wish to address is the meaning of "empathy failures" in cases such as that of Pat. Clinically, an outstanding feature of my interaction with her was my difficulties in being empathic with her. Sessions would begin with her blankly staring at me and then bursting out with a nervous laugh. She would follow this behavior by her asking what I wanted to talk about today. This attempt at humor would often fall flat because it felt neither "cute" nor funny. Instead, it felt irritating. When this interchange first occurred, I took it to reflect her anxiety, and after commenting about it, I waited for her to begin. But instead of taking my cue and proceeding, she seemed to mimic my stance, persisting in wanting me to begin. As we talked about what was going on, she quickly became defensive, saying that she was only making a joke and that I had misunderstood her. However, the same interchanges occurred repeatedly; she seemed unable to shift or to benefit from our discussions as to the meaning of her mode of relating. She discussed her discomfort in beginning as related to her inability to read by state of mind, emphasizing that she could not sense how I was feeling. This, she said, made it difficult for her to begin. Eventually, I was unable to suppress my irritation and shared it with her. Only then would she stop, although as we discussed this later it was more out of compliance and the wish not to "hurt me" as she understood it, rather than because she had developed any insight into the meaning of her behavior.

This vignette illustrates, in part, the difficulty I had with being empathic with her, of going beyond the presenting behavior to the feeling hidden behind it. The failure had its source in my inability to read her nonverbal messages and her inability to read mine. We were obviously not speaking the same language. I experienced her teasing comments as irritating and hostile. For her part, her uncertainty about what I felt and her inability to understand my nonverbal messages led her to an awkward attempt at easing the situation through humor. This form of disrupted dialogue manifested itself in many areas of our interaction. Only as we processed the nonverbal through verbal means could we clarify what went on.

In my mind the problem of my empathic failures loomed large as I either feared alienating her or having her submerge any feelings she might have to avoid making me angry. It raised the larger problem of how to think about what constitutes an empathic failure. I believe that our capacity for empathy is heavily reliant on our ability to "read" the nonverbal messages a patient imparts, which enhances our understanding of what he or she is communicating. However, patients who have these types of neuropsychological deficits are incapable of imparting what they feel nonverbally. Even their verbal efforts at conveying this information is limited by their seeming detachment from what they feel. The situation is fraught with the potential for disjunctions. In spite of a therapist's best efforts at understanding the patient, his or her empathy can fail. A failure such as this exists when the patient experiences the provider of the selfobject function as not available to provide the function—despite the *reality of the availability of the provider to provide such a selfobject function!*

Clinical experiences such as this led me to the conviction that not all empathic failures are alike. There are failures caused by the neglect, abuse, or rejections that caregivers impose on a child. Other failures occur when caregivers have the capacity and opportunity to respond but do not do so. There are also failures that are caused by "circumstance," that is, catastrophes, acts of God, or event that are totally beyond the control of the caregivers. There are also failures, as with the patients we are discussing, where the child's neurological impairment sets a limit to any caregiver's capacity to empathize with the child's state. It seems to me that what is at issue is the significance of the motive behind the unavailability of the caregiver. The meanings of the failure must be understood differentially, depending on the motive behind the caregiver's responses and the child's understanding of that motive. A patient who understands that the limits of the therapist's understanding are caused by the patient's own deficits may feel less traumatized than the patient who feels that the therapist is being cruel or sadistic. If a caregiver were depressed or ill or unable to respond or if the patient were ill or unable to use the functions offered, then it seems to me that a different configuration exists than that described by the concept of "empathic failure." In other words, if a child understands the motives that limit a caregiver's capacity to provide empathic responses, then the child would respond differently than he or she would to the actions of a caregiver who was sadistically withholding and unresponsive. The impact of the absence of a caregiver's understanding would be different.

With my patient, her experience of my inability to understand her was not seen as a failure on my part. It brought the "Saran Wrap" that separated us to our awareness, a barrier caused, not by her unwillingness to be responsive, but by a factor that was beyond her or my control. Her understanding of the source of the barrier brought great relief and clarity to what went on between us and between her and others with whom she tried to form relationships. However, that understanding did not substitute for her need for selfobject responses, nor did it comfort her in her distress at feeling isolated. If anything, it deepened her despair at being able to achieve a sense of intimacy with another person. She could understand intellectually that I was available, concerned, and invested in her, yet this understanding provided cold comfort. Eventually, my understanding of her responses as partially caused by her neuropsychological deficits allowed a deeper level of empathy than would have been possible had I not been aware of those deficits.

Developmentally, although her parents may have been willing and able to respond to her needs, serious selfobject deficits developed because she could not experience their mirroring, soothing, and comforting. Instead, she interpreted their transactions with her as having different meanings than those they might have intended. Her cognitive and affective deficits interfered with the use of the selfobject functions they could have been ready to provide. She experienced the interchanges as failures in empathy. The resulting selfobject deficits imposed severe limits on the range and depth of connection between her and others.

Similar difficulties lay in the path to her acquisition of idealizing selfobject functions. Since most selfobject functions are performed nonverbally, they occurred in a domain that was difficult for her to decode. Along the line of idealizing selfobject functions, experiences such as those of being held safely by a protective caregiver, of being reassured by the modulating influence of a caregiver's regulatory interventions, or of being admired by a caregiver had a different meaning for her than such interactions would have had to others. She could not perceive or she misread the affects the caregivers conveyed. For example, if gestures were misinterpreted, the personal meanings she drew would at best only partially reflect what occurred. As a result, she may, in fact, have experienced the caregiver as unempathic or uncaring. She could not acquire the psychological structures associated with the idealizing selfobject functions. She ended up feeling unsafe and unprotected in ordinary life situations, had difficulties regulating and modulating affects, and was unable to take pride in her own achievements.

Finally, the symptom of withdrawal and isolation from others deserves special attention. Among the factors that lead to defenses and symptomatic behaviors in patients with NVLD is their chronic experience of anxiety that can sometimes be pervasive. The injuries they suffered from others' responses to them and their inability to modulate their affect states lead them to feel repeatedly misunderstood, injured, and bewildered by what occurred. With Pat the absence of alter ego experiences that provide a linkage with others whose humanity she shared left her feeling constantly injured and dehumanized, as though she were an alien in this world. She often spoke of feeling like a color-blind person in a world where neither she nor others knew of her color blindness. Everyone, including herself, assumed that she saw what others saw but when she responded in ways that did not match others' expectations, she saw herself and others saw her as different, if not weird. In some patients with NVLD, this sense of alienation leads them to play up their differences rather than hiding them. The deficits become a badge rather than a shortcoming. Some exaggerate the means through which they communicate, and much like people who when speaking to a foreigner may speak louder in hopes of being understood, they dramatize their responses, unaware of their inappropriateness. Some turn to oppositional behaviors as a way of defining themselves, which makes it difficult for them to get along with others. Some feel a deep sense of shame, fearing that their deficits are evident to everyone. They retreat from social contacts, isolate themselves, and appear uninterested in people. The deficit in alter ego selfobject responses is perhaps the most devastating deficit that manifests in severe self-esteem problems.

These responses must be understood as stemming from the learning disability rather than from other sources exclusively. It would be inaccurate to characterize these responses as stemming from a schizoid personality disorder or an avoidant personality disorder. Such characterization led to different formulations of the patient's dynamics than those arrived at by taking into account the NVLD. The critical factor is that therapeutic interventions geared to addressing the patient's anxieties uncover the sources of those anxieties. What emerges is the history of being misunderstood and inadvertently injured by others' responses. The meanings these themes acquired lead the patient to different responses in social situations than those previously made. However, the residue of anxiety is seldom totally eradicated.

CONCLUSIONS

The study of patients with nonverbal learning disabilities can shed light on the role neuropsychological deficits play in the development of some disorders of the self. These patients suffer from a neurological impairment, which makes it difficult for them to understand, communicate, and process nonverbal cues. These patients allow us to observe some effects of the absence of this dimension of the communicative process on the therapeutic dialogue and draw diagnostic inferences regarding their dynamics. Furthermore, the impairment, by its very nature, is instrumental in producing selfobject deficits because of the disruptions created between the infant and caregiver during development. In the case illustration that follows, I focus on the diagnostic considerations involved in differentiating between the contributions of the neuropsychological deficits and the selfobject deficits to patients' relational problems.

We arrive at three sets of conclusions: First, patients with nonverbal learning disabilities help raise the question of the relationship between etiological and dynamic factors in some disorders of the self. This is an area in which research is badly needed. Our developmental theories do not pay sufficient attention to the role neuropsychological factors play in some disorders. Neither do they consider sufficiently the domain of nonverbal communication in facilitating or interfering with attachment or making use of selfobject functions.

Second, the relationship between nonverbal communication and empathy requires further exploration. Empathy is a tool adapted to nonverbal communication, yet this aspect has received insufficient attention in the literature. Also, examining the meaning of failures in empathy when considering selfobject deficits may enrich our understanding of the nature of the original experience to which the patient responded.

Third, the symptoms of social isolation and the difficulties in forming attachments should be reconsidered in light of the possible contribution of factors related to a patient's endowment. It is incorrect to simply assume that all such symptoms result for a primary disruption in the child/caregiver relationship because of the caregivers' parenting patterns.

REFERENCES

Badian, N. A. (1986), Nonverbal disorders of learning: The reverse of dyslexia? *Annals of Dyslexia*, 36:253–269.

——— (1992), Nonverbal learning disability school behavior and dyslexia. *Annals of Dyslexia*, 42:159–178.

Bruner, J. S. (1990), *Acts of Meaning*. Cambridge: Harvard University Press.

Denckla, M. B. (1983), The neuropsychology of social-emotional learning disabilities. *Arch. Neurol.*, 40:461–462.

Gill, M. M. (1977), Metapsychology is not psychology. *Psychol. vs. Metapsychol.*, 9:7–105.

Johnson, D. J. (1967), Educational principles for children with learning disabilities. *Rehabil. Lit.*, 28:317–322.

——— (1987), Nonverbal learning disabilities. *Ped. Annals*, 16:133–141.

Kohut, H. (1971), *The Analysis of the Self*. New York: International Universities Press.

Palombo, J. (1984), Borderline personality in childhood and its relationship to neurocognitive deficits. *Child & Adolesc. Soc. Work J.*, 1:18–33.

——— (1991), Neurocognitive differences, self cohesion, and incoherent self narratives. *Child & Adolesc. Soc. Work J.*, 8:449–472.

——— (1993), Neurocognitive deficits, developmental distortions, and incoherent narratives. *Psychoanal. Inq.*, 13:85–102.

——— (1995), Psychodynamic and relational problems of children with nonverbal learning disabilities. In: *The Handbook of Infant, Child, and Adolescent Psychotherapy: A Guide to Diagnosis and Treatment, Vol. I*, ed. B. S. Mark & J. A. Incorvaia. Northvale, NJ, Aronson, pp. 147–176.

——— (1996), The diagnosis and treatment of children with nonverbal learning disabilities. *Child & Adolesc. Soc. Work J.*, 13:311–332.

——— & Berenberg, A. H. (1997), Psychotherapy for children with nonverbal learning disabilities. In: *The Handbook of Infant, Child, and Adolescent Psychotherapy: New Directions in Integrative Treatment, Vol. 2*, ed. B. S. Mark & J. A. Incorvaia. Northvale, NJ: Aronson, pp. 25–68.

Pennington, B. F. (1991), *Diagnosing Learning Disorders: A Neuropsychological Framework*. New York: Guilford.

Rourke, B. P. (1989), *Nonverbal Learning Disabilities: The Syndrome and the Model*. New York: Guilford.

Semrud-Clikeman, M. & Hynd, G. W. (1990), Right hemisphere dysfunction in nonverbal learning disabilities: Social, academic and adaptive functioning in adults and children. *Psycholog. Bull.*, 107:196–209.

Voeller, K. K. S. (1995), Clinical neurologic aspects of right-hemisphere deficit syndrome. *J. Child Neurol.*, 10:516–522.

Weintraub, S. M. & Mesulam, M. (1982), Developmental learning disabilities of the right hemisphere: Emotional, interpersonal and cognitive components. *Arch. Neurol.*, 40:463–468.

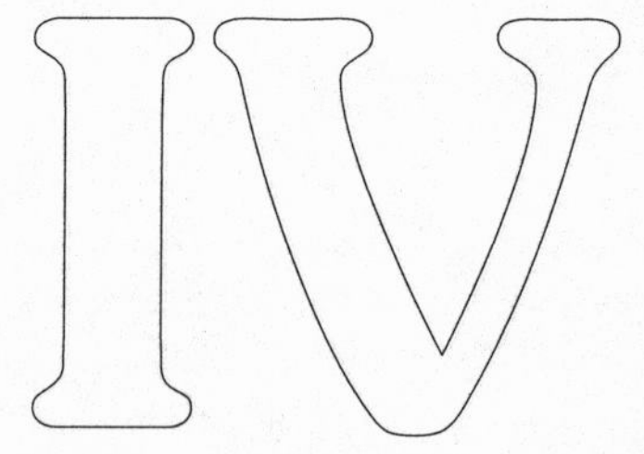

IV Critiques

Chapter 18

Secret Conversations With My Father: The Psychological Dimension of Theoretical Discourse

Maxwell S. Sucharov

This chapter continues my exploration of the multidimensional impact of the analyst's subjectivity on the psychoanalytic enterprise. In a previous paper (Sucharov, 1996), I explored the implications of the central and continuous influence of the therapist's subjectivity on the analytic process. In that context, I presented case material that highlighted the additional dimension of understanding generated by a listening stance that focused on the empathic dance of patient and therapist. I had chosen the metaphor of dance in an earlier paper (Sucharov, 1998) to capture the mutuality of empathy and the interpenetration of experience in the analytic encounter.

The mutuality of the psychoanalytic process and the subsequent inclusion of the therapist's subjectivity as a legitimate focus for analytic investigation has been acknowledged widely in the recent psychoanalytic literature (Hoffman, 1991; Renik, 1993; Doctors, 1995; T. J. Jacobs, 1995; Knoblauch, 1995; Orange, 1995; Aron, 1996; Lachmann and Beebe, 1996; Rustin, 1997; L. M. Jacobs, 1998). However, the clinical importance of the subjectivity of the analyst receives its most extensive elaboration in Atwood and Stolorow's intersubjective systems theory, a broad framework dedicated to the development of a comprehensive theory of subjectivity. Their interest in subjectivity began with the recognition of the embeddedness of all psychological theories in the psychological life of the theorist (Stolorow and Atwood, 1979). A natural corollary to the latter thesis will constitute the principal focus of this chapter: *All psychoanalytic theoretical discourse, both written and oral, cannot be separated from the human subjective contexts in which this discourse takes place.*

It is therefore important that an explication of the role of subjectivity in psychoanalysis needs to include not only case material that illuminates the continuous impact of the therapist's subjectivity on the therapeutic process (the focus of my last paper), but also "case material" that demonstrates the embeddedness of psychoanalytic theoretical discourse in the subjective life of the participants. This chapter constitutes a beginning attempt to meet this need.

In that context I will revisit my own theoretical work with a lens of intersubjective contextualism. Within this perspective, I will attempt to delineate the personal subjective influences that contributed to the choice of problems I explored and to the conceptual and clinical arguments I marshalled in my proposed solutions. Furthermore, I will be looking at my subjectivity, not in isolation, but rather, its articulation within the relational field constituted by the self psychology community in which my clinical and theoretical ideas have evolved. A guiding principle to my exploration is that the content and nature of my theoretical discourse is shaped not just by my own subjectivity, but by a complex interplay between the salient emotional issues of the self psychology community as these issues resonate with the particularities of my own subjective world.

Having contextualized and therefore delimited the generality of my ideas, I will reexamine some of my previous conclusions from within a vantage point that is decentered in part from their intersubjective origins in order to achieve a fresh perspective on the issues with which I have been struggling. My goal is not to achieve a more objective view but, rather, a more informed subjective one that adds a vital dimension of understanding that would be excluded by a perspective that "separates a text from the human context in which it was created" (Stolorow, 1995, p. xv).

This chapter constitutes a natural extension and expansion of the field of inquiry of *Faces in a Cloud* (Atwood and Stolorow, 1993) where the psychobiographical method was restricted to major psychoanalytic theorists. An exploration of the psychological context that has shaped my own modest contributions extends the investigative domain to include the "foot soldier investigators . . . [who] exist within the trenches of the battle surrounded by smoke and fire and trying to catch our breaths in the midst of it all" (Galatzer-Levy, 1997, p. 5).

The "clinical data" I will employ as an entry point into both the subjectivity of the self psychology community and my own personal world consist of a personal dream and a conversation with a psychoanalytic colleague that seemed to contribute to the dream's formation.

The conversation took place between me and a colleague at the self psychology conference in San Francisco in 1995. My colleague is a strong supporter of Atwood and Stolorow's intersubjectivity theory. We were discussing the revolutionary dimension of a fully intersubjective relational approach, and my colleague was lamenting on how few clinicians fully incorporated this point of view into their work.

I did not share my colleague's pessimism, and in that context I asked him what he thought of Frank Lachmann as an example of an innovative thinker. I had a strong respect for Lachmann's contributions. His collaboration with Beatrice Beebe on dyadic systems had strongly influenced my paper on the mutuality of empathy presented at the conference that year. Furthermore, Lachmann had been in "complete agreement" (personal correspondence) with the thesis of an earlier paper of mine that argued for the convergence of self psychology and intersubjectivity theory inside a common general systems paradigm.

My colleague paused as if he were caught off guard with my question. He then acknowledged the progressive innovative nature of Lachmann's work but suggested that the revolutionary potential of his contribution was perhaps restrained by a conservative tendency. (I do not recall the exact words of my colleague. The importance of the conversation is the meaning that I inferred from his response.)

Several days later I had the following dream. In the first part I was looking at the body of my father. Unlike many previous dreams since my father's death in 1972, in which it was unclear whether he was alive or dead, in this dream he was clearly dead and his body was partly decomposed. The dream then shifted, and I was walking down a set of stairs into a living room with a gathering of people from the self psychology community. In the center of the room, Frank Lachmann was on all fours looking at and having a secret conversation with the body of Heinz Kohut, which was laying beneath a glass coffee table.

I say "secret" because Lachmann was disguising Kohut's presence with the use of curtains surrounding the table. I was wondering why he needed to conceal his conversation from the rest of the group. In the transitional space before the next part of the dream, it appeared that some plan was being concocted to create the illusion that Kohut was alive, with the use of embalming make-up.

The second part of the dream began with a dramatic and sudden shift to a bright outdoor space. Kohut had become a rejuvenated King

George III from the movie/play *The Madness of King George.* It was the part of the movie where the psychotic king enters a period of remission and he is presented to his subjects in full majestic splendor. Trumpets were blaring, and in the foreground the king's faithful servant was rubbing his hands with glee, anticipating a return of the "good old days." (The king's rejuvenation strikes a blow to the ambitions of the Prince of Wales who was hoping that a declaration of his father's permanent unfitness to rule would elevate the prince to the throne of England.)

I was observing all this from the outside, and I was thinking that this restoration was an illusion and doomed to failure (King George III eventually deteriorated and spent the last 10 years of his life blind and insane). This part of the dream was experienced as a nightmare, and at this point I woke up.

In a previous paper (Sucharov, 1996), I presented a view of dreams as relational events that reflected the overlapping emotional issues of patient and therapist. This view derives, in part, from the work of Dorpat and Miller (1992), who draw on research in the cognitive sciences to depict a new view of the primary process as a legitimate cognitive perceptual system that engages in unconscious meaning analysis of current events involving self and other. Within this view dreams are not understood to reflect unconscious fantasy (a concept derived from erroneous 19th century theories of perception and memory) but as unconscious perceptions of actual interpersonal events that include *legitimate inferences about the unconscious life of the other.*

Dreams therefore constitute a royal road to the unconscious of *both the dreamer and of persons in his relational world.* I will therefore view my dream as reflecting the mutual entanglement of my own personal world with the subjectivity of the self psychology community of which I am a part. For purposes of explication, I will "crack up" (Bollas, 1995) the dream into its individual component (my own unconscious) and the group component (the unconscious of the self psychology community). This dichotomy is not intended to negate the holistic experiential nature of the dream in which both of these components receive simultaneous expression.

GROUP SUBJECTIVITY

Within this perspective, the dream can be seen as reflecting my unconscious primary process meaning analysis of the self psychology community's unconscious emotional relationship to Kohut and his ideas. The biphasic structure of the dream seems to suggest a dialectical tension between two modes of organizing experience around the themes of loss, need for continuity, and need for creative innovation. The first part of the dream resembles a Jewish "shiva," a gathering at the home of the bereaved that facilitates the mourning process. Lachmann's conversation with Kohut reflects the group's yearnings to reconnect with its departed leader. The secret and disguised nature of the conversation suggests that this yearning for connection is conflictual. Could it be that alliances with innovative factions within the group will be threatened (i.e., he will be viewed as too "conservative")? On the other hand perhaps some advantage will be conferred by this connection. New ideas could be tolerated and supported by factions loyal to Kohut.

The second part of the dream has a bizarre quality that suggests archaic modes of organizing experience. The attempt to restore Kohut to his position of charismatic leader reflects tendencies within the group to resort to massive denial and psychotic restoration as a means of processing loss and maintaining continuity. This constellation will also involve the mobilization of archaic narcissistic configurations, especially around idealizing needs. The primitive nature of this experiential configuration also suggests that the principal fear is not one of loss of needed alliances within a stable group but, rather, dissolution and fragmentation of the group itself.

In summary, I would tentatively propose that the dream, in its reflection of the group's subjectivity, expresses oscillations within the group between two modes of organizing experience in connection to the loss of Kohut and with the need to balance creative expansion with the preservation of continuity to Kohut's seminal work. It is important to emphasize that these two modes of organizing experience do not necessarily refer to different sets of individuals within the group, but reflect the experiential potentiality within each of us. (If I may sneak a little Kleinian theory into this chapter, I would suggest that the two modes represent depressive and paranoid positions, respectively.) I would also suggest that the two fears reflected in these two modes (i.e., fear of loss of needed alliances and fear of group dissolution) constitute group psychic realities that will shape, in part, various solutions to the theoretical task of reconciling new ideas with Kohut's essential contributions.

PERSONAL SUBJECTIVITY

In explicating the personal issues reflected in the dream, I will share an important association that I had to the dream. This association was the phrase, "The crown has fallen from our head." These words constituted the opening statement by the rabbi at my father's funeral in reference to my father's position as a prominent leader of the local Jewish community. The passage is from Lamentations and is spoken by the prophet Jeremiah in the context of his grief over the destruction of Jerusalem by Nebuchadnezzar in 586 B.C. and the subsequent exile of Jews to Babylon. This exile began a 2,500-year odyssey for the Diaspora Jew who strove to maintain continuity and tradition as a minority group in the context of a shifting and often hostile host nation.

The joint participation in Jewish tradition and ritual was the principal mode of connecting with my father. I would usually accompany him to synagogue on the Sabbath, and I was an outstanding student at the local orthodox school. Furthermore, while my father's career was a source of deep disappointment to him, his service to and recognition by our tightly knit Winnipeg Jewish community constituted his main source of pride and accomplishment. My father's Jewish-centered activities therefore provided me with some source of paternal idealizing needs.

As an adult Jew, I have moved beyond the narrow restraints of my father's form of Judaism. I have married outside my faith (this marriage took place after my father's death), and my participation in the social and ritual life of the Jewish community is minimal. To a casual outside observer, I would appear to be an assimilated and secular Jew. However, this superficial appearance fails to convey my personal experience of a powerful Jewish identity, which resonates at the deepest layers of my core self. The manifestations of this vital dimension to my being are, however, mostly private. I enjoy reading the Old Testament, and when alone, I will sing the cantorial tunes that were part of the weekly fare at the synagogue of my childhood. I therefore have "secret conversations with my father."

The personal component to the second part of my dream could reflect my oedipal anxieties with respect to a paternal restoration. The prospect of my father's return to this world could be quite problematic, and I am not so sure he would approve or even understand the shape my life has taken. (This suggests an intriguing question. If Kohut were to return to life, what would he think of current developments within the self psychology/intersubjectivity community? Would we all welcome his return with unqualified enthusiasm?)

In summary, the dream can be seen as a piece of clinical data that supports my contention that the self psychology community's clinical theoretical struggle to balance creative innovation with a respect for Kohut's essential contribution is embedded in the emotional issues of the group's subjective world. These issues are centered around conflictual needs for continuity that are punctuated by fears of loss of important alliances and fears of dissolution of the group. Furthermore, these themes resonate deeply with my own personal struggle to balance my growth beyond the confines of the traditional Judaism of my father with a need to support the survival of Judaism and maintain a connection with my Jewish roots.

It is therefore no surprise that the status of self psychology/intersubjectivity theory, in both its internal tensions and its relations to the wider psychoanalytic community, has been a major focus of my theoretical contributions. I will now revisit these contributions armed with the additional lens of self-reflection, with the purpose of examining to what extent my conclusions and perspectives have been shaped by the overlapping dilemmas of my own personal world and the group subjectivity of the self psychology community. My hope is that this approach will facilitate the emergence of neglected perspectives and therefore provide a more comprehensive understanding to the issues in question.

SUMMARY OF CONTRIBUTIONS

The general strategy I have employed in my struggle to articulate the place of self psychology/intersubjectivity theory in the lexicon of psychoanalytic ideas has been to focus on the epistemological dimension of the two theories. I have consistently argued that this dimension best captures their revolutionary character. Furthermore, I have suggested that the sweeping paradigm change implied by the new epistemology cannot be understood apart from its historical–scientific context.

Freud's thought was embedded in the world of 19th century science based on Newtonian physics. In this worldview the scientist is a detached observer, able to achieve a complete and comprehensive description of a mechanism and predict with certainty its future behavior. Within this perspective, the analyst is an objective observer of the analysand's mental apparatus, understood with the language of clashing forces, redirected energies, and various compromise formations. Countertransference reflects a clouding of the lens of the microscope and, in principle, can be reduced to zero.

Kohut's thought is embedded in the world of 20th-century science, based on the physics of Einstein, Bohr, and Heisenberg. In this worldview the scientist is both spectator and actor, and a complete understanding of phenomena must take into account the interaction between observer and observed. His articulation of the empathic method eventually led him to the insight that the indivisibility of observer and observed is a feature shared by the domains of quantum physics and psychoanalysis (Kohut, 1977).

I have attempted to articulate the link between the epistemologies of Kohut and Bohr by grounding psychoanalysis inside the descriptive framework of complementarity (Sucharov, 1992). This mode of description denies the analyst a firm external ground from which he can gaze with objectivity at the patient's psyche and restricts psychoanalytic knowledge to inferences drawn from a series of shifting (complementary) perspectives that includes the analyst as part of the observational field. Furthermore, the new framework allows for the retention of the old concepts of ego psychology by specifying the limits of their application (i.e., by restricting them to one of a series of perspectives) and thereby giving them a new nonmechanistic meaning.

I have characterized the architects of intersubjectivity theory as representing that component of self psychology that is extending most comprehensively Kohut's epistemological innovations (Sucharov, 1993a). Atwood and Stolorow (1984) have taken (and clarified) Kohut's observational insight as their foundational assumption: "Patient and analyst together form an indissoluble psychological system, and it is this system that constitutes the empirical domain of psychoanalytic inquiry" (p. 64). I strengthened the connection to Bohr's epistemology by suggesting that any theory of psychoanalysis that begins with this assumption embraces a model of the mind as a quantum system inside a quantum domain of investigation.

I developed some general propositions about a quantum system that I claimed to be invariant in any domain of investigation where observer and observed form an indivisible whole. The propositions expanded on the framework of complementarity as a quintessential nonmechanistic descriptive mode that assigns equal validity to the reality of both patient and analyst. The propositions also captured the unique interpenetration of experience in the analytic encounter and formalized a view of mental life as thoroughly relational. Furthermore, the propositions were seen to correspond closely with existing concepts of the intersubjective framework and therefore served to strengthen its conceptual foundations.

In summary, by following the overlapping epistemological journeys of Kohut, Atwood, and Stolorow, I have depicted their respective contributions as existing on a continuum. Kohut emerges as a pivotal figure in the gradual demechanization of psychoanalysis. Atwood and Stolorow are seen as developing this demechanization further along the continuum. Furthermore, I have tightly interwoven their contributions by anchoring them both in the epistemology of modern physics. No attention is focused on potential incompatibilities between the theories.

My narrative of conceptual compatibility and congeniality was disrupted by some minor shockwaves at the 1992 self psychology meeting encapsulated by Gehrie's claim that Stolorow and Atwood were replacing a myth of an isolated mind with a myth of a structureless mind (Gehrie, 1994). I did not view these tensions as reflecting any fundamental differences in theory. I suggested that Gehrie's challenge reflected our collective Cartesian anxiety of groundlessness as we found ourselves in the middle of an emotionally disorganizing epistemological revolution (Sucharov, 1993b). My illumination of the emotional resistance to the integration of the new epistemology deepened my position that self psychology and intersubjectivity theory constituted an important alliance that would facilitate the working through of this resistance.

My constructed alliance was threatened at the 1993 self psychology conference when the minor shockwaves of 1992 approached earthquake dimensions. One of the papers (Trop, 1994) argued for the separateness of the theories, with intersubjectivity being the wider one. Trop claimed that intersubjectivity embraced a wider motivational principle and had redefined a more encompassing method of empathic inquiry. Paul Ornstein countered Trop's argument with a resounding rebuttal and asserted that a change in the method by intersubjectivity theory constituted "leaving the fold" (Ornstein, 1995).

My response to the threat was to articulate a claim that the apparent difference in their motivational theories concealed a deeper truth that the two theories are destined to converge. In that context I argued for the convergence of the two theories inside a general systems paradigm (Sucharov, 1994). I also emphasized that convergence was an inevitable outcome of their common epistemological base. My argument for convergence rested on two claims:

1. The recognition of the bi-directionality of the self–selfobject matrix in the therapeutic encounter (Fosshage, 1993, Bacal and Thomson, 1996) places self psychology inside a systems model.
2. The articulation of the self-delineating selfobject function (Stolorow, Atwood, and Brandchaft, 1992) offers support for the claim that the self–selfobject relationship is the primary relational matrix in which experience is generated, organized, and maintained. I suggested that our set of unconscious organizing principles reflects our particular history of selfobject relationships.

CONTEXTUALIZING THE CONTRIBUTIONS

An examination of my contributions with the lens of intersubjective contextualism requires a response to the following questions: To what extent have my arguments and conclusions been shaped by the overlapping dilemmas of my personal world and the group subjectivity of the self psychology community? Has this shaping obscured relevant perspectives that could deepen our understanding of the issues? We have seen that the group dilemma centers around the struggle to balance creative expansion with a need for continuity with Kohut's essential contributions. This struggle is punctuated by fears of loss of important alliances and of group dissolution. The group dilemma resonates with my own struggle to balance my growth beyond the confines of my father's Judaism with a need to maintain a connection to my Jewish roots.

The above emotional dilemmas suggest the possibility that I would favor conceptual arguments that emphasized revolutionary shifts, would protect group cohesion, would maintain some continuity with earlier conceptualizations, and would obscure, minimize, or even fudge potentially disruptive incompatibilities. My choice to focus on the epistemological dimension of the two theories seems well-suited to accomplish these objectives. The new epistemology constitutes a legitimate revolution, and it moves into the foreground important and compatible elements of the two theories. Furthermore, the framework of complementarity even allows some continuity with Freud's ego psychology by retaining it as one of a series of perspectives and thereby giving it a new nonmechanistic meaning. The driving force behind my argument to converge the two theories inside a systems paradigm is their common epistemological base (holistic systems and a nonobjectivist epistemology imply each other).

Has my conceptual approach obscured relevant perspectives that would illuminate important but disruptive differences in the two theories? I think a safe place to search for an answer is in their clinical application. The abstract experience-distant nature of epistemological arguments creates difficulties in demonstrating the clinical utility of these arguments. In that context, the dyadic systems paradigm provided me with a much needed conceptual bridge from the lofty status of epistemological discussions to the realities of the daily encounters with my patients. In that context, my last two papers have focused on the clinical utility of a systems paradigm by illuminating the mutuality of the empathic process and the importance of a listening stance that acknowledges the continuous entanglement of the subjectivities of both patient and therapist in the process (Sucharov, 1996, 1998).

Dyadic systems, mutuality, and the acknowledgment of the continuous impact of the therapist's subjectivity are all central features of intersubjectivity theory, and these features have, in recent years, profoundly transformed my clinical style. Are these features also part of self psychology? An affirmative answer would require acknowledgment of the uniqueness of each therapeutic dyad. Within this view, transference and countertransference would form an indivisible system and the patients' selfobject transferences would arise not only from their pre-analytic developmental strivings, but would also be shaped in part by the particularities of the therapist's own selfobject needs. The notion of predetermined pathognomonic selfobject transference is therefore incompatible with the mutuality of the analytic process. I will now examine both Kohut's theory and current mainstream self psychology with respect to these issues.

Kohut's (1977) position on the emergence of the selfobject transferences assigns little or no role to the analyst's personality. In *The Restoration of the Self* he states:

> The essential transference is defined by pre-analytically established internal factors in the analysand's personality structure, and the analyst's influence on the course of the analysis is therefore important only insofar as he—through interpretations made on the basis of correct or incorrect empathic closures—either promotes or impedes the patient's progress on his *predetermined path* [p. 217; italics added].

Further on in the same publication, Kohut qualified the above statement: "I will . . . paradoxical as it may seem, admit to the possible occurrence of *rare instances* in which the analyst's personality contributes to influencing the choice between two (or several) equally available valid patterns of structural rehabilitation of a defective self" (pp. 262–263, italics added).

A dyadic systems approach that emphasizes mutuality and that acknowledges the inevitable contribution of the therapist's subjectivity to the selfobject transference does not appear to be part of Kohut's theory. However, the above qualifier does open the door to the possibility of developing a more mutual approach. Has current mainstream self psychology responded to this opening toward mutuality?

In a recent publication devoted to the current status of self psychology, Paul and Anna Ornstein (1995) specified the defining features of the analytic relationship: "What makes this relationship unique and potentially therapeutic is that it provides an opportunity for the patient to develop and sustain a cohesive selfobject transference. Such a transference is specifically (pathognomonically) related to the developmental arrest that gave rise to it" (p. 423). The Ornsteins' position seems to match Kohut's view. With no mention of the impact of the analyst's subjectivity on the nature of the selfobject transference, mutuality does not appear to be a part of their clinical approach. Furthermore, as I have stated above, the notion of pathognomonic selfobject transference is incompatible with a dyadic systems approach.

Notwithstanding the above, I do not think that quotations by themselves, however compelling, can provide an answer to my original question. It is therefore important to include clinical data. In that context, at the 1996 self psychology conference, Diane Martinez presented case material to exemplify the clinical approach from the standpoint of the self–selfobject matrix (Martinez, 1996). The case presentation and the ensuing discussion focused on the problem of identifying the type of selfobject transference. There was no mention of the contribution of the analyst's subjectivity to the transference formation. Mutuality seemed to be a nonissue. The particulars of the analyst's personal world and the patient's empathic access to that world received no discussion.

It would seem reasonable to doubt whether dyadic systems, mutuality, and the acknowledgment of the continuous impact of the therapist's subjectivity on the analytic process are prominent features of current mainstream self psychology. Selfobject transferences are understood to emerge endopsychically and are predetermined by the patient's self-structure. Although the stance of the analyst has shifted from classical neutrality to one of empathic attunement and emotional availability, the analyst's emotional involvement constitutes a nonspecific medium for the emergence of the pathognomonic selfobject transference. With respect to my metaphor of the empathic dance, it would seem that, from the vantage point of self psychology, the analyst, however empathic she may be, is standing still on the dance floor, and the patient is dancing around her.

At this juncture, one might argue that the above stated doubts about mainstream self psychology are oversimplified and do not fairly reflect the complexity and diversity of the self psychology community. I therefore need to qualify my argument by restricting my comments to mainstream self psychology *as espoused in the public domain*. It may very well be that, in the privacy of their consulting rooms, Dr. Martinez and many other clinicians who identify themselves as self psychologists fully acknowledge the contribution of their subjectivity to the transference. If there is a discrepancy between "official theory" and actual practice, it is my hope that this chapter will encourage more case reports that illuminate the impact of the therapist's subjectivity on the analytic process.

Notwithstanding the above qualification, I may still be open to the charge of creating a straw man. My stated position does not account for the possibility that "mainstream self psychologists" can both adhere to the view that preformed internal structures determine the quality and thrust of the transference and also recognize that the internal state of the analyst will affect the shape of a given transference within a given treatment.

I believe that an intersubjectivist would argue that such an approach would still fall short of working within a framework of mutuality and contextuality. The point of contention would be the assumption of preformed internal structures (pathognomonic transference is grounded in this assumption). This assumption would be viewed as a reification of an experiential state and as a remnant of a static Cartesian understanding of mental life. This alleged retention of Cartesian thinking in the mind of the mainstreamer makes it likely that he/she will characterize the impact of the analyst's subjectivity on the transference to be a *linear, unidirectional causal process* that would preserve the pathognomonic core of the transference and affect its secondary features (shape and color) only.

An intersubjectivist who is working at the clinical level within a framework of mutuality and contextualism would assume that, whereas each participant brings to the encounter a unique set of *experiential potentials* (note the difference between the latter term and "preformed internal structure") shaped by his/her history, the actualization of the particulars of analytic experience for both patient and analyst will be highly contingent on the mutual interplay of personal worlds that arises in the field. The notion of pathognomonic transference, even if it is, in part, shaped by the analyst's internal states, would be seen to be incompatible with the fluid mutuality of experience that predicates an intersubjective contextualist view of the analytic encounter.

I respect that a full refutation of the straw man claim may require a more extensive discourse that is beyond the limited scope of this chapter. A more complete discussion would inevitably involve an explication of the differences between a Cartesian and a post-Cartesian psychoanalytic world. These two worlds use different languages, ask different questions, and harbor profoundly different views about both the nature of mental life and how we access that life. At the risk of another oversimplification, I would suggest that intersubjective theorists are attempting to place both of their feet in a post-Cartesian world, and they would view mainstream self psychologists, especially those who are closely identified with Kohut, as having one foot in each world.

It is important to emphasize that it is not the purpose of this chapter to argue for the superiority of either mainstream self psychology or intersubjectivity theory. The point I am trying to make is that a closer examination of the two approaches suggests that there are important and potentially incompatible distinctions that I failed to appreciate in my earlier work. In particular, my earlier claim that self psychology was moving toward a systems model (this claim supported my argument for convergence of the two theories) must now be called into serious question.

In summary, I have suggested that self psychology's reluctance to fully embrace a systems view may be based on a possible incompatibility between mutuality of influence and the assumption of pathognomic selfobject transferences. Furthermore, intersubjectivity theory contextualizes not only the patient's transferences, but also the developmental process. The context-dependent nature of human development transforms the developmental model from one of predetermined linearity to one of emergent nonlinear complexity (see Lachmann, 1995; Stolorow, 1997). The universality of selfobject (narcissistic line of) development from archaic to mature configurations, a central feature of Kohut's theory, would then be called into question.

My second principal claim for converging the two theories (i.e., that the articulation of the self-delineating selfobject transferences supports the centrality of selfobject relationships as the primary relational matrix in which experience is generated, organized, and maintained) would appear to fly in the face of intersubjectivity's unrelenting contextualism. It would seem that my argument for convergence, if not totally collapsed, is resting on shaky ground.

DISCUSSION

Exploration of the psychological dimension of my theoretical discourse on the status of self psychology/intersubjectivity theory has illuminated the extent to which my arguments and conclusions are embedded in the overlapping psychological life of me and of the self psychology community. My choice to focus on the epistemological dimension of the theories served a personal and group need to accentuate similarity and to minimize potentially disruptive differences. My self-reflection facilitated the search for neglected perspectives that brought to the foreground potential incompatibilities at both theoretical and clinical levels.

A central thesis to my argument is that my need to obscure incompatibilities resonates with an analogous tendency within the self psychology community. Paul Ornstein echoed this concern at a recent panel on integration: "In the effort to heal the rift, will we shove under the carpet legitimate differences that divide us?" (Ornstein, 1996). In that context, the claim that intersubjectivity is a "metatheory" or a "broad intellectual sensibility" rather than a clinical one (Orange, 1996; Stolorow, 1996) is, in my view, a linguistic maneuver that finesses disquieting differences at the clinical level.

The metatheoretical process-oriented nature of intersubjectivity theory does not preclude it from also being a clinical theory. Our understanding of the process informs our clinical style. I would think that the acceptance of the mutual regulatory nature of the process *irrevocably alters the understanding of each and every moment in the therapeutic encounter.* I have already suggested that mutuality is not a prominent part of mainstream self psychology and may be incompatible with some of its central assumptions.

A further example of the blurring of important differences is reflected in Stolorow's argument that intersubjectivity has "seamlessly integrated" selfobject theory as a dimension of experience and has therefore provided self psychology with a "comfortable home" (Stolorow, 1996). Notwithstanding the aesthetic and intellectually compelling nature of this position, the argument overlooks the vital implication that, *from the vantage point of self psychology,* an integration of this nature profoundly alters the heart of Kohut's theory.

The *universality and centrality* of the self–selfobject matrix as an organizer of human self-experience is a cardinal and defining feature of mainstream self psychology. This feature, which is incompatible with intersubjectivity's unrelenting contextualism, is therefore a nonnegotiable item in the debate concerning integration. It should be emphasized that my disagreement with Stolorow is not with his articulation of the relationship of intersubjectivity and the selfobject concept per se. His position in this regard is entirely consistent with the structure of his theory. Where I differ is in his claim that this relationship constitutes an *integration.* A true integration would leave the essential features of each theory intact. Stolorow's position is asymmetrical in that his theory remains complete (and strengthened!) and self psychology is required to surrender a core assumption, a price I do not think it is prepared to pay.

CONCLUSION

An examination of theoretical discourse on the status of self psychology and intersubjectivity theory with the lens of intersubjective contextualism has brought to the foreground neglected perspectives that have deepened our understanding of the issues. Both my own arguments for convergence and Stolorow's position on integration fail to take into account potential incompatibilities between the two theories. The emergence of this added dimension of understanding supports the utility of a conceptual approach that acknowledges the embeddedness of theoretical discourse in the psychological lives of the participants.

My conceptual approach is a natural extension and expansion of Stolorow and Atwood's psychobiographical method (Stolorow and Atwood, 1979). In that context, it should be underlined that this chapter is only a beginning exercise. A single reported dream, however rich and evocative it may be, can hardly be expected to illuminate the full complexity of the psychological issues that shape our dialogue. What needs to be developed is a reliable methodology that would facilitate the systematic investigation of theoretical discourse as a psychological product. An important assumption informing this method is that theoretical ideas do not evolve from a single isolated mind, but from a community dialogue. The field of investigation would therefore need to include the complex relational field formed by the interacting subjectivities of a psychoanalytic community.

The emergence of potential incompatibilities between self psychology and intersubjectivity theory leaves open the question of how to reconceptualize their relationship. This would be a topic for another paper. However, at this juncture, I would tentatively propose that self psychology be kept separate from intersubjectivity and other postmodern theories. (Teicholz, 1998) has discussed Kohut's relationship to the postmoderns. I consider intersubjectivity theory to be part of the latter group that includes Mitchell, Hoffman, Aron, and others.)

Postmodern theorists have a love affair with mutuality, contextualism, constructivism, and deconstruction. A danger therefore exists that, in their unbridled enthusiasm, an edifice could be deconstructed and contextualized before the full complexity of its structure has become known. In that context, Kohut's revolution is still relatively new. Given the wide range, depth, and complexity of his writings, more time is needed to fully explore and develop their clinical applications. There is therefore some wisdom in self psychology's current reluctance to fully embrace a view that emphasizes mutuality and the contributions of the analyst's subjectivity. This restraint may allow a more complete explication of a clinical approach focused on the emergence of pathognomic selfobject transferences.

If self psychology has not yet fully matured, then intersubjectivity theory could still be in its adolescence—full of exciting potential, but requiring further growth and development. A clinical approach that emphasizes mutuality and the contributions of the therapist's subjectivity, however helpful it has been in my clinical work, is not without its problematic dimension (see Aron [1996] for a discussion of mutuality in psychoanalysis). We are therefore still in need of much more clinical data to illuminate its utility.

As a final word, it is my hope that we benefit not only from the new perspectives that have emerged in this chapter, but that we also respect the legitimacy of the psychological issues that continuously shape our dialogue. History and continuity, supportive alliances, and group cohesion are all essential human needs that sustain our efforts to continually enrich psychoanalysis. The presence of incompatibilities, if they are openly acknowledged and respected, should not threaten these needs. Furthermore, conversations with our fathers are important, and they need not be kept secret.

REFERENCES

Aron, L. (1996), *A Meeting of Minds: Mutuality in Psychoanalysis.* Hillsdale, NJ: The Analytic Press.

Atwood, G. & Stolorow, R. (1984), *Structures of Subjectivity: Explorations in Psychoanalytic Phenomenology.* Hillsdale, NJ: The Analytic Press.

——— & ——— (1993), Faces in a Cloud: Intersubjectivity in Personality Theory, 2nd ed. Northvale, NJ: Aronson.

Bacal H. & Thomson, P. G. (1996), The psychoanalyst's selfobject needs and the effect of their frustration on the treatment: A new view of countertransference. In: *Basic Ideas Reconsidered: Progress in Self Psychology, Vol. 12,* ed. A Goldberg. Hillsdale, NJ: The Analytic Press, pp. 17–35.

Bollas, C. (1995), *Cracking Up: The Work of Unconscious Experience.* London: Routledge.

Doctors, S. (1995), On the subjectively structured mind of the analyst and its place in the analytic situation. A discussion of analysis, mutual analysis, and self-analysis: On the interplay of minds in the analytic Process. By T. J. Jacobs. Presented at the Toronto Psychoanalytic Society Conference, March 31, 1995.

Dorpat, T. L. & Miller, M. L. (1992), *Clinical Interaction and the Analysis of Meaning: A New Psychoanalytic Theory.* Hillsdale, NJ: The Analytic Pres.

Fosshage, J. (1993), Countertransference: The analyst's experience of the analysand. Presented at the 16th Annual Conference on the Psychology of the Self, October 28–31.

Galatzer-Levy, R. M. (1997), Discussion of Secret Conversations with my Father: The Human Contextualization of Theoretical Discourse. Presented at the 20th Annual Conference on the Psychology of the Self, November 13–16.

Gehrie, M. (1994), Discussion of Stolorow and Atwood's myth of the isolated mind. In: *A Decade of Progress: Progress in Self Psychology, Vol. 10,* ed. A Goldberg, Hillsdale NJ: The Analytic Press, pp. 251–255.

Hoffman, I. Z. (1991), Discussion: Toward a social constructivist view of the psychoanalytic situation. *Psychoanal. Dial.,* 1:74--05.

Jacobs, L. M. (1998), Optimal responsiveness and subject-subject relating. In: *How Therapists Heal Their Patients,* ed. H. Bacal. Northvale, NJ: Aronson, pp. 191–212.

Jacobs, T. J. (1995), Analysis, Mutual Analysis, and Self-Analysis: On the Interplay of Minds in the Analytic Process. Presented at the Toronto Psychoanalytic Society Conference, March, 31, 1995.

Knoblauch, S. H. (1995), From the word to the scene: An expanded context for empathic resonance. Presented at the 18th Annual Conference on The Psychology of the Self, October 19–22.

Kohut, H. (1977), *The Restoration of the Self.* New York: International Universities Press.

Lachmann, F. (1995), From narcissism to self psychology to . . .? Presented at the 18th Annual Conference on the Psychology of the Self, October 19–22.

Lachmann, F. & Beebe B. (1996), The contribution of self- and mutual regulation to therapeutic action. In: *Basic Ideas Reconsidered: Progress in Self Psychology, Vol. 12,* ed. A. Goldberg, Hillsdale NJ: The Analytic Press, pp. 123–140.

Martinez, D. (1996), Reconceptualizing the clinical exchange: From the standpoint of the self-selfobject matrix. Presented at the 19th Annual Conference on the Psychology of the Self, October 17–20.

Orange, D. (1995*),* Emotional Understanding: Studies in Psychoanalytic Epistemology. New York: Guilford.

——— (1996), Reconceptualizing the clinical exchange: From the standpoint of intersubjectivity. Presented at the 19th Annual Conference on the Psychology of the Self, October 17–20.

Ornstein, P. (1995), Critical reflections on a comparative analysis of "Self Psychology and Intersubjectivity Theory." In: *The Impact of New Ideas: Progress in Self Psychology, Vol. 11,* ed. A. Goldberg. Hillsdale, NJ: The Analytic Press, pp. 47–77

——— (1996), Reconceptualizing the clinical exchange: Toward an integration: Is it possible? Is it desirable? Presented at the 19th Annual Conference on the Psychology of the Self, October 19–22.

——— & Ornstein, A. (1995), Some distinguishing features of Heinz Kohut's self psychology. *Psychoanal. Dial.,* 5:385–391.

Renik, O. (1993), Analytic interaction: Conceptualizing technique in light of the analyst's irreducible subjectivity. *Psychoanal. Quart.,* 62:553–571.

Rustin, J. (1997), Infancy, agency, and intersubjectivity: A view of therapeutic action. *Psychoanal. Dial.,* 7:43–62.

Stolorow, R. (1995), Introduction: Tensions between loyalism and expansionism in self psychology. In: *The Impact of New Ideas: Progress in Self Psychology, Vol. II,* ed. A. Goldberg. Hillsdale, NJ: The Analytic Press, pp. xi–xvii.

——— (1996), Reconceptualizing the clinical exchange: Is it possible? Is it desirable? Presented at the 19th Annual Conference on the Psychology of the Self, October 19–22.

——— (1997), Dynamic, dyadic intersubjective systems: An evolving paradigm for psychoanalysis. *Psychoanal. Psychol.,* 14:337–346.

——— & Atwood, G. (1979), *Faces in a Cloud: Subjectivity in Personality Theory.* Northvale, NJ: Aronson.

——— ——— & Brandchaft, B. (1992), Three realms of the unconscious and their therapeutic transformation. *Psychoanal. Rev.,* 79:25–30.

Sucharov, M. (1992), Quantum physics and self psychology: Toward a new epistemology. In: *New Therapeutic Visions: Progress in Self Psychology, Vol. 8,* ed. A. Goldberg, Hillsdale, NJ, The Analytic Press pp. 199–211.

——— (1993a), Psychoanalysis, self psychology, and intersubjectivity. In: *The Intersubjective Perspective,* ed. R. Stolorow, G. Atwood, & B. Brandchaft, Northvale, NJ: Aronson, pp. 187–202.

——— (1993b), The wise man, the sadist, and Cartesian anxiety: A tale of two solutions. Presented at the 16th Annual Conference on the Psychology of the Self, October 28–31.

——— (1994), Self psychology and intersubjectivity: A converging alliance. Presented at the 17th Annual Conference on the Psychology of the Self, October 20–23.

——— (1996), Listening to the empathic dance: A rediscovery of the therapist's subjectivity. Presented at the 19th Annual Conference on the Psychology of the Self, October 17–20.

——— (1998), Optimal responsiveness and a systems view of the empathic process. In: *Optimal Responsiveness: How Therapists Heal Their Patients,* ed. H. Bacal. Northvale, NJ: Aronson, pp. 273–287.

Trop, J. L. (1994), Self psychology and intersubjectivity theory. In: *The Intersubjective Perspective,* ed. R. Stolorow, G. Atwood, & B. Brandchaft, Northvale, NJ: Aronson, pp. 77–91.

Teicholz, J. (1998), Self and relationship: Kohut, Loewald, and the postmoderns. In: *The World of Self Psychology: Progress in Self Psychology, Vol. 14,* ed. A. Goldberg. Hillsdale, NJ: The Analytic Press, pp. 267–292.

Chapter 19

Surviving the Death of Oedipus: Tips for Self Psychologists

Doris Brothers
Ellen Lewinberg

Despite the grievous injuries it has sustained, many personally inflicted by Heinz Kohut, oedipal theory is alive, if not well, within self psychology. By questioning the preeminence of the Oedipus complex in normal development and demonstrating that inadequate selfobject relations, rather than unresolved oedipal conflicts, form the innermost core of psychopathology, Kohut (1959, 1971, 1977, 1980, 1981, 1984) boldly loosened the mainstays of Freudian theory. Yet, in his last writings, Kohut (1981, 1984) affirmed "the near ubiquity of the Oedipus complex" and retained his belief in the existence of an oedipal stage of development. His evident ambivalence about being perceived as "the Pied Piper who leads the young away from the solid ground of the object-libidinal aspects of the Oedipus complex" (Kohut, 1972, p. 622) appears to have exerted a cautionary effect on his followers. Indeed, most references to oedipal concepts in the self psychological literature since Kohut's death have echoed or elaborated upon his views (e.g., P. Ornstein, 1980; A. Ornstein, 1983; Lichtenberg, 1983, Lichtenberg, Lachmann, and Fosshage, 1992 Terman, 1985; Goldberg, 1988, 1995).

Outside the ranks of self psychologists, proponents of widely varying approaches have found fault with every conceivable aspect of oedipal theory (Horney, 1924, 1926, 1939; Adler, 1927; Schafer, 1968; Gilligan, 1982; Stiver, 1991; Chodorow,1992 are notable examples), yet few have called for its complete elimination. Benjamin (1996), for example, argues in favor of a broader view of gender identification than that which is possible according to "the oedipal logic of opposites," yet she states, "No absolute transcendence of the oedipal is possible" (p. 41). Emde (1994) calls attention to the obvious fact that oedipal conflicts and retellings occur in the context of adult development. Despite his claim that research on children fails to support oedipal theory, he, too, retains the Oedipus complex by narrating three versions of it. Only Horney (1939) appears to have argued against the ubiquitous occurrence of the Oedipus complex as a biologically conditioned phenomenon. What remains when the theory is discarded, she observed, is "the highly constructive finding that early relationships *in their totality* mold the character to an extent which can scarcely be overestimated" (p. 87).

In light of recent advances in theory and research that starkly reveal the shortcomings of oedipal theory, we ask self psychologists to consider laying Oedipus to rest once and for all. In what follows we first review the evolution of Kohut's stance on oedipal issues and the positions taken by his followers. Next, we counter a number of problematic assumptions embedded within oedipal theory with research findings on gender and child development, as well as the illuminating perspectives of selfobject theory, intersubjectivity theory, and motivational systems theory, the cumulative effect of which hopefully confirms our belief that psychoanalysis should be released from Oedipus's death grip. Then we propose an alternative view of oedipal phenomena as manifestations of the imposition of dichotomous gender. Finally, we reexamine two case studies written by contemporary self psychologists—one describing the treatment of an adult and one the assessment of a child—in an effort to demonstrate our new understanding of oedipal issues.

KOHUT'S ASSAULT ON OEDIPUS

Simon (quoted in Modell, 1985) observed that, ever since Freud defined the Oedipus complex as the "shibboleth" of psychoanalysis, challenging oedipal theory has become "an act of rebellion equivalent to parricide, or its variant fratricide" (p. 201). Moreover, as Simon suggested, the theory has created such deeply rooted biases in analysts that they have continually found and elaborated upon phenomena predicted by the theory. And using a self psychological perspective, we understand the tendency to cling to oedipal theory despite its vexing problems, as possible attempts to retain highly prized idealizing selfobject experiences in relation to analysts, teachers, supervisors—not to mention our great psychoanalytic forefathers, Freud and Kohut.

Regardless of how one chooses to understand the powerful hold of oedipal theory on analysts, the sheer courage of Kohut's revisions cannot be underestimated. With each step Kohut took in developing self psychological theory, he moved the Oedipus complex further and further away from the heart of psychoanalysis. In his groundbreaking 1959 paper, "Introspection, Empathy and Psychoanalysis: An Examination of the Relationship between Mode of Observation and Theory," Kohut emphasized that it is the introspective, empathic mode of observation that defines psychoanalysis, an assertion that, as Basch pointed out, implicitly contradicts the idea that the analysis of the Oedipus complex demarcates that which may be considered psychoanalytic (in Modell, 1985).

Kohut (1971) postulated "two separate and largely independent developmental lines: one which leads from autoerotism via narcissism to object love; another which leads from autoerotism via narcissism to higher forms and transformations of narcissism" (p. 220). Demonstrating that the analysis of disturbances in the latter line of development could result in a patient's recovery without ever dealing with oedipal issues, he radically altered the perception that psychoanalytic cure must include resolution of the Oedipus complex.

In *The Restoration of the Self,* Kohut (1977) went so far as to suggest that the Oedipus complex does not adequately explain psychoneuroses. The lust and hostility that traditional psychoanalysts take for "normal" oedipal childhood experiences are, according to Kohut, disintegration products of the child's "assertive–affectionate self" in the face of parental competitiveness, seductiveness, and failure to provide needed selfobject experiences. He also observed that some patients, at the end of self psychological treatment, experience a brief but joyful oedipal phase with all the earmarks of a developmental achievement.

Kohut (1980) suggested that it is useful to differentiate among the following: (1) an oedipal phase or oedipal *period* (referring to the occurrence of certain experiences that typify a certain age); (2) an oedipal *stage* (referring to the normal set of experiences at that age); and, finally, (3) the Oedipus complex (the pathological distortion of the normal stage). With reservations, Kohut advocated a return to Freud's original seduction theory. Although he argued against a belief in actual seduction of children, he urged analysts to search for the "basic layer of psychological truth" that Freud first encountered in the stories of parental seduction told by his hysterical patients. In Kohut's view, this psychological truth resides in empathic failures by "oedipal selfobjects."

In his last paper, Kohut (1981) questioned the aptness of the oedipal myth itself. Arguing that analysts have "reversed their usual stance

. . . by taking the manifest content—father murder, incest—as the essence" (p. 564), instead of attending to the "most significant genetic dynamic feature" of the story, namely that "Oedipus was a rejected child" (p. 564), he actually proposed a replacement for the Oedipus story. The "semicircle of mental health" refers to the story of Odysseus and Telemachus, in which a father, feigning madness to avoid fighting in a war, reveals himself a "draft dodger" by making a semicircle with his plow in order to avoid killing his infant son.

Having rejected the oedipal notion that what is "normal and human" is "inter-generational strife and mutual wishes to kill and destroy" (p. 563), Kohut nevertheless went to great lengths to retain remnants of oedipal theory. By separating an oedipal stage of development in which a healthy and joyful outcome is at least possible (provided parents respond empathically to their children's assertiveness and affectionateness) from the pathology-infused Oedipus complex, Kohut appears to have spared himself the painful necessity of calling for the complete destruction of Freud's most cherished construct.

Kohut's followers have largely followed his lead. It was Terman[1] (1985) who first proposed that the Oedipus complex be viewed as a phase of self-development involving specific issues such as differentiation, diminution of need for parental selfobject provision, and identification. A. Ornstein (1983) observed that failure by the same-sex parent to respond to the child's active engagement in the oedipal experience results in a structural deficit. She argued that identification under these circumstances serves to fill in these deficits. Moreover, she indicated that "the presence of sexual themes or triangular configurations in the patient's associations does not indicate that psychopathology is related to a faulty resolution of the Oedipus complex" (p. 390). Rather, she suggested that these seemingly oedipal manifestations are often efforts to establish or restore self-cohesion. Like Kohut, however, Ornstein appears to accept the ubiquity of oedipal-stage phenomena.

Along similar lines, Lichtenberg (1989) asserted that parent–child struggles within the sensual/sexual motivational system inevitably result in selfobject failures in the oedipal stage. As a consequence of their own procedural memories, he explained, caregivers respond negatively to the child's search for sensual enjoyment and sensual excitement. Although he (Lichtenberg, Lachmann, and Fosshage, 1992) rejected the hierarchical concept of development implicit in oedipal theory, he avoided eliminating the Oedipus complex by likening the oedipal

[1] Terman first presented this paper in 1975 before Kohut (1977) suggested that oedipal problems have their genesis in empathic failures of the oedipal period.

drama to "a model scene" whose meaning can be pieced together through the collaborative efforts of patient and analyst.

Stern (1985, 1995) also found ways to sidestep the issue. Complaining that psychoanalytic developmental theories are not supported by the latest research, he argued that "what psychoanalysis has taken to be the Oedipus complex is surely the end result of many developmental transformations that need to be studied" (Stern, 1995, p. 146). Yet he, too, ultimately retained oedipal theory by viewing the oedipal triad as simply one in a long line of developmental triads.

Shane, Shane, and Gales (1997) have stopped just short of calling for Oedipus's demise by asserting that "the Oedipus complex is not a universal organizer of development, but rather it is dependent for its emergence on experiences within the family constellation" (p. 174). They also contend that, because one aspect of the complex is clearly demonstrated in a given patient, not all aspects need be present.

Judging from the relative paucity of references to the Oedipus complex and the oedipal stage in the recent writings of other prominent self psychologists,[2] it appears that most have found it expedient to downplay or simply ignore these concepts without challenging them or, like Lichtenberg; Stern; and Shane, Shane, and Gales, retain them by reinterpreting their meaning as consistent with their own theoretical formulations.

OEDIPUS IN THE ALTOGETHER

In the spirit of the child who fearlessly wondered aloud at the emperor's lack of clothing, we now hope to expose a number of assumptions embedded within oedipal theory to the revealing light provided by recent developments in research and theory.

Human Development Is Best Conceptualized as Proceeding in Invariant Stages or Phases

The premise that any aspect of development follows an invariant sequence of stages has increasingly been challenged by contemporary theorists (e.g., Kohlberg, Yaeger, and Hjertholm, 1968; Franklin, 1981). Even the cognitive–adaptive theory of the preeminent stage theorist, Jean Piaget, has been widely criticized (see Watkins, 1986; Brothers, 1995, p. 46). Stern (1985), for example, questioned the notion of

---

[2] A review of the indexes of *Progress in Self Psychology* reveals only a handful of references to oedipal theory or the Oedipus complex.

phases of development devoted to specific clinical issues. In his developmental scheme, four different senses of self—the sense of an emergent self, the sense of a core self, the sense of a subjective self, and the sense of a verbal self—remain fully functioning and active throughout life. They do not replace one another in successive phases. Rather, once formed, all continue to grow and coexist. Lichtenberg's (1989) motivational systems theory also accounts for developmental transformation without reference to hierarchical stages. Similarly, Shane, Shane, and Gales (1997) propose that body, brain, and mind be viewed as elements in the total nonlinear dynamic system, the self.

To our minds little is gained in attempting to identify stages or "lines" of development. We believe the imposition of these generalizing concepts is a throwback to a deterministic, mechanistic view of human beings that obscures the enormous complexity and individual variation we believe to be true of development in general and of the development of gender and sexuality in particular. As Coates (1997) cogently observed, "The self is not a layer cake . . . with toothpicks keeping each stage tightly aligned with the one underneath it" (p. 44).

Worse still, stage theories perpetuate the "hunt for pathology" characteristic of traditional psychoanalysis (Tolpin, 1996; Brothers and Lewinberg, 1999) insofar as specific outcomes of any given stage are deemed indicators of health and pathology. For example, children have been judged psychologically "healthy" to the extent that they emerge from the so-called oedipal stage with rigid perceptions of themselves as gendered (i.e., masculine or feminine) and heterosexual in sexual orientation. As we explain below, the belief that psychological health is dependent upon fixed gender identification and heterosexual object choice has obscured the underlying causes of so-called oedipal configurations.

All Normally Developing Young Children Develop Sexual Feelings and Fantasies Involving the Opposite-Sex Parent and Rivalrous/ Aggressive Feelings and Fantasies Involving the Same-Sex Parent

As Chodorow (1992) so astutely observed, psychoanalysis lacks a richly detailed developmental and clinical account of "normal" heterosexuality. She noted that what we think we know "comes by reading between the lines of writing about perversion and homosexuality" (p. 268). Our ignorance is compounded by a lack of congruence between recent child development research and the account provided by oedipal theory. For example, the latest studies fail to support Freud's contention that healthy children experience sexual attraction for the opposite-sex parent and rivalrous aggression toward the same-sex parent. In fact, it now seems highly doubtful that healthy young children feel sexual attraction at all. For example, McClintock and Herdt (1996) outlined three steps in the development of sexuality: (1) attraction, (2) actual desire, and (3) a readiness to act on the desire. Using data from three separate studies, they found that, although puberty may start at age 6 with the release of adrenal sex steroids, sexual attraction is first manifested in the fourth grade, from ages 9 to 10, the ages at which Freud suggested the oedipal storms would have given way to the latency period. According to McClintock and Herdt, there is little evidence that sexual development is precipitated by a psychological event or that children ever enter a latency period. Rather, they conclude that sexual development is a continuously unfolding, gradual process.

Provocative research by de Marneffe (1997) on children between the ages of 15 and 36 months found that children recognize their own genitals early on and are able to label themselves as boys or girls. This appears to cast doubt on Freud's notion that, before the oedipal phase, little girls are undifferentiated from little boys and "masculine" in orientation. De Marneffe found that the children's genital recognition does not appear to have a straightforward relationship to their gradually unfolding concepts of gender. They appear to have a working and valued schema of their own bodies and can distinguish them from the bodies of children of the opposite sex without being capable of applying this knowledge to the experience of themselves as gendered. Moreover, children who recognized their own genitals tended to express preferences for dolls like themselves, supporting the possibility of an early and unconflicted "genital egocentrism." These findings run counter to the notion that children invariably develop rivalrous/aggressive feelings and fantasies involving the same-sex parent.

Thus, we are not convinced that normally developing children (i.e., those who have not experienced traumatizing betrayals) between the ages of 3 and 5, the ages typically associated with an oedipal stage, experience sexual feelings and fantasies in relation to their parents. The tendency to confuse children's longings for tender, sensual experiences with adult sexuality has long been observed to be an unfortunate consequence of Freudian theory (see Ferenczi, 1933).

We believe that ascribing sexual/lustful and aggressive/rivalrous motives to all young children in accordance with oedipal theory represents a wrong-headed attempt to universalize what may indeed reflect the self-experience of *some* children. In other words, we do not rule out the possibility that the oedipal metaphor may correspond well to the feelings and fantasies of certain children. For example, some children are experienced by their parents as repositories for their own unacceptable needs, wishes, and fantasies. In order to assure themselves of needed selfobject experiences, these children may comply with their parents' wishes by exhibiting the sexual and/or aggressive behaviors and feelings attributed to them (see also Stiver, 1991). However, we are wary of conceptualizing such a configuration as oedipal insofar as this tends to blame the child's constitution for that which has been imposed by their parents.

A number of Freud scholars have suggested that his theory of childhood sexuality and aggression enabled him to exonerate his parents for the traumas he suffered at their hands. In other words, if children are innately sexual and aggressive, the cause of their psychological pain resides within them; it was not inflicted by their parents (see Brothers, 1995, for a brief review of this literature).

Building on Kohut's discovery that driven sexuality and aggression result from insults to one's sense of self, we reason that sexual and aggressive feelings and fantasies for parents (either same-sex or opposite-sex) among children aged three to five typically develop in response to trauma. The common clinical finding that child trauma survivors seem preoccupied with sexual and aggressive matters supports this hypothesis, as does the latest research. Cohen-Kettenis and van Goozen (1996), for example, found that children clinically referred for a variety of psychiatric problems, including conduct disorders, oppositional disorders, or disorders occurring in the context of sexual abuse, are far more interested in content involving sex and aggression than those who are not clinically referred.[3] Coates (1997) suggested that, for children who have experienced traumas, sex and aggression may be important organizers of experience. Moreover, as Stolorow and Atwood (1992) contended, experiences of abuse and seduction need not be overtly sexual to be concretized and preserved in sexual symbolism.

Children Cannot Develop Equally Passionate Attachments to Both Parents

Restating Freud's oedipal scenario, Kohut observed that the girl entertains the fantasy "that she will be capable of being penetrated, and get the baby, that great gift from daddy, and give it back to him." In the boy's fantasy, "He will be the one that does away with the father and will give that great forward-moving, penetrating and aggressive gift to the mother" (quoted in Elson, 1987, p. 150). Implicit in Kohut's

[3] We hold the view that children with psychiatric problems have usually experienced traumas (see Brothers, 1995).

description, as in all oedipal theory, is the notion that children in the oedipal stage form passionate attachments only to the opposite-sex parent in the case of the positive oedipal complex and to the same-sex parent in the case of the much less favorably regarded negative oedipal complex. Once again, research fails to support this contention.

A vast number of infancy studies indicate that infants learn to relate to more than one person from the beginning (e.g., Schaffer and Emerson, 1964; Parke and Sawin, 1977; Stechler and Kaplan, 1980; Lichtenberg, 1989; Brazelton, 1992; Shane, Shane, & Gales, 1997). Fathers, as well as mothers, have early, qualitatively distinct, affectionate relationships with both girls and boys (e.g., Greenberg and Morris, 1974; Lamb et al., 1982). As Stern (1995) suggested, the process of becoming a triad takes place "roughly parallel with becoming a dyad" (p. 145).

Both Chodorow (1978) and Stiver (1991) emphasized the strong and enduring connection most girls develop with their mothers despite their critical perceptions of them. Research indicates that only when mothers are grossly inadequate do fathers become the main love object for girls around the ages of three to five (e.g., Lester, 1976).

In light of overwhelming evidence that, under optimal circumstances, children form equally passionate bonds with both parents, we believe that the tendency to equate psychological health with the so-called oedipal passions, that is, the boy's love for his mother and the girl's love for her father, deserves careful scrutiny. As we attempt to demonstrate below, much oedipal theorizing seems intertwined with outdated views of gender and sexuality.

Castration Anxiety and Penis Envy Should Be Understood in Literal, Anatomical Terms

Kohut (1975) observed, "It is not the recognition of her lack of a penis, I believe, that is the cause of serious disturbances of self-esteem in women. . . . A woman's protracted and/or recurrent sense of being castrated . . . grows on a soil of broader and deeper narcissistic deprivation" (p. 791). Despite his rejection of penis envy and castration anxiety as primary pathogenetic factors, Kohut nevertheless understood these concepts as inevitable responses to anatomical differences between the sexes. "I have no doubt," he wrote, "that the sight of the male genital will inevitably make a very strong impression on the little girl, that it will become a crystallization point for her envy" (p. 783).

Other theorists have argued against such literal interpretations. Some like Horney (1939) and Thomson (1942) have argued that castration anxiety and penis envy reflect the privileged role of men in our society.

And some, such as Glassgold (1995), argue that castration anxiety and penis envy symbolize children's experiences of smallness in relation to adults and their inability to fulfill their mothers' needs.

We also reject a literal interpretation of castration anxiety and penis envy. Rather, according to the view we explicate below, castration anxiety may give symbolic expression to the experience of having lost aspects of self as gendered through disavowal and dissociation, while genital envy may concretize the fantasy that others embody these disavowed and dissociated aspects of gendered selfhood.

OTHER PROBLEMATIC OEDIPAL ASSUMPTIONS

Contemporary theorists and researchers have so persuasively exposed the flaws in the following oedipal assumptions that we feel little obligation to do more than mention them.

It Is Possible to Conceptualize Children's Development of Sexual and Aggressive Feelings and Fantasies Outside of an Intersubjective Matrix

The attribution of lust and hostility in young children to innate, universal, drive-related phenomena is antithetical to the notion developed by Stolorow and his collaborators that development occurs within "an evolving psychological field constituted by the interplay between the differently organized subjectivities of child and caretakers" (Atwood and Stolorow, 1984, p. 65).

As a Result of Developmental Vicissitudes, Women Are Inferior to Men

An avalanche of research in the last quarter century has countered all notions of female inferiority embedded in oedipal theory. The overestimation of the importance of penis envy and castration anxiety in women's self-experience has also been thoroughly investigated. (See Lang [1989] for a review of this literature, as well as a self psychological perspective on female self-development).

Moral Development Depends on the Resolution of the Oedipus Complex

The preponderance of research on moral development shows that morality has little, if anything, to do with the outcome of the Oedipus complex. As early as 36 months of age, well before the Oedipus stage is thought to begin, children appear to have capacities traditionally associated with superego functioning (see Emde, Johnson, and Easterbrooks, 1988; Lichtenberg, 1989; Buchsbaum and Emde, 1990; Sandler, 1960). Lichtenberg (1989) suggests that ethics, morals, and values constitute the regulatory component of the sensual/sexual regulatory system and that parent–child and peer–peer reciprocity establish the bases for the attainment of values and morals.

In the interest of keeping this discussion brief, we have not attempted an exhaustive compilation of the problematic assumptions contained within oedipal theory. However, we do not doubt the existence of others we have not considered.

EFFECTS OF THE IMPOSITION OF DICHOTOMOUS GENDER: A SELF PSYCHOLOGICAL ALTERNATIVE TO OEDIPAL THEORY

Until very recently, analysts accepted as incontrovertible truth Freud's assumption that gender is a naturally occurring binary system and that qualities stereotypically associated with masculinity and femininity are biologically and anatomically determined and immutable. Moreover, psychological health has been viewed as highly correlated with the person's acceptance of societally ascribed gender qualities. For example, women who failed to embrace images of themselves as passive, narcissistic, and masochistic were thought to manifest a "masculine protest."[4]

Today, thanks to the pioneering work of Aron (1995), Benjamin (1988), Burch (1993), Butler (1989), Crawford (1996), Dimen (1991), Goldner (1991), Harris (1991), Person and Ovesey (1983), and others, Freud's understanding of gender has been largely discredited. Not only is gender now viewed as largely independent of biology, but the consolidation of a stable sense of gender, once the sine qua non of mental health, is now thought to require the activation of trauma-related processes such as disavowal and dissociation (see Goldner, 1991; Brothers, 1998).

We now propose an alternative to oedipal theory based on recent self psychological conceptualizations of gender, specifically Crawford's (1996) view of gender as trauma and Brothers's (1998) suggestion that alter ego selfobject experience maintains gender dichotomies. We contend that the lust and hostility traditionally associated with a

---

[4] We do not agree that gender is disembodied. Rather, we believe that differences in male and female anatomy, procreative functions, and other constitutional endowments affect the experience of self as gendered.

"normal" oedipal stage, so astutely revealed by Kohut to result from trauma, are, in many instances, produced by the imposition of dichotomous gender on young children. In other words, so-called oedipal feelings and fantasies may be reconceptualized as manifestations of gender trauma. According to Brothers (1995), at the heart of all traumas are betrayals of trust in self and others as providers of selfobject experiences. We suggest that young children may experience traumatizing betrayals when aspects of their self-experience are rejected and derided as gender-incongruent. That is, little boys may manifest so-called "normal" oedipal-stage behaviors when they feel compelled to disavow and dissociate aspects of themselves associated with stereotypic femininity in order to maintain needed selfobject connectedness with caretakers, and little girls may manifest such behaviors when they feel compelled to disavow and dissociate aspects of themselves associated with stereotypic masculinity (Crawford, 1996; Brothers, 1998). (Of course, a child compelled to disavow aspects of self as gendered associated with his or her own sex will also experience traumatizing betrayals, but the outcome may not resemble stereotypic oedipal configurations.)

In an effort to fill in the "black holes" in their self-experience (Brothers, 1995) that result from the dissociation of aspects of self as gendered, we suggest that children may find these qualities embodied in others (often, but not always, the opposite-sex parent) who are then experienced as alter ego selfobjects. In other words, closeness with parents who are perceived as embodying one's dissociated gender-linked attributes provide an experience of cohesive wholeness otherwise impossible to attain. Hostility may be felt toward those who not only fail to provide these experiences, but instead, offer themselves as models of renunciated gender (e.g., the same-sex parents). Sexual feelings and fantasies in young children may now be seen as restorative efforts in the face of these traumas. Brothers (1998) observed:

> Frequently, the disavowal of aspects of gender experience is concomitant with efforts to confirm the gender to which the betrayed person now fiercely clings. Sexual feelings, fantasies and activities are commonly employed to confirm gender that has been purged of its disavowed and self-threatening aspects. Indeed, sexuality under these circumstances is likely to assume a driven, addictive quality. . . . On the other hand, sexuality may also provide a means by which the betrayed person achieves a sense of blissful merger with the disavowed aspects of gendered selfhood [p. 240].

In summary, we ask that childhood experiences previously conceptualized as oedipal be considered as possibly reflecting a need to maintain selfobject connectedness in the face of traumatizing betrayals of trust experienced when aspects of self are rejected as gender-incongruent. The extent to which the imposition of dichotomous gender leads to sexual and aggressive feelings and fantasies depends on the the relationships between children and their caretakers. Not every child experiences betrayals of trust in developing a sense of self as gendered. We can conceive of many nontraumatic scenarios in which children organize their self-experience in accordance with prevailing notions of masculinity or feminity. In other words, since we do not view gender dichotomization as invariably traumatizing, we do not intend our conceptualization as a replacement for a universal oedipal complex or stage of development. Moreover, we also recognize the possibility that betrayals of trust other than those associated with dichotomous gender may produce experiences previously construed as oedipal.

CLINICAL UNDERSTANDING SANS OEDIPUS

"Despite my openness to discern the Oedipus complex . . . and thus come face to face with the resistances that constitute clinical manifestations of the defenses against castration anxiety," Kohut (1984) observed in a discussion of clinical material, "I was unable to discover this classically pivotal configuration" (p. 126). Few other clinicians seem willing to acknowledge the absence of oedipal phenomena in long-term treatment cases with anything approaching Kohut's openness. It is much more common to find references to oedipal configurations, particularly when the patient expresses sexual and/or aggressive feelings for the therapist, despite the availability of more experience-near explanations.

Our reviews of the treatment studies that follow are intended as efforts to demonstrate our alternative understanding of clinical material conceptualized as oedipal in nature. We do not presume to possess deeper wisdom or greater truth about the cases presented than the clinicans who authored them. Indeed, we are well aware that it is impossible to truly understand a case from a vantage point outside of the therapeutic relationship.

TERMAN'S CASE OF MISS N

David Terman's[5] (1985) effort to harmonize oedipal theory with self psychology involved his proposal that the archaic aims of the grandiose

---

[5] We suspect that Terman would have written this case somewhat differently today. However, we based our decision to use it on the fact that it so beautifully illustrates our perspective and because his influence on self psychologists who may be attempting to bridge the gap between old and new theoretical perspectives is great.

self are transformed into realizable ambitions and the content of the superego is determined during an oedipal stage of development. To illustrate the deleterious consequences for self-development when "oedipal selfobjects" fail to provide "phase-appropriate mirroring," he presented the case of Miss N, a 26-year-old semiprofessional, who sought treatment for what she considered "highly inappropriate" rage toward her mother.

Throughout his discussion of this analysis, Terman described the patient's rageful rejection of his oedipal interpretations and her poignant gratitude whenever she experienced him as empathic. Her gratitude seems to have coincided with his use of self psychologically informed interpretations that were invariably devoid of oedipal meanings. Nevertheless, as we shall see, Terman persisted in incorporating oedipal theory into his self psychological understanding of the case.

Miss N grew up with a brother, 18 months older than she, toward whom she felt both worshipful and hopelessly rivalrous, and a sister, 4 years younger. Although she initially described her father as "a quiet, rather contented man," who passively accepted her efforts at connection, she later revealed that he had been seductive and "insensitive to the stimulation of her fantasies" during showers they took together. Miss N often opposed her mother, an "irritable" woman who clearly favored her brother and related to him as a "boyfriend."

Early in treatment, Miss N recalled her mother reprimanding her severely for experimenting sexually with a neighbor boy. When her mother falsely accused her of repeating this behavior a second time, she developed the insight that she would have to grow up without relying on her mother[6]. Her initial experiences of Terman as failing to acknowledge her (provide mirroring selfobject experiences) evoked her mother's past hurtfulness. While convinced that she "brought on" these injuries because of her sexual badness, she nevertheless filled the sessions with "blatant associations of conscious wishes to seduce [Terman]" and her unhappiness over the ending of a short affair.

Terman understood the beginning of Miss N's treatment "in terms of the vicissitudes of her object relations in the oedipal and the defenses against their mobilization in the transference to me" (p. 92). However, whenever Terman interpreted her guilt and fear in response to either her sexual experiences outside the analysis or the impulses mobilized inside, Miss N responded with "rage, indifference, or humiliation" (p. 92).

[6] Lichtenberg (1989) would undoubtedly view this as a model scene.

Despite acknowledging that his initial technique, guided by oedipal theory, "aggravated Miss N's narcissistic tensions," Terman described the unfolding of the analysis in oedipal terms as follows:

> The subsequent unfolding of this self in the analysis centered largely around the typical concerns of the oedipal child: the wish for a baby, the wish to be as big as mother, the wish to be important to father, the wish to take mother's place, the wish to be sexually responded to, etc. The fears associated with these wishes were also typical of the oedipal period—the fear that I would be angry, jealous, derisive—the feeling that she was bad or would be punished. . . . In short, she became, psychologically, an oedipal child, and what seemed central in this oedipal child was the wish for recognition of herself as a future woman, welcomed into the club, as it were, and the fear that I would punish her for it [p. 92].

After a year, Terman realized that Miss N experienced his interpretations as humiliations and that "the oedipal tensions—the wish to get a loving response from me of some kind—were in the service of an important self-confirmation" (p. 93). On hearing Terman explain that she wanted to be able to give herself to him as she had to her father and not have him push her aside with his judgments, she cried and wondered how she had made him understand.

Describing a phase in the analysis in which Miss N dreaded telling Terman about her sexual fantasies and wish for pregnancy, Terman noted, "I was essentially the punishing and narcissistically wounding mother" (p. 94). However, Miss N would become enraged at Terman for interpreting her fear of him in terms of her mother's anger. Once again Terman appears to have empathically grasped Miss N's experience without resorting to oedipal explanations:

> What I had learned—and learned again at this point—was that *linking mother's anger with her impulses implied to her that mother wasn't really angry at her.* I had to understand that mother really was angry with her for legitimate needs and wishes. . . . I had to bear witness to her mother's inappropriate anger at her in the past for presentations of her proud and feisty little-girl self [p. 94].

As Terman noted, "The real trauma was that she *was* punished for loving and competitive feelings and fantasies" (p. 94). Whenever he failed to acknowledge this, Miss N reported a resurgence of phobic symptoms such as a fear of the dark.

During a phase in the treatment Terman called "the father transference," Miss N had affairs with "brother-type" men and "an older married roué." Terman observed that his patient "feared that I would expect her to be 'grown up' sexually and not be satisfied with her childhood coquettishness" (p. 96), a formulation that strikes us as the antithesis of an oedipal interpretation. Here Terman seems to understand that Miss N did not want a sexual relationship with him as the oedipal father; she longed for him to cherish her as a loving father might cherish his little girl.

In his summarizing discussion, which he couched in "self-oedipal" terms, Terman states: "What we see here in rather pure culture . . . is a grandiose oedipal self (or a self whose grandiosity has been confined to phallic oedipal claims)—and an idealized parent imago which is not yet a superego" (p. 99). However, embedded within Terman's discussion is a partial understanding of the case that, to our mind, stands well on its own without the infusion of oedipal theory. Terman states that "the narcissistic manifestations of the case are central" (p. 98). He attributes Miss N's problems largely to failures in empathic responsiveness on the part of her mother, for example, her favoritism toward Miss N's brother and her negative reactions to Miss N's proud displays of her initiative and self-assertiveness. Miss N certainly appears to have suffered at her mother's hands. In fact, we suspect that Miss N experienced traumatizing betrayals of trust in her mother to provide selfobject experiences of mirroring, idealized merger, and so on. However, we wonder why Terman insisted that Miss N's proud displays of initiative occurred within "the competitive context of the oedipal situation." To the extent that the patient experienced her mother as hostile, rejecting, and punitive, her oppositional responses to her mother seem understandable without reference to some innate oedipal need to eliminate her mother in order to have her father or brother to herself.

Conspicuously absent from Terman's discussion are the traumatizing betrayals Miss N appears to have experienced at the hands of her father and brother. Her brother aggressively excluded her from play and flaunted his specialness to her mother, and her father was sexually inappropriate, if not abusive. Oedipal theory, as Stiver (1991) points out, consistently ignores the father's contribution to the little girl's seductiveness. In fact, it appears that many little girls comply with their father's wishes for them to behave seductively.

We now attempt to understand Miss N's supposedly oedipal experiences in terms of our thesis that traumatizing betrayals in childhood related to gender produce what is traditionally interpreted as oedipal pathology and profoundly affect the therapeutic relationship. Miss N grew up with the clear understanding that maleness was rewarded by her mother's love and attention. Being female, on the other hand, appears to have contributed to her rejection by her brother and left her vulnerable to her father's sexual seductiveness. It would not have been surprising if, under these circumstances, she developed a wish to possess the stereotypically masculine characteristics she associated with males. Asserting herself oppositionally with her mother and experimenting sexually with the neighbor boy may well have behaviorally expressed masculinity for her. We suspect that her belief that she would have to grow up without her mother's help represented her decision to retain her masculine-ascribed qualities despite her mother's chastisements. She seems to have unconsciously decided that her only hope for her mother's love was to be like her brother. Thus, unlike many little girls, she does not appear to have completely dissociated her masculine attributes or to have fully adopted a stereotypically feminine posture.

We do not view Miss N's demanding, promiscuous sexual behavior as arising solely from her defiance of "the mother's rage," as Terman suggested, but as an effort to rescript her traumatizing betrayals by both parents (Brothers, 1995, 1997). It is possible that she tested the trustworthiness of the therapeutic relationship by presenting herself to Terman with all the unladylike assertiveness she exhibited with the neighbor boy. Perhaps she hoped that he would provide her with mirroring selfobject experiences for her stereotypically masculine qualities as well as her feminine ones. She also clearly longed to be appreciated as a woman without fear of sexual exploitation.

That Miss N developed a wish to be pregnant does not necessarily evidence her oedipal longing to be impregnated by her father. By carrying her own child, she may have hoped to vicariously experience all the specialness and love denied her. Thus, we suggest that oedipal theory often obscures rather than elucidates. What Terman regarded as oedipal in the therapeutic relationship we understand as efforts by Miss N to rescript traumatizing betrayals in her past life and as attempts to protect herself against retraumatization in relation to him.

JULE P. MILLER, III'S CASE OF JACK

One of the few recent clinical discussions by a self psychologist that heavily relies on oedipal theory is Miller's (1996) account of his one-session assessment of Jack, a 5-year-old boy whose mother was perplexed by a resurgence of his highly aggressive behavior at school. His hitting, kicking, pushing, name-calling, running across chairs, and climbing on tables had begun the previous year when he first entered preschool. These behaviors had largely stopped after his mother reduced his attendance from 5 to 3 days a week, but he exhibited similar aggressivity at the outset of the new school year. When a teacher who had helped Jack behave more calmly was hospitalized for a hysterectomy, he became so aggressive, the substitute teacher worried he would hurt himself or the other children.

Jack's early life appears to have been puncutated by much disruption and illness. Born in Germany, Jack was brought to the United States when he was 15 months old. Neither parent was consistently available. Jack's father's job, which involved much traveling, had kept him away from home for a 9-week period when Jack was 3. Jack's mother worked for 3 months of the year, including a period that had ended just 2 weeks before the evaluation. Chronic ear infections beginning at age 1 greatly hampered his speech development. At 12 months his vocabulary contained twelve words, but by 18 months it was reduced to only five. Shortly after tubes were put into his ears, his speech and vocabulary quickly improved. Despite Jack's parents' claim that he got along fairly well with his only sibling—a brother, 4 years older—this child appears to have been physically aggressive as well. Jack told Miller that, although he enjoyed wrestling with his brother on his mother's bed, he had been hit by him frequently.

During the assessment session, the themes of bodily injury and violence were prominent in Jack's play and his verbalizations. Jack often grabbed his crotch, especially when frightened. While his mother spoke to Miller, he built a tower-like figure with clay and smashed it down. Alone with Miller, he showed where a piece of glass had cut his foot when he and his brother had broken his mother's lamp. Following an account of having been knocked down the stairs "like a hot dog" by a pit bull, Jack spoke of feeling sad that his pregnant dog "will have to go to the doctor to get her tummy cut open to take out the puppies." In response to Miller's likening this to his teacher's hysterectomy, Jack noted that the cause for her hospitalization was "having to yell at the kids so much." Jack reported having nightmares after watching the shark movies *Jaws* and *Jaws II*. After telling Miller that he liked to pretend that he was a pirate, he added emphatically, "not Captain Hook, just a captain." He also confided that there was a "Jaws" in a nearby swamp that his father had killed.

Miller interpreted much of the assessment in oedipal terms. Commenting on Jack's preoccupation with bodily injury, Miller contended, "There were also suggestions of oedipal fantasies, notably when he described wrestling on his mother's bed, and when he built and smashed the phallic image while his mother talked to me" (p. 127). For Miller, Jack's description of being knocked down the stairs "like a hot dog" by the pit bull "would be consistent with a metaphorical description of a fantasy of phallic conflict with his father" (p. 127); Jack's introduction of the topic of pregnancy "resonated with possible oedipal meanings" (p. 127); and Jack's finding comfort in his mother's bed after seeing *Jaws* may have, according to Miller, reflected an oedipal wish. Miller also interpreted Jack's pirate fantasy as indicating his "very strong wants," including his wish "to have as close and intimate a relationship with his mother as he had in infancy." Miller added:

> The frustrations of those wishes led to the angry feelings, which then led to fear of retaliation. Jack was careful to point out that he did not want to be Captain Hook. It may be that Captain Hook's missing hand stimulated Jack's own fear of bodily injury, which might come in retaliation for his crocodile hunger for mother's affection [p. 129].

Miller interpreted Jack's talking about his father's having killed the shark as expressing a wish to identify with and feel protected by his strong, ideal, oedipal father. Moreover, in attempting to understand the lack of improvement in Jack's behavior despite being reassured that his teacher was recovering well after her operation, he gave greater weight to "oedipal dynamics at home" than Jack's fear that he had caused his teacher's illness. Miller observed:

> It is possible that, at about the time the teacher became sick, Jack was having fantasies of marrying his mother and having babies with her. These would make the fact that he was not the one "wrestling" with Mommy all the more frustrating. He was shut out from the bedroom when his father was there, which may have made him very angry. He became afraid that if he could feel so angry at his parents, they could feel that angry at him. He had fears of being physically hurt for his fantasies, of losing his mother and of causing her pain. . . . Hence, his oedipal fears were metaphorically confirmed—if you try to get what you want you will lose the woman you love [pp. 129-130].

We believe that Miller's experience-distant oedipal conceptualizations fail to do justice to the material presented to him by Jack and his mother. To our minds, Miller's vivid account poignantly details a child's heroic attempts to reveal the frightening world in which his difficulties arose—most originating before the so-called oedipal period is thought to begin—and his psychological strategies for dealing with them.

Our understanding differs substantially from Miller's. To begin with, we find no reason to attribute Jack's preoccupation with bodily injury to oedipal-phase phenomena; his concerns about his body seem perfectly understandable in light of his traumatic history. We conjecture that the enormous pain Jack undoubtedly suffered in the throes of ear infections serious enough to have delayed his speech obligated his parents to provide him with a great deal of soothing and comforting selfobject experience.[7] Yet there are a number of reasons to suspect that Jack's parents failed to provide the selfobject responsiveness that might have prevented such pain from assuming traumatic meaning. First, both parents appear to have been unpredictable in their physical and emotional availability. Jack's father was absent for a month when he was less than a year old and his mother's work schedule kept her busy for 3 months out of the year. We can only imagine how frightening it must have been for Jack as a toddler to have tubes inserted into his ears by strange nurses and doctors. We suggest that the story of his being knocked downstairs by the pit bull might consititute "a model scene" (Lichtenberg, 1989) that symbolically concretizes Jack's experience of numerous traumatizing betrayals of trust in his parents when they failed to protect or comfort him at times of pain and injury. Second, despite what we consider her supportiveness in limiting his attendance after his initial difficulties at preschool, Jack's mother appears to have been quite lacking in empathic understanding of her son's experience. For example, she attributed Jack's highly aggressive behavior at school to his eating "pancakes for breakfast." She also downplayed her older son's physical aggression toward Jack.

Thus, it seems reasonable to assume that a child who suffered from severe, chronic ear infections and the loss of words with which to communicate his pain; the insertion of tubes into his ears; a major upheaval at 15 months of age when his family moved to this country; and his brother's violence—all without consistently available parental responsiveness—might be inordinately concerned about injury to his body. Furthermore, it is understandable in these circumstances that a child would seek to avoid retraumatization when confronted with blatant imagery involving bodily harm such as that associated with shark movies and one-handed pirates. Reminding himself of his father's strength in killing a shark and attempting to rescript his traumas (Brothers, 1995) in fantasy by portraying himself as a scary pirate whose body was perfectly intact appear to represent such strategies. Given the unavailability of parental responsiveness, it is little wonder that he attempted to soothe himself by touching his genitals when he was frightened.

---

[7] We disagree with Miller's suggestion that Jack's chronic ear infections occurred during the first phase of the "normal fragmentation all children experience" and that the tubes were inserted at the peak of "normal separation anxiety." In light of much current research, the concepts of "normal" fragmentation and "normal" separation anxiety do not stand the test of time (see, for example, Bretherton, 1987). Rather, we view Jack's fragmentation experiences and separation anxiety as occurring in the context of traumatizing betrayals.

Let us now consider Jack's highly aggressive behavior, which first occurred during his separations from his mother on beginning school and recurred with the hospitalization of a teacher who had provided enough comforting responsiveness to calm him. It is easy to see how a child as traumatized by abandonment and injury as Jack might have been threatened with retraumatization on being thrust into the strange environment of a preschool classroom. Why might aggression represent an effort to ward off retraumatization? First of all, by acting aggressively, Jack may well have hoped to rescript the traumatic scenarios involving his helpless passivity and lack of parental care during his painful illnesses and his beatings by his brother. His trust in himself to secure the selfobject responsiveness he needed may well have depended on his demonstrating strength and self-reliance in the face of abandonment and potential harm. Second, we hypothesize that, as a result of his physical fragility (his ear infections), his parents might have been especially concerned with his gender development. That is to say, they might have been strongly inclined to reward the rough-and-tumble behavior stereotypically associated with masculinity. For Jack, behaving in a hypermasculine, aggressive way in this frightening situation might well have represented a means of complying with his parents' wishes, thereby securing the selfobject responsiveness he so urgently needed. Qualities associated with stereotypic femininity such as passivity, vulnerability, and "good" behavior would have been dissociated and disavowed. Rather than indicating a literal fear of castration, touching his penis may have served to remind him of his maleness and consequently, the basis for selfobject connectedness was intact.

Jack's worries about his teacher's hospitalization and the resurgence of his aggressivity in her absence are also readily explainable without recourse to oedipal theory. Research supports our assumption that Jack lacked the anatomical knowedge to link her hysterectomy to pregnancy and birth (e.g., Bem, 1993). Young children are often told that the doctor takes babies (or puppies) out of the mother's tummy. We suspect that Jack associated his teacher's hospitalization with his own painful and frightening experiences. By blaming her hospitalization on "having to yell at the kids so much," Jack may have attempted to rescript traumas involving his helplessness in the face of the incomprehensible disappearances of those he needed to rely on for the provision of selfobject experiences. At the same time, imagining his teacher as weak, passive, and vulnerable in the face of his "badness" may have enabled him to experience her as an alter ego selfobject who embodied the very qualities associated with stereotypic femininity that he disavowed in himself. In other words, his self-blaming fantasy may well have allowed him to restore an experience of cohesive selfhood.

SUMMARY

Citing recent developments in research on child development and gender, as well as the theoretical advances espoused by selfobject theory, intersubjectivity theory, and motivational systems theory, we have exhorted self psychologists to abandon oedipal theory and the problematic assumptions on which it is based. Two cases presented by self psychologists were reinterpreted in light of our alternative conceptualization that views the feelings, fantasies, and behaviors traditionally associated with an oedipal stage of development as products of traumatizing betrayals of trust in parental figures that occur with the imposition of dichotomous gender. We argue that so-called oedipal passions result when children, forced to dissociate aspects of themselves as gendered, find these aspects of their self-experience embodied in caretakers. Moreover, we believe that clinicians automatically assume oedipal configurations when patients display lust and hostility of a triangular nature despite the existence of many experience-near alternatives.

Because of the complexities and difficulties involved in the task we set ourselves in this chapter, we ask that it be read as part of a work in progress; it is intended primarily as a means of stimulating debate and further exploration.

REFERENCES

Adler, A. (1927), *Understanding Human Nature*. New York: Permabooks.

Aron, L. (1995), The internalized primal scene. *Psychoanal. Dial.*, 5:195–238.

Atwood, G. E. & Stolorow, R. D. (1984), *The Sructures of Subjectivity*. Hillsdale, NJ: The Analytic Press.

Bem, S. L. (1993), *The Lens of Gender*. New Haven, CT: Yale University Press.

Benjamin, J. (1988), *The Bonds of Love: Feminism and the Problem of Domination*. New York: Pantheon.

——— (1996), In defense of gender ambiguity. *Gender & Psychoanal.*, 1:27–44.

Brazelton, T. B. (1992), *Touchpoints*. New York: Guilford.

Bretherton, I. (1987), New perspectives on attachment relations: Security, Communications, and internal working models. In: *Handbook of Infant Development*, 2nd ed., ed. J. D. Osofsky. New York: Wiley, pp. 1061–1100.

Brothers, D. (1995), *Falling Backwards: An Exploration of Trust and Self-Experience*. New York: Norton.

——— (1997), The leather princess: Sadomasochism as the rescripting of trauma scenarios. In: *Conversations in Self Psychology: Progress in Self Psychology, Vol. 13*, ed. A. Goldberg. Hillsdale, NJ: The Analytic Press,

——— (1998), Exploring the "bi" ways of self-experience: Dissociation alter ego selfobject experience, and gender. In: *The World of Self Psychology: Progress in Self Psychology, Vol. 14,* ed. A. Goldberg. Hillsdale, NJ: The Analytic Press, pp. 233–252.

——— & Lewinberg, E. (1999), The therapeutic partnership: A developmental view of self-psychological treatment as bilateral healing. In: *Pluralism in Self Psychology: Progress in Self Psychology, Vol. 15,* ed. A. Goldberg. Hillsdale, NJ: The Analytic Press, pp. 259–286.

Buchsbaum, H. K. & Emde, R. N. (1990), Play narratives in 36–month-old children. *The Psychoanalytic Study of the Child,* 45:129–155. New Haven, CT: Yale University Press.

Burch, B. (1993), Gender identities, lesbianism, and potential space. *Psychoanal. Psychol.*, 10:359–376.

Butler, J. (1989), *Gender Trouble.* New York: Routledge.

Chodorow, N. J. (1978), *The Reproduction of Mothering: Psychoanalysis and the Sociology of Gender.* Berkeley, CA: University of California Press.

——— (1992), Heterosexuality as a compromise formation: Reflections on the psychoanalytic theory of sexual development. *Psychoanal. & Contemp. Thought,* 15:267–303.

Coates, S. W. (1997), Is it time to jettison the concept of developmental lines? *Gender & Psychoanal.*, 2:39–54.

Cohen-Kettenis, P. T. & van Goozen, S. H. M. (1996), Preference for and reactions to sexual and aggressive stimuli in children. Poster presented at the International Academy of Sex Research, Twenty-second Annual Meeting, Rotterdam, The Netherlands, June, 1996.

Crawford, J. (1996), The severed self: Gender as trauma. In: *Basic Ideas Reconsidered: Progress in Self Psychology, Vol. 12,* ed. A. Goldberg. Hillsdale, NJ: The Analytic Press, pp. 269–284.

de Marneffe, D. (1997), Bodies and words: A study of young children's genital and gender knowledge. *Gender & Psychoanal.*, 2:3–34.

Dimen, M. (1991), Deconstructing differences: Gender, splitting, and transitional space. *Psychoanal. Dial.*, 1:335–352.

Elson, M. (1987), *The Kohut Seminars.* New York: Norton.

Emde, R. N. (1994), Three roads intersecting: Changing viewpoints in the psychoanalytic study of Oedipus. In: *Psychoanalysis and Development: Representations and Narratives*, ed. M. Ammaniti & D. N. Stern. New York: New York University Press.

——— Johnson, W. F. & Easterbrooks, M. A. (1988), The do's and don'ts of early moral development. In: *The Emergence of Morality,* ed. J. Kagan & S. Lamb. Chicago, IL: University Chicago Press, pp. 245–277.

Ferenczi, S. (1933), Confusion of tongues between adults and the child. In: *Final Contributions to the Problems and Methods of Psycho-Analysis,* ed. M. Balint. New York: Basic, 1955, pp. 156–167.

Franklin, M. (1981), Play as the creation of imaginary situations: The role of language. In: *Toward a Holistic Developmental Psychology,* ed. S. Wapner & B. Kaplan. Hillsdale, NJ: Lawrence Erlbaum, pp. 197–220.

Gilligan, C. (1982), *In a Different Voice: Psychological Theory and Women's Development.* Cambridge:, MA Harvard University Press.

Goldberg, A. (1988), *A Fresh Look at Psychoanlysis: The View from Self Psychology*. Hillsdale, NJ: The Analytic Press.
——— (1995), *The Problem of Perversion*. New Haven, CT: Yale University Press.
Goldner, V. (1991), Toward a critical relational theory of gender. *Psychoanal. Dial.*, 1:249–272.
Greenberg, J. & Morris, N. (1974), Engrossment: The newborn's impact upon the father. *Amer. J. Orthopsychiat.*, 44:520–531.
Harris, A. (1991), Gender as contradiction. *Psychoanal. Dial.*, 1:197–224.
Horney, K. (1924), On the genesis of the castration complex in women. In: *Feminine Psychology*, ed. H. Kelman. New York: Norton, 1967, pp. 37–53.
——— (1926), The flight from womanhood: The masculinity-complex in women as viewed by men and women. In: *Feminine Psychology*, ed. H. Kelman. New York: Norton, pp. 54–70.
——— (1939), *New Ways in Psychoanalysis*. New York: Norton.
Kohlberg, L., Yaeger, J. & Hjertholm, E. (1968), Private speeds: Four studies and a review of theories. *Child Dev.*, 39:691–735.
Kohut, H. (1959), Introspection, empathy, and psychoanalysis: An examination of the relationship between mode of observation and theory. In: *The Search for the Self: Selected Writings of Heinz Kohut, Vol. 1*, ed. P. H. Ornstein. New York: International Universities Press, 1978, pp. 205–232.
——— (1971), *The Analysis of the Self*. New York: International Universities Press.
——— (1972), Thoughts on narcissism and narcissistic rage. In: *The Search for the Self: Selected Writings of Heinz Kohut, Vol. 2*, ed. P. H. Ornstein. New York: International Universities Press, 1978, pp. 615–658.
——— (1975), A note on female sexuality. In: *The Search for the Self: Selected Writings of Heinz Kohut, 1950–1994, Vol. 2*, ed. P. H. Ornstein. New York: International Universities Press, pp. 783–792.
——— (1977), *The Restoration of the Self*. New York: International Universities Press.
——— (1980), Selected problems in self-psychological theory. In: *The Search for the Self: Selected Writings of Heinz Kohut, Vol. 4*, ed. P. H. Ornstein. New York: International Universities Press, pp. 489–524.
——— (1981), Introspection, empathy, and the semicircle of mental health. In: *The Search for the Self: Selected Writings of Heinz Kohut, Vol. 4*, ed. P. H. Ornstein. New York: International Universities Press, pp. 537–568.
———(1984), *How Does Analysis Cure?* Chicago, IL: University of Chicago Press.
Lamb, M. E., Hwang, C. P., Frodi, A. & Frodi, M. (1982), Security of mother– and father–infant attachment and its relation of sociability with strangers in traditional and non-traditional Swedish families. *Infant Behav. & Dev.*, 5:355–367.
Lang, J. (1989), Self Psychology and the understanding and treatment of women. *Rev. Psychiat.*, 8:384–402.
Lester, E. P. (1976), On the psychosexual development of the female child. *J. Amer. Acad. Psychoanal.*, 4:515–527.
Lichtenberg, J. D. (1983), *Psychoanalysis and Infant Research*. Hillsdale, NJ: The Analytic Press.

——— (1989), *Psychoanalysis and Motivation.* Hillsdale, NJ. The Analytic Press.

——— Lachmann, F. & Fossage, J. (1992), *The Self and Motivational Systems.* Hillsdale NJ; The Analytic Press.

McClintock, M. & Herdt, G. (1996), Rethinking puberty: The development of sexual attraction. *Current Dir. Psycholog. Sci.,* 5:178–183.

Miller, J. P. III (1996), *Using Self Psychology in Child Psychotherapy: The Restoration of the Child.* Northvale, NJ: Aronson.

Modell, A. (1985), The Oedipus complex: A re-evaluation. *J. Amer. Psychoanal. Assn.,* 33:201–206.

Ornstein, A. (1983), Fantasy or reality? The unsettled question in pathogenesis and reconstruction in psychoanalysis. In: *The Future of Psychoanalysis,* ed. A. Goldberg. New York: International Universities Press.

Ornstein, P. (1980), Self psychology and the concept of health. In: *Advances in Self Psychology,* ed. A. Goldberg. New York: International Universities Press, pp. 137–160.

Parke, R. & Sawin, D. (1977), The family in early infancy: Social interactional and attitudinal analyses. Presented at meeting of the Society for Research in Child Development. New Orleans, March.

Person, E. & Ovesey, L. (1983), Psychoanalytic theories of gender identity. *J. Amer. Acad. Psychoanal.,* 11:203–227.

Sandler, J. (1960), On the concept of the superego. *The Psychoanalytic Study of the Child,* 15:128–162. Madison, CT: International Universities Press.

Schafer, R. (1968), *Aspects of Internalization.* New York: International Universities Press.

Schaffer, H. R. & Emerson, P. E. (1964) The development of social attachments in infancy. *Monographs of the Society for Research in Child Development,* 29:3.

Shane M., Shane E. & Gales M. (1997) *Intimate Attachments: Towards a New Self Psychology.* New York: Guilford.

Stechler, G. & Kaplan, S. (1980), The development of the self: A psychoanalytic perspective. *The Psychoanalytic Study of the Child,* 35:85–106. New Haven, CT: Yale University Press.

Stern, D. N. (1985). *The Interpersonal World of the Infant: A View from Psychoanalysis and Developmental Psychology.* New York: Basic.

——— (1995), *The Motherhood Constellation: A Unified View of Parent–Infant Psychotherapy.* New York: Basic Books.

Stiver, I. (1991), Beyond the Oedipus complex: Mothers and daughters. In: *Women's Growth in Connection: Writings from the Stone Center,* ed. J. V. Jordan, A. G.Kaplan, J. B. Miller, I. Stiver & J. L. Surry. New York: Guilford, pp. 97–121.

Stolorow, R. D. & Atwood, G. E. (1992), *Contexts of Being: The Intersubjective Foundations of Psychological Life.* Hillsdale, NJ: The Analytic Press.

Terman, D. (1985), The self and the oedipus complex. In: *The Annual of Psychoanalysis,* ed. The Chicago Institute for Psychoanalysis. New York: International Universities Press, pp. 81–104.

Thomson, C. M. (1942), Cultural pressures in the psychology of women. In: *Psychoanalysis and Women,* ed. J. B. Miller. New York: Brunner/Mazel, 1973, pp. 49–64.

Tolpin, M. (1996), Strivings of the healthy self: The psychoanalysis of normal development—Selfobject transferences. Presented at the Toronto Child Psychotherapy Conference, November 14.

Watkins, M. (1986), *Invisible Guests: The Development of Imaginal Dialogues.* Hillsdale, NJ: The Analytic Press.

Author Index

Subject Index

A

V

W